Change and Continuity in the 1988 Elections

Revised Edition

Change and Continuity in the 1988 Elections

Revised Edition

Paul R. Abramson
Michigan State University

John H. Aldrich
Duke University

David W. Rohde
Michigan State University

PRESS

A Division of Congressional Quarterly Inc.

Library of Congress Cataloging-in-Publication Data

Abramson, Paul R.
    Change and continuity in the 1988 elections / Paul R. Abramson,
John H. Aldrich, David W. Rohde. -- Rev. ed.
        p.   cm.
    Includes bibliographical references and index.
    ISBN 0-87187-561-6
    1. Presidents--United States--Election--1988. 2. United States.
Congress--Elections, 1988. 3. United States. Congress--Elections,
1990. 4. Elections--United States. 5. United States--Politics and
government--1945-   I. Aldrich, John Herbert, 1947-   II. Rohde,
David W.   III. Title.
JK526 1988j
324.73'0927--dc20   91-7350
                                                                              CIP

To
David
Heather and Lee
Jennifer and Margaret

Contents

Tables and Figures

Figures

Preface to the Revised Edition

The Republican presidential victory in 1988 was muted by Republican losses in both the Senate and the House of Representatives. Because the president's party had lost strength in the House in thirty-one of the thirty-two midterm elections since the Civil War, history favored the Democrats in 1990. But a year before the midterm election Republicans believed they might beat the historical odds and actually gain seats. Republican prospects of a historical reversal began to fade, however, as controversies between George Bush and the Democratic-controlled Congress over tax increases, friction between Bush and conservative Republicans, as well as a deteriorating economy eroded public approval of the president. In fact, the Republicans suffered a loss of nine seats in the House, one seat in the Senate, and one or two governorships.

With their midterm electoral victory in 1990, the Democrats won control of the U.S. House of Representatives for the nineteenth consecutive general election, by far the longest winning streak in the history of Congress. Our analysis suggests that the Democrats are likely to retain control of the House in 1992 as well. But despite these patterns American politics seemed highly uncertain in early 1991. The Iraqi invasion of Kuwait on August 2, 1990, had little impact on the midterm election, but the war in the Persian Gulf may greatly affect the 1992 presidential election.

The 1990 midterm election provides no definitive guidelines about future Republican prospects, but it raises important questions. Is there an anti-incumbent mood among the electorate that will jeopardize the high success rate of incumbents seeking reelection and perhaps even place at risk future Democratic dominance of the House? What role do national factors play in affecting midterm election outcomes, and what is the importance of local factors? Why do the Democrats continue to enjoy such unprecedented success in U.S. House elections? Will the reapportionment and redistricting to occur before the 1992 election diminish Democratic chances for future congressional control? How will redistricting affect Democratic presidential prospects?

In answering these questions we speak with one voice, because this book is a collective enterprise. As with the first edition, however, we divided the labor. David Rohde had the primary responsibility for

Chapter 12, John Aldrich for the first two sections of Chapter 13, and
Paul Abramson for the last section.

As with our previous books, the staff at CQ Press was a great help in
expeditiously producing this edition. We are grateful to David Tarr and
Nancy Lammers for their encouragement and to Ann O'Malley for her
assistance with the book's production.

Paul R. Abramson
John H. Aldrich
David W. Rohde

Preface

George Bush's 1988 election victory marks the first time in four decades that the party holding the White House has won three elections in a row, and many scholars now believe that the Republicans are clearly the dominant party in winning presidential elections. Yet the Republican victory was muted, for 1988 was the first election since 1960 in which the party winning the presidency lost seats in the House of Representatives. Although Bush carried forty states, the Republicans lost one seat in the Senate and three seats in the House. Interestingly enough, many Americans may be satisfied with this outcome, for public opinion polls show that a majority prefers different parties to control the presidency and the Congress.

For political scientists the mixed pattern of results poses fundamental questions about the American political system. Although divided control may have advantages, partisan conflict between Congress and the president may make it difficult for political leaders to respond to changing economic and social conditions. Divided control also makes it more difficult for voters to assess responsibility, giving credit for success or attaching blame for failure.

Students of electoral politics are puzzled by the continued pattern of divided government. For several decades, many have argued that the United States was ripe for a partisan realignment in which the basic pattern of electoral politics would change. Most political scientists agree that the winning coalition forged by the Democrats in the 1930s no longer exists, but they argue about what, if anything, has replaced it. Has there been a partisan realignment in which new patterns of voting behavior have been formed? Was there a dealignment in which old voting patterns disappeared without new patterns emerging? Or has there been a new type of realignment—some call it a "split-level" alignment—in which the Republicans continue to win the presidency while the Democrats maintain control of Congress?

To answer these questions, one cannot view the 1988 elections as isolated events, but must place them in historical context. To do this, we have examined a broad range of evidence, from past election results to public opinion surveys of the electorate conducted over the past four decades.

Our goal in writing this book was to provide a solid social-scientific analysis of the 1988 elections using the best data available to study voting behavior. We employ many sources, but rely most heavily upon the 1988 survey of the American electorate conducted by the Survey Research Center and the Center for Political Studies of the University of Michigan as part of an ongoing project funded by the National Science Foundation. In the course of our analysis we use every one of the twenty election studies conducted by the Michigan SRC-CPS, a series often referred to as the National Election Studies (NES).

These surveys of the American electorate, which are disseminated by the Inter-university Consortium for Political and Social Research, can be analyzed by scholars throughout the United States. The ICPSR provided a preliminary version of the 1988 election data to scholars in late April 1989; another version, including a study to determine whether respondents actually voted, was provided in mid-July 1989. Unless otherwise indicated, all the tables and figures in Chapters 2, 4 through 8, and 10 are based upon data obtained from the ICPSR. The standard disclaimer holds: the consortium is not responsible for our analyses or interpretations.

We are grateful to Harriet Dhanak of the Politometrics Laboratory at Michigan State University for helping us analyze these surveys. James Meernik and Renée M. Smith of Michigan State University and R. Michael Alvarez and Phil Paolino of Duke University assisted with the data analysis. John Aldrich received a grant from the Council on Research of Duke University to purchase the Gallup data used in Chapter 1. Jerry T. Jennings of the U.S. Bureau of the Census provided us with unpublished information about the Census Bureau's 1988 survey of voter registration and turnout, Walter Dean Burnham of the University of Texas provided us with estimates of turnout in the 1988 election, and Santa A. Traugott of the Center for Political Studies of the University of Michigan provided us with advice on analyzing the 1988 NES vote validation study.

We are also grateful to Nola Healy Lynch for her careful editing of our manuscript and to Kerry Kern, Carolyn Goldinger, and Nancy Lammers of CQ Press for their help in producing our book. As with our two earlier books, Joanne Daniels of CQ Press provided help and encouragement.

This book was a collective enterprise, but we divided the labor. Paul Abramson had primary responsibility for Chapters 3, 4, 5, and 11; John Aldrich for Chapters 1, 6, 7, and 8; and David Rohde for Chapters 2, 9, and 10. None of us is responsible for the presidential election result, since we all voted for Michael S. Dukakis, the first time in three elections that we agreed about the appropriate electoral outcome. But we have consistently agreed about the interpretation of recent elections. The 1988 election, in our view, raises important questions about the nature of American party politics. Although no book can provide definitive answers about the meaning of these elections, a thorough analysis of the data at hand may lead to a better understanding of recent developments.

Paul R. Abramson
John H. Aldrich
David W. Rohde

PART 1

The 1988 Presidential Election Contest

Presidential elections in the United States are partly ritual, reaffirming our democratic values. But they are far more than that. The office confers great powers upon the occupant, and those powers have expanded during the course of American history. It is precisely because of these immense powers that at least some presidential elections have played a major role in determining public policy.

The 1860 election, which brought Abraham Lincoln and the Republicans to power and ousted a divided Democratic party, focused on whether slavery should be extended into the western territories. Following Lincoln's victory, eleven southern states attempted to secede from the Union, the Civil War erupted, and, ultimately, slavery itself was abolished. An antislavery plurality that did not necessarily favor the abolition of slavery (Lincoln received only 40 percent of the popular vote) set in motion a chain of events that freed some 4 million blacks.

The 1896 election, in which the Republican William McKinley defeated the Democrat and Populist Williams Jennings Bryan, beat back the challenge of western and agrarian interests against the prevailing financial and industrial power of the East. Although Bryan mounted a strong campaign, winning 47 percent of the popular vote to McKinley's 51 percent, the election set a clear course for a policy of high tariffs and the continuation of the gold standard for American money.

The twentieth century also has witnessed presidential elections that determined the direction of public policy. In 1936, incumbent Franklin D. Roosevelt won 61 percent of the vote and his Republican opponent, Alfred E. Landon, only 37 percent, allowing the Democrats to continue and consolidate the economic policies of the New Deal.

1

Lyndon B. Johnson's 1964 landslide victory over Republican Barry M. Goldwater probably provided the clearest set of policy alternatives of any election in this century. Johnson, who received 61 percent of the popular vote to Goldwater's 38 percent, saw his triumph as a mandate for his Great Society reforms, the most far-reaching social legislation enacted since World War II.

Goldwater offered "a choice, not an echo," advocating far more conservative social and economic policies than Johnson, but the voters rejected him. Ironically, the election also appeared to offer a choice between escalating American involvement in Vietnam and restraint. As a result of Johnson's subsequent actions, many of Goldwater's policies about the war ultimately were implemented by Johnson himself.

What Did the 1988 Election Mean?

Only the future can determine the ultimate importance of the 1988 election. As an incumbent vice president, George Bush ran largely on the accomplishments of Ronald Reagan. During his eight years as president, Reagan had cut back social programs, slowed down government growth, substantially increased defense spending, and accelerated the government deregulation that had begun under Jimmy Carter. Reagan's 1980 promise to cut federal income taxes by 30 percent was largely implemented by the Economic Recovery Act of 1981, which cut income taxes 25 percent over a three-year period. Although many Democrats argued that Reagan's reforms mainly benefited wealthy Americans, most Americans benefited from relatively low inflation rates. In 1980, when Reagan was elected, the annual inflation rate was 12.5 percent; during the third quarter of 1988, when Bush was seeking to continue the "Reagan-Bush" administration, the annual inflation rate was only 4.7 percent. On the other hand, the national debt had almost tripled during Reagan's presidency, from $908 billion shortly before he took office to $2,600 billion in the fall of 1988.

Although Bush proposed several new programs, such as tax benefits for child care and increased government commitment for education, his major appeals stressed the continuation of Reagan's policies. He emphatically promised not to raise taxes. Budget deficits, he claimed, could be reduced by a "flexible freeze," and he even called for lowering the capital gains tax in order to encourage investments. Michael S. Dukakis did not propose major new programs, stressing instead that he was more competent to govern than Bush. Even so, it was clear that Dukakis would revise, if not abandon, many of Reagan's policies. He proposed dropping several weapons systems, and opposed deploying the Strategic Defense Initiative ("Star Wars"). Dukakis claimed he could increase government revenues by more efficient tax collection, but he made no firm promise not to raise taxes. He specifically opposed Bush's proposal to lower the capital gains tax, a move that, he argued, would benefit wealthy Americans.

In addition to implementing policies, Reagan had also appointed three new justices to the U.S. Supreme Court, and by the end of his presidency 47 percent of all federal judges were Reagan appointees.[1] The 1988 presidential campaign emphasized such social issues as capital punishment, the legality of abortion, and whether teachers must lead children to recite the Pledge of Allegiance. The president has little direct control over these issues, but they are areas in which the U.S. Supreme Court makes major policy decisions. Given that three of the nine justices would be eighty or eighty-one years old by the end of 1988, it seemed likely that the newly elected president would make several Supreme Court appointments.

Clearly, the election offered policy alternatives, and as we shall see, voters saw clear policy differences between Bush and Dukakis. Although voters could not reelect Reagan, they could vote to continue his policies. Electing Dukakis would not overturn Reagan's reforms, but it would clearly lead to major revisions. Americans could also vote to support the traditional values espoused by Bush or the more liberal views advanced by Dukakis. They would also have the opportunity to elect 33 U.S. senators, all 435 members of the U.S. House of Representatives, 12 governors, and nearly 6,000 state legislators.

The election yielded a mixed outcome. Bush was elected, although by a far closer margin than Reagan had won by in 1984. But the Republicans lost one Senate seat and three members of the U.S. House of Representatives—the first election since 1960 in which the party winning the presidency lost seats in the House. As the 101st Congress began, the Democrats held fifty-five Senate seats, compared with forty-five for the Republicans. The Republicans fared even worse in the House, for they began the session with only 175 members, compared with the Democrats' 260. The Republican percentage in the House (only 40.2 percent of the seats) was the smallest share ever won by the party winning the presidency.

Republicans were euphoric after the 1980 election, for they won twelve Senate seats, they got control of the Senate for the first time since the 1952 election, and they gained thirty-three House seats. In Reagan's 1984 landslide the Republicans lost two Senate seats, but they won fourteen House seats. Republican optimists saw Reagan's 1984 triumph as evidence that the Republicans were, or were shortly to become, the majority party. In August 1985 Reagan himself proclaimed that "realignment is at hand."

Neither party was euphoric after the 1988 election. The Democrats despaired over their third consecutive presidential defeat, a defeat made more bitter by their high expectations of only three months earlier. They were defeated not by Reagan, a skilled campaigner who had mastered the art of television, but by Bush, whom they viewed as an ineffective bumbler. The Republicans, on the other hand, saw that after eight years of Republican presidential rule they were further from controlling Congress than when Reagan had taken office.

Many Americans may be satisfied with partisan control divided between the president and Congress. But the mixed pattern of results in 1988, along with similar mixed patterns throughout the 1980s, raises fundamental problems for students of American politics. Did the Republican success in winning the presidency result from conservative policy preferences among the electorate? Were these victories a result of favorable views of Reagan's presidency? And do these Republican victories signal a shift in partisan forces that will establish the Republicans as the dominant party? Will the Republicans continue to occupy the White House for decades to come, and, if so, will they be able to translate their control of the presidency into control of Congress?

As we will show, neither Reagan's landslide in 1984 nor Bush's victory in 1988 resulted from a conservative shift in the policy preferences of the electorate. Reagan's triumph resulted from favorable views toward his presidency and the performance of the government, as well as a belief among many voters that the Republican party might best solve the nation's problems. Bush's election, as we shall see, occurred despite less favorable views of the government's performance and despite less favorable views of the Republican party's ability to solve national problems. But Bush clearly benefited from a marked shift toward Republican party loyalties among the electorate. The growth of Republican party loyalties, along with continued Republican dominance in winning the presidency, raises a more basic question. Has there been, or will there be, a partisan realignment?

Political scientists define realignment in different ways, but all are influenced by the seminal writings of V. O. Key, Jr., who began by developing a theory of "critical elections" that specified the conditions under which "new and durable electoral groupings are formed."[2] He later argued that realignments can take place over a series of elections—a pattern he called "secular realignment." During these periods "shifts in the partisan balance of power" occur.[3]

As James L. Sundquist points out, all scholars agree that durability is an essential element of realignment.[4] Most scholars also agree that realignments seldom if ever involve across-the-board shifts to the same party among all segments of the electorate. Shifts occur instead in the regional bases of party support and in the voting patterns of social groups. Realignments may also be accompanied by the mobilization of new groups into the electorate. Sundquist also stresses the importance of new issues in bringing about a realignment. Moreover, many political scientists argue that partisan realignments result from shifts not just in the way people vote but also in feelings of party loyalty among the electorate.

Most political scientists would agree that the old alignment, formed in the 1930s, that made the Democrats the majority party, no longer exists. But most do not believe that a new partisan realignment has been formed, even though there may be the potential for one. Some believe that the American party system is in a state of "dealignment"—a condition under which old voting patterns break down without being replaced by new ones.[5] Others maintain that a realignment has occurred, but that it is a new type of realignment in which one party will continue to control the presidency, while the other will control the Congress—a "split-level" realignment.[6] And others suggest that partisan politics in America has reached a stage where the very concept of realignment is no longer useful.[7]

The 1988 election provides further evidence about American electoral politics, and thus provides further fuel to arguments about partisan realignment. Gerald M. Pomper, for example, argues that there has been a realignment. According to Pomper, 1988 was a "confirming election, demonstrating the long-term 'secular realignment' of American politics toward a Republican presidential majority.... Republican power is more than the popularity of particular candidates or Presidents. It is the strength of a party that most voting Americans now believe is better able, as a party, to safeguard their peace, prosperity, and political philosophy."[8] But Pomper sees no long-term prospects for the Republicans to gain control of Congress, because, he argues, most Americans prefer divided government.

Other scholars maintain that if a realignment has occurred, it is a new type of partisan alignment, since in previous realignments one party has dominated both the executive and the legislative branches. Dealignment, they claim, no longer describes American politics, because the party system is no longer in flux. Michael Nelson, for example, argues that Republican congressional losses demonstrate that a full-scale realignment has not occurred. However, the term dealignment "implies a virtual randomness of partisan election outcomes over time." But after the 1988 election it has become clear that "voters have settled into a discernible partisan pattern: Republican presidents, Democratic Congresses and state governments." He concludes, "Because neither realignment nor dealignment describes the modern political situation, a new term has to be employed: split-level realignment."[9]

Byron E. Shafer also rejects both terms, realignment and dealignment. Party power, he argues, is clearly divided between a presidency controlled by the Republicans, a House of Representatives controlled by the Democrats, and a Senate for which both parties can effectively compete. Because this division has become institutionalized, the term dealignment does not apply. The 1988 election, Shafer argues, illustrates the extent to which the new system has become stable. Beginning in 1968, with the controversy over the Vietnam War, a new system began. "What was to emerge, instead of realignment," he writes, "was a different *type* of electoral order, one in which there was a new Republican majority to lay claim to the presidency, an old Democratic majority to keep claim to the House, and a wavering Democratic majority to strive to hold on to the Senate." [10]

And in his analysis of the 1988 election, Everett Carll Ladd argues that it is not worth debating whether a realignment has occurred. In his own view, postwar changes do add up to a realignment. But he maintains that the term realignment may no longer be useful. "For over three decades," he maintains, "political scientists have been engaged in an exceptionally unproductive debate over just what criteria must be met before a proper realignment may be officially declared. As this debate has dragged on, the world of American politics has been transformed." According to Ladd, we should bury the concept of realignment, "and get on with a precise charting of the new arrangements and their implications." [11]

Although we agree with Ladd that debates about the precise criteria for realignments are unproductive, we believe that past research and theorizing about the nature of partisan realignments provide important insights for understanding contemporary American politics. Our knowledge of historical patterns provides a guide to understanding the present distribution of partisan forces. Most important, we believe that conclusions about the meaning of the 1988 election must be based upon a careful examination of the best available data.

In our evaluation of the 1988 elections we are interested in the broader implications of the elections for the future of American politics. We ask two basic questions. First, is the current Republican dominance of the presidency likely to continue for the next several decades? Second, will Democratic control of Congress continue, even if the Republicans continue to win presidential elections? To answer these questions we must explain why the Republicans have been successful in winning recent presidential elections and why the Democrats dominate congressional contests.

Survey Research Sampling

Our book relies heavily upon surveys of the American electorate. It draws upon telephone polls held during the election year, exit polls carried out by the television networks outside voting stations, and interviews conducted in respondents' households by the Gallup Organization, the National Opinion Research Center of the University of Chicago, and the

U.S. Bureau of the Census. But we rely mainly upon interviews conducted in the respondents' households during the two months before and two months after the 1988 election by the Survey Research Center-Center for Political Studies (SRC-CPS) of the University of Michigan. The SRC has been conducting surveys of the American electorate in every presidential and midterm election since 1948, and these surveys are generally known as the National Election Studies (NES). We are able to use the NES surveys to study the entire postwar period. Since 1952 the NES surveys have measured party identification and feelings of political efficacy. The CPS, founded in 1970, has developed valuable questions for measuring issue preferences. The NES data provide the best and most comprehensive source of information about the political attitudes and partisan loyalties of the American electorate.

Readers may question our reliance on the 1988 NES survey of 2,040 Americans, when there are some 173 million Americans of voting age.[12] Would we have obtained similar results if all adults had been surveyed?[13] The NES surveys use a procedure called multistage probability sampling to select the specific individuals to be interviewed. These procedures assure that the final sample is very likely to represent the entire U.S. adult citizen population (except for Americans living in institutions, on military installations, or abroad).[14]

Given the probability procedures used to conduct the NES surveys, we are able to assess the likelihood that the results represent the total U.S. resident citizen population. The 1988 survey sampled only about one American in 85,000, but the representativeness of a sample depends far more upon the size of the sample than on the size of the population being sampled. For most purposes, samples of about 1,500 respondents are adequate to study the American electorate. With a sample of this size, we can be fairly confident (confident to a level of .95) that the results we obtain fall within plus or minus 3 percentage points of the results that we would get if the entire adult population were surveyed.[15] For example, when we find that 45 percent of the voters surveyed named an economic issue as the most important problem facing the nation, we can be fairly confident that between 42 percent and 48 percent of the entire electorate considered an economic problem as the most important. The actual result for the electorate could be less than 42 percent or more than 48 percent. But a confidence level of .95 means that the odds are 19 to 1 that the entire electorate falls within this range.

The range of confidence becomes wider when we look at subgroups of the electorate. When we examine groups of 500 respondents, the range of confidence grows to plus or minus 6 percentage points. For only 100 respondents, the range of confidence grows to plus or minus 14 points. Because the likelihood of error grows as our subsamples become smaller, we often supplement our analysis with reports of other surveys.

Somewhat more complicated procedures are necessary to determine whether the difference between groups is likely to reflect the relationship that would obtain if the entire population were surveyed. The probability that such differences reflect real differences in the total population is largely a function of the size of the samples of the groups being compared.[16] Generally speaking, when we compare the results based upon the entire 1988 NES survey with the results of an earlier NES survey, a difference of 4 percentage points is sufficient to be reasonably confident that the differences are real.

When we compare subgroups of the electorate sampled in 1988 (or subgroups sampled in 1988 with the same subgroup sampled in earlier surveys), a larger percentage difference is necessary for us to be reasonably confident that differences did not result from chance. For example, when we compare men with women a difference of about 6 points is necessary. When we compare blacks with whites, a difference of about 9 points is necessary, since only about 200 blacks are sampled in most NES surveys.

These numbers provide only a quick ballpark estimate of the chance that the reported results are likely to represent the entire population. Better estimates can be obtained using formulas presented in statistics textbooks. To make such calculations or even a ballpark estimate of the chance of error, the reader must know the size of the groups being compared. For this reason, we always report in our tables and figures either the number of cases upon which our results are based or the information necessary to approximate the number of cases.

The 1988 Contest

Part 1 of our book follows the chronology of the campaign itself. We begin with the struggle to gain the Republican and Democratic presidential nominations. In 1988, for the first time in eight years, both party nominations were contested, and for the first time in twenty years the incumbent president did not seek his party's nomination.[17] Six major candidates sought the Republican nomination, and eight major candidates sought the Democratic nomination.

Chapter 1 analyzes the contest for both parties. It begins by examining who chose to run, with the goal of understanding the regularities that govern presidential nomination contests. We then examine the rules for selecting delegates and discuss the way in which the massive Super Tuesday contest of March 8, 1988, affected both nomination races. We provide overviews of the Republican and Democratic campaigns, examining the impact of victories and defeats upon public perceptions of the presidential race and upon voting choices in the Super Tuesday primaries. As we will see, Bush virtually won his party's nomination on

Super Tuesday, but, although the Democratic contest was more protracted, Dukakis was well on his way to victory after his more limited Super Tuesday successes. Last, we turn to examine the party conventions, as well as Dukakis's selection of Lloyd Bentsen as his running mate and Bush's selection of Dan Quayle.

Having won their parties' nominations, Bush and Dukakis faced the task of gaining the 270 electoral votes needed to win the general election. In Chapter 2 we will examine the strategies of both candidates. We will see how Dukakis's campaign plans were based upon erroneous assumptions about Bush's weaknesses and why Bush chose an essentially negative campaign designed to damage public perceptions of Dukakis. In our view, the campaign clearly mattered. Although the Republicans began with several major advantages, it is possible that an effective Democratic campaign could have altered the outcome.

Chapter 3 presents and interprets the election results. Because states are the building blocks upon which electoral vote majorities are won, the results are discussed on a state-by-state basis. The 1980, 1984, and 1988 elections should bury the myth that the Democrats are the majority party. These elections suggest that the Republicans have built an electoral vote base that may aid them in continuing to dominate presidential elections. The pattern of Republican electoral vote success during the postwar years presents a bleak outlook for the Democratic party. At the same time, however, the way people vote has become more similar throughout the nation. Although the Democrats may have virtually no electoral vote base, the Republican base may not be as secure as it appears. Despite their electoral vote dominance, the Republicans may not be a majority party either.

Notes

1. For a discussion, see Sheldon Goldman, "Reagan's Judicial Legacy: Completing the Puzzle and Summing Up," *Judicature* 72 (April-May 1989): 318-330.
2. V. O. Key, Jr., "A Theory of Critical Elections," *Journal of Politics* 17 (February 1955): 4.
3. V. O. Key, Jr., "Secular Realignment and the Party System," *Journal of Politics* 21 (May 1959): 198.
4. James L. Sundquist, *Dynamics of the Party System: Alignment and Realignment of Political Parties in the United States,* rev. ed. (Washington, D.C.: Brookings Institution, 1983), 4.
5. For a discussion of dealignment, see Ronald Inglehart and Avram Hochstein, "Alignment and Dealignment of the Electorate in France and the United States," *Comparative Political Studies* 5 (October 1972): 343-372; Paul Allen Beck, "The Dealignment Era in America," in *Electoral Change in Advanced Industrial Democracies: Realignment or Dealignment?* ed. Russell J. Dalton,

Scott C. Flanagan, and Paul Allen Beck (Princeton, N.J.: Princeton University Press, 1984), 240-266; and Bo Särlvik and Ivor Crewe, *Decade of Dealignment: The Conservative Victory of 1979* and *Electoral Trends in the 1970s* (Cambridge: Cambridge University Press, 1983).

6. For a discussion of this concept, see Kevin Phillips, *The American Political Report* 14 (January 11, 1985). See also John A. Ferejohn and Morris P. Fiorina, "Incumbency and Realignment in Congressional Elections," in *The New Direction in American Politics,* ed. John E. Chubb and Paul E. Peterson (Washington, D.C.: Brookings Institution, 1985), 91-115.

7. For example, at the 1989 annual meeting of the American Political Science Association a major symposium was held, "The End of Realignment: Atrophy of a Concept and Death of a Phenomenon."

8. Gerald M. Pomper, "The Presidential Election," in *The Election of 1988: Reports and Interpretations,* Gerald M. Pomper et al. (Chatham, N.J.: Chatham House, 1989), 147.

9. Michael Nelson, "Constitutional Aspects of the Elections," in *The Elections of 1988,* ed. Michael Nelson (Washington, D.C.: CQ Press, 1989), 197, 198.

10. Byron E. Shafer, "The Election of 1988 and the Structure of American Politics: Thoughts on Interpreting an Electoral Order," *Electoral Studies* 8 (April 1989): 11.

11. Everett Carll Ladd, "The 1988 Elections: Continuation of the Post-New Deal System," *Political Science Quarterly* 104 (Spring 1989): 18.

12. Because we are usually analyzing responses to key questions measured only in the postelection interview (for example, how the respondent said he or she voted for president or for Congress), we often confine our analysis to the 1,775 respondents who were included in the 1988 NES postelection survey.

13. For an excellent introduction to public opinion polling, see Herbert Asher, *Polling and the Public: What Every Citizen Should Know* (Washington, D.C.: CQ Press, 1988).

14. For an excellent introduction to the sampling procedures used by the University of Michigan Survey Research Center, see Herbert F. Weisberg and Bruce D. Bowen, *An Introduction to Survey Research and Data Analysis* (San Francisco: W. H. Freeman, 1977), 27-35. For a more detailed analysis, see Survey Research Center, *Interviewer's Manual,* rev. ed. (Ann Arbor, Mich.: Institute for Social Research, 1976).

15. The probability of sampling error is partly a function of the result for any given question. The probability of error is greater for proportions near 50 percent and diminishes somewhat for proportions above 70 percent or below 30 percent. The probability of error diminishes markedly for proportions above 90 percent or below 10 percent. For the sake of simplicity, we report the confidence levels for percentages near 50 percent.

16. For an excellent table that allows us to evaluate differences between groups, see Leslie Kish, *Survey Sampling* (New York: John Wiley & Sons, 1965), 580. Kish defines the difference between two groups to be significant if the results are two standard errors apart.

17. Lyndon B. Johnson announced that he would not seek the Democratic presidential nomination on March 31, 1968, less than three weeks after the New Hampshire primary in which Senator Eugene J. McCarthy of Minnesota, running as an anti-Vietnam War candidate, won 42 percent of the vote.

Chapter 1

The Nomination Struggle

The 1988 presidential nomination campaigns promised to be the most exciting in years. It had been eight years since both parties' nominations were contested, twenty years since both were contested in the absence of an incumbent (at least once President Lyndon B. Johnson had declared his intentions not to seek renomination in 1968), and twenty-eight years since the incumbent president had been ineligible to run for renomination.[1] Not only were both nominations to be contested, but both were to be contested by relatively large numbers of candidates, most of whom were experienced and successful politicians.

As the fields took shape in late 1987, both parties' races were expected to be relatively wide open. To be sure, former Democratic senator Gary Hart of Colorado and Republican vice president George Bush were designated by the media as front-runners. Still, Bush could be seen as beatable, and Hart was soon to be embroiled in scandal.

Hart held a substantial lead over the rest of the field in 1987. Commentators and even the other candidates had come to call the eight Democratic candidates "Gary Hart and the Seven Dwarfs," suggesting that Hart's opponents had little political stature. Once Hart's friendship with Donna Rice suggested that he was no Snow White, the Democratic field was reduced to just the Seven Dwarfs. Later, after Sen. Joseph R. Biden, Jr. (Del.) had withdrawn in late 1987 over a plagiarism controversy and Hart had reentered the race, Hart's status was so greatly reduced that the Seven Dwarfs label was still used. This perception was reinforced when Democrats such as Gov. Mario M. Cuomo (N.Y.), Sen. Sam Nunn (Ga.), and Rep. Patricia Schroeder (Colo.), who some believed would make a stronger field of candidates, refused to enter the race.

Bush, as the obvious successor to continue the Reagan-Bush administration, was the Republican front-runner. Many, however, believed his lead slim or fragile. Sen. Robert Dole (Kan.) was the Senate minority leader, making him both well known and the second most powerful Republican officeholder. A strong case could be made for his nomination prospects. Bush, moreover, had potential weaknesses of his own. Vice presidents have become a major force in presidential nomination politics only since World War II, and not since 1836 had a sitting vice president been elected president. Moreover, social conservatives, a critical part of Ronald Reagan's coalition, were skeptical about Bush. Bush, after all, had been Reagan's strongest nomination opponent in 1980, calling Reagan's supply-side economic policy—the linchpin of Reagan's platform in 1980—"voodoo economics." And, social conservatives considered Bush's newfound emphasis on their concerns to be opportunistic, rather than representing genuine commitment. Further, Bush had not won election to public office on his own since his second House election from Texas in 1968. In 1970, Lloyd Bentsen defeated him by 7 points in the general election race for senator. Bush had held an impressive array of offices since then, but all of them were attained by appointment or on Reagan's coattails. Finally, he was dogged by the "wimp" label, questioning his ability to stand strong in adversity and lead the nation, rather than (competently) execute the wishes of his superiors. Given Dole's candidacy and those of several candidates more satisfactory to the social conservatives, Bush seemed beatable.

The events of 1987, especially the scandals surrounding Hart and Biden and the curiosity over who was—and was not—to run, were exciting. Large fields of active candidates, eight Democrats and six Republicans, promised more. Rarely could so many in both parties imagine a realistic chance at the nomination, foresee room at the top, as it were. Both fields, moreover, were somewhat more varied than usual. The Reverends Jesse Jackson on the Democratic and Pat Robertson on the Republican sides, for example, had never held public office, yet both possessed skills—and eloquence and commitment to beliefs—that added to the anticipation of excitement.

In many ways, that promise was realized. Both Jackson and Robertson affected their parties' campaigns, especially Jackson, who finished in second place and dominated major portions of the Democratic National Convention. Bush did falter early on and lost his lead briefly to Dole in the public opinion polls. On the Democratic side, Rep. Richard A. Gephardt (Mo.), Sen. Paul Simon (Ill.), Sen. Albert Gore, Jr. (Tenn.), Jackson, and, most of all, Gov. Michael S. Dukakis (Mass.) won significant victories during the Democratic campaign.

And yet, looking back on the campaigns, many observers were disappointed over the *absence* of excitement. The Republican contest was all but over when Bush won overwhelmingly on Super Tuesday, March 8, 1988, soon after the primary season had begun. Dukakis's victory took longer to become inevitable. But inevitable it became, long before the convention.

To many, then, the 1988 nomination contests were the same old story, at least the same "old" story of nominations under the "new nomination system," initiated in 1972. Crowded fields of candidates narrow rapidly, usually after the Iowa caucuses and New Hampshire primaries which open the campaign. The nomination is usually won by the middle of the primary season, if not earlier. In all five contests between 1972 and 1988, the Republican nominee has won the New Hampshire primary. Three of the five Democratic nominees won in New Hampshire, and Walter Mondale, who was upset in New Hampshire by Hart, won the Iowa caucuses.[2] The campaigns and their coverage in the media seem to many to be more about the fortunes of the candidates— the horse race as it is called—than about the substance of politics. And the conventions themselves are devoid of excitement, since their major business, selection of nominees, is over before they open.

This description (and more) of regular patterns to presidential nominations is, as we will show, not coincidental. The new nomination system does impose regularities, and we will examine them carefully in the rest of this chapter. And yet, as we will also see, each campaign has its own unique characteristics, such as the nature of the candidates, their appeals, and the evaluations of the public about who is best to lead their party in the general election. We turn next to examine the first step of the nomination process, the decision of politicians to become—or not to become—presidential candidates. Then we will examine the rules of the nomination system they face. Finally, we will consider how the candidates ran and why Dukakis and Bush succeeded in their quests.

Who Ran

Fourteen candidates sought the nomination of their party, eight on the Democratic side and six on the Republican side. This count, by itself, reflects one regularity. In nomination campaigns from 1972 to 1988, unless the president is seeking the nomination, many candidates enter the race.

The Republican field included Bush, the vice president; Dole, the minority leader in the Senate; Pierre ("Pete") duPont, who had recently completed his second term as governor of Delaware; Alexander Haig, Reagan's first secretary of state; Jack Kemp, retiring as representative (N.Y.); and Marion ("Pat") Robertson, minister and social conservative activist. The Democratic field consisted of Bruce Babbitt, who had recently completed his second term as governor of Arizona; Biden, senator; Dukakis, governor; Gephardt, representative; Gore, senator; Hart, former senator; Jackson, minister and civil rights activist; and Simon, senator.

This list shows several other regularities common to campaigns in the new nomination system. First, and remarkably, just over half of these candidates were in office during the nomination campaign. Even discounting the two who never held political office, only eight of the twelve who had were currently in office. Holding public office makes it difficult to face the pressures of mounting a presidential campaign. Hart represents something of an extreme by retiring from the Senate in 1986 (when he probably would have won reelection easily) to run for President, but it is hard to imagine a better illustration of the demands of candidacy.

A second regularity is that most (twelve of fourteen) held or had recently held high political office, and all but one of those held a high elective office. The field included a vice president, five current or recent senators, three current or recent governors, two members of the House of Representatives, and a former secretary of state. "Ambition theory," developed originally by Joseph A. Schlesinger to explain how personal ambition and the pattern and prestige of offices combine to shape political careers, predicts that those who run for office will tend to emerge from political offices that provide the strongest electoral base for such a campaign.[3] This base for the presidency includes the offices of vice president, senator, governor, and, of course, the presidency itself.

In 1988, nine candidates had such a strong electoral base. Haig, as former secretary of state, emerged from what had once been the stepping stone to the presidency. Today appointive office is a far weaker base for a candidacy, although the secretary of state is still the most prestigious cabinet post. Still, Haig's lack of elective office experience was seen as a major weakness of his candidacy, and his early withdrawal seemed to support this assessment. Two members of the House ran for nomination, about the same proportion as in other post-1968 contests. Two factors serve to reduce House members' chances of running. First, they have a small constituency and the House provides little public visibility. Gephardt and Kemp were, however, among the more prominent representatives, and their visibility was primarily due to their championing of public policy positions. Second, representatives running for president labor under the disadvantage of being up for reelection to the House at the same time. None of the other candidates was up for reelection to his current office in 1988. Thus, House members may eventually be forced to choose between a very likely reelection victory and the far less likely chance of winning the presidency. Kemp, however, differed from Gephardt because he had already determined not to seek reelection to the House, and thus did not have to consider this choice.[4]

The regularity with which candidates emerge from offices with strong electoral bases is shown in Table 1-1. The distribution of backgrounds of the fourteen candidates of 1988 is very similar to those of all candidates for presidential nomination over the 1972-1988 period. Overall, three-quarters of all candidates came from offices that provide a strong electoral base. Moreover, in the 1972-1988 period, about three in ten were no longer in office, about the same proportion as in 1988. Of those, the great majority, as in 1988, had left office in favorable circumstances.[5] Finally, as in 1988, the great majority of candidates were not also up for reelection to their current office as they ran for president.[6]

Jackson and Robertson's candidacies are not well described by this set of regularities. Jackson, however, had run a strong race for the 1984 Democratic nomination, coming in third. As we will discuss, he was able to benefit from this experience (one that few presidential candidates have and only his 1984 opponent Hart had in the 1988 Democratic campaign). He was also able to continue the formal organization he helped found in 1984, the Rainbow Coalition, and he was able to extend his base of public support in 1988 from that of 1984. Robertson was, in some respects, in a similar position to Jackson in 1984. Both were well known ministers and political activists. Both represented policy and ideological (and activists') constituencies that had come to play strong roles in the national politics of their parties. Both were, in fact, eloquent spokesmen for these constituencies. And both actively championed their causes as well as fought for the nomination for themselves.

Overall, then, the fields of contenders for the 1988 presidential nominations resembled in most respects those of the other campaigns conducted in the new nomination system, at least in a party without an incumbent seeking renomination. Let us, therefore, describe the system they faced.

The Rules

Two major sets of rules govern presidential nomination campaigns, and both underwent important changes between 1968 and 1972. These rules affect the way delegates are selected to attend the national conventions and how money is raised and allocated in presidential contests. After 1972, these rules were modified further. The basic shape of the rules governing nominations, however, remain intact, and thus we can speak of nominations as under a new system that began in 1972.

Delegate Selection Rules

Since 1832 no person has been elected president without first having been chosen by the votes of delegates at a national nominating convention.[7] In principle, delegates can nominate anyone they want. In

Table 1-1   Current or Most Recent Office Held by Declared
Candidates for President: Two Major Parties, 1972-1988

Office held[a]	Percentage of all candidates holding that office	Number 1972-1988	Number 1988
President	6%	4	0
Vice president	3	2	1
U.S. senator	40	25	5
U.S. representative	15	9	2
Governor	23	14	3
U.S. cabinet	3	2	1
Other	5	3	0
None	5	3	2
Total	100%	62	14

[a]Office held at time of candidacy or office held most recently prior to candidacy.

Source: This list of candidates between 1972 and 1984 is found in *Congressional Quarterly's Guide to U.S. Elections*, 2d ed. (Washington, D.C.: Congressional Quarterly, 1985), 378. The 1988 candidates are listed on pages 13-14 of this chapter.

reality, they have rarely been that free. Most delegates these days are chosen by competition among presidential contenders in the states' primaries or caucuses. The candidates, in other words, campaign to get the public to select delegates who back them.

National convention delegates are chosen by the states' parties in one of two ways. One method is the primary election. A primary is an official election held by the state, in which voters choose which presidential candidate's delegates attend the national convention. Especially in the larger states, presidential candidates campaign for popular support in much the same way as they do in the general election, by direct appeal to the public through expensive and extensive media campaigns.

Other states use the caucus method for choosing delegates. Caucuses are elections run by political parties, and there is a great deal of variation from state to state. While these procedures are often very complex, the key action usually happens in the very first step, often at the precinct level. A precinct caucus is a meeting of those partisans who live in the precinct and are interested enough to attend. At the caucus, partisans declare their preference among presidential candidates. In the Democratic party at least, delegates who back the various presidential candidates are chosen to attend the county, then district, state, and finally national conventions in proportion to the presidential preferences of those at the precinct caucuses. Thus, at least in the Democratic party, the caucus system is like a primary in that all Democrats in the state can go to the caucuses and declare a preference for a presidential candidate, and delegates, when finally chosen, must reflect the results of that "vote." [8] However, caucuses differ from primaries in one crucial respect: very few people attend caucuses. Turnout of 5 to 10 percent is unusually high. Therefore, while candidates might run an electionlike campaign in a caucus state, the important campaign is to find the candidate's supporters and get them to attend the caucuses. Success in caucuses, therefore, often turns less on general popularity, media campaigning, and advertising and much more on a strong, well-financed campaign organization. Many attributed Robertson's strong second place finish in the Iowa caucuses and Jackson's victory in the Michigan caucuses, for example, to their strong state organizations rather than to their overall popularity in the electorate in those states.

There is one more crucial fact about delegate selection. It is a months-long process. In 1988 the Democratic party began delegate selection on February 8 and ended the process on June 7; the Republican process was even longer.[9] As a result, candidates can hope to use success in one state's primary or caucuses to generate enthusiasm, media coverage, and, the candidates hope, greater popular support in a later state's primary or caucuses. The result is a long, rapidly changing, and some would say chaotic campaign. Whatever the case, it is a campaign run by the candidates through the media to obtain grass-roots support. The party leaders play only a small role in selecting the standard bearer. This public campaign makes America unique. In all other democracies, the party leaders have a much greater role in choosing the nominees. How did it happen that our party leaders play such a small role—and the public such a large role—in choosing the parties' nominees?

The basic shape of the Democratic delegate selection reforms was set in reaction to the tumultuous nomination campaign of 1968. In that year, Sens. Eugene J. McCarthy (Minn.) and Robert F. Kennedy (N.Y.) ran public, primary-oriented campaigns. Before the second primary, in Wisconsin, President Johnson surprisingly announced that he would not seek renomination. Vice President Hubert H. Humphrey took his place as a candidate. Humphrey, however, made no *public* campaign, winning nomination without entering a primary. The controversial nomination split the Democratic party and led it to initiate reforms, including those designed to open the nomination process to more diverse candidacies and to more public participation.

The most obvious consequence of these reforms was the rapid increase in the use of primaries to select delegates. In 1968, seventeen states held Democratic presidential primaries. That figure jumped to twenty-three in 1972, climbed to thirty in 1976, and was thirty-one in 1980. In 1984, several states abandoned primaries and chose their delegates by party caucuses, and there were only twenty-five Democratic primaries used to select delegates. In 1988, there was a return to the primary. Thirty-three states used primaries to select delegates to the Democratic party convention, and thirty-five states held such primaries on the Republican side. About two out of three Democratic delegates were chosen by primary, while the figure was three of four on the Republican side. Most delegates not selected in primaries have been chosen by caucuses. However, reforms have succeeded in making them more open to public participation—more timely, better publicized, and, in short, more primarylike. Since 1976, for example, the Iowa caucuses have been the first important public delegate-selection proceedings in the nation. As such, they have become as widely covered in the media and as hotly contested and important to the candidates as any primary.

The important point in these changes has been the greater role played by the public. No candidate can avoid a public campaign. Indeed, the eventual nominees in all campaigns have won *because* they won in the primaries and caucuses. Moreover, candidates discovered not only that they needed to win in the primary season, but also that they could use early primary and caucus events as a launching pad toward prominence, resources, and victory, gathering, in the favored catchword, momentum.[10]

These reforms, and the nomination system they created, have been controversial. The most controversial result has been to move the locus of nomination power from the party leadership to the general public. Indeed, the number of elected and appointed party leaders who were even able to win seats at the convention declined massively in the Democratic party in 1972.[11] In order to bring party leaders back into the selection process, the Democratic party created so-called superdelegates for the 1984 (and 1988) conventions. In 1984 and 1988, about one out of seven of the delegate slots was reserved for party and elected leaders. Moreover, these superdelegates were free to vote for whomever they chose, unbound by popular sentiment expressed in primaries, caucuses, or public opinion polls. In 1984, these superdelegates played a critical role in Mondale's nomination campaign, transforming his slim lead over Hart in delegates won in primaries and caucuses into a clear victory in total delegate support.[12]

The changes discussed so far have been initiated primarily by the Democratic party. The Republican party's nomination procedures have been revised over this period, generally in a direction consistent with the Democratic party reforms. The Republican reforms, however, have been less extensive. For example, the party did not create superdelegates, largely because Republican elected and party officials were already strongly represented at the convention. The party's campaign process closely resembles the Democratic one, therefore, in part because Republicans have followed Democratic reform initiatives and in part because primaries are the product of state legislation. If a state decides to establish a primary, it will generally hold primaries for both parties.[13]

One further important change that was to prove especially significant in 1988 was the decision of increasing numbers of states to move their delegate selection date earlier and earlier in the primary season—so-called frontloading. In 1976, the last primary date of the season selected more delegates than were chosen on any other day. That date, therefore, became known as Super Tuesday. By 1984, Super Tuesday had moved to March 13, two weeks after the New Hampshire primary, since nine states began their delegate selection proceedings on that day and more delegates were selected then than on any other day. In 1988, Super Tuesday was again the second week in March (March 8), three weeks after the New Hampshire primary. This time, however, twenty states began their proceedings on that day on the Democratic side (on the Republican side, eighteen began their proceedings on March 5 or March 8), selecting a third of all Democratic delegates (42 percent on the Republican side were chosen these two days). Frontloading, of course, reflected the importance candidates and media attached to performance in early events, along with the often momentum-driven victories achieved before the primary season had ended. Each state naturally desired to be crucial in the nomination contest and stood to receive a lot of media attention and to have money spent within it if it hosted a prominent campaign event.

In 1988, Super Tuesday was more than just the most important date in the primary season. Many southern and border states had arranged to hold their proceedings then to create a "regional" primary.[14] The idea was to coordinate their primaries—as early as possible in the primary season—so that the southern states could exert maximum impact on the presidential nomination process. To that extent, they were in many ways successful. Bush all but won the nomination with his overwhelming victory in state after state that night. Dukakis's strong showing, especially in the Florida and Texas primaries, also proved crucial in his longer and more difficult run for the nomination. Nonetheless, one of the goals of southern Democrats was to nominate a Democrat more in line with their region's interests. A Massachusetts Democrat who proved vulnerable to charges by Bush of being too liberal was not the kind of candidate the southern Democrats hoped would emerge.

Although the Democratic and Republican nomination procedures are similar in most respects, there are some differences. As we saw, the Democrats set aside one-seventh of their seats for superdelegates to ensure representation of party officials. The Republicans have traditionally selected party leaders as delegates, but the party does not have explicit rules that guarantee them seats. There are usually a few states where the Republicans accept a state's primary procedures for selecting delegates, but where the Democratic party demands that the state party hold a caucus to select delegates. On the other hand, there are some states in which it is very difficult for an average citizen to participate in the Republican delegate selection process. In the 1988 contest, for example, Michigan Republicans began their delegate selection procedure in a statewide party primary held in August 1986 to elect approximately ten thousand precinct delegates. In January 1988, only these precinct delegates were eligible to participate in choosing among the Republican presidential candidates.

The Democratic rules differ from the Republican procedures in another major respect. From 1976 on, the Democrats have refused to accept state rules in which the candidate who wins the most votes in a state primary or caucus can win all of the state's delegates. The Democrats require, instead, that all states follow some form of proportional representation. Under pure proportional representation, a candidate's share of the delegates would be the same as his or her share of the popular vote. Rarely is any electoral system so pure. In 1976, 1984, and 1988, the party allowed states to use various "loophole" or "bonus" procedures that gave the winner more than his or her proportionate share of the delegates, and even states without such procedures required candidates to pass a specified threshold in votes before earning any delegates in that state. (In 1988, the threshold was usually 15 percent.) Despite these deviations from pure proportional representation, losing candidates could often earn some delegates. The Republicans, on the other hand, allow the popular vote winner to earn all the state's delegates. In such cases, of course, losing candidates wind up with no delegates at all.

Financial Rules

The 1970s also brought major changes in campaign financing procedures. The Federal Election Campaign Act of 1971 opened these reforms. The act was substantially amended in 1974 and 1976 and has been revised and interpreted in less important ways since then. In general, the major features of the reforms fell into three areas of immediate concern.[15]

First, individuals and groups (political action committees, or PACs) were severely limited in the contributions they could make to any campaign (to $1,000 per person and $5,000 per group). The old-style "fat cats" who gave thousands or even millions of dollars to a candidate were thereby eliminated. Money would henceforth have to be raised in a massive, broad-based campaign, paralleling the candidates' broad-based campaign for votes.

Second, presidential nomination candidates could receive a dollar-for-dollar match of small ($250 or less), individual contributions, thus providing as much as 50 percent federal funding of their campaigns. While few receive anything close to that large an extent of funding from the government, the federal government has become a very important source of funds.

Third, presidential candidates who accept federal funding (as all did in 1988) are subject to limits on what they can spend. In 1988, candidates could spend only a bit more than $23 million on the primary season (with more for fund-raising expenses). Moreover, there are limits to spending in each state. Because state limits add up to nearly three times the overall limit, candidates who raise the full amount of money have to plan carefully where to spend it.

Clearly, the candidates will spend the most in states crucial to their nomination prospects. The importance of early events, such as those in Iowa and New Hampshire, means that spending is often even more frontloaded than delegate selection. In 1980, for example, the four leading candidates had spent three-quarters of the legal maximum before half the delegates were selected, and a similar pattern held in 1984. The very large number of delegates selected on Super Tuesday in 1988, in so many different states, worsened the problem of early spending. To compete effectively in many of these states virtually required a media-oriented advertising campaign (especially television), and thus an unusually expensive one. Campaigns in Iowa and New Hampshire, both small states, required a disproportionate amount of money but still could be conducted on a "retail" basis (that is, by telephone and doorbell ringing, shaking hands at malls and factories, and so on). Super Tuesday mandated a "wholesale" campaign for votes, looking much like the media-dominated general election campaign. There simply wasn't time to do otherwise.

The Campaigns

On the surface, the two parties' contests looked very different. As we will see, however, there were underlying similarities. We begin with overviews to see how very dissimilar the two campaigns seemed to be and then turn to some similarities.

The Republican Campaign

The Republican contest was short-lived. Bush essentially won the nomination on Super Tuesday by thoroughly routing his remaining opponents. This was, basically, only the third major contest, after the Iowa caucuses and the New Hampshire primary.[16]

This short campaign featured six candidates, but only three had much impact. DuPont's and Haig's campaigns never got on track, and they withdrew early and quietly. Kemp had more success, but even his campaign was far too limited. While more popular than duPont and Haig among Republicans, he was unable to attract enough attention to be a major figure at all. That left a campaign featuring Bush, Dole, and Robertson.

The Iowa caucuses, first in the nation, also featured the first major surprises of the year. Dole won the caucuses (with 37 percent support), which was not a major surprise. Robertson, however, did do surprisingly well by coming in second (25 percent). The biggest loser was front-runner Bush, who came in an embarrassingly weak third place (19 percent).

As attention turned to New Hampshire, Bush's campaign appeared to be in trouble, while Dole's and perhaps Robertson's campaigns seemed to have momentum (called the "Iowa bounce" by journalists in 1988). Would this be like the Democratic campaign in 1984, where Hart's surprisingly strong second-place finish in Iowa gave him enough bounce to defeat Mondale in New Hampshire, or would it be more like the 1980 Republican contest, in which Bush's victory in Iowa made Reagan's campaign appear vulnerable, but in which any Iowa bounce was insufficient for Bush to defeat Reagan in New Hampshire?

Dole's Iowa bounce was short-lived. As in 1980, the Iowa winner took a brief lead in polls in New Hampshire, only to fall back into second place by primary day. Bush defeated Dole that day, 38 to 28 percent, with Robertson garnering only 9 percent of the vote.

Bush and Robertson set their sights on Super Tuesday week. Robertson focused his efforts—indeed, put his campaign on the line—in the South Carolina primary held three days before Super Tuesday.[17] Bush aimed his efforts more broadly at virtually all of the events of March 5 and 8.

Dole, in contrast, sought victories earlier, presumably to obtain a new bounce leading into Super Tuesday. Although Dole did win the South Dakota primary and Minnesota caucuses held the week after New Hampshire's primary, these efforts were not productive. Without the front-runner actively involved, these events received little media attention, Dole's victories were discounted, neither state offered many delegates, and Dole, essentially, wasted time and resources. The net effect was that he was, if anything, farther behind as Super Tuesday neared.

Bush's easy victory over Robertson in South Carolina (Robertson even finished behind Dole) foreshadowed the next Tuesday. On Super Tuesday, Bush won an outright majority in twelve of the sixteen primary states, and he carried a plurality in the other four. Dole came in second in all but two of the primaries (a narrow third to Robertson in Louisiana and Texas), but was close to Bush only in Missouri and Oklahoma. Robertson won the Washington state caucuses, the only GOP caucuses on Super Tuesday; but with only fifteen thousand participants, it attracted little attention. Overall, then, the day was an impressive victory for Bush. While both challengers maintained active candidacies for a time (Dole until March 29, Robertson until May 16), Bush effectively secured nomination on March 8—five months before the Republican nomination convention.

In short, Bush lost in Iowa, righted his campaign with a victory in New Hampshire, and won nomination on Super Tuesday. An obvious interpretation is that Bush was the overwhelming favorite for nomination, and Iowa was simply an aberration. That he was vice president to the most popular incumbent in two decades, serving a country at peace amidst prosperity, made his nomination inevitable.

There is much truth in this easy interpretation. As we will see, however, the story was not quite this simple. The more complex story will point to several similarities with the Democratic contest. First, however, let us consider the differences between the two contests.

The Democratic Campaign

Dukakis's path to victory was longer and more difficult than Bush's. Five Democrats won at least one major primary or caucus. Super Tuesday ended in essentially a three-way draw. Dukakis did not win a majority of the delegates until June 7 (Bush went over the top in the Pennsylvania primary, April 26). And his closest competitor, Jackson, did not withdraw his candidacy until the Democratic Convention was underway.

In Iowa, Gephardt won (with 31 percent support) over Simon (27 percent) and Dukakis (22 percent). In New Hampshire, Dukakis (with 36 percent) defeated Gephardt (20 percent) and Simon (17 percent). After New Hampshire, Babbitt withdrew and Hart's candidacy was effectively ended. Jackson's and Gore's candidacies, however, were about to begin in earnest. Both would find the South more congenial than Iowa and New Hampshire. Gore, in fact, had ceased campaigning in these first two states, while Jackson's 9 and 8 percent support in these overwhelmingly white states was seen as a surprisingly strong showing.

Super Tuesday was effectively a draw among Dukakis, Gore, and Jackson. Gephardt and Simon trailed badly. Indeed, Simon had withdrawn from Super Tuesday competition to focus on his home state. Two third-place finishes had depleted his resources and gave him no bounce to garner more. Gephardt, who won only his home state of Missouri, was the biggest loser. His campaign was reminiscent of Dole's: win in Iowa, get a bounce but come in second in New Hampshire, lose big on Super Tuesday (in part for the same reason, lack of resources), and drop out by the end of March (the day before Dole, in fact). On the Republican side, Super Tuesday was the knockout punch for Bush. On the Democratic side, it raised the fortunes of Gore and Jackson, provided Dukakis with some southern (as well as northern) victories and a lot of delegates, did not further weaken a noncontesting Simon, and therefore hurt only Gephardt.

With no clear pattern emerging and no clear front-runner, the campaign moved to Illinois. There, one favorite son (Simon) defeated another (Jackson), 42 to 32 percent. Seemingly, there was now a fourth candidate. Simon, however, lacked resources to follow his home state victory and effectively ceased campaigning on this high note. Dukakis missed an opportunity for a major victory (coming in with 16 percent); Gore did not contest there. Jackson appeared to be weakened. That perception changed in the next major event, the Michigan caucuses. There, Jackson won an outright majority with Dukakis a distant second. Dukakis, in turn, righted his campaign with victories in Connecticut and Wisconsin. Gore was still not contesting vigorously.

The New York primary on April 19, six weeks after Super Tuesday and Bush's nomination triumph, finally proved the turning point. New York, of course, had a large delegation at stake. Gore had established it as his first major campaign effort outside the South, and both Dukakis and Jackson sorely needed a victory there. Thus, it loomed large strategically as well as in terms of delegates to be won.

Crucial it appeared to be in the offing, and crucial it was in fact. Dukakis won an outright majority (51 percent), well ahead of Jackson (at 37 percent). Gore, with the dubious assistance of New York City Mayor Ed Koch, came in far behind (with only 10 percent).[18] Thus, Gore's candidacy was gravely weakened, and he suspended his campaign two days later. So there were now two candidates remaining.

While Dukakis and Jackson remained as the viable candidates, they were not equal competitors. As expected, Jackson won in the District of Columbia. But Dukakis would go on to win every one of the eleven remaining state primaries, usually by at least a two-to-one margin. In many respects, New York only demonstrated what was in fact a pattern of dominance for Dukakis. New York's primary only served to show that Dukakis's two preceding wins in Connecticut and Wisconsin were the pattern, the losses in Illinois and Michigan the exception.

It is noteworthy that Jackson continued to compete, despite a two-month string of nearly uninterrupted defeats. Most candidates would have ended their campaigning as pointless—or would have exhausted their money and ability to raise more. Jackson was able to continue because he had a core of support that remained despite the inevitability of his defeat. Moreover, he viewed himself as the champion of a cause. The Democratic party rules, however, also facilitated his continued candidacy. Because the party prohibited winner-take-all contests, Jackson gained some delegates during these remaining months. In the final presidential roll call, Jackson won delegate votes from ten of the eleven primary states that he lost after New York.

Similarities Between the Two Campaigns

Beneath the surface dissimilarity of the two campaigns lurked some interesting similarities. We will show this by examining pairs of candidates, one from each side. Let us begin with the victors.

The two winners had the strongest, best organized, and best financed campaign organizations in their respective parties. Organizational might gave them two critical advantages. First, they had the resources to withstand defeats. By the end of 1987, Bush had already raised $18 million and Dukakis $10 million, putting both millions of dollars ahead of their next best financed opponents. Put alternatively, the less well off candidates needed clear-cut victories over strong opponents to be able to generate the enthusiasm and attention to attract resources and activists for the next stage in the competition. Second, Bush and Dukakis had developed widespread enough organizations as the campaign opened to be able to conduct campaigns in many states at once. This proved particularly critical on Super Tuesday. In earlier years without as much frontloading, candidates needed to conduct campaigns in only one or two states at a time in this early period. Super Tuesday was so large that winning only one or two states would pale beside the many defeats in the remaining states. Moreover, the only way to conduct campaigns in so many states at a time was to combine a well-oiled organizational effort within the state with a high-profile, expensive, and nearly national media campaign.

Super Tuesday was critical for both nominees. This point is obvious for Bush. For Dukakis, however, it is also true. In particular, victories in the South enabled him to claim that he alone of the Democrats was a national candidate. Dukakis won pluralities in five primaries and three caucuses that night. Only two were in the South, Florida and Texas, but these were the two biggest states.[19] By the end of Super Tuesday, Dukakis had won in the East, the Midwest (he had won the Minnesota caucuses earlier), the South, and the West (Hawaii, Idaho, and Washington on Super Tuesday). The other candidates could be seen primarily as regional, even at the end of the campaign. Simon won only in his home state. Gephardt won only in his home state and one of its neighbors. With the exception of the Wyoming and Nevada caucuses, in which a total of only eight thousand Democrats participated, Gore won only southern and border states. Jackson had won primaries only in southern states with large black populations, Puerto Rico, and D.C., although he scored caucus victories in Texas, Alaska, South Carolina, Michigan, Delaware, and Vermont, as well as the Virgin Islands. Moreover, the psychological impact of the Democratic governor of Massachusetts (or, as Bush would call him in the fall, the *liberal* Democratic governor of Massachusetts) carrying the two largest prizes in the South was substantial.

There were other similarities between the two contests. Consider another pair of candidates, Jackson and Robertson. We have already noted the similarities (and unusual nature) of their backgrounds and candidacies. They were the last candidates to withdraw from active competition. This fact reflects in large part the nature of their candidacies, that is, their deep commitments to political and ideological priorities and policy agendas (vastly different as the two commitments are). In other words, both ran for reasons beyond their personal ambitions to be president. Their commitments were revealed in another way besides campaigning after any realistic hope of victory was long past. Both won rather surprising and remarkable "victories," Robertson in Iowa (a strong second place) and Jackson in Michigan. In a Gallup poll conducted in Iowa only a little more than a week before the caucuses (January 29 to 31), Robertson was the first choice of only 8 percent of Republicans. And yet he received 25 percent support at the caucuses. The media saw Jackson's majority support in the Michigan caucuses as evidence of widespread popular support, raising the possibility that Jackson might even win nomination. Later analysis revealed that, like Robertson's in Iowa, Jackson's popular support in Michigan was far smaller than the caucus results suggested.

   Their strong showings without strong mass popular support in these states appears to be due to their commitments and, therefore, the commitments of their supporters. Turnout in caucuses is very low, as discussed earlier. Highly committed followers, especially when they can be located through organized groups (churches and ideological groups for both candidates, plus black organizations for Jackson), can be mobilized far more easily than broadly diffused and unorganized support for other candidacies, even when far more in the general public support those candidates. (Labor unions provide another organizational resource, but unlike the 1984 contest, when labor leaders backed Mondale even before the election year began, union leaders did not line up behind a specific candidate in 1988.)

   For a final pair of similar candidates, consider Dole and Gephardt. First, they were similar in being perceived as at least somewhat more centrist or moderate than many of their opponents. They both won in Iowa and lost in New Hampshire (effectively ending their candidacies). They are, of course, both from midwestern states. We will now see that they were similar as well in getting an Iowa bounce or momentum, in having or acquiring a fairly broad base of support in other states, in briefly achieving credibility as a candidate, but in losing that credibility due to their losses in New Hampshire. Their credibility declined, if not their general popularity.

   Consider first the data in Table 1-2, where we present the results of Gallup telephone polls conducted in various states before their caucuses or primary. The data report which candidate was the respondents' first choice as their party's nominee. Consider, especially, the two New Hampshire polls. The first was conducted early in the year, the second between the Iowa caucuses and their primary. Bush and Dole were

Table 1-2 First Choice of Republicans and Democrats for Nomination, Various Gallup Polls, Preprimary or Caucus

Candidate	Iowa I	Iowa II	New Hampshire I	New Hampshire II	Massachusetts I	Massachusetts II	Florida I	Florida II	Texas I	Texas II
Republican										
Bush	27%	26%	28%	23%	47%	56%	52%	58%	59%	63%
Dole	42	40	30	35	32	28	22	19	21	18
Robertson	6	8	3	8	3	3	9	9	10	9
Kemp	6	10	14	10	10	7	6	4	4	5
DuPont	3	6	6	9	—	—	—	—	—	—
Haig	2	1	4	—	—	—	—	—	—	—
None/DK[a]	14	10	16	14	9	7	11	10	5	5
Total percent	100%	101%	101%	99%	101%	101%	100%	100%	99%	100%
Number	(546)	(540)	(882)	(2,257)	(447)	(615)	(402)	(991)	(523)	(1,054)
Democratic										
Dukakis	12%	19%	26%	35%	64%	68%	32%	36%	27%	24%
Gephardt	15	32	5	17	10	6	15	15	17	16
Gore	1	*	3	6	2	2	5	6	9	12
Jackson	7	6	5	6	7	10	15	14	16	21
Simon	16	15	13	12	7	3	4	3	2	2
Babbitt	2	6	3	4	—	—	—	—	—	—
Hart	31	12	20	4	2	1	7	3	11	6
None/DK[a]	15	11	24	17	8	9	23	23	18	20
Total percent	99%	101%	99%	101%	100%	99%	101%	100%	100%	101%
Number	(623)	(590)	(351)	(1,806)	(689)	(1,340)	(421)	(980)	(463)	(1,120)

Notes: The choice of Republican (or Democratic) candidates is among Republican (or Democratic) identifiers.
Dates of polling: Iowa I: 1/1-1/3, II: 1/29-1/31; New Hampshire I: 1/1-1/3, II: 2/12-2/14 (after the Iowa caucuses, 2/8); Massachusetts I: 2/19-2/21 (after the New Hampshire primary, 2/16), II: 3/4-3/6; Florida I: 2/26-2/28, II: 2/26-2/28; Texas I: 2/26-2/28, II: 3/4-3/6.

[a] Includes those with no preference and those who said "don't know."

* Indicates less than 1 percent.

Source: Gallup polls, made available to and analyzed by authors.

essentially tied early in the year. After the Iowa caucuses, Bush's support fell while Dole's increased, garnering Dole a substantial, 12-point lead as the primary neared. An Iowa bounce seems plausible. The same seems to be true on the Democratic side. Gephardt's support more than tripled, although Dukakis's increased by 9 points (mostly due to the falling support for Hart). Note, as well, that Gephardt had a substantial following in Florida and Texas, even in the polls conducted just days before the Super Tuesday vote. Although Dukakis held the lead in both states, Gephardt was as popular as anyone else and held the advantage over his chief competitor, Gore. Moreover, there were many undecided voters in these two states (as in New Hampshire). Perhaps if he had had greater resources, Gephardt could have held his support and competed more strongly among the uncommitted voters. In the actual vote, he edged Gore in Florida, 14 to 13 percent (with Jackson second to Dukakis), while in Texas, he fell behind Gore, 14 to 20 percent (with Jackson again second to Dukakis).

These data suggest that both Dole and Gephardt benefited from their victories in Iowa and that Gephardt, especially, had the potential to be a major figure in at least some key states as Super Tuesday neared. We can get a clearer demonstration of these opportunities—and at least a strong hint about their failures to truly capture momentum—by looking at the National Election Studies (NES) survey of the Super Tuesday states.

This survey was conducted among the residents of the sixteen states holding primaries on Super Tuesday. Instead of conducting a single survey in a short period of time (as in the Gallup polls above), the NES preelection survey was conducted using telephone polls over two months, from January 17 through March 8, and a total of 2,117 respondents were interviewed.[20] Surveys conducted each week were selected so as to consist of a small but random sample of the entire population of the Super Tuesday states.[21] The purpose was to be able to examine changes in public opinion over the course of the campaign, and we will use these surveys in that way.[22]

In Table 1-3 we report three types of information about reactions to principal competitors. The first row for each Republican candidate reports the percentage of Republicans (including independents who leaned toward the Republicans) who said they would support him. This percentage is labeled "vote preference." The second row reports the average evaluation of the candidate (among supporters of his party). This is a response to a 100-point "feeling thermometer," asking respondents how warm (maximum 100 degrees) or cool (minimum 0 degrees) they felt toward that candidate, with 50 indicating neutral (neither warm nor cool) feelings. The third line consists of 100-point "viability" ratings. These are scales on which respondents indicated how likely they thought that

Table 1-3 Dynamics of Vote Preferences, Evaluation of the Candidates, and Perceptions of Candidate Viability Among the Super Tuesday Partisans, NES Super Tuesday Poll

Candidates	Week of the Primary Campaign						
	1	2	3	4 Iowa caucus	5 N.H. primary	6	7 Super Tuesday
Republican							
Bush							
% vote preference	54	58	64	40	56	56	61
Avg. evaluation	67	68	70	66	70	70	69
Avg. viability	73	77	74	67	75	76	73
Dole							
% vote preference	25	26	18	45	30	27	28
Avg. evaluation	63	65	66	67	65	65	67
Avg. viability	64	66	60	71	70	70	66
Number of Republicans interviewed	(108)	(95)	(95)	(185)	(118)	(98)	(173)
Democratic							
Dukakis							
% vote preference	22	22	14	22	32	36	36
Avg. evaluation	60	64	60	56	58	60	61
Avg. viability	56	57	64	59	61	65	67
Gephardt							
% vote preference	6	9	6	28	23	16	11
Avg. evaluation	49	56	58	60	57	57	52
Avg. viability	45	48	51	61	56	56	54
Gore							
% vote preference	18	11	20	18	8	11	18
Avg. evaluation	57	57	57	57	56	54	57
Avg. viability	48	43	50	44	45	43	46
Jackson							
% vote preference	28	15	14	19	24	25	28
Avg. evaluation	57	44	45	49	56	52	57
Avg. viability	46	36	32	36	41	35	43
Number of Democrats interviewed	(106)	(109)	(82)	(179)	(128)	(140)	(180)

Notes: Week 1=1/20-26; 2=1/27-2/2; 3=2/3-8; 4=2/9-16; 5=2/17-23; 6=2/24-3/1; 7=3/2-8. Iowa caucuses held on 2/8. New Hampshire primary held on 2/16. Super Tuesday was 3/8.

Evaluation=100-point "feeling thermometer." Viability=100-point chances for nomination scale. Republicans (Democrats)=strong, weak, and "leaning" Republicans (Democrats). Number of Republicans [Democrats] interviewed is the total number of Republicans [Democrats] who completed the NES interview in that week. This number is also the *N* for vote preference.

The results for voting preferences are based upon all the Republicans and Democrats (including independent leaners) who were interviewed. The number of Republicans and Democrats evaluating the candidates and rating their chances of winning is always lower than the total number interviewed, and varies considerably from week to week.

Source: NES Super Tuesday Survey, analyzed by authors.

candidate was to win his party's nomination, ranging from 0 (no chance) to 100 (certain victory).[23]

Let us begin with the middle line, the feeling thermometer ratings. In general, there is very little change in these from week to week. Bush's ratings average from 66 to 70, Dole's from 63 to 67, for example. Such week-to-week changes are too small, in general, to be statistically meaningful, and they generally change with no apparent pattern.

The differences between Bush and Dole on this measure are also quite small and stable, with evaluations of Dole generally 3 or 4 points lower than those of Bush. These two candidates were far more warmly evaluated than the other Republicans. Ratings of Kemp averaged in the upper 50s, Haig's and duPont's just about 50, and Robertson's in the middle 40s. In short, Republicans liked the two leading contenders, with Bush just slightly ahead of Dole on average, and this changed little over the course of the campaign.[24]

Average viability ratings were different. First, Bush generally held a more substantial lead over Dole by this measure than by the evaluation measure. In other words, most of the time, Republicans liked Dole almost as much as Bush but thought him less likely to be nominated. Second, however, the 10-point or greater average advantage Bush held over Dole in this measure before the Iowa caucuses disappeared completely in the week after Iowa. While, on average, Dole actually was ranked ahead of Bush, the 4-point difference is too small to be meaningful. In short, Dole was seen to be at least as likely to win nomination as Bush after his Iowa victory and Bush's third-place showing. But beginning immediately after his victory in the New Hampshire primary, Bush was once again seen as the more likely to win nomination. Republicans reacted to the campaign events *not* by changing their overall evaluations of these two candidates but by reacting to the changing strategic environment.

Finally, then, we come to the "bottom line" for the candidates, how many said they would support them in these Super Tuesday states. Bush was the first choice of a clear majority of Republicans up to the Iowa caucuses, while about a quarter backed Dole. This changed dramatically the next week, as Dole was the first choice of 45 percent that week, up from 18 percent the week before. Bush's support dropped nearly as dramatically, from 64 to only 40 percent. Dole held a lead that week not only in New Hampshire (see Table 1-2), but throughout these Super Tuesday states as well. After Bush defeated Dole in New Hampshire, however, vote preferences reverted back to almost exactly their pre-Iowa levels.

What are we to make of these patterns? The answer appears to be something like an Iowa bounce or momentum. There are two nearly equally well liked (on average) candidates running for nomination. Pure evaluations might give Bush a small advantage, but it was small at best.

Either would be more than minimally satisfactory to most Republicans. But one candidate seems more likely to win nomination (and election, see note 23). And those perceptions of viability change with actual outcomes of delegate selection events. If evaluations are relatively stable and close together, voters seem likely to support the candidate they view as more likely to win nomination and election.

Political scientists Henry E. Brady and Patricia D. Conley reported exactly the same account of the dynamics of opinion in the 1976 presidential nomination contest in California. They wrote:

> Poll results revealed extraordinary volatility in support for Jimmy Carter, Jerry Brown, and Hubert Humphrey.... Underlying preferences changed very little.... Strategic behavior, on the other hand, was a major determinant of the dynamics of candidate support. Changes in perceptions of candidate viability account for most of the volatility in the polls.[25]

The data about Dukakis and Gephardt reveal a strikingly similar pattern. At least by the second week of the survey, evaluations of the two contenders fluctuated little and sporadically over time. Just as on the Republican side, the evaluations of these two were, on average, little different (with Gephardt just a bit under Dukakis, just as Dole was to Bush). The increasing perceptions of Dukakis's viability, however, were set back the week after the Iowa caucuses, while Gephardt's perceived chances jumped that week. Once again, just as on the Republican side, the aftermath of Iowa showed the winner there to be seen as slightly more likely to win nationally than the erstwhile more viable candidate, reversing a clear lead. The proportion choosing Gephardt as their preferred candidate zoomed that week, from 6 to 28 percent, giving him his first—and last—lead over Dukakis, just as Iowa gave Dole his first—and last—lead in vote preferences over Bush. Dukakis's victory in New Hampshire, like Bush's, reversed his opponent's lead in both viability and vote preference.

What this suggests, then, is that by winning in Iowa both Dole and Gephardt opened a small window of vulnerability against the eventual nominee. There was a bounce or momentum. It was a small opening, perhaps, and certainly brief.

At this point, the story diverges somewhat. Gephardt was facing Dukakis in the latter's neighboring state, one closely tied to Massachusetts.[26] While Bush has New England ties, they are less immediate and direct than Dukakis's. Thus, Dole was able to go well ahead of Bush in the second Gallup poll in New Hampshire as well as in the Super Tuesday poll. While Gephardt was able to edge ahead of Dukakis in the Super Tuesday poll, he was able only to cut a 21-point Dukakis lead to 18 points in the New Hampshire Gallup poll. He was able, however, to move into second place, which he held through the actual vote. Conversely, although Dole's chances in New Hampshire were somewhat better than Gephardt's, the reverse was true in the South. There, Bush had a huge lead, at least after winning in New Hampshire. Gephardt's chances were better mainly because Dukakis was not nearly as strong an opponent in that region. Moreover, in the week after Iowa, Gephardt was the actual leader in the Super Tuesday poll, and if he could have held on to his support, he would have remained a credible contender in the South.

The critical question for Dole, then, is why he lost his briefly held lead in New Hampshire. One account is Dole's own. On national TV the night of the New Hampshire primary, Dole attributed the reversal to ads run by the Bush campaign. In this thirty-second ad, known as the "Straddle" or "Period," the announcer says (in full):

> George Bush and Bob Dole on leadership:
> George Bush led the fight on the INF treaty for Ronald Reagan. Bob Dole straddled, until Iowans pushed him into supporting INF.
> George Bush is against an oil import tax. Bob Dole straddled, but now says he's for an oil import fee.
> George Bush says he won't raise taxes, period. [With portrait of Bush and letters, "Won't Raise Taxes."] Bob Dole straddles, and he just won't promise not to raise taxes. And you know what that means. [With two pictures of Dole facing each other and the letters "Straddled" dissolving to "Taxes—he can't say no."]
> George Bush—ready on Day One to provide presidential leadership.[27]

Bush had earlier vetoed running this ad, but as he fell behind in the polls, he relented. His campaign saturated the airwaves with this ad on the Saturday before the primary, purchasing every available thirty-second spot on television. On national TV on the primary night, Dole regretted that he had not countered these ads, presumably because his failure to do so gave the appearance that the ad was correct. In addition, Dole bitterly responded to Bush's wish of good luck in the South by saying, "Tell George Bush to stop lying about my record!" which also served to re-raise questions about Dole as a bad loser and hatchet man. Still, the argument is that the substance of the campaign is what made the difference.

We do not have polling data to examine Dole's claim directly. We do, however, have some indirect evidence. In the Gallup polls, respondents were given a list of twelve alternatives from which they were asked to choose their perception of the most important problem facing the country. Our analysis of these polls reveals that in the first poll in New Hampshire (in early January), the budget deficit was the problem most commonly chosen by Republicans (39 percent), with taxes as second (18 percent). More of Dole's supporters than Bush's chose deficits (46 to 31 percent), while Bush's supporters were more likely to pick taxes (20 versus 8 percent). By the second New Hampshire poll, after the Iowa caucuses, deficits were chosen by 31 percent (and by 35 and 26 percent among Dole and Bush supporters, respectively). Taxes had declined to a 12 percent selection, and the difference between the supporters of the two candidates had shrunk considerably (15 percent among Bush's and 10 percent among Dole's supporters). Dole may have defused the concern of Republicans that he might raise taxes. Dole argued that Bush's attack reraised this concern, deceptively and at the last minute. We don't know that this is true, but the data suggest Dole's argument is plausible.

Whatever the reasons for his loss that day, Dole's defeat had two effects. It closed the slight opening in the polls and ended his opportunity to raise money enough to compete effectively on Super Tuesday.

Gephardt probably never had an opportunity to win in New Hampshire, even though the Iowa caucus victory increased his support considerably. He, like Dole, needed some way to raise funds to compete effectively on Super Tuesday. Neither had the cash on hand, as their principal competitors did. With a loss in New Hampshire, neither could find a way to raise the money. Both were forced to cut back their Super Tuesday campaign to target a few potential pockets of strength. Such a strategy required help from other candidates, for if other candidates failed to score victories, the front-runner would emerge as dominant. Dole got no help because Kemp and Robertson both fared poorly. Gephardt found some help preventing a Dukakis sweep. Unfortunately for Gephardt, one of the successful candidates was Gore, and Gore became the candidate favored by the more moderate and conservative elements of the Democratic party, in place of Gephardt.

At one level, then, the two nomination contests were very different. One was short and simple, the other long and complicated. At another level, however, there were many striking parallels. These centered on the earliest contests. Super Tuesday was decisive for the Republicans, and we believe that it was nearly as crucial to Dukakis's Democratic victory. In each contest, the Iowa caucuses opened small opportunities for a moderate candidate, Dole and Gephardt, but New Hampshire closed those opportunities and set the stage for Super Tuesday. Moreover, the reaction of voters was rather similar. Relatively stable evaluations of the candidates mixed with rapidly changing appearances of viability, leading to momentumlike dynamics in vote intentions. And, as in all campaigns since 1972, the nominations were won in these dynamic primary contests by the choices of the public, reacting to the strategies of the candidates as reflected in the media. As always in the new nomination system, the nominations were decided before the conventions.

The Conventions and the Running Mates

With the presidential nominations already determined, national party conventions lose much of their excitement. Still, they retain important functions. On the first night, delegates approve the seating of delegations and vote on the party's rules. The most important business of the second night is determining the party's campaign platform. On the third night, the actual roll call of the states for presidential nomination is conducted. On the final night the convention ratifies the nominee's selection of a vice-presidential running mate, and the two standard bearers deliver their acceptance speeches. Throughout the convention there are many opportunities for key party leaders to make speeches and for the party and its leadership to appear before the nation through the media. With so many tasks and such concentrated media coverage of so many ambitious politicians, most conventions have moments of drama and controversy, even though the presidential nominee is known in advance. Such moments occurred in both parties' conventions in 1988.

The Democratic party convened on Monday, July 18, in Atlanta. Here, the main drama centered on Jesse Jackson. The drama began before the convention itself. By this point, Jackson had become a significant force in the Democratic party.

In 1984, Jackson had run a strong third-place campaign to Mondale and Hart. Although he had sought a Rainbow Coalition of people of all races and backgrounds, his support had been concentrated primarily among blacks. In 1988, he sought to expand his base. This time, he was the second-place candidate, and he expanded his support among whites considerably. He often carried 10 percent and more of the white vote, and he regularly carried a quarter of the Democratic vote overall. Moreover he was a very strong presence, in person and on the air. Overall, he was the strongest representative of the liberal wing of the party in 1988. In 1984, he had faced considerable opposition for this position from Mondale. Mondale, in fact, had a following even in Jackson's core constituency, the black electorate. In 1988, only Simon could compete to represent the liberal tradition in the Democratic party, and as we have seen, he failed to make any real impact outside of his home state. Thus, one reason Jackson was able to expand his base from 1984 was the lack of strong opposition from liberal Democrats.

One of the most interesting facts of the 1988 Democratic contest was the shift in the type of candidate running. Only Jackson and Simon could be said to fully represent the liberal, New Deal, Great Society tradition in the Democratic party, a tradition that still motivates many of its most active members. In 1984, of the eight Democrats who ran, four represented that tradition (Jackson, Mondale, Sen. Alan Cranston of California, and former senator and 1972 presidential nominee, George S. McGovern). This pattern in 1984 was typical of previous nominations. Thus, the small number of liberal candidates in 1988 is a major story of the Democratic campaign. The 1988 nomination contest saw the rise of a new breed of Democrats that Hart represented in 1984. Babbitt,

Biden, Gephardt, and of course Hart were very much in this mold. So, too, was Dukakis, whose initial campaign was of a candidate who held to the "new ideas and new leadership" of Hart's campaign theme in 1984, but differed in that as governor he had implemented many of them. In some respects, Gore, too, represented this new breed. Overall, then, as many as six of the eight initial candidates reflected this new breed. The traditional liberal wing of the party was represented solely by Jackson and the relatively ineffective campaign of Simon.

Thus, Jackson came the closest to representing this long tradition in the Democratic party. He was, as well, the first black candidate to have had anything close to the electoral success he achieved in 1988. Finally, his eloquence and presence contributed to his being a force to be reckoned with, even in defeat.

Dukakis began his campaign, as noted, by claiming to be a candidate who had actually implemented new ideas. His drive for nomination, however, meant that he, as the only nationally successful candidate, had to reach out to the various constituencies that make up the Democratic party. Thus, his relations with Jackson were critical.

After winning nomination, Dukakis's major decision was selecting his running mate. Commentators' speculation covered many possible names, of course. Among them was Jackson himself, and it was widely speculated that Dukakis would choose a running mate who was at least acceptable to Jackson. In fact, shortly before the convention opened, Dukakis announced that he had chosen Sen. Lloyd Bentsen of Texas as his running mate. Bentsen had many advantages. He came from, and was a power in, a large state with twenty-nine electoral votes. He was a moderate to conservative Democrat who balanced a ticket headed by a Massachusetts Democrat. He signaled the southern Democrats that Dukakis might be responsive to their concerns. And Bentsen had soundly defeated Bush in Bush's only run at statewide office. None of these credentials were of obvious interest to Jackson or the forces he represented.

The announcement was also bungled. Dukakis's selection was leaked to the press before Dukakis had even had a chance to discuss it with Jackson. The result was that Jackson complained of being ignored in the selection process. He even implied that he might attempt a floor fight over the vice presidential nomination.

Negotiations between the two camps resolved the issue. Jackson agreed to speak before the convention on Tuesday, the night of the platform vote, at which point he announced his support for the Democratic ticket. That night was, essentially, given over to Jackson. He was not just the center of attention; he and the buildup he was given dominated that night, especially on television.

The selection of running mate was also the most controversial part of the Republican convention, which opened on Monday, August 15, in New

Orleans. Early on Tuesday, Bush announced that his running mate would be Sen. Dan Quayle of Indiana. Bush made it clear that this choice was his own, made by himself independently of his advisers. The choice proved controversial. Unlike Bentsen, Quayle was a relatively unknown, junior senator. Journalists quickly raised questions about his record of service in the Vietnam period. Quayle had been a member of the National Guard; it was well known that many had sought to join the National Guard rather than serve in a unit likely to risk combat in Vietnam. Quayle's record as a student in college was less than outstanding. His low grades made entry into law school difficult, and he had made a personal appeal to the School of Law at Indiana University to get admitted, when his record kept him from direct admission. In both the National Guard and law school entry incidents, moreover, there was some suggestion that his family connections (his family had for several generations run a successful newspaper business in Indiana) were used to permit his entry. All in all, it was a less than auspicious beginning. This beginning was compounded by his initial personal appearances before the public and press, in which he appeared ill prepared and, some suggested, ill equipped for the job.

Just like Dukakis, then, Bush seemed to fumble his first key decision. In Dukakis's case, it seemed that he failed to maintain proper relations with his chief competitor and, to make amends, perhaps gave Jackson too much attention just when it should have been Dukakis's shining moment. In Bush's case, it was the person selected as running mate that cast doubt on his judgment. And in both cases attention was diverted in ways that detracted from the successes the candidate had enjoyed in the nomination campaign.

Both candidates, however, had the advantage of prime time televised coverage of the culmination of their nominations and the conventions, their acceptance speeches. These are major events in campaigns. They are the transition for the candidate from intraparty competitor to party standard bearer for the fall. They provide the opportunity for healing whatever wounds may remain in the party as a result of the nomination contests. More important, they set the stage for the fall campaign. In them, the nominees can develop the themes by which they offer their candidacy to the general electorate. In 1988, both rose to the occasion with acceptance speeches that won critical reviews even from skeptical pundits. And so the stage was set for the fall.

Lessons of the Nomination Campaigns

The 1988 nomination campaigns provided two more examples of actively contested nominations without an incumbent seeking renomination in the new nomination system, and they illustrated many of the same patterns as were found in earlier post-1968 contests. First, the large number of contenders for these two nominations was typical. Second, the backgrounds, experiences, and offices held by these hopefuls was also quite typical, including the high proportion of candidates who sought nomination while not currently in office.

We have also seen that the earliest portion of the nomination campaigns is the most dramatic, dynamic, and nearly decisive. One change from previous years was that the earliest events extended to include Super Tuesday. Still, Haig, Babbitt, and duPont withdrew their candidacies before Super Tuesday. Others ended their races because of Super Tuesday, and by the end of March, Kemp, Hart, Gephardt, and Dole had withdrawn. The magnitude of Super Tuesday placed an even greater priority than usual on already established organizations and on resources. Dole, Gephardt, and Simon, for example, were hurt by their inability to conduct broad-based and expensive campaigns for that date. Conversely, Bush and Dukakis were greatly aided by their New Hampshire primary victories, but they also had the most extensive and best-financed organizations.

Over this period, we saw that the electorates in these states changed their vote intentions considerably, making or breaking many candidacies. Underlying this changeability, however, was a great deal of stability in evaluations of the candidates. What made the difference for a candidate, then, was to be highly evaluated, but also to be seen by the public as a viable candidate. It appears that the dynamics of this period in candidate fortunes follow from the perceptions of changing viability of already well liked candidates. And, these perceptions changed with actual outcomes of prior caucuses and primaries—as they were covered or not covered by the media.

In the final analysis, it was these decisions by voters that made the difference. As were all such contests in this period, the 1988 nominations were decided in public and by the public, well before the conventions.

Notes

1. The Twenty-second Amendment, which prevents a person from being elected president more than twice, was ratified in 1951, but it specifically exempted the president in office at the time of its ratification. Dwight D. Eisenhower in 1960 and Ronald Reagan in 1988 were the only two incumbents constitutionally ineligible to seek reelection, although Richard Nixon would have been an ineligible incumbent in 1976 if he had remained president. Franklin D. Roosevelt was the only second-term incumbent who actually ran for reelection.
2. In 1972, Democratic senator George S. McGovern of South Dakota came in second in the New Hampshire primary. His surprisingly strong showing there, however, is ordinarily considered a victory. (The first early Iowa caucus was not held until 1976.)

3. See Joseph A. Schlesinger, *Ambition and Politics: Political Careers in the United States* (Chicago: Rand McNally, 1966).

4. Gephardt did win reelection (easily) to the House. Kemp was appointed as Secretary of Housing and Urban Development in the Bush cabinet.

5. In 1988, only Haig, who had resigned under pressure, could be said to have left office under less than favorable circumstances. The others had chosen not to seek reelection (or were ineligible). Had they sought reelection, they almost certainly would have been reelected. The same is true for Kemp.

6. There are some irregularities, however. Gore and Simon were both first-term senators, and Gore, who was born in 1948, was far younger than most presidential candidates. Dole had run for president unsuccessfully in 1980. Each of these characteristics is something of a liability for the candidate. On the other hand, there were also some further similarities with previous races. Among senators, Biden, Hart, and Simon had all demonstrated the willingness to take political risks by running against an incumbent when they first ran for the Senate, while Gore and Dole ran for open seats. For a further discussion of factors that affect the likelihood of U.S. senators seeking the presidency, see Paul R. Abramson, John H. Aldrich, and David W. Rohde, "Progressive Ambition Among United States Senators: 1972-1988," *Journal of Politics* 49 (February 1987): 3-35.

7. For a discussion of the way nominating conventions began, see Byron E. Shafer, *Bifurcated Politics: Evolution and Reform in the National Party Convention* (Cambridge, Mass.: Harvard University Press, 1988), 9-17.

8. At least, this form is the most common one in the Democratic party. There are many variations. In most Republican caucuses, all Republicans in the state can attend their precinct caucus and "vote" for their favored presidential candidate. The results do not have to lead to delegates reflecting the proportion of presidential preferences expressed in the caucuses, although they often do so imperfectly.

9. Actually, the Michigan Republican party began to select its delegates in August 1986. The second round (county conventions) was held in January 1988. Both attracted candidate and media attention. Kemp and Robertson aligned in 1986 to try to stop Bush. He, in turn, spent about a million dollars there in winning in the January 1988 contests. For an excellent discussion of the Republican contest in Michigan, see Jack W. Germond and Jules Witcover, *Whose Broad Stripes and Bright Stars? The Trivial Pursuit of the Presidency 1988* (New York: Warner, 1989), 80-100.

10. See John H. Aldrich, *Before the Convention: Strategies and Choices in Presidential Nomination Campaigns* (Chicago: University of Chicago Press, 1980); and Larry M. Bartels, *Presidential Primaries and the Dynamics of Public Choice* (Princeton, N.J.: Princeton University Press, 1988).

11. Many have argued that these reforms have weakened the parties. See Nelson W. Polsby, *Consequences of Party Reform* (New York: Oxford University Press, 1983); David S. Broder, *The Party's Over: The Failure of Politics in America* (New York: Harper & Row, 1972); William Crotty and John S. Jackson III, *Presidential Primaries and Nominations* (Washington, D.C.: CQ Press, 1985). Howard L. Reiter, however, has made a strong argument that the decline of party predated the reforms. See his *Selecting the President: The Nominating Process in Transition* (Philadelphia: University of Pennsylvania Press, 1985).

12. See Paul R. Abramson, John H. Aldrich, and David W. Rohde, *Change and*

Continuity in the 1984 Elections, rev. ed. (Washington, D.C.: CQ Press, 1987), 25-26.

13. In some instances, however, the national Democratic party has refused to certify a state's primary as a valid method for selecting delegates because there was no procedure to prevent Republicans from easily voting in the Democratic primary (or for preventing Democrats from easily voting in the Republican primary). The Republicans have accepted these "open" primaries. Although a Democratic primary would still be held, the results would not affect the selection of delegates, with their actual allocation being determined by Democratic caucuses.

14. These states included Alabama, Arkansas, Florida, Georgia, Kentucky, Louisiana, Maryland, Mississippi, Missouri, North Carolina, Oklahoma, Tennessee, Texas, and Virginia (and, three days earlier, South Carolina on the Republican side).

15. For more detailed analysis of these reforms, see Crotty and Jackson, *Presidential Primaries.*

16. Nevada, Minnesota, South Dakota, and Vermont held Republican contests between those of New Hampshire and Super Tuesday. These were not well covered in the media. We consider the Republican primary in South Carolina (March 5) along with Super Tuesday.

17. The Democrats refused to accept the South Carolina primary procedures and allocated their delegates by holding party caucuses a week later.

18. Koch's campaigning for Gore raised charges of racism, something a southerner seeking to demonstrate national appeal hardly needed in New York.

19. He also carried another state south of the Mason-Dixon line that night, Maryland.

20. In addition, 1,688 of these respondents were reinterviewed by telephone after Super Tuesday, but we do not use these postelection interviews in our analysis.

21. The NES surveys tend to oversample respondents at higher socioeconomic levels, but these biases are somewhat greater in telephone polls. Most important for our purposes, only 10 percent of the Super Tuesday respondents were black, even though blacks made up 15 percent of the voting age population in these sixteen states.

22. We used weeks that ran from Wednesday to Tuesday, so January 20 is the first such date (although surveying actually began on January 17). The one exception is that the third "week" is six days long, ending on Monday, February 8, the day of the Iowa caucuses. Hence the next "week" runs from Tuesday, February 9, to the next Tuesday, February 16, the day of the New Hampshire primary. Note that we use the date of completion of the survey, which may be different from the date the survey was begun, to determine what week a survey falls into. While this weakens the randomness of the surveys for each week, it ensures that all surveys—for instance, those assigned to the week preceding the Iowa caucuses—do not include some respondents whose interviews were completed after learning of the outcome of those caucuses.

23. The survey also asked "electability" ratings, which ask respondents to indicate how likely they feel the candidate is to win the general election. These reveal almost exactly the same patterns as the viability ratings.

24. This view of two well-liked—and clearly leading—candidates is reflected as well in our analysis of the Gallup poll data. Large majorities selected one of these two as their first choice, and often near majorities selected them as their two top choices. (Data not shown.)

25. Henry E. Brady and Patricia D. Conley, "Do Strategies Come and Go While Preferences Remain the Same?" Unpublished manuscript, University of Chicago, August 21, 1988, abstract.
26. Increasing numbers of workers in the Boston area live in and commute from New Hampshire, and New Hampshire residents get much of their news from the Massachusetts media.
27. Reported in Gary Maloney, ed., *Almanac of 1988 Presidential Politics* (Falls Church, Va.: American Political Network and LTV Corp., 1989), 40.

Chapter 2

The General Election Campaign

Once nominated, candidates choose their general election campaign strategies based on their perceptions of what the electorate wants, of the relative strengths and weaknesses of their opponents and themselves, and of their chances of winning. A candidate who has a substantial lead in the polls will choose strategies that are very different from those used by a candidate who is far behind. A candidate who believes that his or her opponent has significant weaknesses is more likely to run an aggressive, attacking campaign than one who does not perceive such weaknesses.

Since neither George Bush nor Michael S. Dukakis was an incumbent, analysts anticipated that both parties had a realistic chance of success. This did not mean that the two candidates were equally likely to win, or even that observers believed they were equally likely to win. Rather it meant that unlike the 1984 contest, when Walter F. Mondale faced the juggernaut of Ronald Reagan's reelection campaign, both campaign organizations and outside observers could create plausible scenarios that resulted in either candidate being victorious. The polls—whether conducted for the candidates or for public news organizations—reinforced this perception, since in July and August both candidates held the lead at various times, and the numbers were frequently close. Due in part, however, to the way the polls varied and in part to the makeup of the organizations, the two sides did not perceive their situations in similar ways, and these differences shaped the conduct of their campaigns.

Part 2 of this book will consider in detail the impact of particular factors (like issues or evaluations of Reagan's job performance) on the voters' decisions. This chapter will provide an overview of the campaign—an account of its course and a description of the context within which strategic decisions were made.

Candidates' Perceptions and Strategic Choices

As we said, candidates base their strategies on their perceptions of the political situation. One aspect of that situation is the track record of the electorate in presidential elections, and that did not offer an encouraging picture for the Democrats. From 1952 through 1984 there were nine presidential elections, and the Republicans won six of them. The more recent results were even worse; from 1968 on the Republicans won four out of five elections. Between 1968 and 1984 the Democrats won one close race (1976), lost one close race (1968), and were on the short end of three electoral college landslides.

A closer analysis of these last five elections indicates what a daunting task the Democrats faced in their effort to win enough states to compile the 270 electoral votes that were necessary for victory. As Figure 2-1 reveals, there were twenty-three states that voted Republican in every one of those elections. No state was equally loyal to the Democrats.[1] Only the District of Columbia, with three electoral votes, voted Democratic every time; the twenty-three Republican states had 202 electoral votes, three-fourths of the total necessary to win. In addition there were thirteen other states, with 152 electoral votes, that the Republicans had carried in four of the five elections. Balancing these, the Democrats had won only Minnesota (with 10 votes) four times, and every one of those wins was with a Minnesotan on the ticket. Thus if each state's political leanings were categorized on the basis of the last five elections, 13 electoral votes were likely to go Democratic, and 354 electoral votes were basically Republican (84 more than were needed to win).

Each candidate reacted differently to this strategic context and other relevant circumstances during the summer of 1988. The Democrats largely ignored the previous pattern of electoral votes, and instead took comfort in the poll results. One feature of the polls was what one Dukakis campaign worker called "this incredible security blanket called 43 Negative."[2] Forty-three percent of poll respondents gave Bush negative ratings, a very high figure for a national politician. Based on these numbers, the Dukakis organization convinced itself that Bush was so unpopular that he simply could not be elected.

The Democrats also gained comfort from the results of "trial heats" between the candidates. Even before the Democratic convention, all three national television network polls showed Dukakis with a lead of between 6 and 10 points. This was consistent with the results that had been registered over the previous few months. After the convention, however, the results got even better. In the CBS News/*New York Times* poll the

Figure 2-1   States That Voted Republican at Least Four Out of Five
Times, 1968-1984

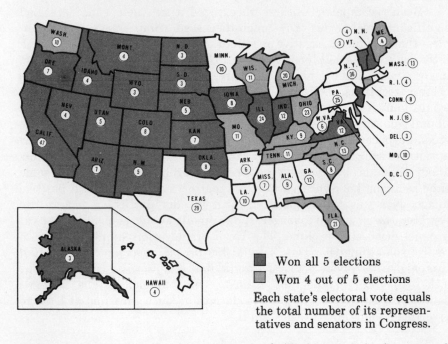

Won all 5 elections

Won 4 out of 5 elections

Each state's electoral vote equals
the total number of its representatives and senators in Congress.

Source: Presidential Elections Since 1789, 4th ed. (Washington, D.C.: Congressional
Quarterly, 1987).

Democrats went from an 8-point to a 17-point lead, at 50 to 33 percent.[3]
Similarly, in the Gallup poll Dukakis's lead grew from 6 points to 17 (54
to 37 percent). Dukakis and his organization seemed to forget that
candidates virtually always get a noticeable positive bounce in the polls
after their convention (at least if it wasn't a total disaster, like the
Democrats in Chicago in 1968), and that much or all of it would melt
away naturally after the Republicans met in August. He believed that he
could just play it safe and sit on his lead. According to Donald Morrison
and his colleagues, Dukakis appeared to be following a strategy of "say
little. Do just enough. Don't rock the boat. Let George Bush self-
destruct."[4]

The Republican campaign organization put more stock in the
electoral vote patterns. They knew that the electorate's previous behavior
was an advantage for them. They also knew that other factors, like the
economy and progress in relations with the Soviets, worked in their favor.
(For example, in early July the Labor Department announced that
unemployment had fallen to the lowest point since 1974.) Despite these

advantages, however, they took seriously what messages they got from polls of potential voters.

Bush's campaign workers recognized that their candidate had significant weaknesses—the much-discussed wimp image, for example—that produced negative reactions. They also discovered, through interviews with small focus groups in May, that many potential voters knew almost nothing about either Bush or Dukakis.[5] In response to these perceptions, the Republicans devised a strategy for victory. They would launch an attack campaign against Dukakis, painting him as a liberal who was out of step with the values of the American people. The second aspect of the strategy was that Bush would launch much of the attack himself. In this way Bush would fill in the blanks for the voters about Dukakis, boosting his opponent's negatives, while at the same time reducing his own negatives by creating a new strong and positive image. Nor was the Republican strategy any particular secret. Lee Atwater, the campaign manager, spoke openly about its basic outlines at a panel discussion in June. The Bush organization simply seemed to realize something that Dukakis and his people never did: presidential campaigns are about choices. Candidates had to give voters reasons either to vote for them or against their opponents. The Dukakis campaign strategy had no plan to do either; Bush intended at least to give them something to vote against.

From the Conventions to the Debates

The Republican Strategy at Work

The Republican strategy demonstrated one disadvantage of Dukakis's long service as governor: he had a long record of decisions that could be searched through for examples that could now be used against him, and a rich supply of enemies to recall such examples. One such enemy was John H. Sununu, the conservative Republican governor of New Hampshire who had represented Bush in drafting the Republican platform. Sununu had served the last six years watching the Massachusetts governor from next door, and detested him. Early in 1987 he had seen a story in a Massachusetts newspaper about a convicted murderer named Willie Horton, who raped a Maryland woman while on furlough from a Massachusetts prison. Sununu filed the story away for later use, and in the spring of 1988 he offered it as ammunition to the Bush campaign. It was ideal, for it could be used to portray Dukakis as soft on crime. Atwater promised an early summer Republican meeting that "by the time this election is over, Willie Horton will be a household name." [6] Through references in speeches, television commercials, and campaign flyers, this promise was fulfilled.

Another issue used by the Republicans in their effort to "Mondalize" Michael Dukakis (that is, to make voters think of him as a liberal in the mold of Mondale) was the Democratic governor's veto in 1977 of a bill requiring public school teachers to lead students in reciting the Pledge of Allegiance. Dukakis, a member of the American Civil Liberties Union (ACLU), had taken the action on constitutional grounds, but the Republicans used his veto to show that the Democratic candidate did not hold the same values as most Americans. They further reinforced this tactic by direct attacks on Dukakis's membership in the ACLU, an organization that Attorney General Edwin Meese once referred to as a "criminal's lobby." To emphasize his own patriotism, Bush led audiences in reciting the Pledge of Allegiance and visited a flag factory.

Even when the attacks came from somewhere else, the Republicans were able to take advantage of them. Followers of extremist political candidate Lyndon H. LaRouche, Jr., circulated a rumor at the Democratic convention that Dukakis had been treated twice for depression by a psychiatrist.[7] Bush aides, while not attesting to the veracity of the rumor, urged reporters to look into it. When Reagan was asked about the matter, he said that he was not going to "pick on an invalid." Reagan later apologized, saying he was only joking, but the damage was already done.

The Bush attack was not limited to these "values issues." The Republicans also claimed that Dukakis did not deserve the credit he was claiming for the economic resurgence of Massachusetts (the Democrats talked of "the Massachusetts miracle"), and that Dukakis was unprepared or wrong on a range of defense and foreign policy issues. On defense they wanted to paint Dukakis as what GOP consultant Charles Black called "a standard pacifist liberal."[8] Bush, for example, attacked his opponent's opposition to the MX and Midgetman strategic nuclear missiles, saying, "I think Gov. Dukakis is just as wrong as he can be in these unilateral strategic cuts."[9] The Republican nominee also frequently claimed that Dukakis and his running mate, Sen. Lloyd Bentsen of Texas, were not compatible, arguing that Bentsen agreed with the Republicans on most important issues.

The Republican campaign was not, however, only negative. While questioning Dukakis's economic accomplishments, Bush continually claimed credit for the Republicans for the nation's more than five years of economic expansion. In his speech on Labor Day, for example, he spoke of "17½ million new jobs the past six years, more disposable income for Americans, lower taxes, increased standard of living. And all my opponent can do is try to tell the American people how bad everything is."[10] Bush also discussed education, child care, and the environment, and in a departure from the Republican platform endorsed some increase in the minimum wage.

The Bush strategy was a resounding success. Shortly after the Republican convention, the Democratic lead had largely melted away, and by early September Bush had surged into the lead in every major published national poll. The Republicans were confident that if they just kept hammering away at Dukakis the rest of the way, victory would be theirs.

Downhill with the Democrats

When the Democratic convention ended in late July, the party's standard bearers immediately went on the road. Reflecting the party's positive feelings about their chances, Dukakis and Bentsen spent their first day of campaigning in Texas—Bush's (and Bentsen's) home ground. They both conveyed their message in English and Spanish, criticizing the imbalance in the federal budget and calling for the creation of "good jobs at good wages."

Buoyed by this positive beginning and by the big lead in the postconvention polls, Dukakis went home to Massachusetts to tend to being governor, while the Republicans carried forward their plan. As we noted, Dukakis believed that he could just sit on his lead and let the Bush effort fall apart. Many in the Democratic campaign did not believe that Bush could make an effective attack. Jill Buckley, a Democratic media consultant, said, "There's something a little tiny bit prissy about [Bush].... He can't afford to go after Dukakis and look small." [11]

But Bush did attack, and the poll numbers began to shift against the Democrats. Some party leaders expressed doubt about Dukakis's failure to counter Bush's charges, but the Democratic nominee trusted in his own judgment that people ultimately wouldn't buy what Bush was selling. He told an interviewer in August:

> It's a judgment you have to make. I've been through campaigns where
> you've got to strike a balance. You know, these are pretty wild charges.
> And it's been going on for weeks and weeks and weeks. This isn't new.
> This is the same kind of rhetoric we heard six or eight weeks ago.
> Personally, I don't think it's going to work. [12]

As the poll numbers continued to turn against them, the campaign organization began to get dispirited and frustrated. Particularly bothersome to Susan Estrich, the campaign manager, was the inability to get Dukakis to spend more time outside of Massachusetts. In late August, for example, he went on a two-day campaign swing through nine cities, making twenty stops—all within his home state.

While Bush continued to raise values issues, Dukakis clung to his previous messages, saying the election was about "competence" and calling for economic growth. On Labor Day in Detroit, he emphasized the "middle-class squeeze," saying:

All across this country, we see two parents working harder and harder to buy what one income could buy before. . . . We see fewer families today able to afford a home than they could eight years ago. [They are] unable to find child care for their children while they go out and work.[13]

Finally Dukakis could no longer avoid the reality of his political slide and the disarray in his campaign. In September, he called John Sasso, his former campaign manager and close friend, back to service. (Sasso had been fired a year earlier because he had provided the press with videotapes showing that the campaign organization of Sen. Joseph R. Biden, Jr., one of Dukakis's opponents for the nomination, had plagiarized a speech from British Labour party leader Neil Kinnock.) Sasso immediately began drawing up a game plan for the rest of the campaign, which would include a firm daily schedule and a set of issues to press. The message was to be primarily economic, emphasizing the "middle-class squeeze" and America's declining competitive edge in the world economy. These are the things he wanted the American people to be thinking about on election day. "If the issues on voters' minds are America's place in the world and the family squeeze," Sasso said, "we win. If it's peace and prosperity, we lose." [14]

The economic emphasis did not, however, directly counter the values issues being raised by Bush, and the limited efforts to deal with them did not always work out. For example, to buttress Dukakis's shaky image on defense, the campaign had their candidate put on military gear and take a ride in the turret of an M-1 tank. Unfortunately, many media people noted that Dukakis bore a striking resemblance to Snoopy, and a poll indicated that voters who knew about the ride were much more likely to shift against the Democrat than toward him.

Despite these problems, Sasso believed that the Democrats had an ace-in-the-hole: the debates. He tried to persuade the Republicans to agree to four debates, but had to settle for two, plus one more for the vice-presidential candidates. Sasso believed that Dukakis, an experienced television performer, would outshine the vice president and set the campaign back on track.

The Debates: Lost Opportunities for Dukakis

Whether or not Sasso's confidence was justified, it was clear that the debates were likely to be the make-or-break chance for the Democratic campaign. Polls conducted in mid-September gave Bush a small lead. An ABC News/*Washington Post* poll showed that both presidential candidates had approximately the same ratio of positive to negative evaluations (about 55 percent positive), whereas in May Dukakis's rating had been about 87 percent positive.[15] The attacks had worked. The Republicans, however, could not yet take victory for granted. Another poll taken shortly before the first debate indicated that Bush was ahead, but also showed that 37 percent of the voters were undecided or weakly committed.[16] The election was still up for grabs.

With so much riding on the outcome, the campaign organizations sparred over the ground rules as if they were negotiating a nuclear arms agreement. The preparations for the first debate in North Carolina on September 25 caused a great deal of tension for the candidates and their handlers. Initially Dukakis was, like Sasso, confident because of his debate experience (he had done forty of them during the nomination campaign).[17] This confidence lasted until the mock debate four days before the real thing. Dukakis had spent little time preparing, and he was routed by Bush's stand-in, a Washington lawyer named Bob Barnett. Barnett anticipated that the Republicans would continue to press the values issues, trying to paint Dukakis as a liberal: "It was raining L-words on the governor's head, the whole Bad-George repertoire from flags to furloughs, and he was caught without an umbrella. His demeanor turned frustrated and defensive; a debate is theater, and he was doing rote news-conference answers." [18] Dukakis and his managers knew there was a lot to do, but there were conflicting views on how to go about it. Should he get angry at Bush? Should he concentrate on offering a positive vision? Should he show more personal warmth?

The Bush campaign's preparation was more polished and effective. In their mock debate, almost every question that came up in the actual debate was anticipated. The preparation did not, however, necessarily make a difference. In the debate Dukakis attacked his opponent on a range of issues, including the Iran-contra affair, solving the drug problem, and the qualifications of Dan Quayle. He called Bush the "Joe Isuzu of American politics," and said he resented Bush's "questioning" his patriotism on the Pledge issue. Bush also attacked, using the values issues again, but most observers judged that Bush had not dealt very effectively with the Democrat's assaults, frequently getting flustered. They awarded the debate to Dukakis "on points." But presidential debates are not won among ringside observers or debate coaches. They are, as the quotation above said, theater, and they are won among the voters who watched and the others who hear the interpretations in subsequent days. The judgments of commentators were mixed. Some thought Dukakis won, others said Bush, and George Will said everybody lost, calling it "a national embarrassment." [19] The public's verdict was also mixed. A *Newsweek* poll indicated that Dukakis had done better, 42 to 41 percent (although other polls gave him a somewhat larger margin).[20] Other results, however, showed that those who watched the debate *liked* Bush better. In the days after the debate, it became clear that Dukakis had not done what he needed to do: score a convincing victory. Politically the debate was essentially a tie—and that meant Bush had won. In a political campaign, ties work to the advantage of the front-runner.

Yet this did not mean that victory was out of reach for the Democrats. There were still two debates to go. The next one was the clash of the vice-presidential candidates in Omaha on October 5, and there was widespread belief within the Democratic campaign that they had the advantage here. After being named the vice-presidential nominee, Quayle had endured much negative press commentary related to his serving in the National Guard during the Vietnam War. Since then the Bush campaign had kept him out of the center of things, sending him largely to safe, friendly locations for campaign stops. Meanwhile the Democrats tried to make Quayle's lack of qualifications to succeed to the presidency a major campaign issue.

In preparing for the debate, the Republicans coached Quayle to expect questions on this issue, telling him to cite his twelve years as representative and senator as adequate preparation. When the matter came up, however, it was with a twist. Quayle was asked what were the first things he would do if he suddenly found himself president. Quayle dutifully recited his résumé as instructed, but this sounded unresponsive and the question was repeated later in the debate. By the third round on this question, Quayle noted his qualifications again but departed from the script by noting: "I have as much experience in the Congress as Jack Kennedy did when he sought the presidency." He had used the comparison on the stump before, but had been warned not to do so in the debate. Bentsen's response yielded what will probably be the most remembered political utterance of 1988: "Senator," he said, "I served with Jack Kennedy. I knew Jack Kennedy. Jack Kennedy was a friend of mine. Senator, you're no Jack Kennedy." Quayle said that the remark was "uncalled for," but Bentsen responded by saying, "You're the one that was making the comparison, *Senator*." [21]

Unlike the first debate, judgments on the second were unequivocal: Bentsen had hit a home run. Polls by CBS News and ABC News both showed the same results: about half of the respondents said Bentsen had won, while only 27 percent said Quayle. Even among people supporting Bush, only 44 percent in the CBS News poll said Quayle had won. [22]

The Democratic camp was exuberant, and Bentsen was a new star. Observers began wondering openly whether the Democratic ticket wasn't upside down. Polls indicated that Bush's margin had been reduced a bit, and the Democrats believed that they could still pull the election out if Dukakis achieved a big win in the final debate in Los Angeles on October 13.

This new enthusiasm was dashed, however, by the night before the event. Dukakis was tired from campaigning and ill from the flu. As

Dukakis was preparing for a mock debate, ABC News came on and most of his staff gathered around a TV to watch.[23] A new poll showed that Bush's lead was only 6 points, but the network analysis indicated that the lead in the electoral college was becoming certain. Most states were allocated to Bush, few to Dukakis. The mood in the room became grim. The candidate refused a ninety-minute practice debate, then also a sixty-minute session. The meeting simply broke up after that. It was as if further preparation was pointless.

Bush too was tired and had a bout with the flu, but the realities of the situation renewed his confidence. After participating in his mock debate, he dismissed his team and went out to watch the National League baseball playoffs. From the outset of the final confrontation, Bush's confidence appeared to be justified. The moderator, Bernard Shaw of Cable News Network, asked Dukakis a hypothetical question about whether he would still oppose capital punishment if his wife were raped and murdered.

> It was a fat pitch disguised as a beanball, a chance for Dukakis to show some core of human emotion; he might, for example, have talked about the rage anyone would feel in such a circumstance, or about how his own father had been mugged in his office at the age of 77, or about his brother having been cut down by a hit and run driver.[24]

Instead he gave his standard academic argument against the death penalty, and renewed a promise to call an international drug summit when elected.

The Democrat never rebounded after that. He seemed to give just rote responses to questions, showing little emotion. In the end, of six issues he had agreed with his advisers to attack Bush on, Dukakis had raised only one.[25] Bush's performance may not have been championship caliber, but he avoided any major gaffes and that is all he had to do. Soon after the debate, Bush's lead in the polls grew to double digits. Dukakis's final major opportunity to shift a large number of voters his way had been lost.

The End Game: Dukakis Finds a Message

Samuel Johnson said that when a man knows he is to be hanged in a fortnight, it concentrates his mind wonderfully. In that spirit, after the last debate the Democrats finally began looking at the electoral landscape in somewhat more realistic terms. The Dukakis organization announced a strategy keyed to economic issues that would target eighteen states plus the District of Columbia, which had a total of 272 electoral votes.[26] The targeted states were California, Connecticut, Hawaii, Illinois, Iowa, Maryland, Massachusetts, Michigan, Minnesota, New York, Ohio, Oregon, Pennsylvania, Rhode Island, Vermont, Washington, West Virginia, and Wisconsin. As our map reveals, five of these states had voted Republican in all five of the elections between 1968 and 1984, and five others had voted Republican in four of these five contests.

Dukakis's new look offered a basically populist appeal. Dukakis told audiences, "I'm on your side," and argued that the Republicans were the champions of greed and privilege. Regarding Bush's proposal to cut the tax on capital gains, Dukakis said: "He wants to play Santa Claus to the rich and Ebenezer Scrooge to the rest of us." [27]

The Democratic candidate also discovered the ability to show his anger at the style of the Republican campaign. He termed "political garbage" two brochures mailed to voters by the Illinois Republican party. One again raised the Willie Horton incident, quoting the rape victim, while the other said, "All the murderers and rapists and drug pushers and child molesters in Massachusetts vote for Michael Dukakis." [28] (The Bush campaign claimed no connection with the brochures.) Echoing the missed opportunity of the second debate, he discussed his own firsthand experience with crime (including his father's being mugged and the killing of his brother), saying, "I don't need any lectures from Mr. Bush on the subject." [29] Perhaps most striking of all, while campaigning in California on October 30 he finally found this response to Bush's bludgeoning him with the "L-word": Dukakis declared that he was indeed "a liberal in the tradition of Franklin Roosevelt and Harry Truman and John Kennedy." [30]

Initially after the debates, the Bush organization intended to have their candidate ease up on the attacks on Dukakis, leaving that aspect of the campaign to ads and surrogates. The inclination didn't last long, however, and Bush launched a new offensive painting his opponent as inexperienced and dangerous on foreign and defense policy. This renewed attack strategy was reinforced by private polls which showed the Republican lead melting away. (This may have been due to sampling error, because Bush's margin stayed around 10 points in all the published polls.) The Bush campaign allocated enormous last-minute resources to a few large battleground states, like California and Ohio, that Dukakis absolutely had to carry to win the election. They also launched a final national media blitz. The new commercials included, perhaps fittingly, an appeal from President Reagan to "vote Republican, up and down the ticket, to continue the change we began in 1981." [31]

Did the Campaign Matter?

It is appropriate to ask whether the general election campaign made any difference. The answer depends on the yardstick used to measure the campaign's effects. Did it determine the winner? Did it affect the choices of voters? Did it put issues and candidates' positions clearly before the voters? Did it produce events that will have a lasting impact on American politics?

Regarding the outcome and voter choices, there are plenty of indications that the campaign did matter. We have seen that early in the campaign, poll respondents indicated by substantial margins an intention to vote for Dukakis. Over the course of the campaign many voters shifted between the candidates, and even very late a large minority indicated that they were undecided or weakly committed to their preferred candidate. These results all support the argument that either candidate could have won, and thus that the campaign made a difference.

Reinforcing this conclusion are data from the 1988 National Election Study (NES) survey presented in Table 2-1. The table shows the percentage voting for Bush, controlling for the respondent's party identification[32] and when he or she claimed the vote choice was made. Overall, only about 15 percent of the sample said they knew all the time how they were going to vote. On the other hand, almost 40 percent said they decided after the conventions, and almost one-fourth claimed they made their choice in the last month or so. Among this last group, Bush received only 51 percent of the votes. One should also note that within each party identification category, those respondents who reported making their decision later in the campaign were generally more likely to defect from their identification than were those who decided earlier.

Whether the campaign revealed candidates' issue positions and whether it had any lasting impact are related questions. In the view of most observers, this was one of the most negative, issueless, and mean-spirited campaigns of all times, and we can expect more of the same in the future. The reason for this conclusion is that the campaign demon-strated how effective such a campaign can be, at least if it is not effectively countered.

To be sure, voters indicate that they are turned off by negative campaigning. In a *Newsweek* poll published at the end of October, 64 percent of the respondents said this campaign was more negative than those in the past, and by 60 percent to 36 percent, they agreed with the statement: "The candidates are not discussing issues that are important to me." [33] But turned off or not, the negative campaigning worked in the view of many analysts. For example, the Gallup organization, which conducted a series of seven surveys for the Times Mirror Company, reached the following conclusion in its final report: "We find the success of the Bush campaign was based on making liberalism, the Pledge of Allegiance and the prison furlough controversies salient, while at the same time making Bush vulnerabilities of less relative importance." [34] Of course, the Republicans were not the only ones to use negative themes; indeed the Democrats tried to fight fire with fire by launching their own attack ads. The important point, however, is that Republican attacks

Table 2-1 Percentage of Major Party Voters Who Voted for Bush, by Time of Vote Decision and Party Identification, 1988

	When voter decided							
	Knew all the time		*Through the conventions*		*After conventions through second debate*		*After second debate*	
	%	*(N)*	%	*(N)*	%	*(N)*	%	*(N)*
Strong Democrat	4	(47)	1	(118)	13	(32)	21	(38)
Weak Democrat	26	(31)	19	(79)	32	(28)	41	(49)
Independent, leans Democrat	0	(18)	11	(56)	11	(18)	20	(40)
Independent, no partisan leanings	[3]	(4)	65	(23)	82	(17)	50	(32)
Independent, leans Republican	100	(13)	97	(64)	86	(22)	65	(43)
Weak Republican	100	(15)	87	(74)	86	(29)	74	(61)
Strong Republican	98	(48)	100	(128)	91	(21)	90	(20)
Total	50	(176)	54	(542)	56	(167)	51	(283)

Note: Numbers in parentheses are the totals on which percentages are based. Numbers in brackets are the number voting for Bush in cases where the total *N* is less than 10.

brought their candidate from behind, and because the Democrats never found a way to deal with them and reverse the trend again, Bush won. We believe that it is reasonable to expect, therefore, that such a negative approach will be used again in the future, at least until a target of the approach demonstrates that it can be blunted and rendered unproductive.

In closing it is worth discussing one other aspect of the campaign that received a good deal of attention in the fall: the impact of the vice-presidential candidates. As we noted above, the Democrats—particularly after the Bentsen-Quayle debate— hoped that their man in the second spot on the ticket would make the difference in the outcome. That of course was not to be, but there is still evidence that the vice-presidential candidates had an effect on the candidates, and vice versa. On the last point, it is apparent that the campaign was kind to the public image of Bentsen relative to the other candidates. In Gallup polls in September and November, respondents were asked whether their overall opinions of the men on the two parties' national tickets were positive or negative. Between the two polls the percentage having a favorable opinion of three of the candidates dropped—Bush by 4 points, and Dukakis and Quayle by 6. Only Bentsen's ratings improved. In November his percentage favorable stood 5 points higher than it had two months before, outpointing the new president by 57 percent to 55 percent.[35]

In terms of the impact on the 1988 election, analysis indicates that Bentsen did have a positive effect relative to Quayle. In a recent paper, Martin P. Wattenberg calculates the net effect on the division of the presidential vote of preferences regarding the vice-presidential candidates, using the NES surveys for the last 6 elections.[36] Between 1968 and 1984 the net effect of vice-presidential preferences never reached 2 percentage points, and in three elections it was less than 1 point. In 1988, according to Wattenberg, public perceptions of the vice-presidential candidates cost the Republicans 2.26 percentage points. Thus if the result of the presidential race had been different, Dukakis might well have owed his success to his Texas running mate. As it was, Bush won with the help of his campaign managers and their attack ads, but despite the impact of Dan Quayle on the voters.

Notes

1. For a discussion of the way the states have changed their voting patterns over the last half century, see Chapter 3.
2. *Newsweek* Election Special, November 21, 1988, 112. For a fuller account by the *Newsweek* writers, see Peter Goldman, Tom Mathews, et al., *The Quest for the Presidency: The 1988 Campaign* (New York: Simon & Schuster, 1989).
3. Unless otherwise indicated, all trial heat results are taken from "Opinion Roundup: George Bush and Michael Dukakis: How They Stand in the National and Regional Polls," *Public Opinion* 11 (November/December 1988): 36-39.
4. Donald Morrison, ed., *The Winning of the White House 1988* (New York: Time, 1988), 217. This book was authored by seven *Time* Magazine writers.
5. See ibid., 219.
6. *Newsweek* Election Special, 117.
7. This description draws on *The Winning of the White House*, 222-223.
8. Paul Taylor, "GOP Sees Dukakis as Vulnerable on Defense," *Washington Post*, August 1, 1988, A6.
9. David Hoffman, "Bush Plans Broad Challenge to Dukakis on Foreign Policy," *Washington Post*, August 5, 1988, A1.
10. David Hoffman, "Bush and Dukakis Stress Jobs, Peace: Protect the Gains, Republican Urges," *Washington Post*, September 6, 1988, A16.
11. Gwen Ifill, "Bush Camp Plans Negative Campaign," *Washington Post*, August 13, 1988, A8.
12. *The Winning of the White House*, 222.
13. Edward Walsh, "Bush and Dukakis Stress Jobs, Peace: Democrat Rips Help to 'Privileged Few,'" *Washington Post*, September 6, 1988, A1.
14. *Newsweek* Election Special, 115.
15. David S. Broder and Richard Morin, "Bush Leading Dukakis 50-46%, as Debate Nears," *Washington Post*, September 21, 1988, A15.
16. Paul Taylor and Gwen Ifill, "Group of Previously Undecided Viewers Leans Closer to Bush," *Washington Post*, September 26, 1988, A17.
17. *Newsweek* Election Special, 123.

18. Ibid.
19. George Will, "A National Embarrassment," *Washington Post*, September 27, 1988, A21.
20. "Debate '88: Playing Hardball," *Newsweek,* October 3, 1988, 22.
21. *Newsweek* Election Special, 137.
22. E. J. Dionne, "The Debates: Revival for Democrats," *New York Times,* October 7, 1988, B6.
23. This account draws on *Newsweek* Election Special, 138-139.
24. Ibid., 139.
25. *The Winning of the White House,* 230.
26. Paul Taylor and David S. Broder, "Dukakis Electoral Strategy Set," *Washington Post*, October 16, 1988, A1.
27. *The Winning of the White House,* 232.
28. Edward Walsh and David Hoffman, "Dukakis Blasts GOP 'Garbage,' Lags 52-45% in Poll," *Washington Post*, October 20, 1988, A28.
29. "Campaign '88: The Smear Campaign," *Newsweek,* October 31, 1988, 18.
30. "It Has Been a Long Road Since Atlanta: A Chronology of Campaign Highlights," *Congressional Quarterly Weekly Report,* November 5, 1988, 3183.
31. Lloyd Grove, "Multimillion-Dollar Ad Blitz," *Washington Post*, November 5, 1988, A10.
32. For a discussion of the concept of party identification, see Chapter 8. For the questions used to measure party identification, see Chapter 4, note 46. The question used to measure the time the respondent decided how to vote was asked in the postelection interview and read as follows: "How long before the election did you decide that you were going to vote the way you did?"
33. "Campaign '88: The Smear Campaign," 19.
34. Thomas B. Edsall, "Poll Shows GOP Attacks Worked Against Dukakis," *Washington Post*, November 16, 1988, A12.
35. All of these figures are from *The Gallup Report,* November 1988, 8-11. They are based upon surveys of registered voters.
36. Martin P. Wattenberg, "And Quayle Too: Examining the Electoral Effect of Vice Presidential Candidates" (Unpublished manuscript, University of California, Irvine, April 1989). Wattenberg uses feeling thermometers designed to measure positive or negative affect for candidates. We are grateful to Professor Wattenberg for his permission to discuss this analysis here.

Chapter 3

The Election Results

By election day, November 8, 1988, Michael S. Dukakis appeared to be closing the wide lead in the polls that George Bush had established after the second presidential debate. Even so, all the national polls showed that Bush retained a lead, and most state polls showed Bush to be leading. By 8 p.m. EST, when the polls closed in many eastern states, it was clear that Bush was amassing an electoral vote lead that would be impossible for Dukakis to overcome. By 9:17 p.m., CBS News, based upon a combination of actual votes counted and its own exit polls, declared that Bush had been elected, and ABC News called the Bush win three minutes later. At the time these networks declared Bush elected, the polls were still open in twelve western states.[1] NBC News, exercising more caution, declared Bush the winner at 10:30 p.m., although the polls were still open in six states.

Bush won forty states, while Dukakis won only ten states and the District of Columbia. Bush won 48.9 million votes to 41.8 million for Dukakis, a 7.7 percentage point margin that was somewhat smaller than Ronald Reagan's 9.7-point margin over Jimmy Carter in 1980, and much smaller than Reagan's 18.2-point win over Walter Mondale in 1984.

All third-party candidates fared poorly. Ron Paul, the Libertarian candidate, was on the ballot in forty-seven states and D.C., but won only 430,000 votes, less than half a percentage point. Together, all third-party candidates combined won just under 1 percent of the popular vote. Third-party candidates fared even worse in 1984, but eight years earlier, independent candidate John Anderson won 5.7 million votes, 6.6 percent of the votes cast.[2] Table 3-1 presents the official election results by state for the 1988 elections.[3]

Table 3-1 Official Presidential Election Results, by States, 1988

State	Total vote	Republican	Democratic	Other*	Percentage of total votes Republican	Percentage of total votes Democratic	Percentage of total votes Other
Alabama	1,378,476	815,576	549,506	13,394	59.2	39.9	1.0
Alaska	200,116	119,251	72,584	8,281	59.6	36.3	4.1
Arizona	1,171,873	702,541	454,029	15,303	60.0	38.7	1.3
Arkansas	827,738	466,578	349,237	11,923	56.4	42.2	1.4
California	9,887,065	5,054,917	4,702,233	129,915	51.1	47.6	1.3
Colorado	1,372,394	728,177	621,453	22,764	53.1	45.3	1.7
Connecticut	1,443,394	750,241	676,584	16,569	52.0	46.9	1.1
Delaware	249,891	139,639	108,647	1,605	55.9	43.5	0.6
Florida	4,302,313	2,618,885	1,656,701	26,727	60.9	38.5	0.6
Georgia	1,809,672	1,081,331	714,792	13,549	59.8	39.5	0.7
Hawaii	354,461	158,625	192,364	3,472	44.8	54.3	1.0
Idaho	408,968	253,881	147,272	7,815	62.1	36.0	1.9
Illinois	4,559,120	2,310,939	2,215,940	32,241	50.7	48.6	0.7
Indiana	2,168,621	1,297,763	860,643	10,215	59.8	39.7	0.5
Iowa	1,225,614	545,355	670,557	9,702	44.5	54.7	0.8
Kansas	993,044	554,049	422,636	16,359	55.8	42.6	1.6
Kentucky	1,322,517	734,281	580,368	7,868	55.5	43.9	0.6
Louisiana	1,628,202	883,702	717,460	27,040	54.3	44.1	1.7
Maine	555,035	307,131	243,569	4,335	55.3	43.9	0.8
Maryland	1,714,358	876,167	826,304	11,887	51.1	48.2	0.7
Massachusetts	2,632,805	1,194,635	1,401,415	36,755	45.4	53.2	1.4
Michigan	3,669,163	1,965,486	1,675,783	27,894	53.6	45.7	0.8
Minnesota	2,096,790	962,337	1,109,471	24,982	45.9	52.9	1.2
Mississippi	931,527	557,890	363,921	9,716	59.9	39.1	1.0
Missouri	2,093,713	1,084,953	1,001,619	7,141	51.8	47.8	0.3
Montana	365,674	190,412	168,936	6,326	52.1	46.2	1.7
Nebraska	661,465	397,956	259,235	4,274	60.2	39.2	0.6
Nevada	350,067	206,040	132,738	11,289	58.9	37.9	3.2

State	Total vote	Republican	Democratic	Other*	Percentage of total votes		
					Republican	*Democratic*	*Other*
New Hampshire	451,074	281,537	163,696	5,841	62.4	36.3	1.3
New Jersey	3,099,553	1,743,192	1,320,352	36,009	56.2	42.6	1.2
New Mexico	521,287	270,341	244,497	6,449	51.9	46.9	1.2
New York	6,485,683	3,081,871	3,347,882	55,930	47.5	51.6	0.9
North Carolina	2,134,370	1,237,258	890,167	6,945	58.0	41.7	0.3
North Dakota	297,261	166,559	127,739	2,963	56.0	43.0	1.0
Ohio	4,393,699	2,416,549	1,939,629	37,521	55.0	44.1	0.9
Oklahoma	1,171,036	678,367	483,423	9,246	57.9	41.3	0.8
Oregon	1,201,694	560,126	616,206	25,362	46.6	51.3	2.1
Pennsylvania	4,536,251	2,300,087	2,194,944	41,220	50.7	48.4	0.9
Rhode Island	404,620	177,761	225,123	1,736	43.9	55.6	0.4
South Carolina	986,009	606,443	370,554	9,012	61.5	37.6	0.9
South Dakota	312,991	165,415	145,560	2,016	52.8	46.5	0.6
Tennessee	1,636,250	947,233	679,794	9,223	57.9	41.5	0.6
Texas	5,427,410	3,036,829	2,352,748	37,833	56.0	43.3	0.7
Utah	647,008	428,442	207,343	11,223	66.2	32.0	1.7
Vermont	243,328	124,331	115,775	3,222	51.1	47.6	1.3
Virginia	2,191,609	1,309,162	859,799	22,648	59.7	39.2	1.0
Washington	1,865,253	903,835	933,516	27,902	48.5	50.0	1.5
West Virginia	653,311	310,065	341,016	2,230	47.5	52.2	0.3
Wisconsin	2,191,608	1,047,499	1,126,794	17,315	47.8	51.4	0.8
Wyoming	176,551	106,867	67,113	2,571	60.5	38.0	1.5
District of Columbia	192,877	27,590	159,407	5,880	14.3	82.6	3.0
United States	91,594,809	48,886,097	41,809,074	899,638	53.4	45.6	1.0

* Other indicates Ron Paul (Libertarian party), who received 432,179 votes; Lenora B. Fulani (New Alliance party), who received 217,219; and a variety of other candidates.

Source: America Votes 18: A Handbook of Contemporary American Election Statistics, compiled and edited by Richard M. Scammon and Alice V. McGillivray (Washington D.C.: Congressional Quarterly, 1989), 6-7.

Bush's electoral vote win was impressive. Figure 3-1 presents the electoral votes by state for the last three presidential elections. As Map 3-1C reveals, Bush won 426 electoral votes, to 111 for Dukakis.[4] Even so, Bush did not fare as well as Reagan. In 1980 Reagan had captured forty-four states and 489 electoral votes (Map 3-1A), while in 1984 he won forty-nine states and 525 electoral votes (Map 3-1B).

The Pattern of Results

The 1988 election may be placed in perspective by comparing it with previous presidential elections and by studying the overall pattern of results. Three conclusions emerge. Bush scored a broadly based win, but his popular vote margin was not impressive. Second, his win continues a pattern of Republican dominance in postwar presidential elections. Last, Bush's win ended the pattern of electoral volatility in presidential elections that began with Dwight D. Eisenhower's 1952 victory.

Because of the geographic breadth of Bush's win, there are some criteria by which his victory could be termed a near-landslide. The term *landslide* has been used very loosely by American political commentators, but Stanley Kelley, Jr., has presented a clear definition: a presidential election is a landslide if the winning candidate wins 53 percent of the popular vote, *or* wins 80 percent of the electoral vote, *or* wins 80 percent of the states.[5] Kelley finds that twenty of the thirty-nine elections held between 1828 and 1980 met at least one of these conditions. In our view, this definition is too loose, as Kelley himself realizes. For example, we do not consider Reagan's 1980 win a landslide because he won only 51 percent of the popular vote. But any election that meets *all three* of these conditions should be classified as a landslide. Reagan's 1984 triumph met all three conditions by a very considerable margin.[6]

Bush's 1988 victory comes very close to meeting all three criteria. He won 53.4 percent of the popular vote, just meeting Kelley's threshold. However, he fell four votes short of winning 80 percent of the electoral vote. If one includes D.C. as a state, as Kelley does, Bush also fell just short of carrying 80 percent of the states.

Despite the geographic breadth of his victory, there were other respects in which his win was unimpressive. As Gerald M. Pomper points out, nearly half of Bush's electoral votes came from states in which he won no more than 55.5 percent of the two-party vote.[7] Pomper also notes that Bush's share of the two-party popular vote (53.9 percent) was relatively low compared with the share won by other Republican winners in the twentieth century.[8] But even without this historical comparison, it is obvious that Bush's win was muted because the Republicans lost three seats in the U.S. House of Representatives, the first time since 1960 that the party winning the presidency has lost seats in the House. The Republicans also lost one seat in the U.S. Senate and one governorship.

The breadth and size of a presidential victory may have few long-term implications, however. Even clear-cut landslide victories do not necessarily lead to partisan realignments. Herbert Hoover's 1928 landslide did not lead to continued Republican dominance, for the Great Depression, along with Franklin D. Roosevelt's policies, made the Republicans the minority party. Most political scientists see Eisenhower's 1952 and 1956 landslides as victories for a popular war hero that had no long-term partisan consequences. And Richard Nixon's 1972 landslide was followed by a narrow Republican defeat four years later.

There is also no necessary connection between the size of an electoral victory and later policy changes by the winner. Some landslide victories, such as Roosevelt's in 1932 and 1936 and Lyndon B. Johnson's in 1964, led to major policy initiatives. Others—Hoover's 1928 victory, Eisenhower's 1952 and 1956 wins, and Nixon's 1972 and Reagan's 1984 landslides—did not. Moreover, some narrow electoral victories have led to major policy changes. In 1860, for example, Abraham Lincoln won only 39.8 percent of the popular vote, only 54.5 percent of the states, and only 59.4 percent of the electoral vote, but his election led to the end of slavery. Woodrow Wilson won only 41 percent of the popular vote in 1912, but during the first year of his presidency there was major tariff reform and the Federal Reserve System was established. Given Democratic gains in the congressional elections, Bush's win may not lead to major policy changes, despite the scope of his victory.

Although the size of Bush's win may not have long-term implications, the postwar pattern of Republican dominance does. Many political scientists still consider the Democrats to be the majority party because public opinion polls show that more people say they are Democrats than Republicans and because the House of Representatives has been dominated by the Democrats since 1930. But elections are not conducted through public opinion polls, and the United States does not have a parliamentary system in which the legislature chooses the key political executives.

The Republicans have now won seven of the eleven elections since World War II, including five of the last six. They have won a majority of the popular vote six times (1952, 1956, 1972, 1980, 1984, and 1988); the Democrats have gained a majority only twice (1964 and 1976). The average (mean) level of Republican presidential support in the eleven postwar elections is 50.9 percent; the average level of Democratic support is only 45.9 percent. Moreover, during these elections, the Republican presidential candidates have won 47 million more votes than the Democrats—a total of 418,113,000 cast for Republican candidates and 370,937,000 cast for the Democrats.

Figure 3-1 Electoral Votes by States, 1980 1984, and 1988

Map 3-1A Electoral Votes by States, 1980

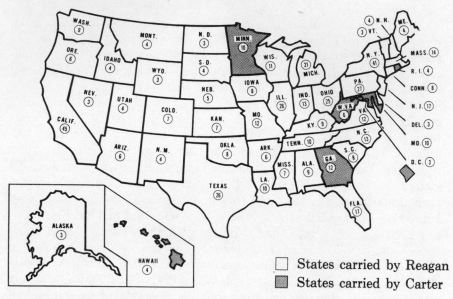

Note: Reagan won 489 electoral votes; Carter won 49 electoral votes.
Source: Congressional Quarterly Weekly Report, Nov. 8, 1980, 3297.

Map 3-1B Electoral Votes by States, 1984

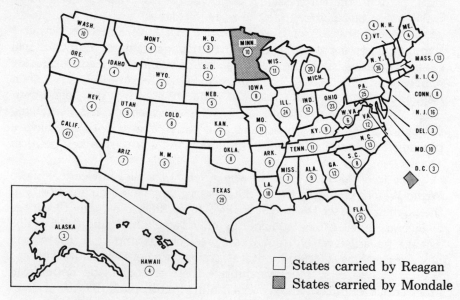

Note: Reagan won 525 electoral votes; Mondale won 13 electoral votes.
Source: Congressional Quarterly Weekly Report, Nov. 10, 1984, 2893.

Map 3-1C   Electoral Votes by States, 1988

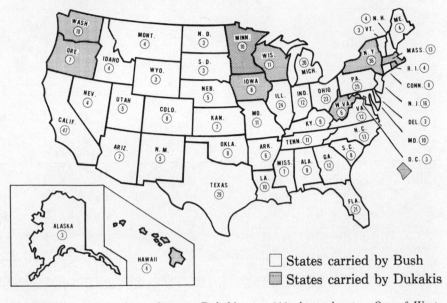

☐ States carried by Bush

▓ States carried by Dukakis

Note: Bush won 426 electoral votes; Dukakis won 111 electoral votes. One of West Virginia's six electors voted for Bentsen.

Source: Congressional Quarterly Weekly Report, Nov. 12, 1988, 3242; Dec. 24, 1988, 3595.

Although the Republicans hold a strong lead over the Democrats, until 1988 the pattern of postwar results reveals considerable electoral volatility. Between 1952 and 1984 no party was able to win three presidential elections in a row. The high level of change during these years set the postwar era in sharp contrast with most of American electoral history. Table 3-2 shows the presidential election results since 1832, the first year the candidate of the modern Democratic party, Andrew Jackson, ran for reelection. Between 1832 and 1948 we find four periods in which a single party won a series of three or more elections. The Republicans won six consecutive elections between 1860 and 1880, although in 1876 Rutherford B. Hayes beat Samuel Tilden by a single electoral vote, and Tilden had a majority of the popular votes. The Republicans also won four elections between 1896 and 1908, as well as three between 1920 and 1928. The Democrats won five straight elections between 1932 and 1948.

After 1948 a period of electoral volatility began. But although no party managed three straight wins, until 1980 the winning party was able to pull off a second presidential victory. The Republicans won in 1952 and 1956, the Democrats in 1960 and 1964, and the Republicans in 1968 and 1972. In all these elections, the second win was by a bigger margin

Table 3-2   Presidential Election Results, 1832-1988

Election	Winning candidate	Party of winning candidate	Success of incumbent political party
1832	Andrew Jackson	Democrat	Won
1836	Martin Van Buren	Democrat	Won
1840	William H. Harrison	Whig	Lost
1844	James K. Polk	Democrat	Lost
1848	Zachary Taylor	Whig	Lost
1852	Franklin Pierce	Democrat	Lost
1856	James Buchanan	Democrat	Won
1860	Abraham Lincoln	Republican	Lost
1864	Abraham Lincoln	Republican	Won
1868	Ulysses S. Grant	Republican	Won
1872	Ulysses S. Grant	Republican	Won
1876	Rutherford B. Hayes	Republican	Won
1880	James A. Garfield	Republican	Won
1884	Grover Cleveland	Democrat	Lost
1888	Benjamin Harrison	Republican	Lost
1892	Grover Cleveland	Democrat	Lost
1896	William McKinley	Republican	Lost
1900	William McKinley	Republican	Won
1904	Theodore Roosevelt	Republican	Won
1908	William H. Taft	Republican	Won
1912	Woodrow Wilson	Democrat	Lost
1916	Woodrow Wilson	Democrat	Won
1920	Warren G. Harding	Republican	Lost
1924	Calvin Coolidge	Republican	Won
1928	Herbert C. Hoover	Republican	Won
1932	Franklin D. Roosevelt	Democrat	Lost
1936	Franklin D. Roosevelt	Democrat	Won
1940	Franklin D. Roosevelt	Democrat	Won
1944	Franklin D. Roosevelt	Democrat	Won
1948	Harry S Truman	Democrat	Won
1952	Dwight D. Eisenhower	Republican	Lost
1956	Dwight D. Eisenhower	Republican	Won
1960	John F. Kennedy	Democrat	Lost
1964	Lyndon B. Johnson	Democrat	Won
1968	Richard M. Nixon	Republican	Lost
1972	Richard M. Nixon	Republican	Won
1976	Jimmy Carter	Democrat	Lost
1980	Ronald Reagan	Republican	Lost
1984	Ronald Reagan	Republican	Won
1988	George Bush	Republican	Won

Sources: Congressional Quarterly's Guide to U.S. Elections, 2d ed. (Washington, D.C.: Congressional Quarterly, 1985), 276-313; *Congressional Quarterly Weekly Report,* November 12, 1988, 3242.

than the first. The Democrats won narrowly in 1976 but failed to hold the White House in 1980. The 1980 and 1984 Republican victories fit the earlier pattern, a win followed by a bigger win. And in 1988, with Bush's victory, the Republicans won their third straight election.

The 1976 and 1980 elections are the only contests in the twentieth century in which the incumbent party lost two elections in a row. There were two similar periods in the nineteenth century, however. The incumbent party lost four elections in a row between 1840 and 1852, a period of alternation between the Democrats and the Whigs, and again between 1884 and 1896, a period of alternation between the Republicans and the Democrats. Both of these intervals preceded major party realignments. After the Whigs lost in 1852, the Republicans replaced them as the second major party. Although many Whigs, including Lincoln, became Republicans, the Republican party was not just the Whig party renamed. The Republicans had transformed the American political agenda by capitalizing upon opposition to extending slavery into the territories.[9] They had a different regional base than the Whigs, for unlike the Whigs, they had no southern support. But they created a base in the Midwest, something the Whigs had never established.

The 1896 contest, the last in a series of four incumbent losses, is usually viewed as a critical election because it solidified Republican dominance. Although the Republicans had won all but two of the elections after the Civil War, many of their victories had been by narrow margins. In 1896 the Republicans emerged as the clearly dominant party, gaining a solid hold in New York, Connecticut, New Jersey, and Indiana, states that they frequently had lost between 1876 and 1892. After William McKinley's defeat of William Jennings Bryan in 1896, the Republicans established a firmer base in the Midwest, New England, and mid-Atlantic states. They lost the presidency only in 1912, when the GOP was split, and in 1916 when Wilson ran for reelection.

The Great Depression ended Republican dominance. The emergence of the Democrats as the majority party was not preceded by a series of incumbent losses. The Democratic coalition, forged between 1932 and 1936, relied heavily upon the emerging industrial working class and the mobilization of new groups into the electorate.[10] A series of incumbent losses is not a prerequisite for a partisan realignment, but it may be an indicator that a realignment is imminent. Now that the 1988 election has established a clear pattern of Republican dominance, the two consecutive incumbent losses of 1976 and 1980 may be seen as a signal that a presidential realignment was underway.

Bush's electoral victory is distinctive in three basic respects. First, it is the first time in four decades that the incumbent party has won the White House for two consecutive elections. Second, the Republicans held the White House without running the incumbent president, something no party had accomplished since Hoover's Republican victory in 1928.[11] Last, Bush was the first sitting vice president to be elected president since Democrat Martin Van Buren's victory in 1836. Many Democrats viewed Bush as a weak candidate. However, even if his opponents underestimated him, the 1988 Republican win can scarcely be viewed as the triumph of a politician who, like Reagan, had mastered the electronic media. Rather, it must be seen as an impressive display of Republican dominance in winning presidential elections.

State-by-State Results

Politicians, journalists, and political scientists are fascinated by how presidential candidates fare in each state because the states deliver the electoral votes needed to win the presidency. The presidential contest can be viewed as fifty-one separate elections, one for each state and one for the District of Columbia.

With the exception of Maine, the candidate with the most votes in each state wins all of its electoral votes.[12] The number of electors for each state is the sum of the number of its senators (two) plus the number of representatives in the House. In 1988, the number of electoral votes per state ran from a low of three in Alaska, Delaware, North Dakota, South Dakota, Vermont, Wyoming, and the District of Columbia, to a high of forty-seven in California. There are 538 electoral votes, and an absolute majority is required to be elected president by the Electoral College. Naturally, the quest for the 270 electoral votes needed to win focuses on the most populous states. Candidates usually concentrate on large states that often switch their allegiance from election to election. In 1988, Dukakis spent a great deal of time and money in California and considered it crucial to his chances, even though California had voted Republican in eight of the previous nine elections. But the vote in California has often been fairly close; thus, a Democratic candidate could hope to carry its forty-seven electoral votes—more than a sixth of the votes needed to win.

States are the building blocks of winning presidential coalitions, but state-by-state results can be overemphasized and may be misleading. First, in thirty-eight of the forty presidential elections between 1832 and 1988, the candidate with the largest number of popular votes has also gained an absolute majority of the electoral votes. (The only two exceptions during these years were in 1876 and 1888.) Thus, candidates can win by gaining broad-based support throughout the nation, even though they must also consider their likelihood of winning specific states. Moreover, given the importance of national television coverage, candidates must run national campaigns. They can make special appeals to states and regions, but these appeals will be broadcast to the entire country through the national media.

Second, comparing state-by-state results can be misleading because it may conceal change. To illustrate this point we can compare such results for two of the closest postwar elections—John F. Kennedy's win over Nixon in 1960 and Carter's win over Gerald R. Ford in 1976.

There are many striking parallels between these two Democratic victories. In 1960 and 1976 the Republicans did well in the West, and both Kennedy and Carter needed southern support to win.[13] Kennedy carried six of the eleven states of the old Confederacy (Arkansas, Georgia, Louisiana, North Carolina, South Carolina, and Texas), as well as 5 of Alabama's 11 electoral votes, for a total of 81 electoral votes. Carter carried ten of these states (all but Virginia) for a total of 118 electoral votes.

The demographic basis of Carter's support was quite different from Kennedy's, however. In 1960 only 29 percent of the black adults in the South were registered to vote, compared with 61 percent of the whites. According to our analysis of survey data from the National Election Studies (NES), only one voter out of fifteen supporting Kennedy in the South was black (Chapter 5). After the Voting Rights Act of 1965, however, black registration and voting increased dramatically. In 1976, 63 percent of black adults were registered to vote, compared with 68 percent of the whites.[14] We estimate that about one out of three southerners who voted for Carter was black. A comparison of state-by-state changes conceals this massive change in the social composition of the Democratic presidential coalition.

Third, state-by-state comparisons do not tell us why a presidential candidate received support. Of course, such analyses can lead to interesting speculation, especially when dominant political issues are clearly related to regional differences. But it is also necessary to turn to surveys, as we do in Part 2, to understand the dynamics of electoral change.

With these qualifications in mind, we now turn to the state results. Figure 3-2 shows Reagan's margin of victory over Carter in 1980, Reagan's margin over Mondale in 1984, and Bush's margin over Dukakis in 1988. These maps clearly reveal differences between these three Republican victories.

As Map 3-2A reveals, Carter did best in his native South. Although he won only one of the eleven states of the old Confederacy, his margin of defeat was 5 points or less in six of the remaining states. Carter fared less poorly in these states because they have a relatively large black population; blacks were the only major group that gave Carter solid support. Carter's margin of defeat was also relatively small in the six New England states, where he won one state and lost by 5 points or less in two others.

In 1980 Reagan did far better in the West than in other regions. We consider eighteen states to be western from the standpoint of presidential

Figure 3-2   The Republican Margin of Victory, 1980, 1984, and 1988

Map 3-2A   Reagan's Margin of Victory Over Carter

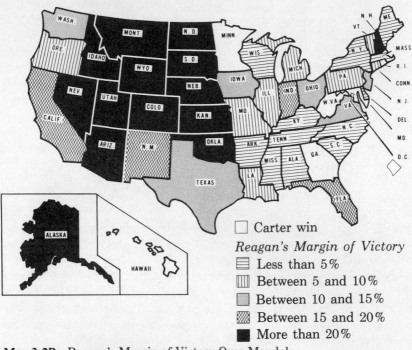

☐ Carter win
Reagan's Margin of Victory
▤ Less than 5%
▥ Between 5 and 10%
▦ Between 10 and 15%
▧ Between 15 and 20%
■ More than 20%

Map 3-2B   Reagan's Margin of Victory Over Mondale

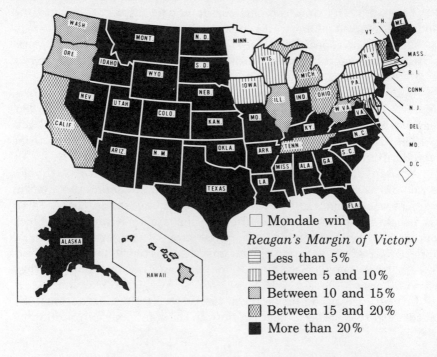

☐ Mondale win
Reagan's Margin of Victory
▤ Less than 5%
▥ Between 5 and 10%
▦ Between 10 and 15%
▧ Between 15 and 20%
■ More than 20%

Map 3-2C Bush's Margin of Victory Over Dukakis

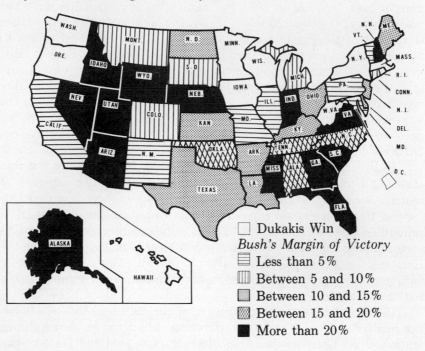

☐ Dukakis Win
Bush's Margin of Victory
▤ Less than 5%
▥ Between 5 and 10%
▦ Between 10 and 15%
▩ Between 15 and 20%
■ More than 20%

elections, and Reagan won thirteen of them by a margin of 20 points or more, while winning two others by 15 to 20 points.[15]

Once we turn to the state-by-state results for 1984 (Map 3-2B), the West no longer appears distinctive. Reagan won by a larger overall margin in 1984, and he had impressive wins in many more states. Although Reagan still had a massive margin of victory in the West, he now carried seventeen states outside the West by a margin of 20 points or more. His biggest gains were in the South. In 1980 he carried none of the eleven southern states by a 20-point margin. In 1984, he carried ten of them by a margin of at least 20 points, and he carried Tennessee by 16 points. Although southern blacks voted overwhelmingly for Mondale, his losses in the South were massive. Whereas in 1980 Carter had won over a third of the southern white votes, only about one white southern voter in four supported Mondale.

The 1988 results show a clear improvement for the Democrats (Map 3-2C). Dukakis won two New England states, gaining nearly half (49.9 percent) of the popular vote in this region. He carried three midwestern states and three western states. Dukakis fared slightly worse than Carter in the border states, where he won only West Virginia. Like Mondale, Dukakis lost all eleven southern states.

Bush's overall margin of victory was much less than Reagan's margin over Mondale in 1984 and somewhat less than Reagan's 1980 margin over Carter. Moreover, Bush's regional strength differs from that of Reagan in his two victories. Bush's best region was the South, and he was far less dominant in the West than Reagan. Bush won five southern states by a margin of over 20 percentage points, and three others by between 15 and 20 points. He won the three remaining states by a margin of between 10 and 15 points. Bush thus won every southern state by more than his national margin (7.7 points) and carried the South as a whole by 17.5 percentage points over Dukakis.

In the eighteen states we view as western, Bush actually lost three states and won by less than 10 percentage points in five others. If we restrict our attention to the eight mountain states,[16] we find that Bush carried five by a margin of greater than 20 points, but he carried the remaining three by less than 10 points. The combined results for these states show a Bush margin of 16.8 points over Dukakis, slightly smaller than his margin in the South. Bush's overall margin in all eighteen western states was only 7.5 percentage points, slightly *less* than his national margin.

Perhaps the most striking feature of the 1984 and 1988 elections is the relative absence of regional differences, which can be shown through statistical analyses. Joseph A. Schlesinger has analyzed state-by-state variation in all the presidential elections from 1824 through 1988. His measure is the standard deviation among the states in the percentage voting Democratic.[17] In 1988, the state-by-state variation was only 5.60 percentage points, the second lowest in all eleven postwar elections, and in 1984 it was 5.84 points, the third lowest.[18] State-by-state variation was somewhat higher (7.95 points) in Reagan's 1980 victory, placing it in the middle range (fifth highest) among the postwar elections. But what is most striking in Schlesinger's analysis is the relatively low level of state-by-state variation in all eleven of the post-World War II elections. According to his analysis, all fifteen of the presidential elections between 1888 and 1944 displayed more state-by-state variation than any of the eleven postwar elections.

As Schlesinger's analysis suggests, the 1980, 1984, and 1988 elections may be seen as part of a trend toward a more nationalized electorate in presidential elections. These elections also continue the trend toward a more Republican electorate.

Viewed from a regional perspective the 1988 election continues two basic trends in American politics. First, the election continues a pattern of Republican dominance in the West, although the pattern was slightly weakened by Dukakis's victories in Oregon and Washington. Second, the election clearly demonstrates the breakdown of Democratic dominance in the South, and shows that the Republicans are now the dominant presidential party in this region.

Figure 3-3 presents six maps that portray this shifting regional strength. Maps 3-3A and 3-3B show election results by state for the five elections between 1932 and 1948; that is, Roosevelt's four wins and Harry S Truman's defeat of Thomas E. Dewey. Maps 3-3C and 3-3D show the results for the three elections between 1952 and 1960; that is, Eisenhower's two wins and Kennedy's win over Nixon. Maps 3-3E and 3-3F present the results for the seven most recent elections, of which the Republicans have won five.

Maps 3-3A, 3-3C, and 3-3E show the states that supported the Democratic candidate most of the time during each of these periods. Maps 3-3B, 3-3D, and 3-3F show the states that supported the Republican candidate most of the time during each of these periods.

The Democrats generally prevailed throughout the country during the Roosevelt-Truman era. The Democratic dominance in the West is particularly noteworthy. The Democrats failed to dominate in the prairie states from North Dakota south through Kansas, but they won six of the mountain states in all five elections, and most of the elections in the remaining two. In addition, the Democrats won Oklahoma, Washington, and California in all five elections, and Oregon in four out of five. Map 3-3A also shows the beginning of a crack in the "Solid South." Alabama, Louisiana, Mississippi, and South Carolina voted for J. Strom Thurmond, the States' Rights Democrat, in 1948, but no southern state went Republican during this era.

The 1932-1948 period was a lean time for the Republicans, as Map 3-3B illustrates. The GOP carried only seven states in three or more of these elections.

The years between 1952 and 1960 show a marked move to the Republicans among the western states (see Map 3-3D). It is not surprising that these states voted Republican during Eisenhower's two landslides. What is more important is that only two western states (Nevada and New Mexico) returned to the Democratic fold in 1960. The two new Western states split, with Alaska voting for Nixon and Hawaii voting for Kennedy.

All the western states except Arizona (Barry M. Goldwater's home state) voted Democratic in Johnson's 1964 landslide. But most western states voted consistently Republican after 1964, as Map 3-3F makes apparent. Hawaii is the only western state that the Republicans have failed to dominate. Dukakis's success in the Pacific Northwest, however, means that the Republicans now enjoy only a narrow edge in Washington (four wins and three losses) and that their edge in Oregon (five wins and two losses) has been reduced.

Maps 3-3E and 3-3F show that the Republicans have dominated the South during the last seven elections, although their dominance is not as

Figure 3-3 How States Voted for President Between 1932 and 1948, 1952 and 1960, 1964 and 1988

Map 3-3A States That Voted Democratic at Least Three out of Five Times, 1932-1948

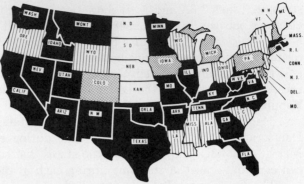

■ Won 5 times
▦ Won 4 times
▨ Won 3 times

Map 3-3B States That Voted Republican at Least Three out of Five Times, 1932-1948

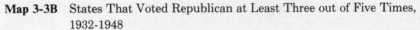

■ Won 5 times
▨ Won 3 times

Map 3-3C States That Voted Democratic at Least Two out of Three Times, 1952-1960

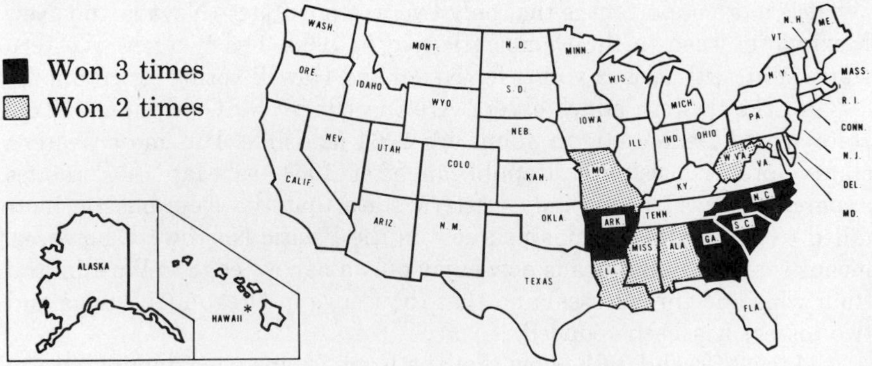

■ Won 3 times
▨ Won 2 times

* Hawaii attained statehood in 1959 and voted Democratic in 1960.

Map 3-3D States That Voted Republican at Least Two out of Three Times, 1952-1960

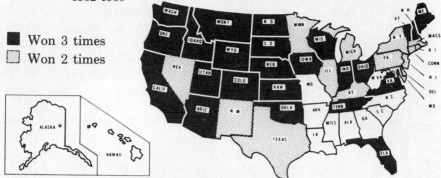

■ Won 3 times
▨ Won 2 times

* Alaska attained statehood in 1959 and voted Republican in 1960.

Map 3-3E States That Voted Republican at Least Four out of Seven Times, 1964-1988

■ Won 6 times
▨ Won 5 times
▥ Won 4 times

(7 times)

Map 3-3F States That Voted Republican at Least Four out of Seven Times, 1964-1988

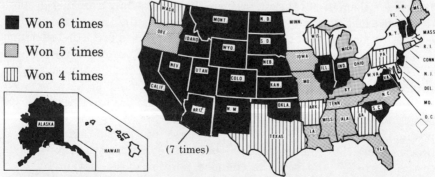

■ Won 6 times
▨ Won 5 times
▥ Won 4 times

(7 times)

Note: States that voted for third party candidates are as follows: Alabama, Louisiana, Mississippi, and South Carolina voted for J. Strom Thurmond in 1948; all of the electors from Mississippi and the majority of the electors from Alabama voted for Harry F. Byrd in 1960; and Alabama, Arkansas, Georgia, Louisiana, and Mississippi voted for George C. Wallace in 1968.

great as their prevalence in the West. The major breakthrough came in 1964, when Goldwater carried Alabama, Georgia, Louisiana, Mississippi, and South Carolina. In 1968 Hubert H. Humphrey carried only one former Confederate state (Texas), while American Independent Party candidate George C. Wallace carried five (Alabama, Arkansas, Georgia, Louisiana, and Mississippi). In 1972 Nixon carried all eleven states of the old Confederacy, but in 1976 Carter carried every one but Virginia. Four years later he carried only his home state, Georgia. In both 1984 and 1988 the Republicans carried all eleven southern states. The Republicans' success in the South does not match their success in the West because of two elections: 1968 and 1976. Even so, they have now won eight of these eleven states in at least five of the last seven elections.

What explains the Republican strength in the West? No simple answer accounts for this regional shift.[19] Historically, the Democratic party enjoyed western support after William Jennings Bryan's Democratic and Populist candidacy in 1896. In the 1920, 1924, and 1928 Republican victories, however, the West voted solidly Republican. Roosevelt's agricultural policies may have earned him western support, and Truman's appeals to farmers may have helped him carry this region. Perhaps Kennedy failed to regain the West partly because he was a Roman Catholic, and most western states have fewer Catholics than the nation as a whole. Another reason may be because Kennedy was an easterner who did not emphasize agricultural issues.[20]

During the Bryan contests of 1896 and 1900 and perhaps during the Roosevelt years, many westerners may have looked to the federal government to protect them from powerful banking and railroad interests in the East. Today, when most social and economic policies emerge from Washington, westerners may resent the federal government and vote for the party that favors less federal regulation. The Democratic reliance on black votes hurts them in this region, because these states have a smaller proportion of blacks than the nation as a whole. Finally, the Democrats tend to emphasize conservation, while the Republicans tend to favor the economic development of federal lands, which are concentrated in the West.

The reason for Democratic losses in the South is more readily apparent. As V. O. Key, Jr., brilliantly demonstrated in his *Southern Politics in State and Nation* (1949), the crucial factor in southern politics is race: "In its grand outlines the politics of the South revolves around the position of the Negro.... Whatever phase of the southern political process one seeks to understand, sooner or later the trail of inquiry leads to the Negro." [21] And it is the changed position of the national Democratic party toward black Americans that smashed Democratic dominance in the South.[22]

During the twelve presidential elections from 1880 (after Reconstruction ended) to 1924, the Democrats won all eleven former

Confederate states, with one exception—Tennessee in 1920. In 1928, when the Democrats ran Alfred E. Smith, a Roman Catholic, six of the most solid southern states voted Democratic (Alabama, Arkansas, Georgia, Louisiana, Mississippi, and South Carolina), even though all but Louisiana are overwhelmingly Protestant.[23] After southern blacks lost the vote during the late nineteenth and early twentieth centuries, the Republicans ceded these states to the Democrats. Although the Republicans, as the party of Lincoln, had black support in the North, they did not attempt to enforce the Fifteenth Amendment that bans restrictions on voting on grounds of "race, color, or previous condition of servitude."

In 1932 a majority of blacks remained loyal to Hoover, although by 1936 Roosevelt won the support of northern blacks. Roosevelt made no effort to win the support of southern blacks, most of whom were effectively disfranchised. Even as late as 1940 about 70 percent of the nation's blacks lived in the eleven states of the old Confederacy. Roosevelt carried all eleven of these states in all four of his elections. His 1944 victory, however, was the last contest in which the Democratic candidate carried all eleven southern states.

World War II led to massive black migration to the North, and by 1948 Truman, through his support of the Fair Employment Practices Commission, made explicit appeals to blacks.[24] These policies led to defections by the "Dixiecrats," and cost Truman four southern states. Adlai E. Stevenson deemphasized appeals to blacks and held most of the deep southern states, although Eisenhower made some inroads. Kennedy also played down appeals to blacks, and southern support was essential to his win over Nixon.[25] By choosing Texan Lyndon B. Johnson as his running mate, Kennedy may have helped himself in the South. Clearly, Johnson's presence on the ticket helped Kennedy narrowly win Texas.

But if Johnson as running mate aided the Democrats in the South, Johnson as president played a different role. His support for the Civil Rights Act of 1964 and his explicit appeal to blacks helped end Democratic dominance in the South. Goldwater, the Republican candidate, had voted against the Civil Rights Act, creating a sharp contrast between the presidential candidates. By 1968, Humphrey, who had long been a champion of black causes, carried only one southern state, Texas, which he won with only 41 percent of the vote. (He was probably aided by Wallace's candidacy, since Wallace gained 19 percent of the Texas vote, and national surveys suggest that he took more votes from Nixon than from Humphrey.) Even in 1976, Carter carried a minority of the vote among white southerners.

Today the South is predominantly Republican, although Carter's 1976 win demonstrates that it is in principle a competitive region. Although Carter lost ten of the eleven southern states in 1980, in six of these states he came within 5 percentage points of winning. In 1984

Reagan did better in the South than in the nation as a whole, and in 1988 the South was Bush's best region.

The 1980, 1984, and 1988 elections underscore the problems the Democrats face in this region. As long as the Democratic party is seen as the supporter of blacks, it will have difficulty winning enough white votes to carry the South. And yet without black support the Democrats are unlikely either to win the South or to carry the northern industrial states they also need to win the presidential elections.

Conclusion

The three elections of the 1980s, when placed in the historical context of postwar presidential elections, present a bleak outlook for the Democrats. The party lacks an electoral vote base. Only the District of Columbia has voted consistently Democratic in the last seven elections, and only one state, Minnesota, has voted Democratic in six of the last seven. Hawaii, Massachusetts, Rhode Island, and West Virginia have voted Democratic in five of the last seven elections. Taken together, these states and D.C. have only forty electoral votes. New York and Maryland, with a total of forty-six electoral votes, have voted Democratic in four of the last seven contests.

The Republican base is impressive. Although the West appears more competitive after the 1988 election, the Republicans still clearly dominate. Among the eighteen states we have classified as western, the Republicans have won fifteen in all five of the last elections. These states provide 116 electoral votes, more than two-fifths of the 270 needed to win the presidency.

But these western states do not provide an insurmountable Republican advantage.[26] Kennedy was elected in 1960 even though he won only three western states (Hawaii, Nevada, and New Mexico) with a total of ten electoral votes, and Carter was elected in 1976 even though he carried only one western state (Hawaii) with four electoral votes. Despite the three reapportionments since the 1960 election and the one reapportionment since 1980, a Democrat could have won in both 1984 and 1988 with the sets of states won by either Kennedy or Carter. Although there will be another reapportionment after the 1990 census, it seems likely that a Democrat could win the 1992 election with these same sets of states.

The Republican base in the West is not as impressive as Map 3-3F makes it appear. Even though Dukakis lost fifteen of these eighteen states in 1988, he came within 6 points of winning in four other western states. One of these close states was California, with its forty-seven electoral votes, which Bush carried by less than 4 percentage points. Thus, while California has voted Republican in nine of the last ten elections, it is not as firmly Republican as this record makes it appear.

Although California has a Republican governor and one Republican senator, it also has one Democratic senator; its congressional delegation has twenty-seven Democrats and eighteen Republicans. Both houses of its state legislature are controlled by the Democratic party.

In presidential elections the popular vote in California has not been very different from the nation as a whole. During the eleven postwar elections, its average level of Republican support has been 51.2 percent, less than half a percentage point more Republican than the nation as a whole. In 1968, it voted 4 percentage points more Republican than the nation as a whole, but in 1956, 1972, 1984, and 1988 it voted less Republican. In every close election, California has been close.

No state can be considered safe for the Democrats. But perhaps very few states are safe for the Republicans either. Even with Bush's broad-based victory, four states that were predominantly Republican in their past voting patterns voted for Dukakis (Iowa, Oregon, Washington, and Wisconsin). In Johnson's 1964 landslide, seven of the eight mountain states voted Democratic. As American presidential elections become increasingly nationalized, no state may be out of reach for either party. Given the high level of volatility in postwar presidential elections, the District of Columbia may be the only electoral unit that cannot be won by both political parties.

The 1980, 1984, and 1988 elections should bury the myth that the Democrats are the majority party. In postwar elections, the Republicans have a clear edge, whether one focuses on elections won, popular votes cast, or states that usually support the same party. We should not judge Republican prospects, however, without a close examination of the attitudes and behavior of individual voters, the subject of Part 2 of our study.

Notes

1. Based upon the poll-closing hours listed in *Congressional Quarterly Weekly Report,* November 5, 1988, 3180. See also "Projections with Polls Still Open Anger West Coast Voters," *New York Times,* November 10, 1988, Y17.
2. For a perceptive analysis of conditions that contribute to third-party voting, see Steven J. Rosenstone, Roy L. Behr, and Edward H. Lazarus, *Third Parties in America: Citizen Response to Major Party Failure* (Princeton, N.J.: Princeton University Press, 1984).
3. We report the results for 1980 in Paul R. Abramson, John H. Aldrich, and David W. Rohde, *Change and Continuity in the 1980 Elections,* rev. ed. (Washington, D.C.: CQ Press, 1983), 52-53; we report the results for 1984 in Abramson, Aldrich, and Rohde, *Change and Continuity in the 1984 Elections,* rev. ed. (Washington, D.C.: CQ Press, 1987), 68-69. These results are widely available in other sources as well. See, for example, *Presidential Elections Since 1789,* 4th ed. (Washington, D.C.: Congressional Quarterly, 1987), 131-132.

4. One West Virginia elector voted for Lloyd Bentsen for president and for Dukakis for vice president. Throughout American history the vast majority of electors have voted for the presidential candidate that they were pledged to support. Between 1796 and 1984 there were only eight "faithless" electors, although some argue that an additional three electors should be classified as faithless. See *Presidential Elections Since 1789,* 4th ed., 147.

5. See Stanley Kelley, Jr., *Interpreting Elections* (Princeton, N.J.: Princeton University Press, 1983), 26-27. Kelley was modifying three criteria advanced by Max Frankel, "Nixon is Re-elected in Landslide Vote," *New York Times,* November 8, 1972, 34.

6. Eight earlier elections met all three conditions. They were Lincoln's victory in 1864, Hoover's in 1928, Roosevelt's in 1932 and 1936, Eisenhower's in 1952 and 1956, Johnson's in 1964, and Nixon's in 1972.

7. Gerald M. Pomper, "The Presidential Election," in *The Election of 1988: Reports and Interpretations,* Gerald M. Pomper et al. (Chatham, N.J.: Chatham House, 1989), 132.

8. Ibid.

9. For an analysis of agenda setting during this era, see William H. Riker, *Liberalism Against Populism: A Confrontation Between the Theory of Democracy and the Theory of Social Choice* (San Francisco: W. H. Freeman, 1982), 213-232. See also Riker, *The Art of Political Manipulation* (New Haven, Conn.: Yale University Press, 1986), 1-9.

10. There has been an interesting controversy in recent years over the extent to which the New Deal realignment was based upon the mobilization of new voters and the extent to which it was based upon converting Republicans to the Democratic party. For the most sustained support for the mobilization thesis, see Kristi Andersen, *The Creation of a Democratic Majority, 1928-1936* (Chicago: University of Chicago Press, 1979). For the evidence supporting the conversion thesis, see Robert S. Erikson and Kent L. Tedin, "The 1928-1936 Partisan Realignment: The Case for the Conversion Hypothesis," *American Political Science Review* 75 (December 1981): 951-962.

11. Between 1932 and 1980 there were three attempts by the incumbent party to hold the White House without running its incumbent president. Adlai E. Stevenson was the Democratic nominee in 1952, Nixon was the Republican nominee in 1960, and Hubert H. Humphrey was the Democratic nominee in 1968. All were defeated.

12. Maine has four electoral votes. Since 1969, Maine has allocated its electoral vote by awarding the candidate who wins the most votes in the state two electoral votes, by awarding the candidate with the most votes in its first congressional district one electoral vote, and by awarding the candidate with the most votes in its second congressional district one electoral vote. In the five elections since Maine adopted this system, the same candidate has won all of these contests, thus winning all of Maine's electoral votes. Any state with more than one member of the U.S. House of Representatives could adopt a similar system if its state legislature so desired. In fact, every state but Maine has a winner-take-all system.

13. Although the U.S. Bureau of the Census classifies several border states and the District of Columbia as southern, we use an explicitly political definition—the eleven states of the old Confederacy—which are Alabama, Arkansas, Florida, Georgia, Louisiana, Mississippi, North Carolina, South Carolina, Tennessee, Texas, and Virginia.

14. U.S. Department of Commerce, Bureau of the Census, *Statistical Abstract of the United States,* 101st ed. (Washington, D.C.: U.S. Government Printing Office, 1980), 514.

15. According to the U.S. Bureau of the Census the West includes thirteen states: Alaska, Arizona, California, Colorado, Hawaii, Idaho, Montana, Nevada, New Mexico, Oregon, Utah, Washington, and Wyoming. But, as Walter Dean Burnham points out, for presidential elections the 96th meridian of longitude provides a dividing line. See Walter Dean Burnham, "The 1980 Earthquake: Realignment, Reaction, or What?" in *The Hidden Elections: Politics and Economics in the 1980 Presidential Campaign,* ed. Thomas Ferguson and Joel Rogers (New York: Pantheon Books, 1981), 111. For our discussion in this chapter, we therefore also consider Kansas, Nebraska, North Dakota, Oklahoma, and South Dakota as western. Even though Texas lies mainly to the west of this meridian, we have classified it as southern since it was a former Confederate state.

16. Arizona, Colorado, Idaho, Montana, Nevada, New Mexico, Utah, and Wyoming are considered the mountain states. Among the western states, they have been the most strongly Republican.

17. Joseph A. Schlesinger, "The American Party System on the Scales," unpublished manuscript, Michigan State University, March 1989. Schlesinger treats each state as an equal unit. His key value for each state is the percentage of voters who voted Democratic, and his overall measure for each election is the standard deviation in the percentage of the Democratic vote among the states. The standard deviation measures the extent to which all states differ from the average (mean) level of Democratic voting in a given election. The standard deviation is considered the best measure of the extent to which the values are dispersed. The actual formula for computing the standard deviation is available in social statistics textbooks and the computation can be performed easily on many desk calculators. Including the District of Columbia, which has voted only since the 1964 election, increases the standard deviation somewhat, since it is always more Democratic than the most Democratic state. We report only Schlesinger's results for states, not the alternative results that include D.C.

18. According to Schlesinger, the postwar election with the lowest variation was 1960, with a state-by-state standard deviation in the Democratic vote of only 5.42 percentage points.

19. Relatively few political scientists have attempted to explain the Republican success in the West. For a good overview of social and political changes in the mountain states, see John G. Francis, "The Political Landscape of the Mountain West," in *The Politics of Realignment: Party Change in the Mountain West,* ed. Peter F. Galderisi, Michael S. Lyons, Randy T. Simmons, and John G. Francis (Boulder, Colo.: Westview Press, 1987), 19-32.

20. Of course the population of the West changed substantially during the postwar years as a result of migration. However, a study of partisan realignment in the mountain states suggests that in-migration did not contribute to the shift of this region to the Republican party. See Walter J. Stone, "Regional Variation in Partisan Change: Realignment in the Mountain West," in *The Politics of Realignment,* 64-68.

21. V. O. Key, Jr., *Southern Politics in State and Nation* (New York: Alfred A. Knopf, 1949), 5.

22. There have been many studies of partisan change in the South. For a recent book that presents state-by-state results, see Alexander P. Lamis, *The Two-*

Party South, expanded ed. (New York: Oxford University Press, 1988). For another excellent study see Earl Black and Merle Black, *Politics and Society in the South* (Cambridge, Mass.: Harvard University Press, 1987).

23. Alabama, Georgia, Louisiana, Mississippi, and South Carolina are generally considered to be the five Deep South states. These are the five southern states with the highest percentage of blacks.

24. Since World War II there has been substantial migration by northern whites to the South. The importance of this migration in weakening the Democratic party is a subject of debate. Raymond E. Wolfinger, for example, argues that migration was a major factor in weakening the Democratic party. See, for example, Wolfinger, "Dealignment, Realignment, and Mandates in the 1984 Election," in *The American Elections of 1984,* ed. Austin Ranney (Durham, N.C.: Duke University Press, 1985), 289. John R. Petrocik, on the other hand, argues that it has played a negligible role. See Petrocik, "Realignment: New Party Coalitions and the Nationalization of the South," *Journal of Politics* 49 (May 1987): 347-375. In our view, the evidence suggests that in-migration to the South contributed somewhat to Republican strength, but that change among native white southerners was more important.

25. Kennedy made a major symbolic gesture that helped him win black votes. Three weeks before the election, Martin Luther King, Jr., was arrested in Atlanta for taking part in a sit-in demonstration. Although all of the other demonstrators were released, King was held on a technicality and sent to the Georgia State Penitentiary. Kennedy telephoned King's wife to express his concern, and his brother, Robert F. Kennedy, made a direct plea to a Georgia judge which led to King's release on bail. This incident received little notice in the press but had a major impact among the black community. For an account, see Theodore H. White, *The Making of the President, 1960* (New York: Atheneum, 1961), 321-323.

26. For a strong argument that the Republicans do not have a lock on the electoral college, see Michael Nelson, "Constitutional Aspects of the Elections" in *The Elections of 1988,* ed. Michael Nelson (Washington, D.C.: CQ Press, 1989), 193-195.

PART 2

Voting Behavior in the 1988 Presidential Election

The collective decision reached on November 8, 1988, was the product of 173 million individual decisions.[1] Two choices faced American citizens eighteen years and older: whether to vote and, if they decided to vote, how to cast their ballots. The way voters make up their minds is one of the most thoroughly studied subjects in political science—and one of the most controversial.[2]

Voting decisions can be studied from at least three theoretical perspectives. First, individuals can be viewed primarily as members of social groups. Voters belong to primary groups of family members and peers; secondary groups, such as private clubs, trade unions, or voluntary associations; and broader reference groups, such as social classes and ethnic groups. Understanding the political behavior of these groups is the key to understanding voting, according to the pioneers of this approach, Paul F. Lazarsfeld, Bernard R. Berelson, and their colleagues. Using a simple "index of political predisposition" they classified voters according to their religion (Catholic or Protestant), socioeconomic level, and residence (urban or rural) to predict how they would vote in the 1940 presidential election. Lazarsfeld and his colleagues maintain that "a person thinks, politically, as he is, socially. Social characteristics determine political preference."[3] This perspective is still very popular, although more so among sociologists than political scientists. The writings of Robert R. Alford, Richard F. Hamilton, and Seymour Martin Lipset provide excellent examples of this sociological approach.[4]

A second approach emphasizes psychological variables. To explain voting choices in the 1952 and 1956 presidential elections, Angus Campbell and his colleagues at the University of Michigan's Survey Research Center (SRC) developed a model of political behavior based upon social-psychological variables.[5] They focused on attitudes likely to have the greatest effect just before the moment of decision, particularly attitudes toward the parties, candidates, and issues. Party identification emerged as the major social-psychological variable that influences voting decisions. The Michigan approach is the most prevalent among political scientists, although many de-emphasize its psychological underpinnings. The SRC has collected data on presidential elections since 1948, and students of political behavior throughout the country often use the questions originally developed by the Michigan researchers. Indeed, in the following chapters we rely upon the National Election Studies (NES) conducted by the Michigan SRC because they clearly provide the best surveys for studying the political attitudes of the American electorate. The writings of Philip E. Converse provide an outstanding example of this research tradition.[6]

A third approach draws heavily from the work of economists. According to this perspective, voters weigh the costs of voting against the expected benefits of voting when deciding whether to go to the polls. And when deciding whom to choose on election day, voters calculate which candidate favors policies closest to their policy preferences. Voters are thus viewed as rational actors who attempt to maximize their expected utility. Anthony Downs and William H. Riker are the major theoretical founders of this rational choice approach.[7] The writings of Riker, Peter C. Ordeshook, John A. Ferejohn, and Morris P. Fiorina provide excellent examples of this tradition.[8]

How, then, do voters decide? In our view none of these perspectives provides a complete answer. Although individuals are members of groups, they are not always influenced by these memberships. Moreover, classifying voters by social groups does not explain why they are influenced by social forces. On the other hand, too great an emphasis on psychologically based variables can lead us away from the important political forces that shape voting behavior. And although the assumptions of economic rationality may lead to clearly testable propositions, the data necessary to test them are often weak, and the propositions that can be tested are sometimes of limited importance.

Although taken separately none of these perspectives adequately explains voting behavior, taken together they are largely complementary. Therefore, we have chosen an eclectic approach that draws upon the most useful insights from each perspective. Where appropriate, we focus on sociological variables, but we also employ social-psychological variables such as party identification and sense of political efficacy. The rational choice approach guides our study of the way issues influence voting decisions.

Part 2 begins by examining the most important decision of all: whether to vote. One of the most profound changes in postwar American politics has been the decline of electoral participation. Although turnout grew fairly consistently between 1920 and 1960, it fell in 1964 and in each of the next four elections. From a high of 63 percent of the adult population voting in 1960, turnout fell to below 53 percent in 1980. Despite massive efforts to get out the vote in 1984, turnout rose by only half a percentage point. In 1988 turnout fell to only 50 percent, a 13 percentage point decline from 1960. But although turnout in 1988 was remarkably low, it was not equally low for all social groups, and we will examine group differences in detail. From a social-psychological perspective, Chapter 4 studies attitudes that contribute to electoral participation and attempts to account for the decline of turnout during the past quarter century. Last, we try to determine whether low turnout has political consequences.

In Chapter 5 we examine how social forces influence the vote. The NES data enable us to analyze the vote for George Bush and Michael S. Dukakis by race, gender, region, age, occupation, union membership, educational level, and religion. As we will see, the impact of these social forces has changed considerably during the last four decades. Support for the Democratic party among the traditional New Deal coalition of southerners, union members, the working class, and Catholics has eroded, and it is very unlikely that this coalition can be restored.

Did Bush's victory result from conservative policy preferences among the electorate? Chapter 6 attempts to answer this important question by looking at how issues influence the way Americans vote. We will compare issue preferences among the electorate in the last five presidential elections and conclude that a major shift toward conservative policy preferences did not occur in the 1980s. Issue preferences contributed to voting choices, but, as we will show, Bush's 1988 election did not result from a pro-Republican shift in issue preferences.

This leads to a consideration of the way presidential performance influences voting choices. Recent research suggests that many voters decide how to vote on the basis of "retrospective" evaluations of incumbents. In other words, what incumbents have done while in office— not what candidates promise to do if elected—affects how voters decide. In Chapter 7 we assess the role of retrospective evaluations in 1972, 1976, 1980, and 1984—four presidential elections in which an incumbent ran, and in 1988, when an incumbent vice president sought election to the White House. As we shall see, voters' evaluations of Gerald R. Ford's and Jimmy Carter's performances played a major role in electing Carter in 1976 and defeating him four years later. In 1984, positive evaluations of Reagan's performance as president, as well as positive evaluations of the government's performance and of the Republican party, contributed to

Reagan's reelection landslide. Although Bush was not an incumbent president, positive evaluations of Reagan contributed to his victory. Less favorable views of the government's performance and of the Republican party's ability to deal with the nation's problems partly account for the relative narrowness of his win.

How closely do voters identify with a political party? And how does this identification shape issue preferences and retrospective evaluations of the incumbent and the incumbent party? Chapter 8 explores the impact of party loyalties on voting choices in the postwar era. We will find that two major changes that occurred in 1984 persisted in 1988. First, there was a sizable shift toward the Republicans in the party loyalties of the electorate in 1984, and the gains scored by the GOP were still present four years later. Second, there was an increase in the impact of partisan loyalties upon presidential voting choices in 1984, and in 1988 there was also a relatively strong relationship between party loyalties and actual voting choices. This shift toward Republican party loyalties contributed to Reagan's victory in 1984 and may have been crucial to Bush's election four years later. And the shift toward Republican party loyalties could create an additional burden for the Democrats in future elections.

Notes

1. Based upon the politically eligible population as of November 1988. See Chapter 4, note 9 for an explanation of how this number was derived.
2. For an excellent collection of articles dealing with some of the major controversies, see Richard G. Niemi and Herbert F. Weisberg, eds., *Controversies in Voting Behavior,* 2d ed. (Washington, D.C.: CQ Press, 1984).
3. Paul F. Lazarsfeld, Bernard Berelson, and Hazel Gaudet, *The People's Choice: How the Voter Makes Up His Mind in a Presidential Campaign,* 2d ed. (New York: Columbia University Press, 1948), 27. See also Bernard R. Berelson, Paul F. Lazarsfeld, and William N. McPhee, *Voting: A Study of Opinion Formation in a Presidential Campaign* (Chicago: University of Chicago Press, 1954).
4. See Robert R. Alford, *Party and Society: The Anglo-American Democracies* (Chicago: Rand McNally, 1963); Richard F. Hamilton, *Class and Politics in the United States* (New York: John Wiley & Sons, 1972); and Seymour Martin Lipset, *Political Man: The Social Bases of Politics,* expanded ed. (Baltimore: Johns Hopkins University Press, 1981).
5. Angus Campbell, Gerald Gurin, and Warren E. Miller, *The Voter Decides* (Evanston, Ill.: Row, Peterson, 1954); and Angus Campbell, Philip E. Converse, Warren E. Miller, and Donald E. Stokes, *The American Voter* (New York: John Wiley & Sons, 1960).
6. For the single best essay summarizing Converse's views on voting behavior, see Philip E. Converse, "Public Opinion and Voting Behavior," in *Handbook of Political Science, Vol. 4: Nongovernmental Politics,* ed. Fred I. Greenstein and Nelson W. Polsby (Reading, Mass.: Addison-Wesley, 1975), 75-169. For an excellent summary of research from a social-psychological point of view, see Donald R. Kinder and David O. Sears, "Public Opinion and Political

Action," in *Handbook of Social Psychology, Vol. 2: Special Fields and Applications,* 3d ed., ed. Gardner Lindzey and Elliot Aronson (New York: Random House, 1985), 659-741.

7. Anthony Downs, *An Economic Theory of Democracy* (New York: Harper & Row, 1957); and William H. Riker, *The Theory of Political Coalitions* (New Haven, Conn.: Yale University Press, 1962).

8. See, for example, William H. Riker and Peter C. Ordeshook, "A Theory of the Calculus of Voting," *American Political Science Review* 62 (March 1968): 25-42; John A. Ferejohn and Morris P. Fiorina, "The Paradox of Not Voting: A Decision Theoretic Analysis," *American Political Science Review* 68 (June 1974): 525-536; and Morris P. Fiorina, *Retrospective Voting in American National Elections* (New Haven, Conn.: Yale University Press, 1981). For a recent introduction to much of this research, see James M. Enelow and Melvin J. Hinich, *The Theory of Spatial Voting: An Introduction* (New York: Cambridge University Press, 1984).

Chapter 4

Who Voted

Before discovering how people voted in the 1988 presidential election, we must answer an even more basic question: Who voted? Only 50 percent of the adult population voted for president, the lowest participation since the 1924 contest between Calvin Coolidge and John W. Davis. If nonvoters had participated in 1988, who would have been elected? Even though George Bush won by over 7 million votes, the 80 million nonvoters could easily have made Michael S. Dukakis the winner. In principle, nonvoters could have selected any alternative candidate, since many more Americans chose not to vote than voted for Bush. Yet, as we will see, it seems unlikely that increased turnout would have changed the outcome of the Bush-Dukakis contest. Before we study turnout in the 1988 election we must place the remarkably low turnout of this contest in a broader historical perspective.

Turnout Between 1828 and 1916

Historical records can be used to determine how many people voted in presidential elections, and we can derive meaningful estimates of turnout as early as 1828. Turnout is calculated by dividing the total number of votes cast for president by the voting-age population. Should the turnout denominator (that is, the voting-age population) include all persons old enough to vote or should it include only those *eligible* to vote? The answer to this question will greatly affect our estimate of turnout in all presidential elections through 1916, for until 1920 few women were legally eligible to vote.

Although women gained the right to vote in the Wyoming Territory as early as 1869, even by the 1916 presidential election only eleven of the forty-eight states had enfranchised women, and these were mainly western states with small populations.[1] The Nineteenth Amendment, which granted women the right to vote in all states, was ratified only a few months before the 1920 election. Because women were already voting in some states, it is difficult to calculate turnout before 1920. Clearly, women should be included in the turnout denominator in those states where they could vote. Including them as part of the denominator in those states where they could not vote leads to very low estimates of turnout.

Table 4-1 presents two sets of estimates of turnout between 1828 and 1916. Both sets of results have been published by the U.S. Bureau of the Census, although for the second set we present more recent estimates published by Walter Dean Burnham. The first column, compiled by Charles E. Johnson, Jr., calculates turnout by dividing the total number of votes cast for president by the voting-age population. The second column, based upon Burnham's tabulations, calculates turnout by dividing the total presidential vote by the total number of Americans eligible to vote. Burnham excludes southern blacks before the Civil War, and from 1870 on he attempts to exclude aliens where they were not able to vote. But the major difference between Burnham's calculations and Johnson's is that Burnham excludes women from his turnout denominator in those states where they were not able to vote.

Most political scientists would consider Burnham's estimates to be more revealing than Johnson's. For example, most political scientists argue that turnout was higher in the nineteenth century than it is today. But even if we reject this interpretation, both sets of estimates reveal the same pattern of change. There clearly is a large jump in turnout after 1836, for the Whigs turned to popular appeals to mobilize the electorate. Turnout jumped markedly in the 1840 election, the famous "Log Cabin and Hard Cider Campaign," in which William Henry Harrison, the hero of Tippecanoe, defeated the incumbent Democrat, Martin Van Buren. Turnout waned after 1840 but rose rapidly after the Republican party, founded in 1854, polarized the nation by taking a clear stand against extending slavery into the territories. In Abraham Lincoln's election in 1860, four white males out of five went to the polls.

Turnout waxed and waned after the Civil War, peaking in the 1876 contest between Rutherford B. Hayes, the Republican winner, and Samuel J. Tilden, the Democrat. As a price of Hayes's contested victory, the Republicans agreed to end Reconstruction in the South. When federal troops were withdrawn, many blacks were prevented from voting. Although some southern blacks could still vote in 1880, overall turnout among blacks dropped sharply, decreasing southern turnout. Turnout began to fall nationwide by 1892, but it rose in the 1896 contest between William Jennings Bryan (Democrat and Populist) and William

Table 4-1   Turnout in Presidential Elections, 1828-1916

Election year	Winning candidate	Party of winning candidate	Percentage of voting-age population who voted	Percentage eligible to vote who voted
1828	Andrew Jackson	Democrat	22.2	57.3
1832	Andrew Jackson	Democrat	20.6	56.7
1836	Martin Van Buren	Democrat	22.4	56.5
1840	William H. Harrison	Whig	31.9	80.3
1844	James K. Polk	Democrat	30.6	79.0
1848	Zachary Taylor	Whig	28.6	72.8
1852	Franklin Pierce	Democrat	27.3	69.5
1856	James Buchanan	Democrat	30.6	79.4
1860	Abraham Lincoln	Republican	31.5	81.8
1864[a]	Abraham Lincoln	Republican	24.4	76.3
1868	Ulysses S. Grant	Republican	31.7	80.9
1872	Ulysses S. Grant	Republican	32.0	72.1
1876	Rutherford B. Hayes	Republican	37.1	82.6
1880	James A. Garfield	Republican	36.2	80.6
1884	Grover Cleveland	Democrat	35.6	78.3
1888	Benjamin Harrison	Republican	36.3	80.5
1892	Grover Cleveland	Democrat	34.9	78.3
1896	William McKinley	Republican	36.8	79.7
1900	William McKinley	Republican	34.0	73.7
1904	Theodore Roosevelt	Republican	29.7	65.5
1908	William H. Taft	Republican	29.8	65.7
1912	Woodrow Wilson	Democrat	27.9	59.0
1916	Woodrow Wilson	Democrat	32.1	61.8

[a]The estimate for the voting-age population is based upon the entire U.S. adult population. The estimate for the eligible population excludes the eleven Confederate states that did not take part in the election.

Sources: The estimates of turnout among the voting-age population are based upon Charles E. Johnson, Jr., *Nonvoting Americans* (U.S. Department of Commerce, Bureau of the Census, Washington, D.C.: U.S. Government Printing Office, Current Population Reports, Series P-23, No. 102, May 1980), 2. The estimates of turnout among the population eligible to vote are based upon calculations by Walter Dean Burnham. Burnham's earlier estimates were published in U.S. Department of Commerce, Bureau of the Census, *Historical Statistics of the United States: Colonial Times to 1970* (Washington, D.C.: U.S. Government Printing Office, 1975), Series Y-27-78, 1071-1072. The results in this table, however, are based upon Burnham, "The Turnout Problem," in *Elections American Style,* ed. A. James Reichley (Washington, D.C.: Brookings Institution, 1987), 113-114.

McKinley. Turnout dropped in the 1900 rerun between the same two contenders.

By the late nineteenth century blacks were denied the franchise throughout the South, and poor whites often found it difficult to vote as well.[2] Throughout the country registration requirements, at least partly designed to discourage voter fraud, became more widespread.[3] Because individuals were responsible for getting their names on the registration rolls before the election, the procedure created an obstacle that reduced electoral participation.

Introducing the secret ballot also reduced turnout. Before this innovation, most voting in U.S. elections was public. Ballots were printed by the political parties, each party producing its own. Ballots differed in size and color, and, because voters usually cast their ballots in public, their choices were obvious. In 1856 Australia adopted a law calling for a secret ballot to be printed and administered by the state. The "Australian ballot" was first used in statewide elections in the United States in Massachusetts, which introduced it in 1888. By the time of the 1896 election, nine out of ten states had followed Massachusetts's lead.[4] Although the secret ballot was introduced to cut fraud, it also reduced turnout. When voting was public, men could sell their votes, but candidates were less willing to pay for a vote if they could not see it delivered. Ballot stuffing was also more difficult when the state printed and distributed the ballot.

As Table 4-1 shows, turnout trailed off rapidly in the early twentieth century. By the time of the three-way contest among Woodrow Wilson (Democrat), William Howard Taft (Republican), and Theodore Roosevelt (Progressive), fewer than three out of five eligible Americans went to the polls. In 1916 turnout rose slightly, but just over three out of five eligible Americans voted, only about a third of the total adult population.

Turnout Between 1920 and 1988

It is easier to calculate turnout after 1920, and we have provided estimates based upon Census Bureau statistics. Although there are alternative ways to measure the turnout denominator, they lead to relatively small differences in the overall estimate of turnout.[5]

In Table 4-2 we show the percentage of the voting-age population that voted for the Democratic, Republican, and minor party candidates in the eighteen elections between 1920 and 1988. The table also shows the percentage that did not vote and the overall size of the voting-age population. In Figure 4-1 we show the percentage of the voting-age population that voted in all eighteen elections.

As Table 4-2 shows, Bush received the votes of only 27 percent of the voting-age population. Eleven of the seventeen winners between 1920 and

Table 4-2 Percentage of Adults Who Voted for Each Major Presidential Candidate, 1920-1988

Election year	Democratic candidate		Republican candidate		Other candidates	Did not vote	Total percent	Voting-age population
1920	14.8	James M. Cox	26.2	Warren G. Harding	2.4	56.6	100	61,639,000
1924	12.7	John W. Davis	23.7	Calvin Coolidge	7.5	56.1	100	66,229,000
1928	21.1	Alfred E. Smith	30.1	Herbert C. Hoover	.6	48.2	100	71,100,000
1932	30.1	Franklin D. Roosevelt	20.8	Herbert C. Hoover	1.5	47.6	100	75,768,000
1936	34.6	Franklin D. Roosevelt	20.8	Alfred M. Landon	1.5	43.1	100	80,174,000
1940	32.2	Franklin D. Roosevelt	26.4	Wendell Willkie	.3	41.1	100	84,728,000
1944	29.9	Franklin D. Roosevelt	25.7	Thomas E. Dewey	.4	44.0	100	85,654,000
1948	25.3	Harry S Truman	23.0	Thomas E. Dewey	2.7	48.9	100	95,573,000
1952	27.3	Adlai E. Stevenson	34.0	Dwight D. Eisenhower	.3	38.4	100	99,929,000
1956	24.9	Adlai E. Stevenson	34.1	Dwight D. Eisenhower	.4	40.7	100	104,515,000
1960	31.2	John F. Kennedy	31.1	Richard M. Nixon	.5	37.2	100	109,672,000
1964	37.8	Lyndon B. Johnson	23.8	Barry M. Goldwater	.3	38.1	100	114,090,000
1968	26.0	Hubert H. Humphrey	26.4	Richard M. Nixon	8.4	39.1	100	120,285,000
1972	20.7	George S. McGovern	33.5	Richard M. Nixon	1.0	44.8	100	140,777,000
1976	26.8	Jimmy Carter	25.7	Gerald R. Ford	1.0	46.5	100	152,308,000
1980	21.6	Jimmy Carter	26.7	Ronald Reagan	4.3	47.4	100	164,595,000
1984	21.5	Walter F. Mondale	31.2	Ronald Reagan	.4	46.9	100	174,447,000
1988	22.9	Michael S. Dukakis	26.8	George Bush	.5	49.8	100	182,628,000

Note: The names of winning candidates are italicized.

Sources: Results for 1920 through 1928 are based upon U.S. Department of Commerce, Bureau of the Census, *Statistical Abstract of the United States, 1972* (Washington, D.C.: U.S. Government Printing Office, 1972), 358, 373; results for 1932 through 1956 are based upon *Statistical Abstract of the United States, 1985* (Washington, D.C.: U.S. Government Printing Office, 1985), 238, 251; results for 1960 through 1984 are based upon *Statistical Abstract of the United States, 1989* (Washington, D.C.: U.S. Government Printing Office, 1989), 240, 258. For 1988 the voting-age population is based upon U.S. Department of Commerce, Bureau of the Census, *Projections of the Population of Voting Age for States: November 1988*, Series P-25, No. 1019 (Washington, D.C.: U.S. Government Printing Office, January 1988), 1; the number of votes cast for each candidate and the total number of votes cast are based upon *America Votes 18: A Handbook of Contemporary American Election Statistics*, compiled and edited by Richard M. Scammon and Alice V. McGillivray (Washington, D.C.: Congressional Quarterly, 1989), 7.

Figure 4-1 Percentage of Voting-Age Population That Voted for President, 1920-1988

Percentage

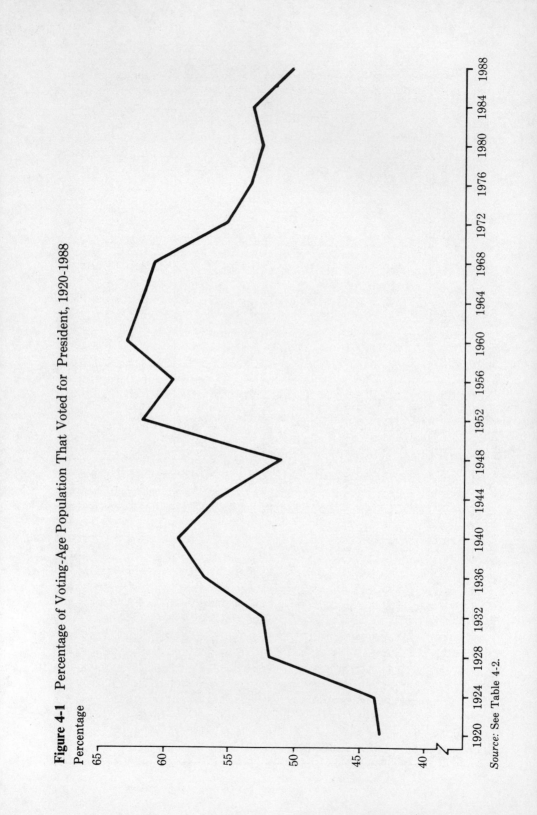

Source: See Table 4-2.

1984 exceeded this total. Bush's share of the total voting-age population was similar to Jimmy Carter's share in 1976 and to Ronald Reagan's in 1980. In the fifteen elections between 1928 and 1984, the only winners to gain a smaller share than Bush were Harry S Truman in 1948 and Richard Nixon in 1968. In fact, two *losing* candidates (Adlai E. Stevenson in 1952 and Nixon in 1960) exceeded Bush's total, and four others came close (Wendell Willkie in 1940, Thomas E. Dewey in 1944, Hubert H. Humphrey in 1968, and Gerald R. Ford in 1976).

Bush's low overall total is a combination of two factors: he received only 53 percent of the popular vote, and only half the adult population voted. That Bush won just over a fourth of the total adult vote reinforces our conclusion in Chapter 3 that his popular vote victory was not impressive. We should bear in mind, however, that fewer than one in four adults voted for Dukakis.

As Figure 4-1 makes clear, turnout has been falling since 1960. However, turnout increased in seven of the ten elections held between 1920 and 1960. Two of the exceptions—1944 and 1948—resulted largely from the social dislocations during and shortly after World War II. Specific political events explain why more people voted in certain elections. The jump in turnout between 1924 and 1928 resulted from the candidacy of Alfred E. Smith, the first Roman Catholic to receive a major party nomination, and the increase between 1932 and 1936 resulted from Franklin D. Roosevelt's efforts to mobilize the lower social strata, particularly the industrial working class. The extremely close race between Nixon and another Catholic candidate, John F. Kennedy, partly accounts for the high turnout in 1960. Turnout rose to 62.8 percent. This was far below the percentage of eligible Americans that voted between 1840 and 1900, although it was the highest percentage of the voting-age population that had ever voted in a presidential election (Table 4-1). But U.S. turnout in 1960 was still far below the average level of turnout attained in recent years in most Western democracies.[6]

Although short-term factors account for the rise of turnout in specific elections, long-term changes were also driving turnout upward. The changing social characteristics of the electorate contributed toward increasing turnout. For example, women who came of age before the Nineteenth Amendment often failed to exercise their right to vote, but women who came of age after 1920 had higher levels of turnout. Generational replacement gradually has replaced these older women with women who had the right to vote when they reached voting age. Because it was necessary to be a citizen to vote (a requirement imposed by state law, not by the Constitution), many immigrants failed to enter the electorate. But after 1921, as a result of restrictive immigration laws, the percentage of the population that was foreign born declined. Moreover, levels of formal education have been growing throughout the twentieth century, a change that boosted turnout. Americans with higher educational levels are much more likely to vote than those with lower levels.

By 1960 the first two trends had run their course and no longer played an important role in increasing turnout. However, educational levels continued to increase, a change that might have been expected to push turnout upward. Political changes might also have been expected to increase turnout. After the passage of the Voting Rights Act of 1965, turnout rose dramatically among southern blacks, which often led to increased voting among southern whites. Less restrictive registration requirements during the last quarter century have made it easier to vote. Despite these changes, turnout declined after 1960 and continued to decline through 1980.

Given the low turnout in 1980, many political leaders saw the potential for increasing electoral participation as a way to win elections. As was widely recognized, nonvoters tend to have social characteristics that would make them likely Democratic voters. They are, for example, more likely to be black, Hispanic, and poor. By 1984, many Democratic leaders, along with groups sympathetic to the Democrats, launched massive registration drives. Fearing Democratic efforts, the Republicans also attempted to register potential GOP voters. Because potential Republican voters are more likely to be registered already, adding Republicans to the voting rolls is more difficult, and the Republicans often used computer-aided techniques to identify potential Republican voters and to screen out potential Democratic supporters. The Republicans also received some help from evangelical groups, especially in registering southern whites. By most estimates the Republicans more than matched Democratic registration efforts.[7] In addition to partisan efforts, private foundations supported voter registration efforts, and state governments frequently used public agencies to facilitate voter registration.

Despite the massive get-out-the vote efforts in 1984, turnout rose by only about half a percentage point. In 1988 both parties cut back their efforts on voter registration, and private foundations cut back their funding for voter registration drives. Although Jesse Jackson stressed the need for increased voter registration, his efforts to register voters were less intensive than they had been before the 1984 election.[8]

Even before the general election it was apparent that voter registration was lagging, and experts expected turnout to decline. Few expected the massive decline in turnout that actually occurred, for voter participation fell a full 3 points, to only 50.2 percent of the voting-age population. Even if one takes into account that about 10 million persons of voting age are not eligible to vote, turnout among eligible Americans was only 53.0 percent.[9] Between 1960 and 1988 turnout among the voting-age population had declined 12.6 points, whereas turnout among the politically eligible population had declined 12.4 points. If turnout among the politically eligible population had been as high in 1988 as it was in 1960, an additional 21 million Americans would have voted, a number three times greater than Bush's popular vote margin over Dukakis.

Turnout Among Social Groups

Although turnout was very low in 1988, it was not equally low among all social groups. Because respondents sometimes claim to have voted when they have not, reports of electoral participation derived from postelection surveys can lead to substantial overestimates of turnout. Fortunately, the 1988 National Election Study (NES) included a check of local registration and voting records to determine whether respondents were registered and whether they voted. In this chapter we will rely upon this actual check of voting records for most of our analysis.[10] Even this check of the registration records reveals an overall turnout of 59 percent, about 6 points higher than the overall turnout among the citizen population. But this is substantially less than the 69 percent reported turnout registered by the NES survey.[11]

There are two basic reasons the NES survey exaggerates turnout, even when turnout is measured using the vote validation studies. In the first place, the NES surveys undersample the lower socioeconomic groups, which have very low turnout. Second, during presidential years the same individuals are interviewed both before and after the election. Being interviewed before an election provides a stimulus to vote, and thus increases voting within the NES sample.[12] Despite these problems, the NES surveys can be used to study relative levels of turnout among social groups. Of course, biases are greater when reported participation is used to measure turnout. Even though respondents are asked a question that explicitly provides reasons for not voting, some persons who have not voted falsely claim to have voted.[13]

Although we rely on the NES vote validation study, wherever possible we will supplement our analysis with Census Bureau studies of turnout. Beginning in 1964, and in every subsequent midterm and presidential election, the Census Bureau has conducted a survey to determine who voted. As a government agency, the bureau cannot ask some of the more important questions posed by political scientists. The bureau asks no questions about political attitudes or about religion, for example. These surveys cannot be used to determine *how* people voted, for such a question would be inappropriate for a government agency.

Despite these limitations, these studies have two major advantages. First, the Census Bureau is able to survey the lower social strata more effectively than the NES. This partly explains why the overall level of turnout in the census surveys is always much lower than reported turnout in the NES surveys.[14] In 1988, for example, reported turnout in the bureau survey was 57.4 percent, only 7 points higher than the actual turnout among the voting-age population.[15] Second, the Census Bureau surveys are much larger than the NES surveys. In 1988, for example, interviews were conducted in 54,132 households, and registration and voting information was gathered on 110,452 individuals.[16] Because the sample is larger, subgroups will also be larger in this survey. This allows for comparisons that are not practical with the NES surveys. For example, with the NES survey we can compare only 68 black men with 148 black women. The Census Bureau survey includes information for approximately 5,400 black men and 6,800 black women.

Race, Gender, Region, and Age

Table 4-3 compares turnout among basic social groups in the NES vote validation study. Our analysis begins with a comparison of blacks and whites. As the table shows, whites were much more likely to vote than blacks, a gap of 23 percentage points. Our analyses of both validated and reported turnout show that turnout dropped among both blacks and whites, but that it fell more among blacks. According to the Census Bureau survey, reported turnout was 59.1 percent among whites and 51.5 percent among blacks, a 7.6-point gap. Like the NES survey, the bureau study found that between 1984 and 1988 turnout had dropped more among blacks than among whites. Among whites, turnout dropped only 2 points, whereas among blacks it fell 4 points. Although the decline in turnout was only slightly greater among blacks than whites, the Census Bureau results suggest that the 1988 election ended a two-decade trend toward reducing racial differences.

Because relatively few blacks were sampled in the NES surveys, we will rely upon the census surveys to make comparisons among blacks. According to the census survey, 54.2 percent of black women and 48.2 percent of black men voted. Reported turnout was 48.0 percent among southern blacks but 55.6 percent among blacks outside the South. And young blacks were far less likely to vote than middle-aged blacks, or even blacks above the age of seventy-five. Among all blacks between the ages of eighteen and twenty-four, reported turnout was only 35.0 percent; among black men of this age it was 32.4 percent.

As Table 4-3 shows, among whites,[17] those who identified as Hispanic were less likely to vote than non-Hispanics, mainly because turnout was low among Mexican-Americans.[18] Although the Census Bureau results are not comparable to those based upon NES data, their survey shows that reported turnout among Hispanics was only 28.8 percent, although turnout rises to 46 percent among Hispanics who were citizens. The census study suggests that there was a 4-point drop in turnout among Hispanics and a 2-point drop among Hispanic citizens.[19]

Our table shows that white men and white women were equally likely to vote. Surveys show that men consistently outvoted women in all presidential elections through 1976. By 1980 these differences were negligible. The 1980 vote validation study revealed that white men were more likely to vote than white women, although the census survey showed reported turnout to be the same for both groups. The 1984 vote validation study revealed no differences in turnout between white men and white women, but the 1984 census survey found white women were marginally more likely to vote than white men. The 1988 census survey also found white women to be more likely to vote than white men. Among white women reported turnout was 59.8 percent; among white men it was 58.4 percent. Among the entire electorate, the census survey found that 58.3 percent of women voted, while 56.4 percent of the men did. Both the NES survey and the Census Bureau study suggest that between 1984 and 1988 turnout declined among both sexes. The Census Bureau survey reveals a 2-point decline in turnout among both white men and white women; among the entire electorate turnout had declined 3 points among both sexes. Despite the decline in turnout among women in 1988, the three elections of the 1980s mark a historical turning point, for the participation advantage among men was eliminated.

Of course, we do not need surveys to study turnout in the various regions of the country. Because the Census Bureau estimates the total voting-age population for each state, we can measure turnout merely by dividing the total number of votes cast for president within each state by its voting-age population. Turnout varies greatly from state to state, from a low of 38.8 percent in Georgia to a high of 66.3 percent in Minnesota.[20] Official statistics clearly show that turnout was lowest in the South, where only 44.7 percent of the voting-age population voted.

Official election statistics do not present results according to race, so we need surveys to study the relative level of turnout among whites and blacks within the regions. As Table 4-3 shows, white turnout in the South was lower than it was outside the South.[21] Fifty-three percent of the whites in the South voted; outside the South, 66 percent did.[22] The Census Bureau survey also shows turnout to be low among white southerners. According to their survey, 56.4 percent of the whites in the South voted; outside the South, 60.4 percent did. The relatively low turnout in the South results partly from the low educational levels in that region.[23] But regional differences have declined dramatically during the past quarter century. According to the 1964 census survey, southern whites were 15 percentage points less likely to vote than whites outside the South, and nonwhite southerners were 28 points less likely to vote than nonwhites outside the South.[24]

The 1988 NES survey reveals the same general pattern by age as previous studies show. Turnout was very low among the young (born

Table 4-3   Percentage That Voted for President According to Vote Validation Study, by Social Group, 1988

Social group	Voted (%)	Did not vote (%)	Total percent	(N)
Electorate, by race				
White	63	37	100	(1,495)
Black	40	60	100	(216)
Whites by Hispanic identification				
Identify as Hispanic	55	45	100	(125)
Do not identify	64	36	100	(1,370)
Whites, by gender				
Male	64	36	100	(675)
Female	62	38	100	(820)
Whites, by region				
New England and mid-Atlantic	61	39	100	(289)
North Central	72	28	100	(440)
South	53	47	100	(309)
Border	45	55	100	(154)
Mountain and Pacific	70	30	100	(303)
Whites, by birth cohort				
Before 1924	72	28	100	(289)
1924-1939	71	29	100	(312)
1940-1954	66	34	100	(479)
1955-1962	54	46	100	(262)
1963-1970	35	65	100	(150)
Whites, by social class				
Working class	52	48	100	(616)
Middle class	73	27	100	(719)
Farmers	62	38	100	(74)
Whites, by occupation of head of household				
Unskilled manual	48	52	100	(175)
Skilled, semiskilled manual	54	46	100	(441)
Clerical, sales, other white collar	67	33	100	(248)
Managerial	73	27	100	(284)
Professional and semiprofessional	81	19	100	(187)
Whites, by level of education				
Eight grades or less	47	53	100	(139)
Some high school	46	54	100	(149)
High school graduate	56	44	100	(518)
Some college	69	31	100	(336)
College graduate	83	17	100	(229)
Advanced degree	81	19	100	(101)

Table 4-3 (continued)

Social group	Voted (%)	Did not vote (%)	Total percent	(N)
Whites, by annual family income				
Less than $10,000	45	55	100	(202)
$10,000 to $14,999	54	46	100	(190)
$15,000 to $19,999	63	37	100	(137)
$20,000 to $24,999	62	38	100	(160)
$25,000 to $29,999	64	36	100	(118)
$30,000 to $34,999	68	32	100	(123)
$35,000 to $39,999	70	30	100	(102)
$40,000 to $49,999	72	28	100	(153)
$50,000 to $59,999	71	29	100	(94)
$60,000 to $74,999	76	24	100	(83)
$75,000 and over	78	22	100	(92)
Whites by union membership[a]				
Member	67	33	100	(284)
Nonmember	62	38	100	(1,205)
Whites, by religion				
Protestant	63	37	100	(927)
Catholic	65	35	100	(388)
Jewish	68	32	100	(28)
None, no preference	51	49	100	(124)
Whites, by social class and religion				
Middle-class Protestants	75	25	100	(421)
Working-class Protestants	51	49	100	(395)
Middle-class Catholics	73	27	100	(197)
Working-class Catholics	59	41	100	(154)

Notes: Percentages read across. Seven validated voters who said they did not vote for president have been classified as nonvoters.

[a]Whether respondent or family member in union.

between 1963 and 1970), and highest among the cohort born between 1924 and 1939 and the cohort born before 1924. The 1988 census survey presents reported turnout by age among whites. Among whites between the ages of eighteen and twenty-four years, reported turnout was only 37.0 percent. But turnout rose to 50.0 percent among whites between twenty-five and thirty-four, and to 65.0 percent among those between thirty-five and fifty-four. Among whites between fifty-five and sixty-four turnout was 70.6 percent, and among those between sixty-five and seventy-four it was 73.8 percent. Turnout falls only among the very old, those seventy-five years and over. But even among this group reported turnout, at 63.6 percent, was much higher than turnout among the young. As Raymond E. Wolfinger and Steven J. Rosenstone's analysis of census surveys shows, low turnout among the elderly results from their relatively low level of formal education.[25]

Although the somewhat lower turnout among the elderly is consistent with the relationship between level of education and turnout, the low turnout by the young is not. Young Americans have relatively high levels of formal education. However, low turnout by the young is clearly a function of their youth—as young people age, marry, have children, and develop community ties, their turnout tends to increase.

Social Class, Income, and Union Membership

As Table 4-3 shows, social class differences in turnout were pronounced in 1988, a finding consistent with the relationship of formal education to turnout. Middle-class whites (nonmanually employed workers and their dependents) were substantially more likely to vote than working-class whites (manually employed workers and their dependents).[26] Farmers registered average levels of turnout, but the number of farmers sampled was too small to lead to reliable conclusions. Although the distinction between the middle class and the working class is crude, it appears to capture a politically meaningful division, for when we further divide respondents according to occupation, we find that turnout among clerical, sales, and other white collar workers (the lowest level of the middle class), is markedly higher than among skilled and semiskilled manual workers.

Annual family income also was related to turnout, with very low turnout among whites with family incomes below $10,000 a year.[27] Turnout was very high among whites with annual family incomes of $60,000 and above. The Census Bureau survey also discovered a strong relationship between income and turnout. Among whites with family incomes below $10,000 a year, reported turnout was only 37.6 percent; among whites with annual family incomes above $50,000, 77.2 percent voted. Americans with high family incomes tend to have higher levels of formal education, and both income and education contribute to turnout; however, education appears to have a greater impact on turnout than income does.[28]

Surveys over the years have found only a weak and inconsistent relationship between union membership and turnout. Although being in a household with a union member leads to organizational ties that should stimulate turnout, members of union households tend to have somewhat lower levels of formal education. As Table 4-3 reveals, in 1988 whites in union households were somewhat more likely to vote than whites in households with no union members.

Religion

In most postwar elections, white Catholics have voted more than white Protestants, but these differences have eroded. The 1980 vote validation study revealed no difference in turnout between these two groups, although the 1984 study showed that Catholics were once again more likely to vote than Protestants. As Table 4-3 shows, in 1988 white Catholics and white Protestants were equally likely to vote. Jews have much higher levels of formal education than gentiles and have always had higher turnout. They registered high turnout in 1988, but the number of Jews sampled is too small to reach reliable conclusions. Whites with no religious preference had lower than average turnout.

Because fundamentalist leaders have attempted to register their followers in recent elections, we examined turnout among white Protestants in some detail. We found little evidence that these leaders were successful in the 1980 election, but there was some evidence that they succeeded in 1984. The 1988 survey found only limited evidence that fundamentalist leaders were successful in mobilizing their followers. Among the major Protestant denominations, turnout was highest among white Presbyterians and Lutherans. Turnout was only 52 percent among white Southern Baptists ($N = 129$), the most fundamentalist of the major Protestant denominations.

We also explored turnout among white Protestants with differing religious values, and here we found some evidence of successful mobilization among fundamentalists. Among those who felt close to Christian fundamentalists ($N = 176$), 69 percent voted, whereas among the small number who felt close to "evangelical groups active in politics" ($N = 57$), 81 percent voted.[29] But turnout was somewhat lower among white Protestants who claimed to have been "born again" than among those who said they had not had this religious experience.[30]

In Table 4-3 we also present the combined effect of social class and religion. Among middle-class whites, religion is weakly related to turnout. Middle-class Protestants were about as likely to vote as middle-class Catholics. Among the working class, however, religion is clearly related to turnout. Working-class Catholics were 8 percentage points more likely to vote than working-class Protestants.

Education

We found a strong relationship between formal education and turnout. As Wolfinger and Rosenstone document, education is the most important variable in explaining differences in turnout in the United States.[31] Better educated Americans are more likely to develop attitudes that contribute to participation in politics, especially feelings that citizens have a duty to vote and can be politically effective.

Among whites who had not graduated from high school, only 46 percent voted. Among whites who had graduated from college, 82 percent voted. The census survey also shows a strong relationship between education and turnout. Among whites with eight grades of education or less, reported turnout was only 36.3 percent; among those with some high school, 41.5 percent voted; among those with four years of high school, 56.2 percent voted. Among whites with one to three years of college, reported turnout was 66.3 percent, while among those with four or more years of college it rose to 79.9 percent.

Why Has Turnout Declined?

Clearly, turnout within educational groups must have declined so fast that it canceled out the impact of rising educational levels.[32] We examined the relationship of educational levels and *reported* turnout among whites in all the presidential elections from 1952 through 1988, dividing the white electorate into five groups: college graduate, some college, high school graduate, some high school, and eight grades or less.[33] Blacks have substantially lower levels of formal education than whites, and southern blacks have been enfranchised only since 1965. Therefore, including blacks in our analysis of trends would partly obscure the relationships we are studying.

College graduates have maintained their high levels of turnout throughout the postwar years, and were as likely to vote in 1988 as they were in 1960, when overall turnout was highest. But turnout declined within all four of the remaining educational categories, and it dropped markedly within the three groups that had not attended college. Therefore, consistent with patterns found in examining Census Bureau data, the greatest declines in turnout have been among Americans who are relatively disadvantaged.[34]

Although increased education within the electorate did not prevent turnout from declining, it played a major role in slowing down the decline. Between 1960 and 1988, the level of education of the white electorate rose substantially, an increase that resulted almost entirely from generational replacement.[35] According to the NES surveys, the percentage of the white electorate that had not graduated from high school fell from 47 percent in 1960 to 20 percent in 1988. During the same period, the percentage who were college graduates rose from 11 percent to 20 percent. Nevertheless, reported turnout among whites dropped 10 points. An estimate based upon a simple algebraic standardization procedure suggests that if educational levels had not increased, turnout among whites would have declined 18 points.[36] Although this procedure provides only a preliminary estimate of the impact of rising educational levels, our analysis suggests that if educational levels had not increased, the overall decline of turnout among white Americans would have been about 80 percent greater than the actual decline.

Other social changes also tended to push turnout upward. In a comprehensive attempt to explain the decline of turnout between 1960 and 1980, Ruy A. Teixeira analyzes changes in reported electoral participation using the NES surveys.[37] He found that increases in income, the movement of women into the work force, and the growth of white collar employment all tended to retard the decline of turnout.[38] But the impact of rising educational levels was over three times as important as these three other changes combined.

There were also social changes that contributed to the decline of electoral participation. In Table 4-3 and in our examination of the census survey we saw that young adults are much less likely to vote than their elders. Because young adults seldom vote, the enfranchisement of eighteen-, nineteen-, and twenty-year-olds in 1971 reduced turnout. The total number of voting-age adults increased by definition (increasing the turnout denominator); the total number of voters increased at a smaller rate. Wolfinger and Rosenstone estimate that about one-fifth (1 percentage point) of the decline of turnout between 1968 and 1972 results from enfranchising eighteen-, nineteen-, and twenty-year-olds.[39] Moreover, as the "baby boom" generation entered the electorate, young adults made up a larger share of the voting-age population. Teixeira estimates that about a fourth of the decline of turnout between 1960 and 1980 results from the changing age distribution of the electorate. It should be noted, however, that between 1980 and 1988 the proportion of eighteen- through twenty-four-year-olds declined, while the proportion over the age of sixty-four increased.[40] The electorate will grow older for the next several decades, a change that may retard further declines of turnout and that could lead to increased electoral participation.

Although the changing age distribution has been the most important social factor in reducing turnout, several other factors have also contributed. The proportion of the population that is single has increased, residential mobility has increased, the proportion of nonwhites has grown, and a larger share of Americans live in the South.[41]

Our own analysis focused on the impact of attitudinal change, and we examined the erosion of party loyalties and the decline in feelings that the government is responsive, or what George I. Balch and others have called feelings of "external" political efficacy.[42] These are the same two attitudes studied by Teixeira.[43] We found these attitudinal changes to be major factors contributing to the decline of turnout between 1960 and 1980, as did Teixeira.[44] We both found that the importance of these attitudinal changes diminished in 1984.[45] However, as we shall see, these attitudinal changes appear to play an important role in contributing to the decline of turnout between 1960 and 1988.

The measure of party identification we employ is based upon a series of questions designed to gauge psychological attachment to a partisan reference group.[46] The percentage of whites who strongly identified with either the Republican or the Democratic party dropped from 36 percent in 1960 and 1964 to 23 percent in 1980. Since then, it has rebounded somewhat, and in 1988, 30 percent of whites were strong party identifiers, a proportion still 6 points lower than it was two decades earlier. In all the NES surveys between 1952 and 1964, the percentage of independents with no party leanings never rose above 9 percent. The figure rose to 14 percent in 1980, and in 1988 12 percent were independents with no partisan leanings. For a more detailed discussion of party loyalties and tables showing the distribution of party identification between 1952 and 1988, see Chapter 8.

Strong feelings of partisan identification contribute to psychological involvement in politics, as Angus Campbell and his colleagues argue.[47] Partisan loyalties also reduce the time and effort needed to learn how to vote and thus reduce the costs of voting.[48] Indeed, in every presidential election since 1952, strong partisans have been more likely to report voting than any other partisan strength category. In every election since 1960, independents with no party leanings have been the least likely to say that they voted.

Between 1960 and 1980 feelings of political effectiveness declined markedly. Scores on our measure are based upon responses to these two statements: "I don't think public officials care much what people like me think" and "People like me don't have any say about what the government does."[49] In 1956 and 1960, 64 percent of the white electorate scored as highly efficacious. The decline in external political efficacy began in 1964. By 1980, only 39 percent scored high. Feelings of political efficacy rose between 1980 and 1984, however, and by the time of the Reagan-Mondale contest 52 percent scored high on our measure. But feelings of political efficacy appear to have declined during the next four years,[50] and in 1988, only 38 percent scored as highly efficacious.[51] The percentage scoring low on our measure was only 15 percent in 1956 and 1960, but it rose fairly steadily through 1976. In 1980, 30 percent scored low. The percentage of whites with low political efficacy fell to 23 percent in 1984, but in 1988, 37 percent scored low on our measure.

Feelings of political effectiveness also contribute to electoral participation. Persons who feel politically capable may feel psychologically motivated to participate. Those who feel overwhelmed by the political process may withdraw from political activity. In addition, citizens are more likely to see benefits from voting if they believe the government is responsive to citizen demands. In every presidential election since 1952, persons scoring high on our measure have been the most likely to report voting, and those scoring low, the least likely.

Table 4-4 Percentage That Voted for President According to Vote Validation Study, by Strength of Party Identification and Sense of "External" Political Efficacy, 1988

Scores on external political efficacy index	Strength of party identification							
	Strong partisan		Weak partisan		Independent who leans toward a party		Independent with no partisan leaning	
	%	(N)	%	(N)	%	(N)	%	(N)
High	81	(232)	67	(202)	64	(145)	66	(53)
Medium	72	(141)	63	(124)	63	(121)	37	(41)
Low	60	(182)	48	(243)	44	(172)	29	(84)

Note: Numbers in parentheses are the totals upon which percentages are based.

Although feelings of partisan loyalty and feelings of political efficacy are both related to turnout, they are only weakly related to each other. In other words, there is little tendency for persons who have strong party loyalties to have high levels of external political efficacy. Table 4-4 examines the combined effect of these political attitudes upon turnout in 1988.

By reading across each row of Table 4-4 we see that strength of party identification is related to turnout, regardless of scores on our measure of political efficacy. By reading down each column, we see that feelings of political efficacy are related to electoral participation, regardless of partisan strength. These attitudinal variables have a strong cumulative effect. Four out of five strong party identifiers with high feelings of political efficacy voted; among independents with no partisan leanings who scored low on political efficacy, only three out of ten voted.

The decline in party loyalties and the erosion in feelings of political efficacy clearly contribute to the decline of turnout. A preliminary assessment of their impact can be derived through a simple algebraic standardization procedure. According to our calculations, the decline in feelings of party identification accounts for 18 percent of the decline of reported turnout among white Americans between 1960 and 1988, while the decline of feelings of political efficacy accounts for 55 percent of the decline.[52] The combined effects of the decline of party loyalties and the decline in feelings of political efficacy appear to account for 62 percent of the decline in reported turnout.

These estimates clearly demonstrate that these attitudinal changes were important, but they are not final estimates of the impact of these changes. As Teixeira demonstrates, a comprehensive estimate of the impact of attitudinal change can be derived by calculating the contribution of attitude change to the decline that would have occurred if there had been no social forces retarding the decline of electoral participation. Moreover, a comprehensive assessment should take into account the total impact of other relevant social and attitudinal changes. In Teixeira's analysis, for example, the decline of party loyalties and the erosion of political efficacy accounted for 62 percent of the decline of turnout between 1960 and 1980. But these attitudinal changes accounted for only 38 percent of the larger decline that would have occurred if changes in educational levels, income, and occupational patterns had not slowed down the decline of turnout. We analyzed the combined impact of rising educational levels, the erosion of feelings of political efficacy, and the decline of partisan loyalties upon levels of reported turnout among whites between 1960 and 1988. Our estimates suggest that attitude change accounted for 33 percent of the decline in electoral participation that would have occurred if rising educational levels had not slowed down the decline of turnout.[53]

A complete assessment of the reasons turnout declined must also take note of factors specific to the 1988 election. Some critics have argued that negative campaigning may have led some potential voters to abstain, but the NES survey provides no questions that would allow us to examine this proposition directly. In addition, both parties fielded dull campaigners who failed to excite the electorate. On the other hand, there were some ways in which the campaign might have been expected to stimulate turnout. As we will show in Chapter 6, the electorate saw clear policy differences between Bush and Dukakis. Moreover, concern with the election's outcome was relatively high. Concern was measured by responses to the question, "Generally speaking, would you say that you personally care a good deal which party wins the presidential election this fall?"—a question asked in every NES presidential election survey since 1952. The highest level of concern among whites was recorded in 1960, when 69 percent said they cared which party won. In 1980, only 54 percent of the whites cared a good deal which party won, but the percentage rose to 66 percent in 1984. In 1988, concern fell slightly, and 62 percent of the whites said they "cared a good deal" which party won.[54] In 1988, as in every previous election, Americans who cared a good deal which party would win were more likely to vote than those who did not care. Among whites who cared ($N = 932$), 72 percent voted; among those who did not ($N = 541$), only 48 percent voted. The decline in concern with the electoral outcome could in principle account for about a fifth of the fall in reported turnout between 1960 and 1988.[55]

Another short-term factor that might have depressed turnout was the widespread expectation that Bush would win. As the media concentrated on the horse race aspect of the election, attentive citizens knew that Bush was ahead by a comfortable margin throughout the entire fall campaign. Even so, between September 6 and November 7, 1988, when the NES preelection interviews were conducted, 74 percent of the whites and 71 percent of the blacks thought the election would be close.[56] During the Reagan-Carter contest in 1980, 85 percent of the whites and 76 percent of the blacks thought the election would be close, a perception that corresponded with the predictions of most pollsters. On the other hand, four years later, when the polls showed Reagan to be ahead of Mondale by a huge margin, only 49 percent of the whites thought the election would be close, although 65 percent of the blacks did.

In most elections, voters who think the election will be close are more likely to vote than those who think the winner will win by a large margin.[57] Even though these differences are usually not large, the percentage viewing the upcoming election as close has varied greatly from contest to contest. Orley Ashenfelter and Stanley Kelley, Jr., report that the single most important factor accounting for the decline in turnout between 1960 and 1972 was "the dramatic shift in voter expectations about the closeness of the race in these two elections." [58] In 1988 whites who thought the election would be close were more likely to vote than those who did not, but differences were small. Among whites who thought the election would be close ($N = 1055$), 66 percent voted; among those who thought the winner would prevail by "quite a bit" ($N = 362$), 59 percent voted.

During the Kennedy-Nixon contest in 1960, 85 percent of the whites and 70 percent of the blacks thought the contest would be close. But even though a smaller proportion of whites thought the 1988 election would be close, these changed perceptions made only a negligible contribution to the decline of turnout between 1960 and 1988. The relationship between perceptions of closeness and electoral participation was simply too weak in 1988 for changed perceptions to have much of an impact upon overall levels of turnout.

Although it is difficult to measure short-term forces that may have depressed turnout in 1988, we suspect that the exceptionally low turnout may at least partly result from conditions that will not necessarily be repeated in future elections. But the bulk of the evidence suggests that the decline of turnout during the past quarter century results mainly from long-term trends. Of course, there are several long-term trends that may lead to higher turnout in future elections. Educational levels will continue to rise for the next several decades, and the proportion of young adults will decline. But even if the remarkably low turnout of 1988 is not repeated, it will be difficult to restore even the modest level of participation that America achieved in 1960.

Does Low Turnout Matter?

Nonvoters, in principle, could have elected Dukakis, but their turnout would have changed the outcome only if they had voted heavily Democratic. Little evidence suggests that nonvoters tended to prefer Dukakis, and there is some evidence that they preferred Bush. For example, during its preelection interview the NES survey asked respondents whom they planned to vote for. Most of these same respondents were also interviewed after the election. Respondents who favored Dukakis and those who favored Bush were equally likely to vote. The NES postelection survey also asked respondents who said that they did not vote whom they preferred, and Bush held a clear edge. Forty-eight percent of the acknowledged nonvoters preferred Bush; only 41 percent favored Dukakis.

It is true, however, that Dukakis tended to do well among two relatively large groups with below average turnout: blacks and Hispanics. There are over 20 million voting-age blacks, and over 95 percent are citizens. It seems likely that about 12 million eligible blacks did not vote. If all of these blacks had voted, and if they had all voted for Dukakis, Dukakis would have prevailed—if more whites did not vote as well. But the conditions that would lead to massive increases in turnout among blacks would almost certainly also lead to dramatic increases in voting among whites. A more reasonable question to ask is how many votes Dukakis would have gained if black turnout had been as high as white turnout. And, rather than assuming that all the new black voters would support Dukakis, it would be more reasonable to assume that the new black voters would split their votes pretty much the same way as the blacks who did vote—about nine Dukakis voters for every Bush voter (see Chapter 5). Assuming that blacks were actually about 15 percentage points less likely to vote than whites, an additional 3 million blacks would be brought to the polls, and Dukakis would score a net gain of 2.4 million votes.[59]

The Census Bureau estimates that there are 13 million Hispanics of voting age, but only 63 percent are citizens. Yet, as we saw, even among Hispanic citizens turnout was very low, and there may have been 4.5 million nonvoters among Hispanics eligible to vote. If all these nonvoting Hispanics had voted, and if all had voted Democratic, Dukakis would have made substantial gains. If we assume that turnout among Hispanic citizens was about 15 percentage points less than white turnout, and if we assume that Hispanic citizens had voted at the same rate as whites, an additional 675,000 voters would have been brought to the polls. And if we assume that Dukakis's share of these new Hispanic voters was about the same as that of Hispanics who did vote, Dukakis would have gained about two new votes to every one new vote for Bush (see Chapter 5). Dukakis would have scored a net gain of only 225,000 votes.[60] Even the combined impact of increased black and Hispanic voting would have probably yielded Dukakis only 2.6 million votes, far fewer than the 7 million votes Bush won by.

Some scholars have argued that low turnout matters little unless the partisan or policy preferences of voters and nonvoters differ markedly. Wolfinger and Rosenstone's analysis of the 1972 NES survey suggests that there were negligible differences in the policy preferences of voters and nonvoters.[61] Similarly, analyses of NES surveys by Paul Kleppner and Stephen D. Shaffer suggest that policy differences between voters and nonvoters differed only slightly during the postwar years.[62] Our analysis of the 1980 NES survey demonstrated that voters and nonvoters differed little in their policy preferences.[63] But our analysis of the 1984 survey revealed that respondents who had pro-Democratic policy preferences were somewhat more likely to vote than those who had pro-Republican preferences.[64]

Our analysis of the 1988 NES survey shows that, as in 1984, there were differences in the partisan loyalties and policy preferences of voters and nonvoters. Table 4-5 summarizes our results. First, we examined turnout according to party identification. Strong Republicans were more likely to vote than strong Democrats, and weak Republicans were more likely to vote than weak Democrats. Among independents, those who leaned toward the Republicans and those who leaned Democratic were equally likely to vote. But even if strong Democrats had voted as often as strong Republicans and if weak Democrats had voted as often as weak Republicans, and assuming these extra Democratic voters were as likely to vote for Dukakis as strong and weak Democrats who did vote, this increased turnout would have added only about 2 percentage points to Dukakis's total share of the vote.

Second, as in 1984, we found policy differences in the preferences of voters and nonvoters. In Chapter 6 we analyze policy preferences on seven major issues—domestic spending, government health insurance, government support for guaranteed jobs, government aid for minorities, whether women should have an equal role, defense spending, and cooperation with Russia. We found that on the first four of these issues respondents who favored an active government were somewhat more likely to vote than those who favored conservative policies, but for the remaining three issues there was virtually no relationship between policy preferences and turnout. The relationships between policy preferences and turnout are presented in Table 4-5, where we use our balance of issues measure, which summarizes the overall policy preferences on all seven issues for each respondent (see Chapter 6). As we can see, the small number who were strongly pro-Republican on the issues were slightly less likely to vote than those who were strongly pro-Democratic. However, those who were moderately pro-Republican were much more likely to

Table 4-5   Percentage That Voted for President According to Vote Validation Study, by Party Identification, Issue Preferences, and Retrospective Evaluations, 1988

Attitude	Voted (%)	Did not vote (%)	Total percent	(N)
Electorate, by party identification				
Strong Democrat	68	32	100	(307)
Weak Democrat	54	46	100	(324)
Independent, leans Democratic	56	44	100	(209)
Independent, no partisan leaning	41	59	100	(180)
Independent, leans Republican	56	44	100	(233)
Weak Republican	63	37	100	(246)
Strong Republican	76	24	100	(251)
Electorate, by balance of issues measure				
Strongly Democratic	72	28	100	(92)
Moderately Democratic	53	47	100	(190)
Slightly Democratic	59	41	100	(338)
Neutral	55	45	100	(685)
Slightly Republican	61	39	100	(293)
Moderately Republican	76	24	100	(142)
Strongly Republican	69	31	100	(35)
Electorate, by summary measure of retrospective evaluations				
Strongly Democratic	72	28	100	(190)
Moderately Democratic	56	44	100	(309)
Leans Democratic	53	47	100	(204)
Neutral	54	46	100	(385)
Leans Republican	65	35	100	(351)
Moderately Republican	67	33	100	(190)
Strongly Republican	76	24	100	(58)

vote than those who were moderately pro-Democratic. Respondents who were slightly Republican on the issues were only marginally more likely to vote than those who were slightly pro-Democratic. These turnout differences had little effect on the overall result. Even if Americans who were pro-Democratic on the issues were as likely to vote as those who were pro-Republican, and assuming they were as likely to vote Democratic as pro-Democratic respondents in each category who did vote, Dukakis's overall share of the vote would have increased only 2 percentage points.

Last, we found that respondents with a positive evaluation of Reagan's performance in office were slightly more likely to vote than those who disapproved of Reagan; those who thought the government was doing a good job solving the most important problem facing the country were slightly more likely to vote than those who thought it was doing a poor job. Respondents who thought the Republicans would do a better job of solving the most important problem facing the country were somewhat more likely to vote than those who thought the Democrats would do a better job. In Table 4-5 we present the percentage that voted according to scores on our summary measure of "retrospective" evaluations, which combines the responses to all three questions (see Chapter 7). As the table shows, respondents with strongly pro-Republican evaluations were slightly more likely to vote than those with strongly pro-Democratic evaluations; those who were moderately pro-Republican were clearly more likely to vote than those who were moderately Democratic; and those who leaned toward the Republicans were clearly more likely to vote than those who leaned toward the Democrats. We estimated what Dukakis's share of the vote would have been if respondents with pro-Democratic views were as likely to vote as those who were pro-Republican, and assumed these new voters would vote for Dukakis at the same rate as the strongly, moderately, and slightly pro-Democratic respondents who did vote. Once again, Dukakis's overall share of the vote would have increased by only 2 percentage points.

Of course these 2-point gains from increased turnout cannot simply be added up to yield Dukakis a 6-point gain. Democratic identifiers are more likely to have pro-Democratic views on the issues and to have pro-Democratic retrospective evaluations. Because these pro-Democratic categories overlap, the potential gains from all these changes is limited.

On balance, there is no reasonable scenario under which increased turnout would have altered the outcome of the presidential election. Indeed, it seems reasonable to conclude that the major problem for the Democrats is not low turnout but low levels of support. Simple arithmetic dictates that relying upon increased turnout to win has a fundamental disadvantage. It takes two new voters to match every one voter who switches to the opposition. Or, to put the matter differently, one voter converted from the opponent is worth just as much as two new voters. During the postwar years millions of traditionally Democratic voters have been voting Republican, at least in presidential elections. Recouping these losses through increased turnout is not a practical strategy.

Given that increased turnout would not have altered the election's outcome, some might argue that low turnout does not matter. Some scholars point out that in most elections (though not 1984 and 1988), the policy preferences of voters have been similar to the preferences of those who did not go to the polls. Turnout has been low in postwar elections, but, in most of these, the voters reflected the sentiments of the electorate as a whole.

Despite this evidence, we cannot accept the conclusion that low turnout is unimportant. We are concerned that turnout is especially low among disadvantaged Americans. From the Johnson-Goldwater contest of 1964 through 1980 turnout declined most among disadvantaged Americans. The decline of turnout was temporarily halted in 1984, but in 1988 turnout once again dropped most among the disadvantaged. Although black turnout is up from the early 1960s as a result of the enfranchisement of southern blacks, turnout among disadvantaged whites is much lower than it was a quarter of a century ago. During the past quarter century turnout declined among blacks outside the South, and in 1988 turnout dropped more among black Americans than it did among whites. Some believe that turnout is declining among the disadvantaged because political leaders structure policy alternatives in a way that provides disadvantaged Americans with little choice. Frances Fox Piven and Richard Cloward, for example, acknowledge that the policy preferences of voters and nonvoters are similar, but argue that this similarity results from the way elites have structured policy choices. "Political attitudes would inevitably change over time," they argue, "if the allegiance of voters from the bottom became the object of partisan competition, for then politicians would be prodded to identify and articulate the grievances and aspirations of lower-income voters in order to win their support, thus helping to give form and voice to a distinctive political class." [65]

We cannot accept this argument either, mainly because it is highly speculative and there is little empirical evidence to support it. The difficulty in supporting this point of view may result from the nature of survey research, because questions about policy preferences are usually framed along the lines of controversy as defined by mainstream political leaders. Occasionally, however, surveys pose radical policy alternatives, and they often ask open-ended questions that allow respondents to state their policy preferences. We find little concrete evidence that current political leaders are ignoring the policy preferences of the electorate.

Nevertheless, the very low turnout of Americans can scarcely be healthy for a democracy. Even if low levels of turnout seldom affect electoral outcomes, they may undermine the legitimacy of elected political leaders. Moreover, the large bloc of nonparticipants in the electorate may be potentially dangerous because this means that many Americans may have weak ties to established political leaders. The prospects for electoral instability, and perhaps political instability, thus increase.[66]

Does the low turnout in 1988 have implications for continued Republican dominance in presidential elections? Eight years ago the low turnout led some scholars to question whether Reagan's victory presaged a pro-Republican realignment. As Gerald M. Pomper then argued, "Elections that involve upheavals in party coalitions have certain hall-marks, such as popular enthusiasm." [67] Indeed, past realignments have been characterized by increases in turnout. As Table 4-1 shows, turnout rose markedly between 1852 and 1860, a period during which the Republican party was formed, replaced the Whigs, and gained control of the presidency. Turnout also rose in the Bryan-McKinley contest of 1896, generally considered a realigning election. As both Table 4-2 and Figure 4-1 show, turnout rose markedly after 1924, increasing in 1928 and again in 1936, a period when the Democrats emerged as the majority party.

But the historical evidence may not provide a guide for the future. Although past realignments were characterized by increased turnout, future realignments—if they occur at all—may not be. At the same time, it is difficult to view any alignment as stable when such a large percentage of the electorate does not vote. Burnham has called the nonparticipants the "party of nonvoters." [68] Nonvoters could alter the balance of power, either by voting Democratic or, as Burnham hopes, by supporting a genuine party of the left. We view these prospects as highly unlikely, however. After the 1984 and 1988 elections it appears that the Republicans could attain long-term dominance despite the ever-present threat of future participation by some 80 million nonvoting Americans.

Notes

1. During the 1916 presidential election women could vote only in Arizona, California, Colorado, Idaho, Kansas, Montana, Nevada, Oregon, Utah, Washington, and Wyoming. Only 10 percent of the U.S. population lived in these states. For a provocative discussion of the struggle for women's right to vote, see Alan P. Grimes, *The Puritan Ethic and Woman Suffrage* (New York: Oxford University Press, 1967).
2. See J. Morgan Kousser, *The Shaping of Southern Politics: Suffrage Restriction and the Establishment of the One-Party South, 1880-1910* (New Haven, Conn.: Yale University Press, 1974). For a more general discussion of the decline of turnout in the late nineteenth and early twentieth century, see Paul Kleppner, *Who Voted? The Dynamics of Electoral Turnout, 1870-1980* (New York: Praeger, 1982), 55-82.
3. There has been a great deal of controversy over the reasons for and the consequences of these registration requirements. For some of the more interesting arguments, see Walter Dean Burnham, "The Changing Shape of the American Political Universe," *American Political Science Review* 59 (March 1965): 7-28; Philip E. Converse, "Change in the American Electorate," in *The Human Meaning of Social Change*, ed. Angus Campbell and Philip E. Converse (New York: Russell Sage, 1972), 266-301; Burnham, "Theory and Voting Research: Some Reflections on Converse's 'Change in the American Electorate,'" *American Political Science Review* 68 (September 1974): 1002-1023, as well as a comment by Converse and a rejoinder by Burnham in the same issue. For a provocative recent discussion, see Frances Fox Piven and Richard A. Cloward, *Why Americans Don't Vote* (New York: Pantheon, 1988), 26-95.

4. For a rich source of information about the introduction of the Australian ballot and its effects, see Jerrold G. Rusk, "The Effect of the Australian Ballot Reform on Split Ticket Voting: 1876-1908," *American Political Science Review* 64 (December 1970): 1220-1238. Rusk's analysis has also led to an interesting interchange with Burnham. See a comment by Burnham and a rejoinder by Rusk in the *American Political Science Review* 65 (December 1971): 1149-1157, as well as further discussion by both authors in the September 1974 issue, 1028-1049, 1052-1057.

5. For example, see Burnham's estimates of turnout among the voting-age citizen population, which include results through 1984. These appear in Burnham, "The Turnout Problem," in *Elections American Style,* ed. A. James Reichley (Washington, D.C.: Brookings Institution, 1987), 113-114. Burnham estimates that the voting-age citizen population in 1988 was 176,700,000 and that turnout was 51.8 percent (personal communication, June 8, 1989).

Because Burnham's turnout denominator is smaller than ours, his estimates of turnout are always somewhat higher. Although there are advantages to Burnham's calculations, we use the total voting-age population as our base for two reasons. First, it is very difficult to estimate the size of the noncitizen population, and official estimates of turnout by the U.S. Bureau of the Census use the voting-age population as the turnout denominator. Second, even though only citizens can vote in present-day U.S. elections, citizenship is not a constitutional requirement for voting. The time it takes to become a citizen is a matter of national legislation, and imposing citizenship as a condition of voting is a matter of state law.

6. See G. Bingham Powell, Jr., "American Voter Turnout in Comparative Perspective," *American Political Science Review* 80 (March 1986): 17-43.

7. For a discussion of voter registration strategies between 1980 and 1984, see Piven and Cloward, *Why Americans Don't Vote,* 181-208.

8. For a discussion of the decreased registration efforts in 1988, see James A. Barnes, "Tuned-Out Turnout," *National Journal,* July 2, 1988, 1743-1747.

9. As the U.S. Bureau of the Census points out, their estimate of the voting-age population includes about 6.5 million legal aliens and about 2.5 million undocumented aliens. In addition, they estimate that about 680,000 citizens are ineligible to vote because they are in prisons or mental hospitals. See U.S. Department of Commerce, Bureau of the Census, *Projections of the Population of Voting Age for States: November 1988,* Series P-25, No. 1019 (Washington, D.C.: U.S. Government Printing Office, January 1988), 1-3.

10. We use the vote validation results released by the Center for Political Studies of the University of Michigan in July 1989. We are grateful to Santa Traugott for her advice in analyzing this study. In our analysis we rely upon the summary variable that reflects the judgment of the Center for Political Studies staff on whether the respondent should be classified as a voter or a nonvoter. We analyze the results only for respondents who were included in the postelection interview.

The main reason for being classified as a nonvoter in the vote validation study is that the researchers fail to find a record that the respondent is registered. There will always be some cases where the researchers' failure to find a registration record leads to classifying an actual voter as a validated nonvoter. The Survey Research Center has varied its procedures over the years in an attempt to improve its validation procedures. As a result of these changes, it is difficult to compare overall levels of validated turnout from year to year. Thus overall levels of turnout for groups in Tables 4-3 through 4-5 should not be compared directly with similar tables in our earlier books. While relative levels of turnout among social and attitudinal groups can be compared, any comparisons of absolute levels of turnout between 1980, 1984, and 1988 will be misleading. Since changing procedures make comparisons over time very difficult, we rely upon our analysis of reported turnout to study postwar trends.

11. There are biases in the extent of voting overreports. In addition to the 1988 vote validation study, similar studies were conducted by the NES researchers as part of the 1964, 1976, 1978, 1980, 1984, and 1986 election studies. Most analyses that compare results of reported turnout and turnout as measured by these vote validation studies suggest that relative levels of turnout among most social groups can be measured using reported turnout. However, research suggests that blacks are consistently more likely to falsely report voting than whites, and turnout differences between the races are always greater when turnout is measured by the vote validation studies. See Paul R. Abramson and William Claggett, "Race-Related Differences in Self-Reported and Validated Turnout in 1986," *Journal of Politics* 51 (May 1989): 397-408.

    For an extensive analysis of the factors that contribute to false reports of voting, see Brian D. Silver, Barbara A. Anderson, and Paul R. Abramson, "Who Overreports Voting?" *American Political Science Review* 80 (June 1986): 613-624.

12. See Michael W. Traugott and John P. Katosh, "Response Validity in Surveys of Voting Behavior," *Public Opinion Quarterly* 43 (Fall 1979): 359-377; and Barbara A. Anderson, Brian D. Silver, and Paul R. Abramson, "The Effects of Race of the Interviewer on Measures of Electoral Participation by Blacks in SRC National Election Studies," *Public Opinion Quarterly* 52 (Spring 1988): 53-83.

13. Respondents are asked the following question: "In talking to people about elections, we often find that a lot of people were not able to vote because they weren't registered, they were sick, or they just didn't have time. How about you—did you vote in the elections this November?"

14. Another factor that may contribute to relatively lower turnout is that the Census Bureau does not interview the respondents before the election. The bureau's procedures for classifying respondents as nonvoters also contributes to lower reported turnout. Nonrespondents and persons who said they did not know if they voted are classified as nonvoters.

15. We must compare the NES and the Census Bureau results with different real-world populations. The census surveys are based upon the total noninstitutionalized civilian voting-age population, and the NES surveys are based upon the total noninstitutionalized politically eligible civilian population.

16. We are grateful to Jerry T. Jennings of the U.S. Census Bureau for providing us with the information about the size of the 1988 sample. In addition, he provided us with unpublished tables that appeared in the final version of the Census Bureau report. For that report, see U.S. Department of Commerce, Bureau of the Census, *Voting and Registration in the Election of November 1988*, Series P-20, No. 440 (Washington, D.C.: U.S. Government Printing Office, 1989).

    It should be noted that the census surveys use the respondent to report information about registration and voting for all voting-age respondents of the household. Studies by the bureau indicate that relying upon this information about how other adults voted leads to no significant biases.

17. Hispanics may be of any race, but far more Hispanics are white than black. Among the 165 respondents classified as Hispanic in the SRC-CPS survey, 88 percent were white and only 5 percent were black.

18. The NES provides a detailed breakdown among Hispanics. Respondents are classified as Mexican, Puerto Rican, Cuban, Latin American, Central American, Spanish, and other. However, the total number of Hispanics sampled was too small to permit careful analysis of their political behavior.

19. In making comparisons of turnout in the 1984 and 1988 elections, we often rely upon the more detailed 1984 results presented in U.S. Department of Commerce, Bureau of the Census, *Voting and Registration in the Election of November 1984,* Series P-20, No. 405 (Washington, D.C.: U.S. Government Printing Office, 1986).

20. Rhodes Cook, "Turnout Hits 64-Year Low in Presidential Race," *Congressional Quarterly Weekly Report,* January 21, 1989, 136.

21. As we state in Chapter 3, we consider the South to include the eleven states of the Old Confederacy. In our analysis of NES surveys, however, we do not classify residents of Tennessee as southerners because the SRC samples respondents in Tennessee to represent the border states. In the following analysis, as well as in our analyses of regional differences using the NES surveys later in our book, we classify the following ten states as southern: Alabama, Arkansas, Florida, Georgia, Louisiana, Mississippi, North Carolina, South Carolina, Texas, and Virginia.

22. The very low level of turnout among border state whites clearly results from sampling error. The SRC classifies Kentucky, Maryland, Oklahoma, Tennessee, West Virginia, and the District of Columbia as border states. Official election statistics show that actual turnout in these states was 47.1 percent, only 3.0 percent below the national average. The voting-age population of these states is 83.2 percent white and only 14.5 percent black. Therefore, white turnout in the border states cannot be dramatically lower than it is for the nation as a whole.

23. See Raymond E. Wolfinger and Steven J. Rosenstone, *Who Votes?* (New Haven, Conn.: Yale University Press, 1980), 93-94.

24. The 1964 census survey used the category nonwhite, rather than black.

25. Wolfinger and Rosenstone, *Who Votes?* 46-50.

26. We use this distinction mainly because it allows us to make comparisons over many elections, and thus is especially valuable for studying change during the entire postwar period, as we do in our analysis of presidential voting in Chapter 5. However, there is one difference between our measure of social class in 1988 and that in previous election year surveys. In all previous surveys, we classified respondents according to the head of household's occupation. Classification according to head of household's occupation is generally considered a more valid measure of a woman's social class position than her own occupation. Many women employed at relatively unskilled nonmanual jobs are married to manually employed men. Their social and political behavior appears to be affected more by their husbands' occupations than by their own occupations. In the 1988 NES, there was no attempt to determine whether the respondent was the "head of household." We have therefore classified married women according to their husband's occupation. A reanalysis of the 1984 NES suggests that we are coming very close to replicating our earlier measure, which was directly based upon the occupation of the head of household.

27. Our measure of family income is based upon the respondent's estimate of his or her family's 1987 annual family income before taxes. For respondents who refused to answer this question and for those the interviewer thought answered dishonestly, we relied upon the interviewer's assessment of family income.
28. See Wolfinger and Rosenstone, *Who Votes?* 13-36.
29. Respondents were handed a list and asked the following question: "Here is a list of groups. Please read over the list and tell me the letter for those groups that you feel particularly close to—people who are most like you in their ideas and interests and feelings about things."
30. Respondents were asked, "Do you consider yourself a born-again Christian?"
31. Wolfinger and Rosenstone, *Who Votes?* 13-36.
32. Precisely because there are some factors that should have increased turnout, the decline of turnout constitutes a puzzle for students of electoral behavior. For an excellent discussion, see Richard A. Brody, "The Puzzle of Political Participation in America," in *The New American Political System*, ed. Anthony King (Washington, D.C.: American Enterprise Institute, 1978), 287-324.
33. Given the problems of over-time comparability in using the vote validation studies, we rely upon reported turnout to study change over time.
34. Walter Dean Burnham, "The 1976 Election: Has the Crisis Been Adjourned?" in *American Politics and Public Policy*, ed. Walter Dean Burnham and Martha Wagner Weinberg (Cambridge, Mass.: MIT Press, 1978), 24; and Thomas E. Cavanagh, "Changes in American Voter Turnout, 1964-1976," *Political Science Quarterly* 96 (Spring 1981): 53-65.
35. For estimates of the effects of replacement between 1956 and 1980, see Paul R. Abramson, *Political Attitudes in America: Formation and Change* (San Francisco: W. H. Freeman, 1983), 56-61.
36. This procedure assumes that overall educational levels were the same in 1988 as they were in 1960, but that reported turnout was the same as the level actually observed in the 1988 survey.
37. Ruy A. Teixeira, *Why Americans Don't Vote: Turnout Decline in the United States, 1960-1984* (New York: Greenwood Press, 1987). Most of Teixeira's study analyzes change between 1960 and 1980, although he does update his analysis by using the 1984 NES survey.
38. Teixeira uses a probability technique called probit analysis for his estimates.
39. Wolfinger and Rosenstone, *Who Votes?* 58.
40. See Census Bureau, *Projections of the Population of Voting Age for States, November 1988*, 2.
41. Teixeira also notes that the proportion of women has grown, but since women are now as likely to vote as men, this change should not be included as a factor that decreased turnout.
42. George I. Balch, "Multiple Indicators in Survey Research: The Concept 'Sense of Political Efficacy,'" *Political Methodology* 1 (Spring 1974): 1-43. For an extensive discussion of feelings of political efficacy, see Abramson, *Political Attitudes*, 135-189.
43. Teixeira also includes the declining percentage of Americans who read about the campaign in newspapers as a "socio-political" change that reduced turnout. Other scholars have identified the decline of newspaper readership as an important factor. See Stephen D. Shaffer, "A Multivariate Explanation of Decreasing Turnout in Presidential Elections, 1960-1976," *American Journal of Political Science* 25 (February 1981): 68-95. However, reading

about politics in newspapers is a form of political behavior, and we do not think it is appropriate to include newspaper readership as an attitudinal variable. Moreover, we do not understand the theoretical basis for including the decline of newspaper reading as a cause of declining turnout. It is true that Americans who read about the campaign in newspapers are more likely to vote than those who do not. But it does not seem reasonable to conclude that reading newspapers causes people to vote. It seems just as reasonable to conclude that people who are more likely to vote are more likely to read newspapers.

44. See Paul R. Abramson, John H. Aldrich, and David W. Rohde, *Change and Continuity in the 1980 Elections,* rev. ed. (Washington, D.C.: CQ Press, 1983), 85-87. For a more detailed analysis using probability techniques to estimate the impact of these attitudinal changes, see Paul R. Abramson and John H. Aldrich, "The Decline of Electoral Participation in America," *American Political Science Review* 76 (September 1982): 502-521.

45. Paul R. Abramson, John H. Aldrich, and David W. Rohde, *Change and Continuity in the 1984 Elections,* rev. ed. (Washington, D.C.: CQ Press, 1987), 115-118; Teixeira, *Why Americans Don't Vote,* 115-123.

46. Respondents are asked, "Generally speaking, do you usually think of yourself as a Republican, a Democrat, an independent, or what?" Persons who call themselves Republicans or Democrats are asked, "Would you call yourself a strong (Republican, Democrat) or a not very strong (Republican, Democrat)?" Respondents who call themselves independents, answer "no preference," or name another party are asked, "Do you think of yourself as closer to the Republican Party or to the Democratic Party?" Respondents who have no partisan preference are usually classified as independents. They are classified as "apoliticals" only if they have low levels of political interest and involvement.

47. Angus Campbell, Philip E. Converse, Warren E. Miller, and Donald E. Stokes, *The American Voter* (New York: John Wiley & Sons, 1960), 120-167.

48. This expectation follows from a rational-choice perspective. For the most extensive discussion of party identification from this point of view, see Morris P. Fiorina, *Retrospective Voting in American National Elections* (New Haven, Conn.: Yale University Press, 1981), 84-105.

49. Respondents who disagreed with both of these statements were scored as highly efficacious; those who disagreed with one but agreed with the other were scored as medium; and those who agreed with both questions were scored as low. Respondents with "don't know" or "not ascertained" responses to one question were scored as high or low depending upon their responses to the remaining question, and those with "don't know" or "not ascertained" responses to both questions were excluded from the analysis.

50. Our measure of sense of external political efficacy cannot be constructed with the 1986 NES survey because the "don't have any say" question was not asked.

51. We stress that feelings of efficacy appear to have declined, since there was a change in the way the political efficacy questions were measured. In all previous surveys except the 1966 midterm study, respondents were asked whether they agreed or disagreed with the political efficacy questions. In 1988, as in 1966, they were asked to reply to a five-point response. In 1988 respondents were asked whether they agree strongly, agree somewhat, neither agree nor disagree, disagree somewhat, or strongly disagree. As we are attempting to build a comparable measure over time, we cannot make use of

the distinction between strongly agreeing and agreeing somewhat or the distinction between disagreeing somewhat and strongly disagreeing. Changing the way the question was asked raises two problems. First, we cannot tell how changing the response alternatives affects the distribution of respondents who basically agree or disagree. Some respondents who might otherwise agree or disagree might answer "neither agree nor disagree" when explicitly provided this alternative. Second, we must decide how to classify respondents who answer both questions "neither agree nor disagree." We must either exclude these respondents altogether for having two ambiguous responses, or include them as "medium" on our measure.

Despite these problems, we believe that the decline in efficacy is real, even though the exact extent of the decline might have been somewhat different if there had been no change in the responses offered. We reach this conclusion for three reasons. First, there was only a small change in scores on "external" political efficacy between 1964 (when a simple agree-disagree format was used) and 1966 (when a five-point response was employed). Second, in 1966 only about 5 percent of the respondents chose the "not sure, it depends" category for each of these questions and in 1988 only about 10 percent of the respondents chose the "neither agree nor disagree" response. Moreover, very few chose these responses for both the political efficacy questions. In 1966, only 2 percent answered both questions "not sure, it depends," and in 1988, only 3 percent answered both questions "neither agree nor disagree."

We conducted all of our 1988 analyses with alternative scoring for the sense of political efficacy measure. In one analysis we excluded respondents with two "neither agree nor disagree" responses; in the other, we scored these respondents as "medium." The differences between the two sets of results are negligible. We present our results for the scoring in which the respondents with two such answers are included. Our main reason for this decision is that the "neither agree nor disagree" response was an explicit category in the response booklet used as a visual aid with each interview.

52. This calculation is based upon the assumption that each partisan strength and each sense of political efficacy category was the same as that observed in 1960, but that for each group reported turnout was the same as that observed in 1988. For a full explanation of this technique, see Abramson, *Political Attitudes,* 296.

53. Our estimates used our algebraic standardization procedures. To simplify the analysis we combined whites with an eighth-grade education or less with those who had not graduated from high school and combined weak partisans with independents who leaned toward a party.

54. In all presidential elections between 1964 and 1984, blacks have been more likely to be concerned about the electoral outcome than whites. In 1988, however, there were no racial differences on this question.

55. The declining concern with electoral outcomes is in our view only partly an election-specific attitude. The question asks whether the respondent cares which *party* wins the presidential election, and there is evidence that the decline in party identification accounts for the trend toward declining concern with electoral outcomes. See Abramson and Aldrich, "The Decline of Electoral Participation," 519-520.

56. Respondents were first asked who they thought would win the upcoming presidential election. Those who predicted a winner were asked, "Do you think the presidential race will be close, or will (name of predicted winner) win by quite a bit?" Those who did not predict a winner were asked, "Do you

think the presidential race will be close or will one candidate win by quite a bit?"

57. See John H. Aldrich, "Some Problems in Testing Two Rational Models of Participation," *American Journal of Political Science* 20 (November 1976): 713-733.
58. Orley Ashenfelter and Stanley Kelley, Jr., "Determinants of Participation in Presidential Elections," *Journal of Law and Economics* 18 (December 1975): 721.
59. Ruy A. Teixeira presents similar estimates but assumes that blacks were only 6 percentage points less likely to vote than whites. He estimates that Dukakis would have scored a net gain of 862,000 votes if black turnout had equaled white turnout. See Teixeira, "Election '88: Registration and Turnout," *Public Opinion* 11 (January/February 1989): 13.
60. Teixeira projects that Dukakis would have scored a net gain of 1,483,000 votes if Hispanics had voted at the same rate as whites (see ibid., 13). However, as he notes, he is not taking into account that a substantial percentage of Hispanics are not citizens.
61. Wolfinger and Rosenstone, *Who Votes?* 109-114.
62. Kleppner, *Who Voted?* 160-161; Stephen D. Shaffer, "Policy Differences Between Voters and Non-Voters in American Elections," *Western Political Quarterly* 35 (December 1982): 496-510.
63. Abramson, Aldrich, and Rohde, *Change and Continuity in the 1980 Elections,* rev. ed., 89-90.
64. Abramson, Aldrich, and Rohde, *Change and Continuity in the 1984 Elections,* rev. ed., 121-122.
65. Piven and Cloward, *Why Americans Don't Vote,* 21. For similar arguments, see Walter Dean Burnham, "Shifting Patterns of Congressional Voting Participation," in *The Current Crisis in American Politics,* ed. Walter Dean Burnham (New York: Oxford University Press, 1982), 166-203.
66. See Seymour Martin Lipset, *Political Man: The Social Bases of Politics,* expanded ed. (Baltimore: Johns Hopkins University Press, 1981), 226-229. Lipset emphasizes the dangers of sudden increases in political participation.
67. Gerald M. Pomper, "The Presidential Election," in *The Election of 1980: Reports and Interpretations,* ed. Gerald M. Pomper et al. (Chatham, N.J.: Chatham House, 1981), 86.
68. Walter Dean Burnham, "The Eclipse of the Democratic Party," *Democracy* 2 (July 1982): 7-17.

Chapter 5

Social Forces and the Vote

Ninety-one million individuals voted in 1988. But most Americans are not simply individuals; they also belong to primary groups composed of families and friends and to secondary groups such as social classes, ethnic groups, and religions. Many belong to voluntary associations such as unions, churches, or professional associations, and thus are formal members of a group.

Voting is an individual act, but social group memberships influence voting choices. People who share social characteristics may share political interests. Group similarities in voting behavior may reflect political conditions that existed generations earlier. The partisan loyalties of blacks, for example, were shaped by the Civil War and postwar Reconstruction, with black loyalties to the party of Lincoln lasting through the 1932 presidential election. The Democratic voting of southern whites, a product of those same historical conditions, lasted even longer, perhaps through 1960.

It is easy to see why group-based loyalties persist over time. Studies of pre-adult political learning suggest that partisan loyalties are often transmitted from generation to generation. And because religion, ethnicity, and, to a lesser extent, social class are also transmitted from generation to generation, social divisions have considerable staying power. Moreover, the interaction of social group members with each other may reinforce similarities in political attitudes and behavior.

Politicians often think in group terms. They recognize that to win they must mobilize the social groups that have supported their party in the past and that it is helpful to cut into their opponent's established bases of support. The Democrats think in group terms more than the

Republicans do, for the Democrats are a coalition of minority groups. To win they must earn high levels of support from the social groups that have traditionally supported their broad-based coalition.

In 1988 many traditionally Democratic groups cast a majority of their vote for George Bush, and others split their vote about evenly between Bush and Michael S. Dukakis. The decline of the Democratic party during the past six presidential elections may be attributed to the failure to hold the basic loyalties of the social groups that made up the winning coalition forged by Franklin D. Roosevelt during the 1930s.

This chapter examines the voting patterns of social groups in the 1988 presidential election. To put the 1988 results in perspective, we then examine voting choices of key social groups for the entire postwar period. By studying the social bases of party support since 1944, we will show how the 1988 election was part of a long-term trend that has severely weakened the New Deal coalition upon which Democratic victories have historically depended.

How Social Groups Voted in 1988

Our basic results are presented in Table 5-1, which shows how various social groups voted for president in 1988.[1] Excluding respondents for whom the direction of vote was not ascertained, 52.3 percent voted for Bush, 46.6 percent for Dukakis, and 1.2 percent for other candidates— results that are very close to the official voting statistics (Table 3-1). The 1988 National Election Study (NES) survey, based upon 1,227 voters, is the single best source of survey data and is especially valuable for studying change over time.[2] However, once we begin to examine sub- groups of the electorate, the number of persons sampled in some social groups becomes rather small. Therefore, we supplement our analysis by referring to the exit polls conducted by the television networks,[3] as well as the final Gallup preelection survey.[4]

Race, Gender, Region, and Age

Political differences between blacks and whites are far sharper than any other social cleavage. According to the NES survey, 90 percent of the black voters supported Dukakis, compared with only 41 percent of the white voters. The CBS News/*New York Times,* the Cable News Network/ *Los Angeles Times,* and the NBC News/*Wall Street Journal* polls all show 89 percent of the blacks voting for Dukakis, but show only between 40 and 43 percent of the whites voting Democratic. The ABC News/ *Washington Post* poll reports that 91 percent of the blacks voted for Dukakis, while only 44 percent of the whites did. The Gallup preelection poll showed Dukakis winning 82 percent support among "nonwhites," while gaining only 41 percent among whites. Even though blacks make up only one-ninth of the electorate, and even though they have relatively low turnout, a fifth of Dukakis's support came from black voters.[5] Dukakis received 41.8 million votes; about 8 million of these were from black voters.

Because race is such a profound social division, our analysis in this chapter will examine divisions among blacks and whites separately. Among blacks, social divisions were relatively unimportant, and we do not present the results in Table 5-1. Among blacks, as among whites, women were more likely to vote Democratic than men. According to the CBS News/*New York Times* survey, one black man in seven voted for Bush; among black women only one in eleven did.[6] However, blacks do not mirror regional differences found among whites. Among whites, southerners were more likely to vote for Bush than whites outside the South, but there were no differences between blacks in the South and blacks outside this region. As is true for whites, older blacks were the most likely age group to vote Democratic, but Dukakis fared very well among blacks between the ages of eighteen and thirty, winning 86 percent of their vote. Given the small number of black voters, we cannot comment further on differences among blacks. But one finding seems clear. Among every subset of blacks we examined, a large majority voted for Dukakis. Blacks who objected to the Democratic ticket may have defected by not going to the polls. But among those who did turn out, only about one in ten voted for Bush.

Among whites, the small number who identified as Hispanic were much more likely to vote for Dukakis than non-Hispanics. Dukakis's success among all Hispanics[7] ranged from 62 percent support in the Cable News Network/*Los Angeles Times* poll to 70 percent in the CBS News/*New York Times* and the ABC News/*Washington Post* polls. Both Dukakis and Lloyd Bentsen spoke Spanish, which may have given the Democratic ticket a special appeal to Hispanics. Even so, Bush gained a substantial minority of the Hispanic vote. Among Cubans, who are heavily concentrated in South Florida, Bush won a clear majority.[8]

Gender differences in voting behavior have been pronounced in some European countries, but historically they have been negligible in the United States.[9] In both 1980 and 1984 women were less likely than men to vote for Reagan, and throughout his presidency they were less likely to approve of his performance as president. These differences between men and women led to the much discussed "gender gap," and some feminists hoped that women would play a major role in defeating the Republicans. However, most discussions of the gender gap ignored an obvious fact: a difference in the voting behavior of men and women would not necessarily aid the Democrats.[10]

Early in the 1988 election contest, polls showed that women were much less likely to support Bush than men were, although the difference narrowed later in the campaign. The NES data reveal that women were

Table 5-1   How Social Groups Voted for President, 1988

Social group	Bush (%)	Dukakis (%)	Other (%)	Total percent	(N)
Electorate, by race					
White	58	41	1	100	(1,052)
Black	8	90	2	100	(125)
Whites, by Hispanic identification					
Identify as Hispanic	36	64	0	100	(83)
Do not identify	60	39	1	100	(969)
Whites, by gender					
Male	60	38	2	100	(486)
Female	57	43	1	101	(566)
Whites, by region					
New England and mid-Atlantic	57	42	1	100	(202)
North Central	59	40	1	100	(340)
South	63	37	0	100	(198)
Border	55	43	1	99	(76)
Mountain and Pacific	55	43	2	100	(236)
Whites, by birth cohort					
Before 1924	55	43	2	100	(219)
1924-1939	62	38	0	100	(247)
1940-1954	57	42	1	100	(364)
1955-1962	58	41	2	101	(158)
1963-1970	62	36	2	100	(64)
Whites, by social class					
Working class	55	43	2	100	(356)
Middle class	60	39	1	100	(593)
Farmers	56	42	2	100	(52)
Whites, by occupation of head of household					
Unskilled manual	49	48	3	100	(102)
Skilled, semiskilled manual	57	41	1	99	(254)
Clerical, sales, other white collar	67	33	0	100	(192)
Managerial	62	36	1	99	(228)
Professional and semiprofessional	50	49	1	100	(172)
Whites, by level of education					
Eight grades or less	46	53	1	100	(70)
Some high school	51	49	0	100	(76)
High school graduate	55	45	0	100	(326)
Some college	67	33	1	101	(263)
College graduate	64	32	3	99	(211)
Advanced degree	48	51	1	100	(91)

Table 5-1 (continued)

Social group	Bush (%)	Dukakis (%)	Other (%)	Total percent	(N)
Whites, by annual family income					
Less than $10,000	54	46	0	100	(95)
$10,000 to $14,999	50	49	1	100	(113)
$15,000 to $19,999	56	43	1	100	(97)
$20,000 to $24,999	52	47	1	100	(111)
$25,000 to $29,999	47	52	1	100	(89)
$30,000 to $34,999	64	36	0	100	(91)
$35,000 to $39,999	52	45	3	100	(75)
$40,000 to $49,999	63	36	1	100	(127)
$50,000 to $59,999	70	29	1	100	(76)
$60,000 to $74,999	68	31	1	100	(71)
$75,000 and over	75	23	2	100	(84)
Whites by union membership[a]					
Member	46	53	*	99	(210)
Nonmember	61	37	1	99	(838)
Whites, by religion					
Protestant	66	33	1	100	(646)
Catholic	48	51	1	100	(290)
Jewish	27	73	0	100	(22)
None, no preference	41	55	4	100	(73)
Whites, by social class and religion					
Middle-class Protestants	68	32	1	101	(351)
Working-class Protestants	64	35	1	100	(220)
Middle-class Catholics	56	44	0	100	(164)
Working-class Catholics	37	60	3	100	(103)

Note: Percentages read across. The eighteen voters for whom direction of vote was not ascertained have been excluded from these calculations.

[a]Whether respondent or family member in union.

* Less than one percent.

slightly more likely to vote for Dukakis than men were, but differences were small—a gender gap of only 6 points.[11] The gender gap in the exit polls ranges from a low of 7 points in the CBS News/*New York Times* and the NBC News/*Wall Street Journal* polls to a high of 10 points in the Cable News Network/*Los Angeles Times* poll. The Gallup poll reveals a gender gap of only 4 points.

Although interpretations of the gender gap will be controversial, it could be argued that the gap aided Bush. The NES survey found that among women, Bush and Dukakis each won 50 percent of the vote, whereas Bush held a 56 percent to 43 percent lead over Dukakis among men. The CBS News/*New York Times* poll shows Bush winning 51 percent of the female vote, and the Gallup poll shows him winning 52 percent. The three other exit polls all found Dukakis to hold a slight lead among women. His best showing was in the ABC News/*Washington Post* poll, which gave him 53 percent of the female vote. But all these polls revealed that Bush won a clear majority of the vote among men—ranging from 55 percent of the male vote in the ABC News/*Washington Post* and the NBC News/*Wall Street Journal* surveys to 59 percent in the Cable News Network/*Los Angeles Times* study. These results suggest that if the vote had been restricted to women, the election result would have been very close, and that Dukakis might have emerged with a slight majority of the popular vote. But even though there were more female voters than male voters, Bush's sizable lead among men led to a clear majority in the popular vote.

As Table 5-1 reveals there was a gender gap among whites, with white women being 5 percentage points more likely to vote for Dukakis than white men. The CBS News/*New York Times* exit poll explicitly compares white women and white men. Among white women, 43 percent voted for Dukakis, while among white men only 36 percent did—a gap of 7 points.

Everett Carll Ladd argues that the exit polls reveal the gender gap was largest among voters of higher socioeconomic status,[12] and our analysis of the NES survey confirms this finding. We found a relatively high gender gap (10 points) among whites with annual family incomes of $50,000 or more a year, and a very high gender gap (31 points) among voters with advanced degrees. Among white women with advanced degrees ($N = 35$), 69 percent voted for Dukakis.

As with our analysis of the 1984 NES survey, we found clear differences among women who were married and those who were single.[13] Among all women who had never been married ($N = 88$), 59 percent voted for Dukakis; among all married women ($N = 364$), only 46 percent voted Democratic. But these differences resulted mainly from the large number of single black women, and differences among whites were relatively small. Among white women who had never been married ($N = 59$), 47 percent voted for Dukakis, among white married women ($N = 330$), 42 percent voted Democratic. The CBS News/*New York Times* exit poll found clear differences according to marital status. Among unmarried women 57 percent voted for Dukakis; among married women only 46 percent did, but the survey results did not introduce controls for race. Differences according to marital status were also found among men. Both the NES survey and the CBS News/*New York Times* poll found that single men were more likely to vote for Dukakis than married men were.

Our analysis in Chapter 3 shows that regional differences were relatively small. There were, however, more pronounced regional differences among whites. As Table 5-1 reveals, among whites in the states of the old Confederacy 63 percent voted for Bush, only 37 percent for Dukakis. The CBS News/*New York Times* exit poll reports that Bush won 67 percent of the vote among southern whites, while Dukakis won only 32 percent, and the Cable News Network/*Los Angeles Times* poll reports a similar result, giving Bush a 68 percent to 31 percent lead over Dukakis among southern whites. As we will see, of all the groups that have shifted to the Republicans in recent years, southern whites have made the most dramatic shift.

In recent years, political scientists have noted that young Americans are now more likely to identify with the Republican party than older Americans,[14] and some expected Bush to do especially well among young voters. The NES survey revealed that Bush did relatively well among the small number of white voters who entered the electorate after the 1980 election (born between 1963 and 1970), but age group differences were small. Dukakis fared best among whites who entered the electorate before or during World War II (born before 1924). The CBS News/*New York Times*, ABC News/*Washington Post*, and Cable News Network/*Los Angeles Times* polls all report that Dukakis did best among older voters, and the Gallup preelection poll reports a similar result. But only the ABC News/*Washington Post* poll reports Dukakis actually gaining a majority of the vote among older Americans; among voters sixty years old or older, 52 percent supported Dukakis. The NBC News/*Wall Street Journal* poll, which finds the smallest age group differences, reports that Bush did slightly better among older voters than among the young.

The CBS News/*New York Times* reports the results by age among white voters, and reveals that Dukakis fared best among the elderly. Among whites sixty years old and older, Dukakis won 45 percent of the vote. Among whites between eighteen and twenty-nine years of age, Dukakis won 39 percent, among those between thirty and forty-four he won 39 percent, and among whites between the ages of forty-five and fifty-nine he won 36 percent. There is considerable evidence that age group differences in support for the Republican and Democratic party result from differences in the formative socialization experiences of voters who entered the electorate during different historical periods.[15] The gradual replacement of relatively Democratic birth cohorts with younger cohorts that entered the electorate during the Reagan and Bush presidencies may lead to a gradual erosion in future Democratic support.

Social Class, Income, Education, and Union Membership

Traditionally, the Democratic party has done well among the relatively disadvantaged. It has done better among the working class, the poor, and voters with lower levels of formal education. Moreover, since the 1930s most union leaders have supported the Democratic party, and union members have traditionally been a mainstay of the Democratic presidential coalition. These bases of social support persisted in 1988, but most of these relationships were weak.

As we will see, the weak relationship between social class and voting behavior is part of a long-term trend that has eroded class voting. Dukakis was a liberal who had strong support from union leaders. The Reagan administration was viewed as hostile to organized labor. Reagan's firing of striking federal air traffic controllers in 1981 led union leaders to establish official ties to the Democratic National Committee. The Reagan administration had opposed an increase in the minimum wage, and in May of 1988 Reagan had vetoed a bill requiring employers to give workers a sixty-day notification before layoffs or a factory closing. In August he allowed a similar bill to become law without his signature, mainly because of pressure from Bush not to allow the plant closing bill to become a campaign issue. Late in the general election campaign Dukakis's claim to be "on your side" directly appealed to working-class voters. On the other hand, Bush's appeals on social issues such as patriotism, his support for the death penalty, and his charges that Dukakis was soft on criminals may have been attractive to working-class voters.

When we examine the relationship of social class, occupation, income, union membership, and level of education to voting behavior, we find few groups that gave Dukakis a majority of the vote. A majority of working-class whites (manually employed workers and their dependents) voted for Bush, although Bush did somewhat better among the middle class. Part of the reason for this weak relationship is that Dukakis did best among both the lowest and highest occupational groups—gaining nearly half the vote among whites who were unskilled manual workers and among whites who were professionals or semi-professionals. The CBS News/*New York Times* poll also shows that occupation was weakly related to electoral choice, but the poll does not find Dukakis doing well among the higher occupational groups. According to the poll Dukakis garnered the votes of 50 percent of the blue-collar workers, 42 percent of the white-collar workers, and 40 percent of the professionals.[16]

Dukakis clearly fared better among the poor than among the most affluent. But as Table 5-1 shows, the relationship between family income and electoral choice was relatively weak among white voters, mainly because Dukakis failed to gain a majority even among the poor. On the other hand, support for Bush was very high among voters with family incomes of $50,000 a year or greater.

Income differences are sharper when the entire electorate is examined, because blacks are relatively poor and because, as we saw, an overwhelming majority of blacks voted for Dukakis. Most poll results do not present the results for whites and blacks separately, and thus the relationship between income and the vote will appear stronger than the results in our table. Although the polls all use different income categories, all four exit polls, as well as the Gallup preelection poll, show Dukakis gaining a majority of the vote in their lowest income category. The highest level of Dukakis voting is reported by the ABC News/*Washington Post* poll, which shows Dukakis winning 69 percent of the vote among Americans with incomes below $5,000 a year. But at this income level a substantial percentage of the voters are black. For example, the NES survey shows that among white voters with family incomes below $5,000 a year ($N = 33$), Dukakis won 48 percent of the vote; among all voters in that income group ($N = 51$), he won 63 percent.

Less educated whites were more likely to vote for Dukakis than better educated whites, and, among whites with an eighth-grade education or less, Dukakis won a slight majority of the vote. But Table 5-1 also shows that Dukakis did relatively well among whites with advanced degrees, winning half of the vote. Thus, as with our measure of occupation, there appears to be an inverted relationship between the voters' social ranking and their presidential vote. The CBS News/*New York Times* poll reports relatively detailed results for level of education (although controls for racial differences are not reported). The study also reveals an inverted relationship between level of education and voting choices. Among voters who were not high school graduates, Dukakis won 56 percent of the vote, while he won 49 percent among high school graduates with no college education. Dukakis's support fell to 42 percent among voters with some college education and to 37 percent among college graduates with no postgraduate education. But among voters with a postgraduate education, he gained 48 percent of the vote. The Cable News Network/*Los Angeles Times* poll reveals a similar pattern. Among voters who did not finish high school, Dukakis won 60 percent of the vote. His share fell to 46 percent among high school graduates, to 42 percent among voters with some college, and to 39 percent among college graduates. But among voters with a postgraduate education, Dukakis won 49 percent of the vote.[17]

Some scholars of American politics, such as Walter Dean Burnham and Everett Carll Ladd, have argued that the Democrats now tend to fare best among upper and lower socioeconomic status groups.[18] The results for both occupation and level of education support their thesis. The Democrats may be appealing to disadvantaged Americans because of their economic policies, while better educated Americans may reject the traditional values emphasized by the Republicans in recent elections.

Dukakis clearly did better among union households than nonunion households. As Table 5-1 shows, Dukakis won a slight majority of the vote in white union households, but just over a third of the vote among white nonunion households. All four exit polls, as well as the Gallup poll, show that Dukakis won a majority of the union vote, ranging from 56 percent in the Cable News Network/*Los Angeles Times* poll to 63 percent in the Gallup poll.[19] Put differently, it would appear that despite the strong endorsement Dukakis received from organized labor, Bush won about two out of five union votes, and close to half the vote among white union households.

Religion

Religious differences, which partly reflect ethnic differences between Catholics and Protestants, also have played a major role in American politics. Roman Catholics have tended to support the Democratic party, and white Protestants, especially outside the South, have tended to favor the Republicans. In all of Roosevelt's elections, and in every postwar election through 1976, Jews strongly supported the Democratic presidential candidate. In 1980, a substantial minority of Jews voted for John B. Anderson, depriving Carter of an absolute majority of the Jewish vote, but Carter still won a plurality. And in 1984, about three out of four Jews voted for Mondale.

As Table 5-1 shows, Dukakis won a bare majority of the vote among white Catholics, while winning only a third of the vote among white Protestants. As most blacks are Protestants, the Democratic share of the vote among all Protestants is higher than the vote among white Protestants, and the CBS News/*New York Times* results are especially valuable since they present results for whites. The results for the exit poll are similar to those of the NES survey. Dukakis won 47 percent of the Catholic vote, but only 33 percent among white Protestants. According to the Cable News Network/*Los Angeles Times* exit poll, Dukakis won only 25 percent of the vote among white Protestants in the South.[20]

Bush's appeals to patriotism, his support for the death penalty, and his opposition to abortion may have had special appeal to white fundamentalists and to evangelicals. According to the NES survey, however, Bush did only marginally better among white Protestants who said they had been "born again" than among those who had not had this religious experience. On the other hand, Bush did very well among white Protestants who felt close to fundamentalists and evangelicals. Among those who felt close to "Christian fundamentalists" ($N = 137$), 76 percent voted for Bush, while among those who felt close to "evangelical groups active in politics" ($N = 47$), 83 percent did.

Exit poll results also suggest that Bush did very well among fundamentalists and evangelical whites. According to the CBS News/*New York Times* poll, Bush won 81 percent of the vote among white fundamentalists or evangelical Christians. And the Cable News

Network/*Los Angeles Times* poll found that 71 percent of the white born again Protestants voted for Bush.

In 1988 Jews had few reasons to defect from their Democratic loyalties. Both Dukakis and Bush pledged strong support for Israel. Dukakis pledged to move the U.S. embassy from Tel Aviv to Jerusalem. Bush made no such promise, but took a stronger stand against establishing a Palestinian state. That Dukakis's wife, Kitty, was Jewish may have been attractive to some Jewish voters. The NES survey shows that nearly three out of four Jews voted Democratic. Given the small number of Jews sampled, we must turn to other surveys. The CBS News/*New York Times* survey found that 64 percent of the Jews voted for Dukakis, while the Cable News Network/*Los Angeles Times* poll reports that 74 percent did.

Although Jews were politically distinctive, the differences between Catholics and Protestants were relatively small. However, when religion and social class are combined, our ability to predict how people will vote is improved. Because working-class voters are more likely to vote Democratic than middle-class voters, and because Catholics are more likely to vote Democratic than Protestants, the tendency to vote Democratic is higher among those who are both working class and Catholic and the Republicans do very well among middle-class Protestants. As Table 5-1 shows, Dukakis won three out of five votes among working-class Catholics; Bush fared somewhat better among middle-class Protestants, winning two-thirds of the vote. And a demographic reality compounded Dukakis's relatively poor showing: there were more than three middle-class Protestants for every one working-class Catholic.

How Social Groups Voted During the Postwar Years

Although there were sharp racial differences, most social differences in voting behavior were relatively small in 1988. How does this compare with other presidential elections? Were the weak relationships in 1988 atypical, or did they result from a long-term trend that eroded the impact of social forces? To answer these questions we will examine the voting behavior of social groups that have been an important part of the Democratic coalition during the postwar years. Our analysis begins with the 1944 presidential contest between Roosevelt and Thomas E. Dewey and uses a simple measure of social cleavage to assess the impact of social forces over time.

In his lucid discussion of the logic of party coalitions, Robert Axelrod analyzes the behavior of six basic groups that made up the Democratic presidential coalition: the poor, blacks (and other nonwhites), union members (and members of their families), Catholics (including other non-Protestants), southerners (including residents of the border states), and residents of the twelve largest metropolitan areas.[21] John R. Petrocik's more comprehensive study identifies fifteen party coalition groups, and classifies seven of them as predominantly Democratic: blacks, lower-status native southerners, middle- and upper-status southerners, Jews, Polish and Irish Catholics, union members, and lower-status border state whites.[22] A more recent study, by Harold W. Stanley, William T. Bianco, and Richard G. Niemi, analyzes seven pro-Democratic groups: blacks, Catholics, Jews, females, native white southerners, members of union households, and the working class.[23] Our analysis focuses on race, region, union membership, social class, and religion.[24]

The contribution that a social group can make to a party's total coalition depends upon three factors: the relative size of the group in the total electorate, its level of turnout compared with that of the electorate as a whole, and its relative loyalty to a party.[25] The larger a social group, the greater its contribution can be.

Blacks, for example, make up about 11 percent of the electorate, and the white working class makes up 35 percent. Thus, the contribution that blacks can make to a political party is limited compared with the potential contribution of working-class whites. The electoral power of blacks is diminished further by their relatively low turnout. However, because blacks vote overwhelmingly Democratic, their contribution to the party can be greater than their size would indicate. And their contribution will grow as whites desert the Democratic party.

Let us begin by examining racial differences, which we can trace back to 1944 by using the National Opinion Research Center (NORC) study for that year.[26] Figure 5-1 shows the percentage of white and black major party voters who voted Democratic for president from 1944 through 1988. Although most blacks voted Democratic between 1944 and 1960, a substantial minority voted Republican. The political mobilization of blacks caused by the civil rights movement and the candidacy of Barry M. Goldwater ended this Republican voting, and the residual Republican loyalties of older blacks were discarded between 1962 and 1964.[27]

While the Democrats made substantial gains among blacks, they lost ground among whites. Between 1944 and 1964, the Democrats gained a majority of the white vote in three of six elections, but from 1968 on they have never won a majority from white voters. However, the Democrats can win with just under half the white vote, as the 1960 and 1976 elections demonstrate.

The gap between the two trend lines in Figure 5-1 illustrates the overall difference between white and black voting. Table 5-2 shows levels of "racial voting" during all twelve elections and also presents four other measures of social cleavage.[28]

Not only did black loyalty to the Democratic party increase sharply after 1960, but black turnout rose dramatically between 1960 and 1968

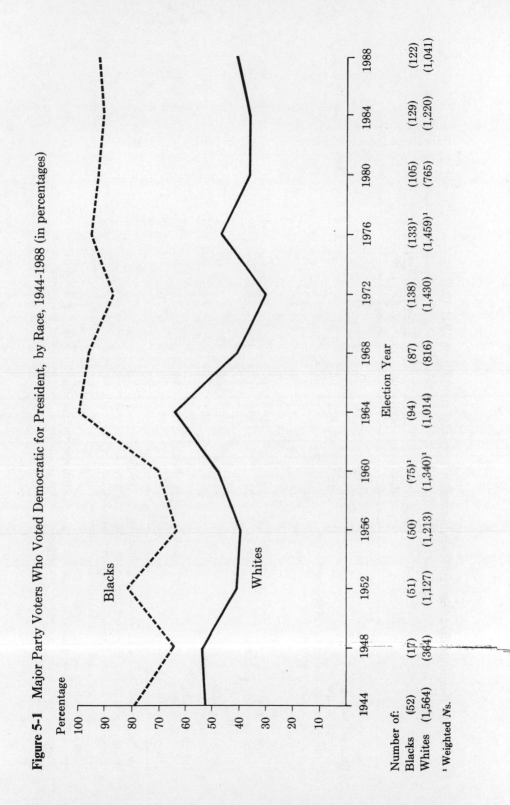

Figure 5-1 Major Party Voters Who Voted Democratic for President, by Race, 1944-1988 (in percentages)

Percentage

	1944	1948	1952	1956	1960	1964	1968	1972	1976	1980	1984	1988
Election Year												

Number of:

	1944	1948	1952	1956	1960	1964	1968	1972	1976	1980	1984	1988
Blacks	(52)	(17)	(51)	(50)	(75)[1]	(94)	(87)	(138)	(133)[1]	(105)	(129)	(122)
Whites	(1,564)	(364)	(1,127)	(1,213)	(1,340)[1]	(1,014)	(816)	(1,430)	(1,459)[1]	(765)	(1,220)	(1,041)

[1] Weighted *N*s.

Table 5-2 Relationship of Social Characteristics to Presidential Voting, 1944-1988[a]

	Election Year											
	1944	1948	1952	1956	1960	1964	1968	1972	1976	1980	1984	1988
Racial voting[b]	27	12	40	25	23	36	56	57	48	56	54	51
Regional voting[c]												
Among whites	—	—	12	17	6	−11	−4	−13	1	1	−9	−5
Among entire electorate (NES surveys)	—	—	9	15	4	−5	6	−3	7	3	3	2
Among entire electorate (official election results)	23	14	8	8	3	−13	−3	−11	5	2	−5	−7
Union voting[d]												
Among whites	20	37	18	15	21	23	13	11	18	15	20	16
Among entire electorate	20	37	20	17	19	22	13	10	17	16	19	15
Class voting[e]												
Among whites	19	44	20	8	12	19	10	2	17	9	8	5
Among entire electorate	20	44	22	11	13	20	15	4	21	15	12	8
Religious voting[f]												
Among whites	25	21	18	10	48	21	30	13	15	10	16	18
Among entire electorate	24	19	15	10	46	16	21	8	11	3	9	11

[a] All calculations based upon major party voters.
[b] Percentage of blacks who voted Democratic minus the percentage of whites who voted Democratic.
[c] Percentage of southerners who voted Democratic minus the percentage of voters outside the South who voted Democratic.
[d] Percentage of members of union households who voted Democratic minus the percentage of members of households with no union members who voted Democratic.
[e] Percentage of working class that voted Democratic minus the percentage of middle class that voted Democratic.
[f] Percentage of Catholics who voted Democratic minus the percentage of Protestants who voted Democratic.

because southern blacks (about half the black population during this period) were enfranchised. Moreover, the relative size of the black population grew somewhat during the postwar years. Between 1960 and 1980 white turnout dropped about 10 percentage points. As we saw in Chapter 4, black turnout dropped more than white turnout in 1988, but the difference between black and white turnout was still far less than it was before the civil rights movement and the Voting Rights Act of 1965.

Between 1948 and 1960, blacks never made up more than one Democratic vote out of twelve.[29] In 1964, however, Lyndon B. Johnson received about one in seven of his votes from black voters, and blacks contributed a fifth of the Democratic totals in 1968 and 1972. In 1976, with Democratic gains among whites, the black total fell to just over one in seven. In 1980, Carter received about one in four of his total vote from blacks, and in 1984 about one Mondale voter in five was black. As we saw, a fifth of Dukakis's total vote came from blacks.[30]

Region

The desertion of the Democratic party by white southerners is among the most dramatic changes in postwar American politics. As we saw in Chapter 3, regional differences can be analyzed using official election statistics. But official election returns are of limited utility in examining race-related differences in regional voting patterns because election returns are not tabulated by race. Survey data allow us to document the dramatic shift in the voting behavior of white southerners.

As the data in Figure 5-2 reveal, white southerners were clearly more Democratic than whites outside the South in the 1952 and 1956 Eisenhower-Stevenson contests and were somewhat more Democratic in the 1960 Kennedy-Nixon contest.[31] But in the next three presidential elections, regional differences were reversed, with white southerners voting Republican more often than whites outside the South. In 1976 and 1980, white southerners and whites outside the South voted very much alike. In both 1984 and 1988 white southerners were less likely to vote Democratic than whites in any other region.

Regional differences in voting among whites from 1952 through 1988 are presented in Table 5-2. The negative signs for 1964, 1968, 1972, 1984, and 1988 reveal that the Democratic candidate fared better among whites outside the South than he did among white southerners. Table 5-2 also presents "regional voting" for the entire electorate. Here, however, we present two sets of estimates: (1) NES results from 1952 through 1988 and (2) results based upon official election statistics. Both sets of figures show that regional differences in voting have declined, but the NES surveys somewhat overestimated the Democratic advantage in the South in 1956 and somewhat underestimated the Republican advantage in 1964 and 1972. In 1968, 1984, and 1988, the NES surveys registered a slight

Figure 5-2 White Major Party Voters Who Voted Democratic for President, by Region, 1952-1988 (in percentages)

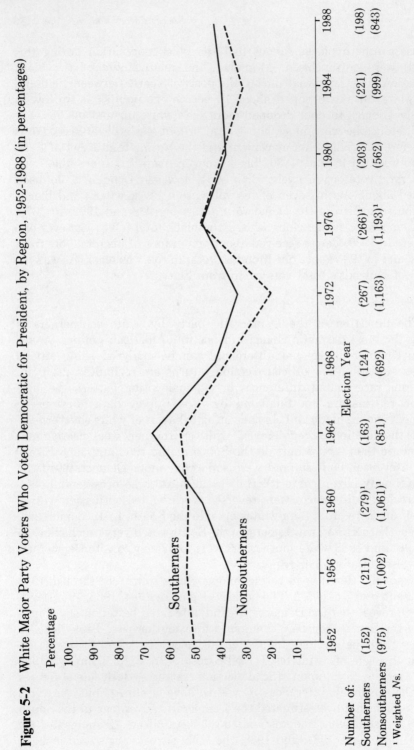

Number of:										
Southerners	(152)	(211)	(279)[1]	(163)	(124)	(267)	(266)[1]	(203)	(221)	(198)
Nonsoutherners	(975)	(1,002)	(1,061)[1]	(851)	(692)	(1,163)	(1,193)[1]	(562)	(999)	(843)

[1] Weighted *N*s.

Democratic advantage in the South, while official election statistics show that the Democrats actually fared somewhat better outside the South.[32] Because most voters in both regions are white, it seems likely that the Republican advantage among white southerners in 1964, 1968, 1972, 1984, and 1988 was somewhat greater than the NES surveys reveal.

The mobilization of southern blacks and the defection of white southerners from the Democratic party dramatically transformed the demographic composition of the Democratic coalition in the South. Democratic presidential candidates between 1952 and 1960 never received more than one vote out of fifteen from black voters. In 1964 nearly three out of ten of Johnson's southern votes came from blacks, and in 1968 Hubert H. Humphrey received nearly as many votes from southern blacks as from southern whites. In 1972, according to these data, George S. McGovern received more votes from southern blacks than from southern whites. In 1976 black voters were crucial to Carter's success in the South. He received about one out of three of his southern votes from blacks in 1976 and again in 1980. In 1984, Mondale received about four in ten of his southern votes from black voters. About one out of three of the votes Dukakis received in the South came from blacks. Dukakis received 9.5 million votes in the eleven states of the old Confederacy. According to our estimates, over 3 million of these votes came from blacks.[33]

Union Membership

Figure 5-3 shows the percentage of white union members and nonmembers who voted Democratic for president from 1944 through 1988. In all six elections between 1944 and 1964, a majority of white union members (and members of their families) voted Democratic. Since then, the Democrats have been less successful. In 1968 Humphrey received a slight majority of the major party vote cast by white union members, although his total would be cut to 43 percent if Wallace voters were included. The Democrats appear to have gained a slight majority of the white union vote in 1988. However, they fell short of the 61 percent they attained in 1976, the only election in this period that they won. At the same time, however, the Republicans gained an absolute majority of the union vote in only one of the last six elections, during Richard Nixon's 1972 landslide.

Differences in the voting of union members and nonmembers fell slightly in 1988 (Table 5-2), because the Democratic performance among voters who were not in union households improved more than the party's performance among union members. "Union voting" was clearly below the average (mean) level between 1944 and 1964. We have also reported union voting for the entire electorate, but, because blacks are as likely to live in union households as whites are, including blacks has little effect on our results.

Figure 5-3 White Major Party Voters Who Voted Democratic for President, by Union Membership, 1944-1988 (in percentages)

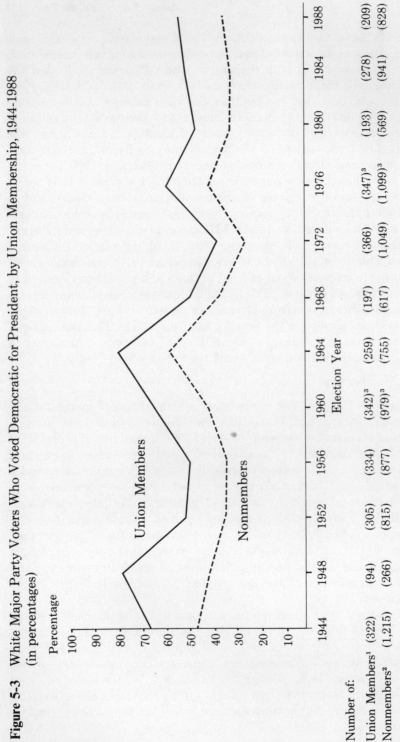

Number of:

	1944	1948	1952	1956	1960	1964	1968	1972	1976	1980	1984	1988
Union Members[1]	(322)	(94)	(305)	(334)	(342)[3]	(259)	(197)	(366)	(347)[3]	(193)	(278)	(209)
Nonmembers[2]	(1,215)	(266)	(815)	(877)	(979)[3]	(755)	(617)	(1,049)	(1,099)[3]	(569)	(941)	(828)

[1] Union members or in household with union member.
[2] Not a union member and not in household with union member.
[3] Weighted Ns.

The percentage of the total electorate composed of white union members and their families has declined during the postwar years, and their turnout has declined at the same rate as that of nonunion whites. These changes have not been as dramatic as the decline in union support for Democratic presidential candidates. All of the above factors, as well as increased turnout among blacks, have reduced the total contribution of white union members to the Democratic presidential coalition. Through 1960, a third of the total Democratic vote came from white union members (and members of their families). Between 1964 and 1984, only about one Democratic vote in four came from white union members. In 1988, about one out of five votes Dukakis received came from white union members. Despite these changes during the postwar years, union members remain an important part of the Democratic presidential coalition.

Social Class

The broad cleavage between the political behavior of manually employed workers (and their dependents) and that of nonmanually employed workers (and their dependents) is especially valuable for studying comparative voting behavior.[34] In every presidential election since 1936, the working class has voted more Democratic than the middle class. But, as Figure 5-4 shows, the percentage of working-class whites voting Democratic has varied considerably from election to election. It fell to its lowest level in 1972. Carter regained a majority of the white working-class vote in 1976, but he lost it four years later. The Democrats failed to win a majority of the white working class in both 1984 and 1988.

Although levels of "class voting" have varied since 1944, they are following a downward trend, as Table 5-2 reveals.[35] In 1988 working-class whites were only 5 points more Democratic than middle-class whites. Blacks are disproportionately working class, and, as we have seen, they vote overwhelmingly Democratic. In four of the last six elections, including blacks clearly raises class voting, and the trend toward declining class voting is dampened substantially if we study the entire electorate. However, black workers voted Democratic because they were black. Among blacks, class differences were negligible, because middle-class blacks also voted Democratic. It seems reasonable, therefore, to focus on changing levels of class voting among the white electorate.

During the postwar years, the proportion of the electorate made up of working-class whites has remained relatively constant, while the proportion of middle-class whites has grown. The percentage of whites in the agricultural sector has declined dramatically. After 1960, turnout fell among whites of both social classes, but it fell more among the working class. As we saw in Chapter 4, only 52 percent of the working-class whites voted in 1988, compared with 73 percent of the middle-class whites. De-

Figure 5-4 White Major Party Voters Who Voted Democratic for President, by Social Class, 1944-1988 (in percentages)

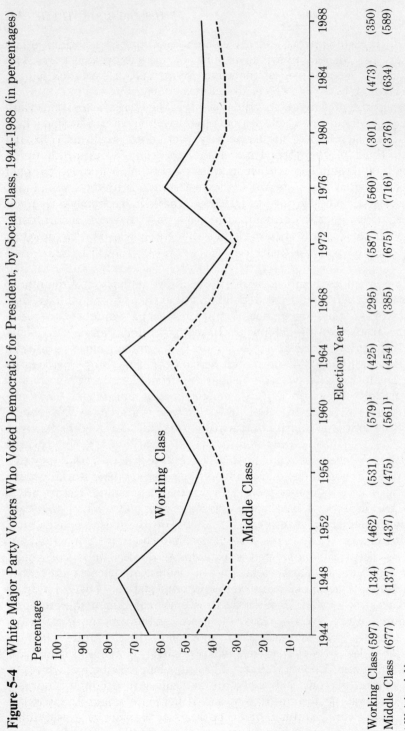

clining turnout and defections from the Democrats among working-class whites, along with increased turnout by blacks, have reduced the total contribution of working-class whites to the Democratic presidential coalition.

In 1948 and 1952, about half the total Democratic vote came from working-class whites, and between 1956 and 1964 more than four Democratic votes out of ten came from this social group. In 1968, the white working-class contribution fell to 35 percent, and then to only 32 percent in 1972. In 1976, with the rise of class voting, the white working class provided 39 percent of Carter's total vote, but in 1980 just over a third of Carter's total support came from working-class whites. In 1984, 36 percent of Mondale's total support came from working-class whites. Given the low levels of class voting in 1988, as well as the low turnout among the working class, only 28 percent of Dukakis's total support came from the white working class.[36] The middle-class contribution to the Democratic presidential coalition was fewer than three votes in ten in 1952, and just under one-third in 1956, stabilizing at just over one-third in the next five elections. In 1980, 33 percent of Carter's total vote came from middle-class whites, and in 1984 Mondale received 39 percent of his total from the white middle class. In 1988, Dukakis received 41 percent of his total vote from the white middle class, a larger share than he received from the white working class.

Religion

Voting differences among religious groups also have declined during the postwar years. As Figure 5-5 reveals, in every election since 1944, Jews have been more likely to vote Democratic than Catholics, and Catholics have been more likely to vote Democratic than Protestants.

A large majority of Jews voted Democratic in every election from 1944 through 1968, and although the Jewish vote for the Democrats dropped during Nixon's 1972 landslide, even McGovern won a majority of the Jewish vote. In fact, from 1972 on, the Republicans have won a sizable minority of the Jewish vote. In 1980 Carter actually failed to gain an absolute majority of the Jewish vote, although he still outpolled Reagan. Both Mondale in 1984 and Dukakis in 1988 won a clear majority of the Jewish vote. Both the NES surveys and exit poll results suggest that the Republicans won between a fourth and a third of the Jewish vote during the last five elections.

A majority of white Catholics voted Democratic in six of the seven elections between 1944 and 1968. The percentage of Catholics voting Democratic peaked in 1960, when the Democrats fielded a Roman Catholic candidate, but it was also very high in Johnson's landslide victory four years later. Since then, Democratic voting among Catholics has declined precipitously. In 1968, a majority of white Catholics voted

Democratic, although Humphrey's total would be reduced from 60 percent to 55 percent if Wallace voters were included. In three of the last five elections a majority of white Catholics have voted Republican. The erosion of Democratic support among Catholics during the postwar years is also documented by Gallup data.

Our simple measure of "religious voting" shows considerable change from election to election, but, as the results in Table 5-2 show, there appears to be a downward trend. Although religious voting rose in 1984 and 1988, as a result of very low levels of Democratic voting by white Protestants, it was still clearly below the average level for the years between 1944 and 1968. Including blacks in our calculations substantially reduces religious voting. Blacks are much more likely to be Protestant than Catholic, and including blacks adds a substantial number of Protestant Democrats. The effect of including blacks is greater from 1964 on because black turnout was higher. In 1988 religious voting is reduced to 11 points if blacks are included.

Throughout the postwar years, the total proportion of the electorate made up of white Catholics has remained constant, but between 1960 and 1980 turnout declined faster among Catholics than among white Protestants. In every election between 1948 and 1972, white Catholics had higher turnout than white Protestants, but the Catholic advantage was negligible in 1976 and erased in 1980. In 1980, only one in five of Carter's total vote came from white Catholics, a record low. In 1984, however, turnout rose among white Catholics, and, once again, Catholics had higher turnout than Protestants. Moreover, Catholic support for the Democrats remained constant between 1980 and 1984, while support among white Protestants fell. As a result the Catholic share of the Democratic presidential vote rose to 28 percent. In 1988 turnout declined among both Catholics and Protestants, but it declined somewhat more among Catholics, and religious differences were once again eliminated. Catholics moved toward the Democratic candidate, but white Protestants were somewhat more Democratic as well. Twenty-six percent of Dukakis's total vote came from white Catholics. The overall contribution of white Catholics to the Democratic presidential coalition in 1988 was very close to the postwar average, although it was far below the level attained in the Kennedy-Nixon contest of 1960, when 37 percent of Kennedy's total vote came from white Catholics.

The Jewish contribution to the Democratic presidential coalition has also declined, partly because Jews have not voted overwhelmingly Democratic in the last five elections and partly because the proportion of Jews in the electorate has declined. In the last five elections, Jews made up only about a twentieth of the total Democratic presidential coalition. However, since most Jews live in a few states with a large number of electoral votes, their contribution may be more important than these numbers suggest.

Figure 5-5 White Major Party Voters Who Voted Democratic for President, 1944-1988 (in percentages)

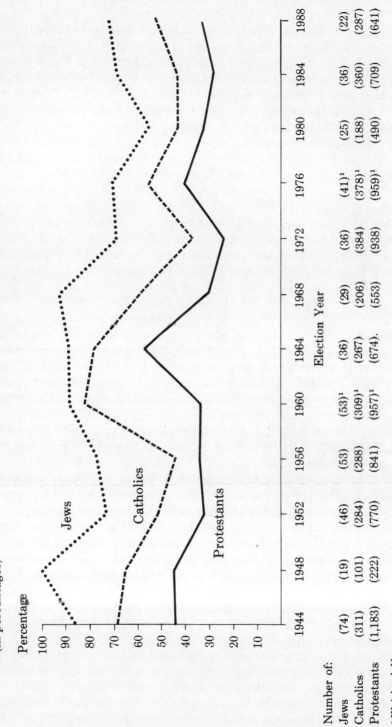

	1944	1948	1952	1956	1960	1964	1968	1972	1976	1980	1984	1988
Number of:												
Jews	(74)	(19)	(46)	(53)	(53)[1]	(36)	(29)	(36)	(41)[1]	(25)	(36)	(22)
Catholics	(311)	(101)	(284)	(288)	(309)[1]	(267)	(206)	(384)	(378)[1]	(188)	(360)	(287)
Protestants	(1,183)	(222)	(770)	(841)	(957)[1]	(674).	(553)	(938)	(959)[1]	(490)	(709)	(641)

[1] Weighted Ns.

As the data in Figure 5-6 reveal, the effects of social class and religion are cumulative. In every election from 1944 through 1988, working-class Catholics have been more likely to vote Democratic than any other class-religion combination. In all twelve elections, white middle-class Protestants have been the least likely to vote Democratic. Of all the groups we studied, they show the most constancy in their vote. An absolute majority voted Republican in all twelve elections.

The relative importance of social class and religion can be assessed by comparing the voting behavior of middle-class Catholics with that of working-class Protestants. Religion was more important than social class in predicting voting choices in 1944, 1956, 1960 (by a considerable margin), 1968, 1972, 1984, and 1988. Social class was more important than religion in 1948 (by a great margin), 1952, 1976, and 1980. And class and religion were equally important in 1964. However, during the last six elections all these trend lines have tended to converge, suggesting that both class and religion have declined in importance.

Why the New Deal Coalition Broke Down

Except for race, all of the social factors we have examined—region, union membership, social class, and religion—have declined in importance as predictors of the vote during the postwar years. The decline in regional differences directly parallels the increase in racial differences. As the national Democratic party strengthened its appeals to blacks during the 1960s, party leaders endorsed policies opposed by southern whites. Several studies suggest that issue preferences contributed to a breakdown of Democratic support among white southerners.[37] The migration of northern whites to the South also reduced regional differences somewhat.

The Democratic party's appeals to blacks may have weakened its hold on white groups that traditionally supported it. A recent study by Robert Huckfeldt and Carol Weitzel Kohfeld strongly suggests that Democratic appeals to blacks weakened their support among working-class whites.[38] But the erosion of Democratic support among union members, the working class, and Catholics results from other factors as well. During the postwar years, these groups have changed. Although union members do not hold high-paying professional and managerial jobs, they have gained substantial economic advantages. Differences in income between the working class and the middle class have diminished. And Catholics, who often came from more recent immigrant groups than Protestants, have grown increasingly middle class as the proportion of second- and third-generation Americans grew. During the 1950s and 1960s white Catholics were more likely than white Protestants to be working class. This is no longer true. From 1976 through 1988 they have been as likely as white Protestants to be middle class.

Figure 5-6 White Major Party Voters Who Voted Democratic for President, by Social Class and Religion, 1944-1988 (in percentages)

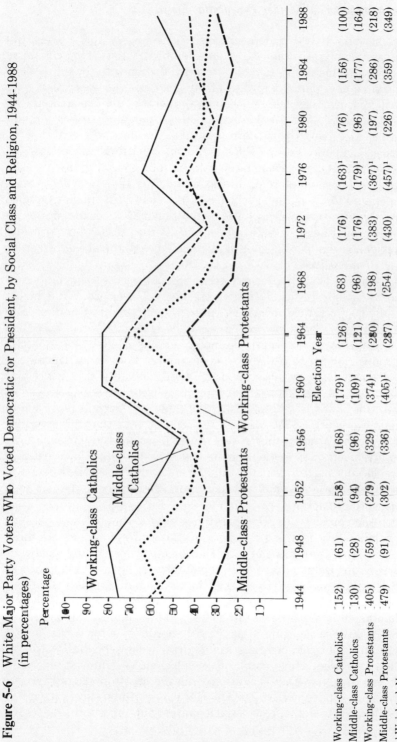

	1944	1948	1952	1956	1960	1964	1968	1972	1976	1980	1984	1988
Working-class Catholics	(152)	(61)	(158)	(168)	(179)[1]	(126)	(83)	(176)	(163)[1]	(76)	(156)	(100)
Middle-class Catholics	(130)	(28)	(94)	(96)	(109)[1]	(121)	(96)	(176)	(179)[1]	(96)	(177)	(164)
Working-class Protestants	(405)	(59)	(279)	(329)	(374)[1]	(280)	(198)	(383)	(367)[1]	(197)	(286)	(218)
Middle-class Protestants	(479)	(91)	(302)	(336)	(405)[1]	(287)	(254)	(430)	(457)[1]	(226)	(359)	(349)

[1] Weighted *N*s.

Not only have these groups changed economically and socially, but the historical conditions that led union members, the working class, and Catholics to become Democrats have receded further into the past. While the transmission of partisan loyalties from generation to generation gives historically based coalitions some staying power, the ability of the family to transmit party loyalties has declined as party identification has weakened.[39] Moreover, the total proportion of the electorate that directly experienced the politics of the Roosevelt years has progressively declined due to generational replacement. By 1988 only one voter in five had entered the electorate before or during World War II. New policy issues, often unrelated to the political conflicts of the New Deal era, have tended to erode Democratic loyalties among traditional Democratic groups. A recent book by Edward G. Carmines and James A. Stimson provides strong evidence that race-related issues have been crucial in weakening the New Deal coalition.[40]

Our study of changing social forces suggest that the Democrats may continue to have problems in winning presidential elections. While blacks vote solidly Democratic, they are a relatively small group with lower than average turnout. Blacks provide a weak base upon which to build a national coalition. A coalition of minority groups needs the support of many groups, and it needs high levels of support from them. During the twelve elections between 1944 and 1988, the Democrats have never won without *at least* three-fifths of the vote of white union members and *at least* two-thirds of the vote of white working-class Catholics. And they have never won without an absolute majority of both the white working class and white Catholics. Moreover, the Democrats have never won an election in which blacks made up more than 15 percent of their coalition. Our calculations suggest that it would be difficult for the Democrats to win a two-candidate election in which more than a sixth of their total vote came from blacks.

Can the erosion of Democratic support among southerners, union members, the working class, and Catholics be reversed? Southern whites are no longer part of the Democratic presidential coalition. Even when the Democrats fielded a southerner against an unelected Republican incumbent in 1976, they failed to gain a majority among white southerners. On the other hand, the Democrats still do relatively better among unionists, the working class, and Catholics, demonstrating that the New Deal coalition is not totally defunct. After Carter's 1976 victory, some political scientists saw signs of renewed vitality for the New Deal coalition. But given the social changes among the groups making up the New Deal coalition and the weak feelings of party identification that contribute to volatile voting preferences, it will be difficult to resurrect the New Deal coalition into a winning electoral alliance.

Notes

1. The basic social categories used in this chapter are the same as we used in Chapter 4. The variables are described in the notes to that chapter.
2. We rely in this and all subsequent chapters (as well as in Table 2-1) on the way people said they voted. If we presented results only for validated voters, our analysis would not be comparable with the vast majority of previous analyses of NES surveys, and we would not be able to compare our results with a majority of earlier NES surveys. In any event, the overall distribution of the presidential vote is virtually identical regardless of whether one analyzes all respondents who said they voted or the subset of the respondents who were classified as voters by the vote validation study. Dukakis's share of the vote declines by two-tenths of a percentage point when only validated voters are studied. Differences are marginally greater in the distribution of the congressional vote, but even here they are minimal. The total Democratic share of the House vote is reduced 1.3 points when the analysis is restricted to validated voters.
3. Television network exit polls were each conducted in cooperation with a major newspaper, and all are based upon very large samples. The CBS News/*New York Times* poll surveyed 11,645 voters, the ABC News/*Washington Post* poll questioned 23,030 voters, the NBC News/*Wall Street Journal* poll surveyed 11,703 voters, and the Cable News Network/*Los Angeles Times* poll sampled 6,043 voters.

   Results for all four surveys are reported in "Opinion Roundup: The Exit Poll Results," *Public Opinion* 11 (January/February 1989): 24-26. The most comprehensive report of the CBS/*New York Times* survey appears in "Portrait of the Electorate," *New York Times,* November 10, 1988, B6. Results for the Cable News Network/*Los Angeles Times* poll are also found in William Schneider, "Solidarity's Not Enough," *National Journal,* 46, November 12, 1988, 2853-2855.

   Exit polls have three main advantages. First, they are far less expensive than the multistage probability samples conducted by the University of Michigan Survey Research Center. Second, partly as a result of their lower cost, a large number of people can be sampled. Third, because persons are interviewed shortly after they have left the voting area, the vast majority will have actually voted for president.

   Despite their large size, these surveys have four major disadvantages. First, the questionnaires must be brief. Second, it is difficult to supervise the field work and to ensure that interviewers are using the proper procedures to sample respondents. Third, many voters, especially in the West, refuse to participate, partly because they resent the early network projections. Last, these surveys are of relatively little value in studying turnout, since persons who do not go to the polls are not sampled.
4. For the Gallup results see *Gallup Report,* November 1988, 5-7. The final Gallup poll was based upon telephone interviews with 3,369 likely voters conducted between November 3 and November 6. Although Gallup surveys generally do not ask as many politically relevant questions as the NES surveys, they provide a valuable source of information about change between 1952 and 1988. Although Gallup presidential polls were conducted as early as 1936, the quality of the sampling improved markedly after the 1948 election.
5. This analysis is based both upon our analysis of the NES survey and upon our recalculations using the four exit polls.

6. Given the small number of blacks sampled in the NES, we report results based upon the CBS News/*New York Times* exit polls. The results for the NES survey are similar, except that it shows black men to be marginally more likely to vote for Dukakis than black women were.

7. Both blacks and whites may identify as Hispanics. However, none of the four exit polls differentiated among blacks who were classified as Hispanic and whites who were so classified. As we saw in Chapter 4 (n. 17), far more Hispanics are white than black.

8. Based upon exit poll results reported in Everett Carll Ladd, "The 1988 Elections: Continuation of the Post-New Deal System," *Political Science Quarterly* 104 (Spring 1989): 14. Ladd bases his results upon the NBC News/*Wall Street Journal* exit poll, but also reports that there were large independent polls in each of the ten southern states for which he presents results.

9. This brief discussion cannot do justice to the growing research on women in politics. For additional information, see Sandra Baxter and Marjorie Lansing, *Women and Politics: The Visible Majority*, rev. ed. (Ann Arbor: University of Michigan Press, 1983); Ethel Klein, *Gender Politics: From Consciousness to Mass Politics* (Cambridge, Mass.: Harvard University Press, 1984); Keith T. Poole and L. Harmon Zeigler, *Women, Public Opinion, and Politics: The Changing Political Attitudes of American Women* (New York: Longman, 1985); and Virginia Sapiro, *The Political Integration of Women: Roles, Socialization, and Politics* (Urbana: University of Illinois Press, 1983).

10. We make this point in Paul R. Abramson, John H. Aldrich, and David W. Rohde, *Change and Continuity in the 1980 Elections*, rev. ed. (Washington, D.C.: CQ Press, 1983), 290.

11. We are defining the gender gap as the percentage of women who voted Democratic minus the percentage of men who voted Democratic. This method of computing differences is similar to our calculations of group differences over time (see Table 5-2). As in these other calculations, we compare differences among major-party voters.

12. Ladd, "The 1988 Elections," 16. Ladd computes the gender gap by subtracting Bush's margin over Dukakis among women from his margin over Dukakis among men. This method of calculation, in our view, tends to exaggerate the extent of differences between social groups.

13. The NES reports six types of marital status: married and living with spouse, never married, divorced, separated, widowed, and partners who are not married. In this paragraph we compare the first two of these groups.

14. Paul R. Abramson, "Generations and Political Change in the United States," *Research in Political Sociology* 4 (1989): 235-280; Helmut Norpoth, "Under Way and Here to Stay: Party Realignment in the 1980s?" *Public Opinion Quarterly* 51 (Fall 1987): 376-391; Ladd, "The 1988 Elections," 10-13.

15. Philip E. Converse, *The Dynamics of Party Support: Cohort-Analyzing Party Identification* (Beverly Hills, Calif.: Sage, 1976), 121-142; Paul R. Abramson, *Political Attitudes in America: Formation and Change* (San Francisco: W. H. Freeman, 1983), 119-126; and Abramson, "Generations and Political Change," 263-270.

16. The poll results as presented by the *New York Times* do not show the results for occupation among whites.

17. Results for level of education were not reported for the two other exit polls. The *Gallup Report* presents results for level of education. It reports that Dukakis won a majority of the vote (55 percent) among voters who had not

graduated from high school, but does not report results for voters with postgraduate educations.

18. See, for example, Walter Dean Burnham, *Critical Elections and the Main-springs of American Politics* (New York: W. W. Norton, 1970); Everett Carll Ladd, Jr., with Charles D. Hadley, Jr., *Transformations of the American Party System: Political Coalitions from the New Deal to the 1970s,* 2d ed. (New York: W. W. Norton, 1978).

19. The ABC News/*Washington Post* poll finds that 65 percent voted for Dukakis, but this result is suspect. The other polls report that 18 to 31 percent of the respondents belong to union households, whereas the ABC News/*Washington Post* poll reports that 10 percent do.

20. Reported in Ladd, "The 1988 Elections," 15. According to the NES survey, among southern white Protestants ($N = 149$), Dukakis won only 31 percent of the vote.

21. Robert Axelrod, "Where the Votes Come From: An Analysis of Electoral Coalitions, 1952-1968," *American Political Science Review* 66 (March 1972), 11-20. Axelrod has also provided updates of his analysis through 1984. For his update of the 1984 results, which includes the cumulative results from 1952 through 1984, see Robert Axelrod, "Presidential Election Coalitions in 1984," *American Political Science Review* 80 (March 1986): 281-284.

22. John R. Petrocik, *Party Coalitions: Realignment and the Decline of the New Deal Party System* (Chicago: University of Chicago Press, 1981).

23. Harold W. Stanley, William T. Bianco, and Richard G. Niemi, "Partisanship and Group Support Over Time: A Multivariate Analysis," *American Political Science Review* 80 (September 1986): 969-976. Stanley and his colleagues developed a measure that assesses the independent contribution that group memberships make toward Democratic party loyalties after controls are introduced for membership in other pro-Democratic groups. For an alternative approach, see Robert S. Erikson, Thomas D. Lancaster, and David W. Romero, "Group Components of the Presidential Vote, 1952-1984," *Journal of Politics* 51 (May 1989): 337-346.

24. For a discussion of the importance of working-class whites to the Democratic presidential coalition, see Paul R. Abramson, *Generational Change in American Politics* (Lexington, Mass.: D.C. Heath, 1975).

25. See Axelrod, "Where the Votes Come From."

26. The NORC survey, based upon 2,564 civilians, used a quota sample that does not follow the probability procedures employed by the University of Michigan Survey Research Center. Following quota sampling procedures common at the time, southern blacks were not sampled. Because the NORC survey overrepresented upper income and occupational groups, it cannot be used to estimate the contribution of social groups to the Democratic and Republican presidential coalitions.

27. Abramson, *Generational Change,* 65-68.

28. The results in Table 5-2 are based upon major party voters. In 1968 about one voter out of seven supported George C. Wallace, the American Independent party candidate, and in 1980 about one voter in fifteen supported the independent candidacy of John B. Anderson. Including Wallace voters in 1968 and Anderson voters in 1980 affects these measures somewhat. For a report on the way including these voters affects these scores, see Abramson, Aldrich, and Rohde, *Change and Continuity in the 1980 Elections,* rev. ed., 102-115.

29. As note 26 explains, we cannot use the 1944 NORC survey to estimate the contribution of social groups to a party's electoral coalition.

30. Because blacks appear to be more likely to falsely report voting than whites, we examined the racial composition of the Democratic presidential coalition using the 1964, 1976, 1980, 1984, and 1988 vote validation studies. If we calculate the composition of the Democratic coalition based upon respondents who actually voted, we find that the black contribution drops from 13 to 11 percent in 1964, from 15 to 13 percent in 1976, from 26 to 24 percent in 1980, from 20 to 17 percent in 1984, and from 20 to 15 percent in 1988.

31. As we explained in Chapter 3, we consider the South to include the eleven states of the old Confederacy. Because we could not use our definition of the South with either the 1944 NORC survey or the 1948 University of Michigan Survey Research Center survey, we have not included these years in our analysis of regional differences among the white electorate.

32. The main source of error arises from the relatively small number of southern voters upon which these estimates are based. In 1988, for example, there were only 258 southern voters sampled, among whom 48.4 percent said they voted for Dukakis. In fact, only 40.9 percent of all white southerners did. The survey was far closer in estimating the vote outside the South. Among the 951 nonsouthern voters, 47.3 percent said they voted for Dukakis. Dukakis's actual share of the vote outside the South was 47.1 percent.

33. We base this estimate on both the 1988 NES survey and the CBS News/*New York Times* exit poll, which uses a somewhat broader definition of the South. The NES survey reports only 125 Dukakis voters in the South, of whom 38 percent were black. But our recalculation of the exit poll results suggests that 32 percent of Dukakis's southern vote was black. These latter calculations, however, include some border states.

34. See Robert R. Alford, *Party and Society: The Anglo-American Democracies* (Chicago: Rand McNally, 1963); Ronald Inglehart, *The Silent Revolution: Changing Values and Political Styles Among Western Publics* (Princeton, N.J.: Princeton University Press, 1977); Seymour Martin Lipset, *Political Man: The Social Bases of Politics,* expanded ed. (Baltimore: Johns Hopkins University Press, 1981); and Ronald Inglehart, *Culture Shift in Advanced Industrial Society* (Princeton, N.J.: Princeton University Press, 1990).

35. Variation in class voting is smaller if one focuses on class differences in the congressional vote, but the trend clearly shows a gradual decline in class voting between 1952 and 1984. See Russell J. Dalton, *Citizen Politics in Western Democracies: Public Opinion and Political Parties in the United States, Great Britain, West Germany, and France* (Chatham, N.J.: Chatham House, 1988), 156-157.

36. As we noted in Chapter 4, the procedures used to measure the respondent's social class differed somewhat in the 1988 survey because the study did not indicate whether the respondent was the head of household. This change may have led to a slightly smaller number of respondents being classified as working class. However, the differences in scoring procedures were not great and are not likely to affect our substantive conclusion that the contribution of the white working class to the Democratic presidential coalition was relatively low in the 1988 election.

37. Paul Allen Beck, "Partisan Dealignment in the Postwar South," *American Political Science Review* 71 (June 1977): 477-496; and Bruce A. Campbell, "Realignment, Party Decomposition, and Issue Voting," in *Realignment in American Politics: Toward a Theory,* ed. Bruce A. Campbell and Richard J.

Trilling (Austin: University of Texas Press, 1980), 82-109. For an alternative view, see Raymond E. Wolfinger, "Dealignment, Realignment, and Mandates in the 1984 Election," in *The American Elections of 1984,* ed. Austin Ranney (Durham, N.C.: Duke University Press, 1985), 287-290.

38. Robert Huckfeldt and Carol Weitzel Kohfeld, *Race and the Decline of Class in American Politics* (Urbana: University of Illinois Press, 1989).

39. For evidence on this point, see Abramson, *Political Attitudes in America,* 94-96.

40. Edward G. Carmines and James A. Stimson, *Issue Evolution: Race and the Transformation of American Politics* (Princeton, N.J.: Princeton University Press, 1989).

Chapter 6

Issues, Candidates, and Voter Choice

In Chapter 5, we demonstrated that social forces were weakly related to voter choice in 1988. Except for blacks, the social and demographic groups that made up the Democratic coalition largely deserted Michael S. Dukakis, giving him only slightly more support than they gave to Walter F. Mondale four years earlier. Only a handful of social groups among whites gave him a majority of their vote, and, except for Hispanics and Jews, those groups gave him only a small majority.

The Democratic presidential coalition has been eroding for some time now, perhaps indicating a long-term breakup of the New Deal coalition. But this decline in the social divisions that defined the New Deal coalition does not in itself demonstrate that the Republicans will become the majority party. It certainly does not mean that the Republicans can translate their hold on the presidency into control of Congress or the nation's statehouses. Indeed, although the Republicans solidified their dominance of the presidency, the Democrats' control of Congress and statehouses strengthened.

It is generally agreed that new political alignments are forged when a party captures the majority position on issues. In our analysis of the 1980 election, we found little evidence that the election was an endorsement of Ronald Reagan's policy proposals, even though he claimed a mandate for them—and received congressional support in enacting many of them. Instead, we found that the typical voter stood in between where Jimmy Carter and Reagan were seen to stand on most major issues. The 1984 election provided an opportunity for voters to choose between Reagan's brand of Republican policies and Mondale's representation of New Deal Democratic proposals. We found that Reagan's landslide victory was not

153

an endorsement of the Republican policy platform. In fact, the average voter was, if anything, slightly closer to Mondale's than to Reagan's stances on issues, but generally was in between the two offerings. In 1984, the public saw clear differences between the two candidates, but the typical voter saw Reagan as being as far to the right of himself or herself as Mondale was seen as being to the left.

We viewed the 1980 election largely as a rejection of Carter's performance as president, coupled with the choice of an acceptable alternative. And we viewed the 1984 election as an endorsement of Reagan's conduct in office, combined with the perception that Mondale would not be any better.

The 1988 election presented the public with another opportunity to choose between two candidates seen to offer distinctly different policies. It also provided voters with another opportunity to reward the current administration for its performance in office. Although voters could not choose the incumbent president, they could select his vice president or could turn to the Democrat as an alternative. The questions we will examine in this chapter and the next are to what extent the 1988 election was a referendum that endorsed the performance of Reagan and his vice president, and to what extent the Republican victory resulted from issue preferences among the electorate that favored the conservative candidate.

Retrospective and Prospective Evaluations

Public policy concerns enter into the voting decision in two very different ways. In an election such as 1988, one approach asks three questions: How has the incumbent president done on policy? Should the incumbent vice president be attributed the same or similar evaluations on what has been done? How likely is it that his opponent would be any better? Voting based on this form of policy appraisal is called retrospective voting and will be analyzed in Chapter 7. The second form of policy-based voting involves an examination of the policy platforms advanced by the two candidates and an assessment of which of these policy promises is more similar to what the individual believes the government should be doing. Policy voting, therefore, involves comparing two sets of promises and voting for the set that is most like the voter's own preferences. Voting based on these kinds of decisions may be referred to as prospective voting, for it involves examining the promises of the candidates about future actions. In this chapter, we will examine prospective evaluations of the two candidates and how these evaluations relate to voter choice.

The three elections of the 1980s show some remarkable similarities in terms of prospective evaluations and voting. Perhaps the most important similarity is the perception of where the Democratic and Republican candidates stood on issues. In these three elections, the public saw clear differences between the major party nominees. In all cases, the public saw the Republican candidates as conservatives on most issues, and most citizens saw them as more conservative than they saw themselves. And, in all three elections, the public saw the Democratic candidates as liberals on most issues, and most citizens saw the Democrats as more liberal than they saw themselves. As a result, many voters perceived a clear choice based on their understanding of the candidates' policy positions. The candidates presented, in the 1964 campaign slogan of Republican nominee Barry M. Goldwater, "a choice, not an echo." The *average* citizen, however, faced a difficult choice. For many, the Democratic nominees were seen to be as far to the left as the Republicans were seen to be to the right. On balance, the net effect of prospective issues was to give neither party a clear advantage.

There were also significant differences among these elections. One of the most important of these was the mixture of just what issues concerned the public. Each election presented a unique mixture of such policy concerns. Moreover, the general strategies of the candidates on issues differed in each election.[1] In 1980, Carter's incumbency was marked by a general perception of his inability to solve pressing concerns. Reagan attacked that weakness both directly (for example, by the question he posed in his debate with Carter, "Are you better off today than you were four years ago?") and indirectly. The indirect attack was more future oriented, articulating a clear set of proposals designed to convince the public he would be a better bet for solving the nation's problems because he had his own proposals to end soaring inflation, to strengthen the United States militarily, and to regain respect and influence for the United States abroad.

In 1984, Reagan was perceived to be a far more successful president than Carter had been. He chose to run a campaign focused primarily on the theme of how much better things were by 1984 (thus his ad slogan, "It's morning in America"). Mondale attacked that claim by arguing that Reagan's policies were unfair and by pointing to the rapidly growing budget deficits. Reagan's counter to Mondale's pledge to increase taxes to reduce the deficits was that he, Reagan, would not raise taxes, and that Mondale would do so only to spend them on increased government programs (he said that Mondale was another "tax and spend, tax and spend" Democrat).

The 1988 campaign was more similar to the 1984 than to the 1980 campaign. Bush continued to run on the successes of the Reagan-Bush administration and promised no new taxes. ("Read my lips," he said. "No new taxes!") Dukakis attempted initially to portray the election as one about "competence," on the grounds that he had demonstrated competence as governor of Massachusetts, rather than as one based on "ideology." By competent management, he would be able to solve the budget and trade deficit problems, for example. Bush, by implication, was less competent. He either participated in the bungled Iran-contra affair or was "out of the loop," that is, not involved in a critical policy decision of the Reagan administration. His administration had for too long supported the "drug-running dictator" of Panama, Gen. Manuel Noriega, according to Dukakis. In addition, the Reagan-Bush administration had run up larger budget deficits in eight years than all preceding administrations added together. Bush countered that it really was an election based on ideology, that Dukakis was just another *liberal* Democrat from Massachusetts. Only at the end did Dukakis agree that he was a liberal Democrat, but one in the mold of Franklin D. Roosevelt, Harry S Truman, and John F. Kennedy (rather than the less popular liberal Democrats such as George S. McGovern, Edward M. "Ted" Kennedy, and Mondale), and that he wanted to use the resources of the government to help the disadvantaged, those struggling to make ends meet, and to improve the lot of average Americans.

Notice that each of these general overviews of campaign strategies provides a mixture of prospective and retrospective strategies. All challengers attempted to hold nominees of the incumbent party accountable for the failings of the current administration, and in 1984 and 1988 Reagan and then Bush ran mainly by emphasizing Republican successes. These were clearly retrospective strategies. But in all three elections the challenger relied heavily on promises of what he would do in office, and all three incumbent party candidates attacked those promises. In 1988, Bush tried to focus the campaign on both kinds of policy evaluations. If voters respond to the campaigns of the candidates, we might expect, therefore, to see both retrospective and prospective policy concerns figure prominently in their decisions.[2]

The Concerns of the Electorate

The first question to ask about prospective voting is what kinds of concerns moved the public. The National Election Studies (NES) survey asks, "What do you think are the most important problems facing this country?" In Table 6-1, we have listed the percentage of responses to what respondents claimed was the single most important problem in broad categories of concerns over the five most recent elections.[3]

In 1988 concerns were concentrated in two of the general categories, economics and social issues. Beginning in 1976, more respondents named economic problems than any other type, and concerns about the economy have remained the most important category ever since. Nonetheless, the proportion citing an economic concern in 1988 continued to decline from its peak in 1976. Moreover, the nature of economic concerns has changed

Table 6-1 Most Important Problem as Seen by the Electorate, 1972-1988 (in percentages)

Problem	1972	1976	1980	1984	1988
Economics	27%	76%	56%	49%	45%
Unemployment/ recession	9	33	10	16	5
Inflation/prices	14	27	33	5	2
Deficit/govt. spending	1	9	3	19	32
Social issues	34	14	7	13	38
Social welfare	7	4	3	9	11
Public order	20	8	1	4	19
(Narcotics)					(13)
Foreign defense	31	4	32	34	10
Foreign	4	3	9	17	6
Defense	1	1	8	17	3
Functioning of government (competence, corruption, trust, power, etc.)	4	4	2	2	1
All others	4	3	3	3	6
Total percent	100%	101%	100%	101%	100%
N	(842)	(2,337)	(1,352)	(1,780)	(1,657)
"Missing"	(63)	(203)	(56)	(163)	(118)
Percent missing	7	7	4	7	7

Notes: Foreign in 1972 includes 25 percent who cited Vietnam. Foreign in 1980 includes 15 percent who cited Iran. Questions asked of randomly selected half sample in 1972. Weighted *N* in 1976. All of the subcategories are not included. The total percentages for the subcategories, therefore, will not equal the percentages for the main categories. The narcotics entry in 1988 is a subcategory of the public order entry.

substantially over these years. In 1976, unemployment and inflation were the two most commonly cited concerns, as befits a condition economists describe as "*stag*flation," a stagnant economy with both high unemployment and high in*flation* rates. In 1980, inflation was the most commonly cited concern, also fitting in a year with double-digit inflation rates. By 1984, concern had shifted to the budget deficit and extent of government spending and to unemployment. This also makes sense, two years after the deepest recession since World War II and well into the great increase in budget deficits.

In 1988, the single most commonly cited concern was the budget deficits and government spending. Nearly a third of the respondents cited this specific category. Again, this is sensible since both unemployment and inflation were relatively low, while massive deficits persisted.

The social issues category was cited by nearly two of five respondents, the largest proportion in this period, and more than double the proportion in any of the three preceding elections. As in 1972, the largest proportion was in the public order subcategory. The particular concern in 1988, however, was drugs, cited by one respondent in seven (in 1972, the most common public order concern was "law and order," one of Richard M. Nixon's campaign themes). The drug problem was not only a commonly cited campaign theme in 1988; it had also received a lot of media attention in the last few years. Note that the proportion citing social welfare issues has increased slowly over the 1980s, reaching a peak in 1988. The greatest increase in this area in 1988 was concern over housing and the homeless, another common campaign theme that had received greatly increased attention in the news.

Not only did the typical economic concerns about inflation and unemployment decrease greatly in 1988, so too did concern over foreign affairs and defense policy. In this regard, 1988 is closer to 1976 than any other recent election. Perhaps due to the leveling off of increased spending for defense and improvement in our relations with the Soviet Union in an era of *glasnost,* the high degree of concern in this area had ebbed considerably. Note, however, that 1984 was a sort of anomaly in this regard. Concerns about foreign affairs and defense were high even though there were no particular hot spots, such as the Vietnam War in 1972 and the Iranian hostage crisis and the Soviet invasion of Afghanistan in 1980.

These findings indicate only what problems concern the electorate. It does not necessarily follow that concern about the budget deficit translates into support for Dukakis's—or Bush's—deficit reduction program, let alone a vote for the favored candidate. A vote, after all, is an expression of a comparison between the alternatives. To investigate these questions, we must look at the voters' issues preferences and their perceptions of where candidates stood on these issues.

Issue Positions and Perceptions

The NES surveys have, beginning in 1972, included numerous issue scales designed to measure the preferences of the electorate and their perceptions of the positions the candidates took on these issues.[4] These questions, therefore, are especially appropriate for examining prospective issue evaluations. We hasten to add, however, that the perceptions of where the incumbent party's nominee stands may well be based in part on what the president has done in office, as well as the campaign promises of that party's nominee. The policy promises of the opposition party candidate may also be judged partly by what his party did when it last held the White House. Bush attempted to paint Dukakis as another liberal Democrat, in the mold of Carter and his vice president, Mondale. Some respondents may have agreed and seen Dukakis as taking positions similar to those of the past Democratic administrations, even when Dukakis did not specifically endorse past Democratic policies. Nevertheless, these issue scales tend to focus mainly on prospective evaluations and are very different from the retrospective judgments that we will analyze in Chapter 7. These issue scales appear to tap different aspects of policy-based evaluations than those we analyze in the next chapter.

These issue scales will be used to examine several questions. Just what alternatives did the voters perceive the candidates to be offering? To what extent did the voters have issue preferences of their own and relatively clear perceptions of candidates' positions? Finally, how strongly were voters' preferences and perceptions related to their choice of candidates?

Figure 6-1 presents the text of one of the seven-point issue scale questions along with a facsimile of the scale presented to respondents as they considered their responses. Figure 6-2 shows the set of issue scales asked in the 1988 NES survey. It also presents the average (median) position of the respondents and the average (median) perception of the positions of Bush and Dukakis.[5] The seven issue scales asked in 1988 probe a large variety of concerns.[6] One dealt with U.S. relations with the Soviet Union and another with defense spending. Five questions concerned domestic policy: Should government spending for social services be increased or decreased, should the government provide for jobs and a good standard of living, provide health insurance, and aid minorities,[7] and should women play an equal role in business, government, and society?[8] Although these issue scales are not a perfect mirror of the problems the public saw as most important (for example, there is no measure related to the drug problem), they do tap many of the public's concerns.

What, then, of the average respondent? These issues were selected precisely because they were controversial and generally measured long-standing partisan divisions. As a result, the average citizen comes out looking moderate on six of the seven issues. The average respondent was at, or very close to, the midpoint (4) on four issues: government spending and social services, defense spending, health insurance, and cooperation with Russia. On the jobs/standard of living and the aid to minorities scales, the average citizen was about halfway between points 4 and 5, that is, at a moderate to moderately conservative position. Most of the public, however, took a distinctly liberal stance on the role of women scale, with the average respondent located about point 2. This is a more extreme self-placement than on any such issue scale asked in recent NES surveys. Excepting this last issue scale, the moderate position reflects a nearly

Figure 6-1   Example of a 7-Point Issue Scale: Jobs and Standard of Living Guarantees

Question asked by interviewers:
"Some people feel the government in Washington should see to it that every person has a job and a good standard of living." [For the first issue scale only, the following is added: "Suppose these people are at one end of the scale at point 1."] "Others think the government should just let each person get ahead on their own." [For the first issue scale only, the interviewer says, "Suppose these people are at the other end, at point 7. And of course, some other people have opinions somewhere in between at points 2, 3, 4, 5, or 6."]

The interviewer refers the respondent to the appropriate page in the respondent booklet (see scale below) and asks, "Where would you place yourself on this scale, or haven't you thought much about this?"

If the respondent places himself or herself on the scale, the interviewer asks, "Where would you place [Michael Dukakis, George Bush, etc.] on this scale?"

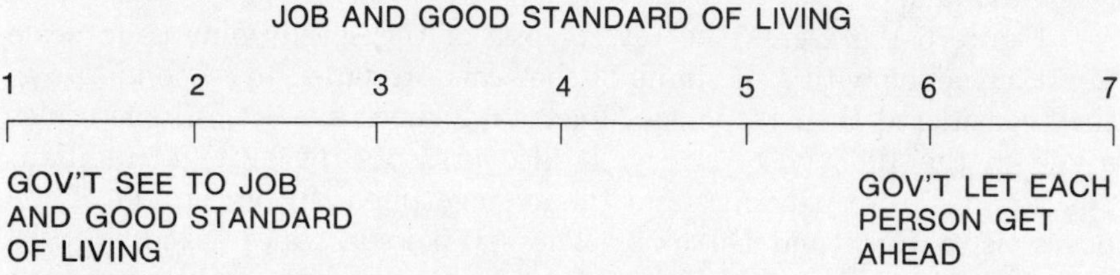

JOB AND GOOD STANDARD OF LIVING

1	2	3	4	5	6	7

GOV'T SEE TO JOB   GOV'T LET EACH
AND GOOD STANDARD   PERSON GET
OF LIVING   AHEAD

Source: Center for Political Studies, *American National Election Study, 1988: Pre- and Post-presidential Election Survey Interviewer Schedules* (Ann Arbor, Mich., November 1988), 33.

equal balancing of liberal and conservative responses, but also reflects the large number of respondents expressing a preference for moderate policies. On five of these scales, the midpoint was the most commonly selected alternative, followed by either (or both) of points 3 and 5 (see the numbers reported in Table 6-3). Only on the health insurance scale did the moderate average position reflect wide divisions. On that scale, each of the seven points was selected by between 10 and 20 percent of those expressing a preference.

The positions of this average respondent in 1988 are very similar to those of the average respondent in 1984.[9] The average is virtually identical in both years on government services and spending and on defense spending. The average respondent in 1988 is more liberal on the relations with Russia scale and more conservative on the aid to minorities and jobs scales, but none of these differences is as large as one-half point.[10] On balance, then, there was very little movement toward either the liberal or conservative positions among the electorate between 1984 and 1988.

Figure 6-2 Median Self-Placement of the Electorate and the Electorate's Placement of Candidates on Issue Scales, 1988

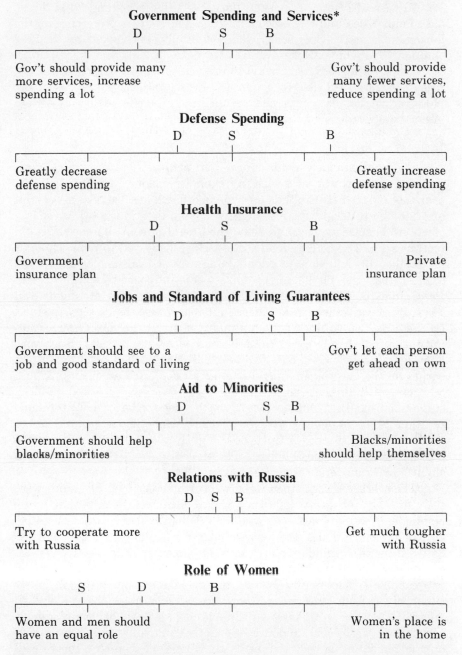

Note: S = median self-placement of electorate; D = median placement of Dukakis; B = median placement of Bush.
* Reversed from actual scoring to make a "liberal" response closer to "1" and a conservative response closer to "7."

Three scales have been asked since 1972, the jobs/standard of living, aid to minorities, and role of women scale. The average preference on the jobs/standard of living scale was essentially unchanged from 1972 through 1988 (the extreme averages were 4.2 in 1984 and 4.5 in 1988). The average self placement on aid to minorities was 4.2 in 1972 and 1976, rose to 4.5 in 1980, fell to 4.1 in 1984, and returned to 4.5 in 1988. However, virtually all of the change in these responses might result from minor modifications in the way the question was asked.[11] The role of women scale showed rapid change from 3.6 in 1972, to 2.9 in 1976, 2.4 in 1980, 2.6 in 1984, and 1.9 in 1988.[12]

The public saw clear differences between the two candidates' positions on six of the seven scales (all except relations with Russia). The average distance between the perceptions of Bush and Dukakis was about one and two-thirds points, just slightly smaller than in the two preceding elections. Dukakis was seen to be on the liberal side on all issue scales (in fact, between 2.5 and 3.5 on all scales). Bush had tried to paint Dukakis as another liberal, akin to Mondale four years earlier. These results suggest that the public might have been influenced by that claim. Perceptions of his positions were quite similar to those of Mondale in 1984. Bush was generally considered a conservative, being seen to stand on the conservative side of the midpoint on six of the seven issue scales (although only barely so on the relations with Russia scale). Bush was, however, seen to be less conservative than Reagan had been four years earlier on the government spending and services, defense spending, and relations with Russia scales. On the two other scales asked in both surveys, jobs and aid to minorities, Bush was seen to be at about the same position as the public saw Reagan in 1984. That the two candidates of 1988 were seen to be distinct but slightly closer together than the nominees in 1984 is mostly due to the perception that Bush in 1988 was slightly more moderate than Reagan in 1984.

The average citizen stood in between where Bush and Dukakis were seen to stand on every issue but the role of women. On that issue, respondents were on average more liberal than Dukakis was seen to be. On the other six issues, the average citizen was almost exactly halfway between the two candidate placements. On no other issue was the average citizen as much as one-half point from being exactly halfway between the two candidate placements. Overall, the average respondent was slightly closer to Bush on three issues (government spending, jobs, and aid to minorities), closer to Dukakis on three issues (defense, health insurance, and the role of women), and almost exactly equidistant between the two on the remaining issue (relations with Russia). Except for the role of women scale, however, neither candidate held any significant advantage.

With the exceptions of the relations with Russia and role of women scales, then, the typical citizen saw clear differences between the two candidates, but saw Dukakis about as far to the left of himself or herself as Bush was seen to be to the right. This near balancing of the two candidates is very similar to the situation of the 1980 and 1984 elections—clear differences seen between the two candidates with the average citizen right in between them. If these issues were typical of all issues in the campaign, then people were no closer to Bush than to Dukakis. While these issue preferences and perceptions might be closely related to the vote, the number of citizens casting a prospective, issue-based vote for Bush should have been just about the same as for Dukakis. Of course, we must look beyond the preferences and perceptions of the respondents before we can assess the role of these issues in electoral choice.

Issue Voting Criteria

The Problem

Since voting is an individual action, we must look at the preferences of individuals to see if prospective issues influenced their vote. In fact, the question of prospective voting is controversial. The authors of the classic study of the American electorate, *The American Voter,* point out that the public is often ill informed about public policy and may not be able to vote on the basis of issues.[13] They asked what information voters would need before an issue could influence the decision of how to vote, and they specified three conditions. First, the voters must hold an opinion on the issue; second, they must see what the government is doing on the issue; and third, they must see a difference between the policies of the two major parties. According to their analysis, only about one-quarter to one-third of the electorate in 1956 could meet these three conditions.

Although it is impossible to replicate their analysis, we can adapt their procedures to the 1988 electorate. In some ways, more recent NES data focus more directly on the actual choice citizens must make, a choice between the candidates. The first criterion is whether the respondent claims to have an opinion on the issue. This is measured by whether respondents placed themselves on the issue scale. (If they did not, they were asked no more questions about the issue.) Second, the respondents should have some perception of the positions taken by both candidates on that issue. This is measured by whether they could place both candidates on the issue.[14] Although some might perceive the position of one candidate and vote on that basis, prospective voting involves a comparison between alternatives. Third, the voter must see a difference between the positions of the two candidates. Failing to see a difference means that the voter perceived no choice on the issue.

A voter might be able to satisfy these criteria but misperceive the offerings of the two candidates. This leads to a fourth condition that we are able to measure more systematically than was possible in 1956. Does the respondent accurately perceive the *relative* positions of the two candidates; that is, see Bush as more "conservative" than Dukakis? This criterion does not demand that the voter have an accurate perception of just what the candidate proposes, but it does expect the voter to see that Dukakis, for instance, favored more spending on social services than Bush did.[15]

The Data

In Table 6-2 we report the percentages of the sample that met the four criteria on each issue scale in 1988. We also show the average proportion meeting these criteria for all seven scales and compare those averages to comparable averages in the four preceding elections.[16] As can be seen in column I, most people felt capable of placing themselves on each issue scale, and this capability was common to all five election years.[17]

Fewer people could place both candidates on an issue scale than could place just themselves, as can be seen in column II. Nonetheless, two of three respondents met these two criteria in 1988, a proportion that is a bit lower than in 1984 but about the same or higher than the other three earlier elections. Notice that there was relatively little variation across issues; from 61 to 72 percent met these criteria on each issue scale. This relatively constant ability to satisfy these criteria is similar to 1984 but different from earlier elections. In 1980, for instance, the highest percentage was the same 72 percent as in 1988, but on three issue scales fewer than half placed both Carter and Reagan.

As can be seen in column III, just over half the sample met the first two criteria and also saw a difference between the positions of Bush and Dukakis on all but two issues. Slightly more than half the sample satisfied these criteria in 1988, but nearly half did not.

More striking, perhaps, is the variation in these percentages from election to election. The figures in column III indicate that 1988 was rather similar to 1972 and 1980. The 1984 figures, however, are higher, while those for 1976 are much lower. What are we to conclude about these differences in the ability of the electorate to satisfy these criteria and thus be able to vote on the basis of issues? It seems highly unlikely that the public's ability to comprehend the electoral process varies so greatly from election to election. Note that there is very little difference from election to election in self-placement on issue scales. Rather, the differences result from perceptions of candidate positions. The differences between the extreme elections of 1976 and 1984 first appear in the ability to place both candidates on the scales. Perhaps 1976 was relatively low

Table 6-2 Four Criteria for Issue Voting, 1988, and Comparisons with 1972-1984 Presidential Elections (in percentages)

			Percentage of sample who:	
	I	II	III	IV
Issue scale	*Placed self on scale*	*Placed both candidates on scale*[a]	*Saw differences between Dukakis and Bush*	*Saw Dukakis more "liberal" than Bush*
Government spending/ services	80	66	57	47
Defense spending	86	71	63	57
Health insurance	84	62	52	44
Jobs and standard of living	85	72	59	49
Aid to minorities[b]	89	66	51	43
Relations with Russia	84	61	44	30
Role of women	94	63	39	30
Average[c]				
1988 (7)	86	66	52	43
1984 (7)	84	73	62	53
1980 (9)	82	61	51	43
1976 (9)	84	58	36	26
1972 (8)	90	65	49	41

Note: Columns II, III, and IV compare the Democratic and Republican nominees (Anderson excluded in 1980).

[a] If respondent could not place self on scale, respondent was not questioned further on that issue.

[b] Aid to blacks and aid to minorities scales (asked of separate halves of sample) combined here.

[c] Number in parentheses is the number of issue scales included in the average for each election year survey.

because Gerald R. Ford had not run for president before and had been the incumbent for only two years, while Carter was a relatively unknown challenger. And perhaps 1984 was so high not only because Reagan had served four years as president, but also because Mondale had served as vice president and thus was unusually well known for a challenger. The differences become especially pronounced, however, in the electorate's ability to see differences between the candidates' positions. In 1984, the candidates adopted particularly distinctive positions on issues, and this relative clarity was picked up by the electorate. In 1972, 1980, and 1988, the candidates were only slightly less distinct, and the electorate saw these differences only slightly less clearly. In 1976, by contrast, Ford and

Carter were generally described as moderates, albeit moderately conservative and moderately liberal, respectively. And the electorate also reacted to this relatively less distinct pair of alternatives.

In sum, we support Morris P. Fiorina's argument that failure to satisfy the criteria for issue voting does not mean that the electorate has ill-formed preferences and perceptions.[18] Rather, the ability of the electorate to perceive differences between the candidates varies because political conditions differ from election to election, and these differences result mainly from differences in the strategies candidates follow. Thus, the "quality" of the responses to these issue questions is based in part on how clearly the candidates articulate their issue positions.

The data in column IV reflect the ability of the electorate to discern distinctions between the candidates' policy offerings. Averaging these issues together, we see that in 1988 more than two of five respondents saw Dukakis as more liberal than Bush. The 1988 data continue to look much like those of 1980 and 1972 in these terms, and 1984 remains the high water mark in meeting this criterion. The 1976 election stands out in even sharper contrast, as barely more than one in four could assess the relative positions of the two candidates.

The data in Table 6-2 suggest that the potential for prospective issue voting was relatively high in 1988. We might, therefore, expect these issues to be closely related to voter choice. We will examine voter choice on these issues in two ways. First, how often did people vote for the closer candidate on each issue? Second, how strongly related to the vote is the set of all issues taken together?

Apparent Issue Voting in 1988

Issue Criteria and Voting on Each Issue

The first question is, to what extent did people who were closer to a candidate on a given issue actually vote for that candidate? That is, how strong is apparent issue voting?[19] In Table 6-3 we report the proportion of major party voters who voted for Bush by where they placed themselves on the issue scales. We also indicate which of the seven points on each issue were closer to where the average citizen placed Dukakis and which points were closer to where the average citizen placed Bush (see Figure 6-2). Many individuals, of course, thought the candidates were at different positions than the public did on average. Using these average perceptions, however, reduces the impact of voters' rationalizing their perceptions to be consistent with their vote, rather than voting for the candidate whose views are closer to their preferences.[20]

As can be seen in Table 6-3, on most issues there is a strong relationship between the voters' issue positions and the candidate they supported. There are two exceptions. One is the scale concerning the role of women, but as we have noted (note 8), this scale is only indirectly related to government action, let alone the candidates' campaign strategies or the public's expressed concerns. The other is the relations with the Soviet Union scale, which was much more strongly related to the vote in 1980 and 1984 than in 1988.[21] These issues are also the two on which the candidates are seen as closest together. If we exclude the midpoint, 4, on the government spending and services scale, voters who were closer to where Bush was seen to stand on the first five issues gave him at least 63 percent of the vote and often voted for him in much higher proportions. As we saw in Chapter 5, 52 percent of the voters in the NES survey voted for Bush, and he received 53 percent of the major party vote, so this represents at least 10 percentage points more than Bush's overall level of support. And if we also exclude the midpoints of 4, voters closer to where Dukakis was seen to stand on these five issues gave him at least 57 percent support, 10 points higher than his 47 percent of major party voters in the NES sample. Thus, in general, the relationship between issue preferences and the vote is quite strong.

The richness of information in Table 6-3 can be summarized to present the relationships more clearly. In the first column of Table 6-4, we report the percentage of major party voters who placed themselves closer to the average perception of Dukakis or Bush and who voted for the closer candidate. To be more specific, the denominator is the total number of major party voters who placed themselves closer to the electorate's perception of Bush and Dukakis.[22] The numerator is the total number of major party voters who were closer to Bush and voted for him plus the total number of major party voters who were closer to Dukakis and voted for him.

If voting were unrelated to issue positions, we would expect that on average 50 percent would vote for the closer candidate. In 1988, 62 percent voted for the closer candidate. Again, this is a higher percentage on average than in 1976, but it is about the same as in 1980 and lower than in the two other elections. Note, however, that the six issues, excepting the role of women issue, have much higher percentages voting for the closer candidate. On the women's role scale, the percentage is quite close to what we would expect by chance. The issues that measure the longstanding divisions between the two parties—government involvement in social services, jobs, health, and assistance to minorities—were more strongly related to the vote.

These figures do not tell the whole story, however, for those who placed themselves on an issue but failed to meet some other criterion were unlikely to have cast a vote based on that issue. In the second column of Table 6-4, we report the percentage of those who voted for the closer candidate on each issue, among voters who met all four conditions

Table 6-3 Percentage of Major Party Voters Who Voted for Bush, by Seven-Point Issue Scales, 1988

Issue scale	Closer to median perception of Dukakis			Closer to median perception of Bush				(N)
	1	2	3	4	5	6	7	
Government spending/services[a]	22	28	37	55	70	77	81	
(N)	(63)	(108)	(185)	(302)	(191)	(115)	(54)	(1,018)
Defense spending	14	26	43	60	74	68	71	
(N)	(85)	(118)	(147)	(378)	(201)	(101)	(58)	(1,088)
Health insurance	38	32	39	51[b]	67	72	76	
(N)	(167)	(95)	(127)	(218)	(158)	(131)	(140)	(1,036)
Jobs and standard of living	23	28	31	45	65	72	71	
(N)	(75)	(61)	(114)	(228)	(213)	(197)	(164)	(1,052)
Aid to minorities	20	23	36	56	70	63	65	
(N)	(85)	(61)	(130)	(285)	(186)	(149)	(181)	(1,077)
Relations with Russia	43	43	47	61	69	56	62	
(N)	(123)	(150)	(199)	(256)	(151)	(102)	(84)	(1,065)
Role of women	49	48	63	56	59	67	57	
(N)	(494)	(187)	(117)	(174)	(59)	(52)	(65)	(1,148)

Note: Numbers in parentheses are the totals on which percentages are based.

[a] Reversed from actual scoring to make a "liberal" response closer to 1 and a "conservative" response closer to 7.

[b] Equidistant between the median perception of Dukakis's position on health insurance and the median perception of Bush's position on health insurance.

on that issue. The third column reports the percentage voting for the closer candidate among voters who placed themselves on the scale but failed to meet all of the three remaining conditions.

Those who met all four conditions were much more likely to vote for the closer candidate on any issue. Indeed, there is relatively little difference, on average, across all five elections. In each case, at least seven of ten such voters supported the closer candidate. For those who failed to meet all of the last three conditions on issue voting, in contrast, voting was essentially random with respect to the issues.

The strong similarity of all five election averages in the second and third columns suggests that the major reason that issue voting seems more prevalent in some elections than others depends primarily on the number of people who clearly perceive differences between the candidates. In all elections, at least seven in ten who satisfied all four conditions voted consistently with their issue preferences, while in all elections, those who did not satisfy all the conditions on perceptions of candidates voted essentially randomly with respect to individual issues. As we saw earlier, the degree to which such perceptions vary from election to election depends more on the strategies of the candidates than on the qualities of the voters. Therefore, the relatively low level of apparent issue voting in 1976, for instance, resulted from the perception of small differences between the two rather moderate candidates. The high level of apparent issue voting in 1984 resulted from the remarkable clarity with which most people saw the positions of Reagan and Mondale. The 1988 election fell in between these two elections, because the distinctiveness of the candidate positions was greater than in 1976, but less than in 1984.

Overall Apparent Issue Voting

Most people held a more liberal position on the role of women than they believed either candidate espoused. If this were the only basis of voter choice, Dukakis would have won the election easily, because far more people saw him rather than Bush as standing closer to their own position. Thus, many who voted for Bush did so even though they saw Dukakis as the closer candidate on this issue. This reminds us that there are many factors involved in voting, and it is the rare voter who finds every factor pushing him or her in one candidate's direction. In later chapters, we will compare the impact of these prospective issues with other factors. Here we will look at the entire set of these issues.

We constructed an overall assessment of these seven issue scales, what we call the "balance of issues measure," by giving individuals a score of $+1$ if their positions on an issue scale were closer to the average perception of Bush, a -1 if their positions were closer to the average

Table 6-4 Apparent Issue Voting, 1988, and Comparisons with 1984, 1980, 1976, and 1972 (in percentages)

	Percent of voters who voted for closer candidate and:		
Issue scale	Placed self on issue scale	Met all four issue voting criteria	Placed self but failed to meet all three other criteria
Government spending/ services	66	78	46
Defense spending	60	86	26
Health insurance	67	71	30
Jobs and standard of living	67	75	52
Aid to minorities[a]	62	69	51
Relations with Russia	59	60	59
Role of women	52	55	49
Average			
1988	62	71	45
1984	65	73	46
1980	63	71	48
1976	57	70	50
1972	66	76	55

Note: An "apparent issue vote" is a vote for the candidate closer to one's position on an issue scale. The closer candidate is determined by comparing self-placement with the median placements of the two candidates on the scale as a whole. Respondents who did not place themselves or who were equidistant from the two candidates are excluded from the calculations.

[a] Aid to blacks and aid to minorities scales (asked of separate half samples) are combined.

perception of Dukakis, and a score of zero if they were equally close to the two candidates or if they had no preference on an issue. These scores were added up for all seven issue scales, creating a measure that ranged from -7 to +7. For instance, respondents who were closer to the average perception of Dukakis's positions on all seven scales received a score of -7. A negative score indicated that the respondent was, on balance, closer to the public's perception of Dukakis, while a positive score indicated the respondent was, overall, closer to the public's perception of Bush.[23]

In Figure 6-3, we collapse this summary measure of prospective issues into seven categories, ranging from strongly Democratic to strongly Republican, and display the distribution of respondents on this measure for all five most recent elections.[24] There is a consistent trend in the five

Figure 6-3 Distribution of Electorate on Net Balance of Issues, 1972-1988

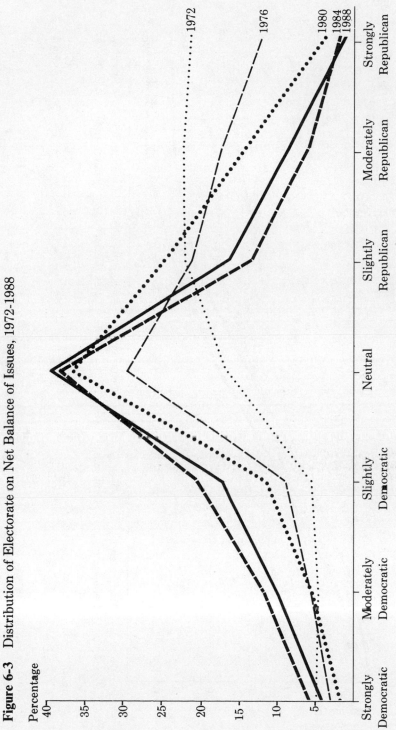

Figure 6–4 Major Party Voters Who Voted Democratic for President, by Net Balance of Issues Measure, 1972–1988

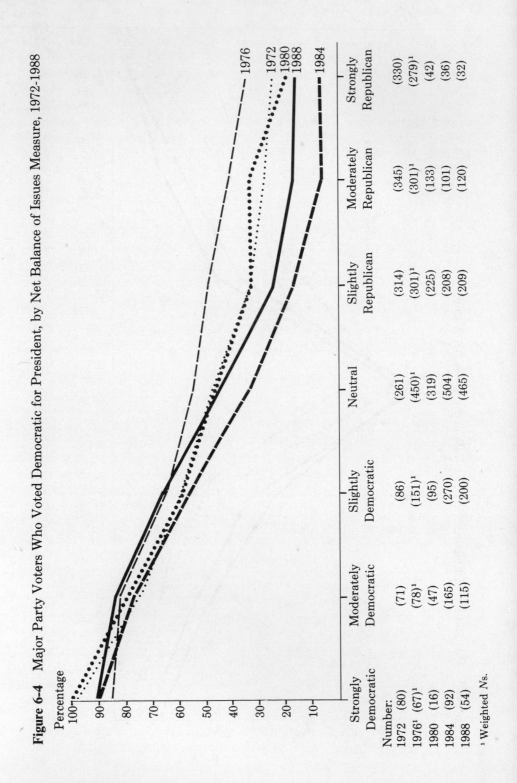

Percentage

						1976
						1972
						1980
						1988
						1984

Number:
1972 (80)
1976[1] (67)[1]
1980 (16)
1984 (92)
1988 (54)

[1] Weighted *N*s.

Strongly Democratic	Moderately Democratic	Slightly Democratic	Neutral	Slightly Republican	Moderately Republican	Strongly Republican
	(71)	(86)	(261)	(314)	(345)	(330)
	(78)[1]	(151)[1]	(450)[1]	(301)[1]	(301)[1]	(279)[1]
	(47)	(95)	(319)	(225)	(133)	(42)
	(165)	(270)	(504)	(208)	(101)	(36)
	(115)	(200)	(465)	(209)	(120)	(32)

elections. In 1972, Americans stood closer, overall, to Nixon than to McGovern. While they were closer to the Republican in 1976 as well, Ford held less of an advantage than Nixon. Rather, there were more people in the neutral category than in any other and rather fewer, overall, closer to Ford than Carter, compared with 1972. By 1980, the relative conservatism of Reagan meant that even more people were in the neutral category than earlier and, consequently, fewer found that issues pushed them strongly in the Republican direction. Still, Reagan held a slight advantage in 1980. By 1984, the Democrat held a slight advantage on issues for the first time. In general, the neutral category continued to grow to over a third of the sample.

In 1988 the same trends continued. Two in five were in the neutral category, the largest proportion of any of these five elections. There were more in the slightly Democratic category than in any of the preceding elections except 1984. Thus, Dukakis held about the same advantage on these issues as Mondale did in 1984, and both surely held a better position than the preceding Democrats, who were at a disadvantage.[25] Still, the overall impression is the concentration of the public in the neutral category—and the overall great similarity between 1984 and 1988.

As can be seen in Figure 6-4, the relationship between the net balance of issues measure and the vote was strong in all five elections. In all elections, when these issues pushed strongly in one candidate's direction or the other, that voter was very likely to vote consistently with these issues. In 1988, for example, over nine of ten in the strongly Democratic category voted consistently with their issue preferences, and about seven out of eight voters in the moderately partisan categories and the strongly Republican category did so. Even in 1976, two-thirds of the voters who were strongly Republican supported Ford. The results for 1984 and 1988 are very similar, for these elections show the strongest relationship between the balance of issues measure and the vote. Moreover, in both 1984 and 1988 a majority who were neutral on our measure voted Republican, and in both these elections these neutral voters were by far the most numerous category. This suggests that many voters were looking at other factors in determining their voting choices.

Conclusion

These findings suggest that prospective issues were quite important in the 1988 election, but they cannot account for Bush's victory. Those for whom prospective issues gave a clear choice voted consistently with those issues. Most people, however, were located between where they saw the candidates standing. Indeed, on most issues, more people were relatively moderate, and Dukakis and Bush were seen as more liberal and more conservative, respectively. In 1980, Carter lost because, compared with his 1976 victory, he fared worse among voters who were slightly Democratic, neutral, or in any of the pro-Republican categories. In 1984, Mondale did even worse among all these groups but the slightly pro-Democratic one. This line of reasoning suggests that people voted against an unpopular incumbent in 1980, unless issues pushed strongly in his direction; they voted for a popular incumbent in 1984, unless issues strongly impelled them otherwise. In 1988 Dukakis had virtually the same level of support as Mondale had among strongly pro-Democratic voters, but he fared somewhat better among all of the other six categories. On balance, voters supported the vice president of a popular incumbent, unless issues impelled them otherwise, but the pull of Reagan's popularity was not quite as strong for his vice president as it had been when he was reelected. In the next chapter, we will see that such an interpretation seems most reasonable.

Notes

1. For more on the strategies of the candidates in the 1980 and 1984 elections, see Paul R. Abramson, John H. Aldrich, and David W. Rohde, *Change and Continuity in the 1980 Elections,* rev. ed. (Washington, D.C.: CQ Press, 1983), chap. 2, and *Change and Continuity in the 1984 Elections,* rev. ed. (Washington, D.C.: CQ Press, 1987), chap. 2, respectively.
2. For an analysis of how the candidates' campaign strategies in 1984 shaped the voters' decisions, see John H. Aldrich and Thomas Weko, "The Presidency and the Election Process: Campaign Strategy, Voting, and Governance," in *The Presidency and the Political System,* 2d ed., ed. Michael Nelson (Washington, D.C.: CQ Press, 1988), 251-267.
3. Respondents are encouraged to name several problems, but they are then asked which is "the single most important problem." The responses in Table 6-1 are from the latter question. Looking at the full array of responses, we find a broader range of alternatives suggested, yet the same outlines are apparent. It should be noted that the wording to the question about national problems was different in 1980 than in the other four elections. In 1980 respondents were asked, "As you know, the government faces many serious problems in this country and other parts of the world. What do you personally feel are the most important problems the government in Washington should try to take care of?"
4. These measures were first used in the NES survey of the 1968 election, but were used extensively in presidential election surveys beginning in 1972. The issue measures used in Chapter 7 were also used extensively beginning in the 1970s. Therefore in this chapter and in Chapter 7, we restrict our attention to the last five elections at most.
5. The median is based on the assumption that respondents can be ranked from most conservative to most liberal. The number of respondents who are more liberal than the median (or who see a candidate as more liberal than the median) is equal to the number who are more conservative (or who see the candidate as more conservative) than the median. Because there are only seven points on these scales, and because many respondents will choose any given point, we use a procedure that derives a median for grouped data. That procedure is described in many statistics texts.

6. The wordings for the remaining issue scales are as follows:

a. "Some people think the government should provide fewer services, even in areas such as health and education in order to reduce spending. . . . Other people feel it is important for the government to provide many more services even if it means an increase in spending."

b. "Some people believe that we should spend much less money for defense. Others feel that defense spending should be greatly increased."

c. "There is much concern about the rapid rise in medical and hospital costs. Some people feel there should be a government insurance plan which would cover all medical and hospital expenses for everyone. Others feel that all medical expenses should be paid by individuals, and through private insurance plans like Blue Cross or other company paid plans."

d. "Some people feel that the government in Washington should make every effort to improve the social and economic position of blacks [and other minorities]. Others feel that the government should not make any special effort to help blacks [minorities] because they should help themselves." (For differences in wording, see notes 7 and 10.)

e. "Some people feel it is important for us to try to cooperate more with Russia, while others believe we should be much tougher in our dealings with Russia."

f. "Recently there has been a lot of talk about women's rights. Some people feel that women should have an equal role with men in running business, industry, and government. Others feel that women's place is in the home."

After each of these statements, respondents were asked, "Where would you place yourself on this scale, or haven't you thought much about this?" Those who placed themselves on the issue scale were asked, "Where would you place Michael Dukakis on this scale?" which was followed by the same question about George Bush and then about other political actors or groups.

7. Two versions of the aid to minorities scale were asked, each of a separate, randomly chosen, half of the sample. One question used the words "aid to blacks and other minorities," the other used the words "aid to blacks." While there are differences in the wording—and some differences in responses—we combined the two questions as if they were the same.

8. The "equal role for women" question is different from the other six scales. Unlike these six other scales, it does not directly measure preferences about government policy options. Rather, it asks for a judgment about gender differences in society. This question, therefore, is not as easily assessed in a campaign context, nor did the candidates discuss it directly in the campaign. Government policy might be related to this issue, however. For example, political elites could provide symbolic leadership. More directly, politicians could appeal for an equal rights amendment to the Constitution, though this possibility was not discussed much in the 1988 campaign. Some policy issues that are directly or tangentially relevant were discussed, such as government provision of day care facilities. Still, this question does differ from the others, which might explain why responses to it are weakly related to the way people voted for president (see Tables 6-3 and 6-4).

9. See Abramson, Aldrich, and Rohde, *Change and Continuity in the 1984 Elections,* rev. ed., 171-172, and Figure 6-2, 170.

10. As explained in note 7, there were two versions of the aid to minorities question, each asked of a randomly selected half sample. For the version similar to that used in past surveys, "aid for blacks and other minorities," the

median self-placement is 4.3 (compared to a median of 4.1 in 1984). For the other version, "aid for blacks," the median is 4.7.

11. We have already noted that there were two versions of this question in 1988. The relatively conservative response in 1980 might result from the respondents' having been asked whether the government should help blacks and other minority groups "even if it means giving them preferential treatment." This phrase was not included in the 1984 and 1988 versions of this scale.

12. In 1984 respondents were asked the role of women issue scale, but were not asked to rate the candidates on it. This question was not used in our analysis of issue voting in the 1984 election, although another issue scale concerning gender was.

13. Angus Campbell, Philip E. Converse, Warren E. Miller, and Donald E. Stokes, *The American Voter* (New York: John Wiley & Sons, 1960), 168-187.

14. The NES interviewers did not ask those who failed to place themselves on an issue scale where they thought the candidates stood. Therefore, those who failed to meet the first criterion were unable to meet any of the remaining ones. Although some with no preference on an issue might know the positions of one or both candidates, it is difficult to see how they could vote based on those perceptions if they had no opinion about what policy should be followed.

15. The arguments made by Campbell et al. in *The American Voter* about issue voting criteria are critiqued by Morris P. Fiorina, *Retrospective Voting in American National Elections* (New Haven, Conn.: Yale University Press, 1981), 9-11. Although many scholars have interpreted failure to meet these criteria as akin to failing a test, he argues that the criteria imply no such thing. We agree. Failure to satisfy these criteria in no way impugns the citizen. As we show, the failure to satisfy these criteria is related to the strategies followed by the candidates in the campaign.

16. For details for 1980 and 1984, see Abramson, Aldrich, and Rohde, *Change and Continuity in the 1980 Elections*, rev. ed., Table 6-3, 130; and *Change and Continuity in the 1984 Elections*, rev. ed., Table 6-2, 174.

17. While this is evidence that most people *claim* to have issue preferences, it does not demonstrate that they *do*. For example, evidence indicates that some use the midpoint of the scale (point 4) as a means of answering the question even if they have ill-formed preferences. See John H. Aldrich, Richard G. Niemi, George Rabinowitz, and David W. Rohde, "The Measurement of Public Opinion about Public Policy: A Report on Some New Issue Question Formats," *American Journal of Political Science* 26 (May 1982): 391-414.

18. Fiorina, *Retrospective Voting*, 9-11.

19. We call it "apparent" issue voting to emphasize several points. First, voting involves too many factors to infer that closeness to a candidate on any one issue was the cause of the voter's choice. The issue similarity may have been purely coincidental or but one of many reasons the voter supported that candidate. Second, we use the median perception of the candidates' positions rather than the voter's own perception. Third, the relationship between issues and the vote may be due to "rationalization." Voters may have decided to support a candidate for other reasons and may also have altered their own issue preferences or misperceived the positions of the candidates to align themselves more closely with their already favored candidate on these issues. See Richard A. Brody and Benjamin I. Page, "Comment: The Assessment of Policy Voting," *American Political Science Review* 66 (June 1972): 450-458.

20. Ibid.

21. This weaker relationship could be because of the remarkable changes occurring within the Soviet Union and its relations with the United States, as well as the change in the Reagan administration's policies from seeing the U.S.S.R. as the "evil empire" to negotiating with the Soviets on a variety of major concerns. For the 1980 data, see Abramson, Aldrich, and Rohde, *Change and Continuity in the 1980 Elections,* rev. ed., Table 6-4, 133; for the 1984 data, see Abramson, Aldrich, and Rohde, *Change and Continuity in the 1984 Elections,* rev. ed., Table 6-3, 177.
22. Those who placed themselves at point 4 on the health insurance scale, and thus are equidistant between the average perceptions of the two candidates' positions, are excluded from both the numerator and denominator (as are those who did not place themselves on the issue scale).
23. This procedure counts every issue as equal in importance. It also assumes that all that matters is that the voter is closer to the candidate on an issue; it does not consider how much closer the voter is to one candidate or the other.
24. Scores of +6 and +7 were called strongly Republican, while similarly negative scores were called strongly Democratic. Scores of +4 and +5 were considered moderately Republican (and -4 and -5 moderately Democratic). Scores of +2 and +3 were considered slightly Republican (and -2 and -3 slightly Democratic). Scores of -1, 0, and +1 were called neutral. Note that the number of issue scales differed from election to election, making comparisons across elections at least somewhat problematic. For details on our procedures for 1972, 1976, and 1980, see Abramson, Aldrich, and Rohde, *Change and Continuity in the 1980 Elections,* rev. ed., 140. Since there were seven issue scales in the 1984 survey, the procedure for that year was the same as for 1988.
25. It is worth noting that Dukakis's advantage on the balance of issues measure is due in large part to the role of women issue, on which the distribution of voters' preferences greatly favored him. Excluding that scale, the balance of issues measure would slightly favor Bush (especially in a reduction in the proportion in the slightly Democratic category and increase in the slightly Republican category). Given that scale's remove from direct political implications, as well as its (probably related) weak relationship to the vote, it is therefore safer to emphasize the large proportion of neutrals on the balance of issues measure and the overall lack of a clear advantage to either candidate due to prospective issues.

Chapter 7

Presidential Performance and Candidate Choice

If voters chose only on the basis of prospective issues, then, according to the balance of issues measures analyzed in the last chapter, more voters should have favored Michael S. Dukakis than favored George Bush. Moreover, nearly four out of ten were exactly or nearly neutral on this measure.

Bush won, of course. Although he won by a smaller margin than any candidate since Jimmy Carter twelve years earlier, his margin of victory was, nonetheless, comfortable. Clearly, there is more to voter choice than decisions based on prospective issues. In 1980 and 1984, the typical voter was also not strongly disposed toward one candidate or the other on prospective issues. The explanation for Ronald Reagan's triumphs in those years was the public's perceptions of how good a job the incumbent had done. In 1980, we attributed Reagan's victory to perceptions that Carter had not done a good enough job as president. In 1984, we concluded that Reagan won reelection largely because people thought he had done a good job as president in his first term. Perhaps Bush's victory in 1988 could be attributed to the public's continuing belief that Reagan was doing a good job as president.[1] This sort of voting decision is termed retrospective voting, a phenomenon we will examine in this chapter.

What Is "Retrospective" Voting?

An individual who voted for the incumbent party's candidate because the incumbent was, in the voter's opinion, a successful president is said to have cast a retrospective vote. The voter decided that "one good term deserves another." A voter casting a ballot for the opposition because, in the voter's opinion, the incumbent had been *un*successful also cast a retrospective vote, in this case to "throw the rascals out" of office. In other words, retrospective voting decisions are based on evaluations of the course of politics over the last term in office and on evaluations of how much the incumbent should be held responsible for what good or ill occurred. V. O. Key, Jr., popularized this argument by suggesting that the voter might be a "rational god of vengeance and of reward." [2]

Obviously, the closer the candidate of one party can be tied to the actions of the incumbent, the more likely it is that voters will decide retrospectively. The incumbent president cannot escape such evaluations, and the incumbent vice president is often identified with (and often identifies himself with) the administration's performance. In nineteen of the twenty-three presidential elections since 1900 (all but 1908, 1920, 1928, and 1952), an incumbent president or vice president stood for election.

George Bush ran in 1988 as the incumbent vice president. He not only stood, therefore, to benefit or pay the price of voters' evaluations of the two Reagan-Bush terms of office, he also actively sought to remind voters that he was the vice president and that he stood as a candidate for president to continue the policies of the Reagan-Bush administration. Thus, he sought to accentuate the importance of retrospective evaluations. This position puts him in marked contrast to the last vice president running to succeed his president, Hubert H. Humphrey in 1968. In that campaign, Humphrey attempted to downplay the role of retrospective evaluations, obviously knowing that Lyndon B. Johnson's policies in Vietnam were unpopular. Bush, on the other hand, had good reasons to assume that retrospective evaluations would be largely positive in 1988, as we will see later in this chapter.

In the perspective offered by Key, retrospective voters are outcome-oriented and evaluate only the performance of the incumbent, all but ignoring the opposition. The retrospective voter in this view also evaluates what has been done, not what might be done in the future.

Anthony Downs presents a different picture of retrospective voting.[3] He argues that voters look to the past to understand what the incumbent party's candidate will do in the future. According to Downs, parties are basically consistent in their goals, methods, and ideologies over time. Therefore, past performance by both parties' candidates, but especially that of the incumbent, may prove relevant for projections about their future conduct. Because it takes time and effort to evaluate candidates' campaign promises and because promises are just words, the voters find it faster, easier, and safer to use past performance to project what the administration's actions for the next four years will be. Downs also emphasizes that retrospective evaluations are used to make comparisons between the alternatives standing for election. Key's view is that of a retrospective referendum on the incumbent's party alone. Downs's view is that such evaluations are used to make comparisons between the candidates as well as to provide a guide to the future. In 1988, for example, Bush attempted to tie Dukakis to past Democratic candidates, such as George S. McGovern and Walter F. Mondale, and to the most recent Democratic administration, that of Jimmy Carter, while Dukakis pointed to the budget deficits and to the Iran-contra scandal as evidence that the Republicans could not govern effectively. Thus, both candidates encouraged voters to make comparative retrospective evaluations.

Another view of retrospective voting is advanced by Morris P. Fiorina. His view is in many respects an elaboration and extension of Downs's point of view. One of the most important of Fiorina's extensions concerns partisan identification. He argues that "citizens monitor party promises and performances over time, encapsulate their observations in a summary judgment termed 'party identification,' and rely on this core of previous experience when they assign responsibility for current societal conditions and evaluate ambiguous platforms designed to deal with uncertain futures."⁴ We will return to Fiorina's views on partisanship in the next chapter.

Retrospective voting and voting according to issue positions, as analyzed in Chapter 6, differ significantly. The difference lies in how concerned people are with societal outcomes and how concerned they are with the means to achieve desired outcomes. For example, everyone prefers economic prosperity. The disagreement among political decision makers lies in how best to achieve it. At the voters' level, however, the central question is whether people care only about achieving prosperity or whether they care, or even are able to judge, how to achieve this desired goal. Perhaps they looked at high inflation and interest rates in 1980 and said: "We tried Carter's approach, and it failed. Let's try something else—anything else." Or, they noted the long run of relative economic prosperity from 1983 to 1988 and said: "Whatever Reagan did, it worked. Let's keep it going by putting his vice president in office." Or, perhaps, they agreed with Dukakis and said: "Sure, the recovery is terrific, but Reagan's programs have led to huge budget deficits, and his administration has had too many scandals such as Iran-contra; let's try Dukakis's approach."

Economic policies and foreign affairs issues are especially likely to be discussed in these terms because they share several characteristics. First, the outcomes are clear, and most voters can judge whether they approve of the results. Inflation and unemployment are high or low; the economy is growing or it is not. The country is at war or at peace; the world is stable or unstable. Second, there is often near consensus on what the desired outcomes are; no one disagrees with peace or prosperity, with world stability or low unemployment. Third, the means to achieve these ends are often very complex, and information is hard to understand; experts as well as candidates and parties disagree over the specific ways to achieve the desired ends.

As issues, therefore, peace and prosperity differ sharply from policy areas, such as abortion and gun control, in which there is vigorous disagreement over ends among experts, leaders, and the public. On still other issues, people value means as well as ends. The classic cases often involve the question of whether it is appropriate for government to take action in that area at all. President Reagan was fond of saying, "Government isn't the solution to our problems, government *is* the problem." For instance, should the government provide national health insurance? Few disagree with the end, health protection, but they do disagree over whether government insurance is the appropriate means to achieve it. Does affirmative action risk "reverse discrimination," and is that acceptable? Should the government provide day care for children of working parents? The choice of means involves some of the basic philosophic and ideological differences that have divided the Republicans from the Democrats for decades.[5] For example, in 1984 and 1988 the Democratic nominees did not argue that we were not in a period of economic prosperity or that prosperity is a bad thing. Mondale in 1984 emphasized that Reagan's policies were unfair to the disadvantaged. Both Mondale and Dukakis claimed that these policies, by creating such large deficits, were sowing the seeds for future woes. Disagreement was not over the ends, but over the means and the consequences that would result from following different means to the shared ends.

Two basic conditions are necessary for retrospective evaluations to affect voting choices. First, the individual must connect his or her concern (for example, the problem felt to be the most important one facing the nation) with the incumbent and the actions he took in office. One might blame earlier administrations for sowing the seeds that grew into the huge deficits of the 1980s, or blame a profligate Congress, or even believe that deficits are totally beyond anyone's control. Moreover, in an election such as 1988, the voter must not only see the current incumbent as responsible for the good or ills of society, but also believe that the current nominee of the incumbent party should be given credit or be held responsible. In 1988, giving credit or attaching blame was facilitated because the nominee was the vice president. Second, individuals (in the Downs-Fiorina view) must compare their evaluations of past performance with what they believe the nominee of the opposition party would do. For example, even if voters held Reagan responsible for budget deficits, and even if they held his vice president responsible, they might conclude that Dukakis's programs would not be any better at reducing the deficit.

We will now examine some illustrative retrospective evaluations and study their impact on voter choice. We will pay special attention to how similar patterns in 1988 are to prior elections (such as 1980 and 1984) in which the incumbent president was seeking reelection directly. In Chapter 6 we looked at issue scales designed to measure what the public saw the candidates as promising to do in office. Of course, the public can evaluate not only the incumbent party's promises but also its actions. We will compare promises with performance in this chapter, but one must remember that the distinctions are not as sharp in practice as they are in principle.[6] Of course, the Downs-Fiorina view is that past actions and projections about the future are necessarily intertwined.

Evaluations of Governmental Performance

What do you consider the "most important problem" facing the country, and how do you feel the "government in Washington" has been handling the problem? These questions are designed to measure retrospective judgments. Table 7-1 uses the National Election Study (NES) surveys to compare the respondents' evaluations of governmental performance on the problem that each respondent identified as the single most important problem facing the country. We are able to track such evaluations for the past five elections.[7] The most striking finding is that in 1988, a majority of respondents thought the government was doing a poor job in handling the problem. Granted, overall evaluations were even lower in 1980 than in 1988, but these elections were clearly the contests with the lowest approval of the government's performance.[8]

If the voter is a rational god of vengeance and reward, we can expect a strong relationship between the evaluation of government performance and the vote. Such is indeed the case for all elections, as seen in Table 7-1B. From seven to nine people in ten who thought the government was doing a good job on the most important problem voted for the incumbent party's nominee in each election. That Bush was the only incumbent vice president (rather than incumbent president) to run in this period appears relatively immaterial, as four of five who thought the government was doing a good job voted for him, three in five who thought the government's performance only fair supported him, and a bit more than two in five who thought it was poor voted for him. Bush, in fact, did better among this last group of voters than any candidate of the incumbent party since Richard Nixon.

According to Downs and Fiorina, it is important not just to know how things have been going, but also to assess how that evaluation compares with the alternative. In recent elections respondents have been asked which party would do a better job solving the problem they

Table 7-1　Evaluation of Governmental Performance on Most Important Problem and Major Party Vote, 1972-1988

	1972[a]	1976	1980	1984	1988
A. Evaluation of Performance on Most Important Problem					
Government is doing:					
Good job	12%	8%	4%	16%	8%
Only fair job	58	46	35	46	37
Poor job	30	46	61	39	56
Total percent	100%	100%	100%	101%	101%
(N)	(993)	(2,156)[b]	(1,319)	(1,797)	(1,672)
B. Percentage of Major Party Vote for Incumbent Party's Nominee					
Government is doing:					
Good job	85	72	81	89	82
(N)	(91)	(128)[b]	(43)	(214)	(93)
Only fair job	69	53	55	65	61
(N)	(390)	(695)[b]	(289)	(579)	(429)
Poor job	46	39	33	37	44
(N)	(209)	(684)[b]	(505)	(494)	(631)

Note: Numbers in parentheses are totals upon which percentages are based.

[a]These questions were asked of a randomly selected half of the sample in 1972. In 1972, the question wording and responses were different. Respondents were asked whether the government was being (a) very helpful, (b) somewhat helpful, or (c) not helpful at all in solving this most important problem.
[b]Weighted *N*s.

named as the most important, and Table 7-2A shows the responses to this question.[9] This question is clearly future oriented, but it may call for judgments about past performance, consistent with the Downs-Fiorina view. It does not ask the respondent to evaluate policy alternatives, and thus responses are likely to be based on a retrospective comparison of how the incumbent party has handled things with a projection about how the opposition would fare. We therefore view this question as a measure of comparative retrospective evaluations to make future projections.

By comparing Tables 7-1A and 7-2A, we can see that in 1988 nearly three times as many people thought the Republican party would be better at handling the most important problem as thought the government was already doing a good job with it. Based upon the results in Table 7-1A, one might have guessed that 1988 would be a bad year for the incumbent Republicans. The data in Table 7-2A indicate something different. A majority, the largest proportion in these recent elections, thought neither party would do a better job handling the most important problem. The rest were nearly evenly divided between the two parties. In Table 7-1A, the 1988 data are most like the data from 1980, a year in which the incumbent was defeated for reelection. The data for these two elections in Table 7-2A are very different, since in 1980 many more saw the opposition party as the better bet for handling the most important problem. The data in this table indicate that 1988 was most like 1972, an election in which neither party was, on balance, advantaged on this measure, and an election in which the incumbent was reelected by a landslide. Clearly, there is more going on here than a mere judgment of the performance of the incumbent. The comparative assessment of the two parties' expected performance, while strongly related to the evaluation of the government, goes beyond merely repeating that judgment.

As Table 7-2B reveals, the relationship between the party seen as better on the most important problem and the vote is very strong—stronger than that found in Table 7-1B, examining voters and their perception of governmental handling of that problem. In this case, 1988 looks most like 1984, an overwhelming relationship. Over nine in ten who thought the Democratic party was the better bet for handling the voter's most important concern voted for the Democratic candidate, while more than nine in ten who thought the Republican party was better voted for its nominee. The majority who thought there was little difference between the parties on this concern voted pretty much the way the electorate as a whole did, giving Bush an edge. It appears that one way to win a vote is to convince the voter your party will be better at handling whatever concerns that voter the most. If neither candidate convinces the voter that his or her party is better, the voter apparently looks to other factors.

The data presented in Tables 7-1 and 7-2 have two limitations. First, as we saw in Chapter 6, there was considerable diversity, especially in 1988, over what problems most concerned respondents. It is therefore harder to make comparisons and interpret the findings. Are those who expressed concern about the budget deficits, for example, similar to those who were concerned about drugs, about international relations, or about social welfare? Second, in the first question, the reference is to "the government" and not to the incumbent president (is it the president, Congress, both, or even others such as the bureaucracy or the courts who are handling the job poorly?), and it is to the "political party" and not the candidate in the second question. So, we will look a bit more carefully at the incumbent and at people's evaluations of comparable problems where there are data to permit such comparisons.

Table 7-2 Evaluation of Party Seen as Better on Most Important Problem and Major Party Vote, 1972-1988

	1972[a]	1976	1980	1984	1988
A. Distribution of Responses on Party Better on Most Important Problem					
Republican	28%	14%	43%	32%	22%
No difference	46	50	46	44	54
Democratic	26	37	11	25	24
Total percent	100%	101%	100%	101%	100%
(*N*)	(931)	(2,054)[b]	(1,251)	(1,785)	(1,655)
B. Percentage of Major Party Voters Who Voted Democratic for President					
Republican	6	3	12	5	5
(*N*)	(207)	(231)[b]	(391)	(464)	(295)
No difference	32	35	63	41	46
(*N*)	(275)	(673)[b]	(320)	(493)	(564)
Democratic	75	89	95	91	92
(*N*)	(180)	(565)[b]	(93)	(331)	(284)

Note: Numbers in parentheses are totals upon which percentages are based.

[a]These questions were asked of a randomly selected half of the sample in 1972. In 1972, respondents were asked which party would be more likely to get the government to be helpful in solving the most important problem.
[b]Weighted *N*s.

Economic Evaluations and the Vote for the Incumbent

More than any others, economic issues have received attention as retrospective issues. The impact of economic conditions on congressional and presidential elections has been studied extensively.[10] Popular evaluations of presidential effectiveness, John E. Mueller has pointed out, are strongly influenced by the economy.[11] Edward R. Tufte has suggested that because the incumbent realizes his fate may hinge on the performance of the economy, he may attempt to manipulate it, leading to what is known as a "political business cycle."[12] Carter's defeat in the 1980 election was due largely to the perception that economic performance was weak during his administration. Reagan's rhetorical question in the 1980 debate with Carter, "Are you better off than you were four years ago?" indicates that politicians realize the power such arguments have with the

Table 7-3   Assessments of Personal Financial Situation and Major
Party Vote, 1972-1988

QUESTION: Would you say that you (and your family here) are better off or
worse off financially than you were a year ago?

	1972[a]	1976	1980	1984	1988
A. Distribution of Responses					
Better now	36%	34%	33%	44%	42%
Same	42	35	25	28	33
Worse now	23	31	42	27	25
Total percent	101%	100%	100%	99%	100%
(*N*)	(955)	(2,828)[b]	(1,393)	(1,956)	(2,025)

**B. Percentage of Major Party Voters Who Voted for the Incumbent
Party's Nominee**

	1972	1976	1980	1984	1988
Better now	69	55	46	74	63
(*N*)	(247)	(574)[b]	(295)	(612)	(489)
Same	70	52	46	55	50
(*N*)	(279)	(571)[b]	(226)	(407)	(405)
Worse now	52	38	40	33	40
(*N*)	(153)	(475)[b]	(351)	(338)	(283)

Note: Numbers in parentheses are totals upon which percentages are based.

[a]These questions were asked of a randomly selected half of the sample in 1972.
[b]Weighted *N*s.

electorate. And, Reagan's sweeping reelection victory in 1984 was due
largely to the very different and more positive perception that economic
performance during his first term was, in spite of a deep midterm
recession, much stronger.

If people are concerned about economic outcomes, especially those
that affect them directly, they should start by looking for an answer to
the sort of question Reagan asked. Table 7-3A presents respondents'
perceptions of whether they were financially better off than one year
earlier. From 1972 to 1980, about a third of the sample felt they were
better off. Over that period, however, more and more of the remainder
felt they were worse off. By 1980 "worse now" was the most common
response. By 1984 the economic recovery was felt by many, and more
than two of five felt they were better off than the previous year; only a
little more than one in four felt worse off. Of course, 1984 was only two
years after a deep recession. Therefore, many may have seen their

economic fortunes improve considerably over the preceding year or so. In 1988 that recovery had been sustained. So, too, were the responses to the question. The distribution of responses to this question in 1988 are very similar to those of 1984. These views were as good news for Bush as they had been for Reagan in 1984, but they were bad news for their Democratic opponents.

Just how good or bad the news was is shown in Table 7-3B, in which the responses to this question are related to the two-party presidential vote. We can see that the relationship between the respondents' financial situations and their vote is often not particularly strong. Even so, those who felt their financial status had become worse in the last year were always the least likely to support the incumbent. Moreover, the relationship between this variable and the vote became considerably stronger in 1984 and only slightly less so in 1988. Thus, there is some relationship between the voters' pocketbooks and their vote, and the Republicans have benefited from a relatively strong relationship in the last two elections.

People may vote their pocketbooks, but people are even more likely to vote retrospectively based on their judgments of how the economy as a whole has been faring. In 1980, about 40 percent thought their own financial situation was worse than the year before, but twice as many (84 percent) thought the national economy was worse off than the year before. In the first two columns of Table 7-4A, we see that there was quite a change in the perceptions of the fortunes of the national economy between 1984 and 1988. In 1984, the improved status of personal finances almost matched perceptions of the status of the economy as a whole. If anything, there was a more positive view of the status of the national economy than of respondents' personal finances. In 1988, the personal financial situation was quite like that in 1984, but perceptions of the national economy were clearly more negative. Half the sample thought the national economy was about the same in 1988 as a year earlier, nearly a third thought it was worse, and only one in five thought it had improved. Thus, perceptions of one's personal fortunes may be very different from those of the economy as a whole.

The next question is whether the respondents believe that the federal government and its policies have shaped these economic fortunes. For both personal and national economic well being, more thought that the federal government policies had made the situation better in 1984 than in 1988. Thus, the good news for Reagan was a bit less positive for Bush. Notice, too, that in both years, people were likely to see federal government policies as having less effect on their own fortunes than on the nation's economy.

In Table 7-4B, we show the relationship between responses to these items and the two-party vote for president. As we can see, this

Table 7-4 Public's View of the State of the Economy, Government Economic Policies, and Major Party Vote, 1984, 1988

	Would you say that over the past year the nation's economy has gotten [responses]?		Would you say that the economic policies of the federal government have made you [responses]?		Would you say that the economic policies of the federal government have made the nation's economy [responses]?	
	1984	1988	1984	1988	1984	1988
A. Distribution of Responses						
Better [off]	44%	19%	19%	12%	38%	20%
Stayed same/have not made much difference	33	50	59	67	40	57
Worse [off]	23	31	22	22	22	23
Total percent	100%	100%	100%	101%	100%	100%
(N)	(1,904)	(1,956)	(1,891)	(1,992)	(1,841)	(1,895)

B. Percentage of Major Party Voters Who Voted for the Incumbent Party's Nominee

	1984	1988	1984	1988	1984	1988
Better [off]	80	77	86	79	84	83
(N)	(646)	(249)	(282)	(153)	(544)	(258)
Stayed same/have not made much difference	53	53	58	55	52	50
(N)	(413)	(568)	(757)	(742)	(457)	(606)
Worse [off]	21	34	30	34	23	30
(N)	(282)	(348)	(281)	(276)	(302)	(275)

Note: Numbers in parentheses are the totals upon which percentages are based.

relationship between these measures and the vote is always quite strong, somewhat more so in 1984 than in 1988, but still quite robust in 1988. Moreover, comparing the bottom halves of Tables 7-3B and 7-4B shows that, in general, the vote is more closely associated with perceptions of the nation's economy and the role the government has been seen to play in it than it is with perceptions of one's personal economic well-being.

To this point, we have looked at personal and national economic conditions and the role of the government in shaping them. We have not

Table 7-5   Evaluations of the Government's/Incumbent's Handling of the Economy and Major Party Vote, 1972-1988

	Government performance on inflation/ unemployment		Approval of incumbent's handling of the economy		
	1972[a]	1976[b]	1980[c]	1984[d]	1988[d]

A. Distribution of Responses

Positive view	22%	15%	18%	58%	54%
Neutral/balanced	59	45	17	—	—
Negative view	19	39	65	42	46
Total percent	100%	99%	100%	100%	100%
(N)	(941)	(2,664)[e]	(1,097)	(1,858)	(1,897)

B. Percentage of Major Party Voters Who Voted for the Incumbent Party's Nominee

Positive view	91	79	88	86	80
(N)	(149)	(247)[e]	(130)	(801)	(645)
Neutral/balanced	68	57	60	—	—
(N)	(401)	(688)[e]	(114)		
Negative view	30	26	23	16	17
(N)	(122)	(597)[e]	(451)	(515)	(492)

[a]Questions asked of randomly selected half sample, asking whether the government had done a good (positive), fair (neutral), or poor (negative) job on handling inflation and unemployment, combined.

[b]Two questions asked in fashion similar to 1972. A "positive (negative) view" was good (poor) on both, or on one, "fair" on the other. Neutral/balanced was any other combination of nonmissing responses.

[c]In 1980 the questions asked whether the respondent approved or disapproved of Carter's handling of inflation (unemployment). A positive (negative) view was approve (disapprove) on both; balanced responses were approve on one, disapprove on the other.

[d]In 1984 and 1988 the question was whether the respondent approved of Reagan's handling of the economy.

[e]Weighted N's.

yet looked at the extent to which such evaluations are attributed to the incumbent. In Table 7-5, we report responses to the question of whether people approved of Reagan's handling of the economy in 1984 and 1988 and of Carter's handling of the economy in 1980. We also include perceptions respondents held of government performance on inflation and unemployment in the 1972 and 1976 NES surveys. These comparisons are difficult to make because different questions were asked in the earlier surveys. Still, even with different questions, it seems quite reasonable to conclude that the public held far more positive views of Reagan's performance than of that of any of the three administrations that preceded his. While a majority approved of Reagan's handling of the economy in both election years, less than one in four held positive views of economic performance in the Nixon, Ford, and Carter years. Clearly, Carter was perceived the most negatively, but no other administration was seen in nearly as positive a light as Reagan's.

The bottom-line questions are whether these views are related to voter choice, and, for 1988, whether the positive views of Reagan transferred to his vice president. As the data in Table 7-5B show, the answer to both questions is yes. Those who held a positive view of the incumbents' performance on the economy were very likely to vote for the incumbent party's candidate; that eight of ten backed Bush in 1988 is only a bit lower than the norm. Large majorities of those with negative views voted to "throw the rascals out." Notice that this was as true for Bush as for any incumbent. The relatively closer vote in 1988 than in 1984, then, is due to the somewhat less positive marks for Reagan in 1988 and a slightly lower ability of Bush to win the support of those approving of Reagan's handling of the economy.

Other Retrospective Evaluations

Although economic concerns have been central to all recent elections and have dominated studies of retrospective voting, other retrospective judgments also have influenced voters.

Foreign affairs is another important area for retrospective evaluations. Peace shares with prosperity many of the same properties that make it an important retrospective concern. In general, the public's views of Reagan's handling of relations with foreign countries in 1984 and 1988 were mixed but slightly positive. In 1984, 53 percent approved of his handling of foreign relations, while this figure increased to a higher 61 percent in 1988. However, in 1988, 37 percent thought that the chances that the United States would get involved in a war had increased, while 34 percent said the chances were the same, and 29 percent thought they had decreased. Also, 38 percent thought the U.S. position in the world had weakened over the past year, compared with 24 percent who thought it had gotten stronger and 39 percent who thought it had stayed the same. These figures are about comparable to the concern people expressed in 1984 about the chances for a nuclear war, with one-third saying they were very worried about "our country getting into a nuclear war at this time," a third saying they were somewhat worried, and the final third saying they were not worried. As we found before, there is a difference between seeing a problem with current policies and thinking the opposition party would be better at solving it. In 1988, a majority (54 percent) thought the two parties were about equally likely to keep the United States out of war, but among the rest, the Republicans held a 10-point advantage. That is, 18 percent thought the Democrats would be better at keeping the United States out of war, but 28 percent thought the Republican party would be better. Moreover, this latter measure is more strongly related to the vote than the assessment of the current situation, just as we found for economic issues. Eighty-nine percent of those who thought the Republican party better at keeping the U.S. out of war voted for Bush, while 90 percent who thought the Democrats better voted for Dukakis. Fifty-five percent of those who saw no difference between the parties on this measure voted for Dukakis.[13]

Specific events, policies, or problems also serve as a basis for retrospective evaluations, and these are sometimes very strongly related to the vote. Prominent examples are Gerald R. Ford's pardon of Nixon and its role in the 1976 election, and Carter's handling of the Iranian hostage crisis and of the Soviet invasion of Afghanistan, both in 1980.[14] In other words, the importance of retrospective economic evaluations has been due to the nature of the times and to the importance of economic concerns, not to their being the sole basis on which the public can form retrospective judgments.

Evaluations of the Incumbent

Fiorina distinguishes between "simple" and "mediated" retrospective evaluations. By *simple* Fiorina means evaluations of the direct effects of social outcomes on the person, such as one's financial status or direct perceptions of the nation's economic well-being. *Mediated* retrospective evaluations are evaluations seen through or mediated by the perceptions of political actors and institutions. Approval of Reagan's handling of foreign relations or the assessment of which party would better handle the most important problem facing the country are examples.[15]

As we have seen, the more politically mediated the question, the more closely responses align with voting behavior. Perhaps the ultimate in mediated evaluations is the presidential approval question: "Do you approve or disapprove of the way (the incumbent) is handling his job as president?" (Sometimes the evaluation is erroneously referred to as presidential popularity, especially in the media.) From a retrospective voting standpoint, this evaluation is a summary of all aspects of his service in office. Table 7-6 reports the distribution of these evaluations and their relationship to major party voting in the last five elections.[16]

As can be seen in Table 7-6A, the three Republican incumbents have enjoyed widespread approval whereas only two respondents in five

Table 7-6 Distribution of Responses on President's Handling of Job and Major Party Vote, 1972-1988

QUESTION: Do you approve or disapprove of the way (the incumbent) is handling his job as president?

	1972[a]	1976	1980	1984	1988
A. Distribution of Responses					
Approve	71%	63%	41%	63%	60%
Disapprove	29	37	59	37	40
Total percent	100%	100%	100%	100%	100%
(N)	(1,215)	(2,439)[b]	(1,475)	(2,091)	(1,935)

B. Percentage of Major Party Voters Who Voted for the Incumbent Party's Nominee

	1972	1976	1980	1984	1988
Approve	83	74	81	87	79
(N)	(553)	(935)[b]	(315)	(863)	(722)
Disapprove	14	9	18	7	12
(N)	(203)	(523)[b]	(491)	(449)	(442)

Note: Numbers in parentheses are totals upon which percentages are based.

[a]Question was asked of a randomly selected half sample in 1972.
[b]Weighted Ns.

approved of Carter's handling of his job. As can be seen in Table 7-6B, there is a very strong relationship between approval of the incumbent and the vote for that incumbent—or his vice president. Like all actual incumbent presidents, Bush as vice president held a great proportion of the support of those who approved of the incumbent—and lost a vast majority of the votes of those who disapproved. We can see why Bush would seek to accentuate his ties to Reagan, so that he could be the beneficiary of the president's high approval ratings.

The Impact of Retrospective Evaluations

Our evidence strongly suggests that retrospective voting was widespread in all recent elections. Moreover, as far as data permit us to judge, the evidence is clearly on the side of the Downs-Fiorina view. Retrospective evaluations appear to be used to make comparative judgments. Presumably, voters find it easier, less time consuming, and less risky to evaluate the incumbent party on what its president did in the most recent term or terms in office than on the nominees' promises for the future. And yet that evaluation is used not as a referendum, as a rational god of vengeance or reward, but for making comparisons between the two major contenders. Thus, the strongest relationships between retrospective evaluations and the vote are found in Table 7-2, where voters are asked to compare the two major political parties. In 1988, many believed that the government had performed poorly on their most important concern but that the incumbent president had done well. Dukakis was, however, unable to convince people that Bush did not deserve much of the credit for the successes of the Republican administration and also, and more important, as Table 7-2 reveals, he failed to convince the public that the Democratic party would better handle their concerns.

We can strengthen the overall assessment of retrospective voting in the last few elections by forming a combined index of retrospective evaluations common to the four most recent presidential election surveys. In Figure 7-1, we report the result of combining the presidential approval measure with the evaluation of the job the government has done on the most important problem and the assessment of which party would better handle that problem.[17] This creates a seven-point scale ranging from strongly supportive of the job the incumbent and his party have done to strongly opposed to that performance. For instance, in 1984 and 1988, those who approved of Reagan's job performance, thought the government was doing a good job of handling the nation's most important problem, and thought the Republican party would better handle that problem scored as strongly supportive of the incumbent party in their retrospective evaluations.

In Figure 7-1, we report the distribution of responses on this combined measure. As these figures make clear, respondents had very negative evaluations of the incumbent and his party in 1980, the only year in which the incumbent lost by a sizable margin. In 1984, there was clear support for the incumbent party, and nearly half of the respondents had a pro-incumbent orientation, while only slightly more than one in three had evaluations that favored the opposition. In both 1976, when the incumbent narrowly lost, and in 1988, when the incumbent vice president won the second closest of these elections, the electorate tended to favor the opposition, but by a relatively narrow margin. Moreover, 1976 and 1988 were the two contests in which over a fifth of the electorate held a neutral position on this measure.

As Figure 7-2 shows, respondents who have positive retrospective evaluations of the incumbent party are much more likely to vote for that party than those with negative evaluations. In this case, the support for Bush in 1988 looks similar to that for Reagan in 1984 and Ford in 1976. Carter, in 1980, generally fared better than Republican incumbents, especially among voters negatively disposed to the Democrats. But in

1980 there were far too many voters who were negatively disposed to his party. Reagan's 1984 election can clearly be seen as a result of favorable retrospective evaluations. In 1976, Ford failed to overcome the negative evaluations of government performance and of his party, and he narrowly lost the election. Overall evaluations were about the same in 1988, but Bush fared better than Ford among voters who were slightly favorable to the incumbent party and did not fare as poorly among voters who were moderately against the incumbent.

In sum, the 1976 election, with its razor-thin edge for Carter, was a very narrow rejection of Ford's incumbency, and 1980 was a clear and strong rejection of Carter's. In 1984, Reagan won in large part because he was seen as having performed well and because Mondale was unable to convince the public his party would do better. In 1988, Bush won in large part because Reagan was seen as having performed well—and people thought Bush would stay the course, but such evaluations, especially of performance on the most important problem, were less positive than four years earlier. Hence, the vote was closer in 1988 than in 1984.

There is obviously more to the differences between these elections than retrospective evaluations alone. In particular, there are also prospective issues. As you may recall from Chapter 6, especially Figure 6-4, this measure is also strongly related to the vote, and its effect seems to have been stronger in the last two elections than in the others. Table 7-7 presents the joint relationship of both types of policy evaluation measures with the vote for Bush, collapsing both measures into pro-Republican, neutral, and pro-Democratic categories. Reading across each row, we see that retrospective evaluations are strongly related to the way people voted, even when one controls for overall prospective evaluations. Reading down each column, we see that prospective issue preferences are related to the vote, even when one controls for retrospective judgments. For the 1976 and 1980 elections, we found little relationship between prospective issues and the vote, once retrospective measures were taken into account. For 1984, we found that prospective measures had some effect on the vote.[18] For 1988, however, the effect is even more pronounced. Retrospective evaluations were more important than prospective ones, but the latter remained an important factor in the vote, and a factor that has grown increasingly important over the 1980s.

Although these two measures together suggest that policy voting was very strong in 1988, the explanation is as yet incomplete. In the first place, the results so far do not account for Ford's failure to win in 1976 and for Bush's modest popular vote victory twelve years later. More important, we have not accounted for why people held the views they did on these two measures. We cannot provide a complete account of the origins of people's views, but there is one important source we can examine. Party identification, a variable we have already used in other

Figure 7-1 Distribution of Electorate on Summary Measure of Retrospective Evaluations, 1976-1988

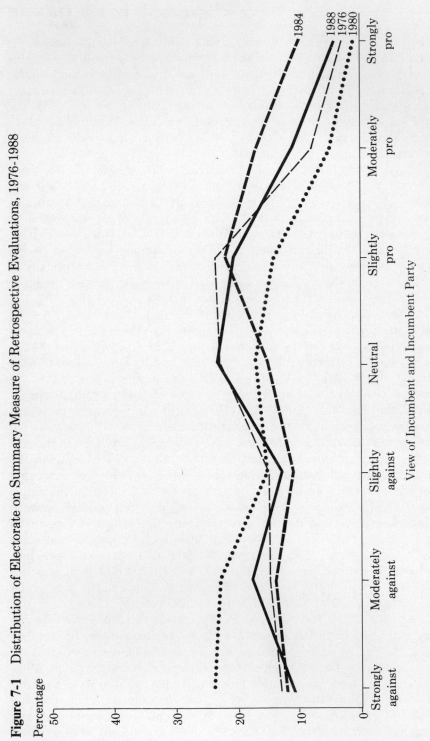

Note: The total number of cases: 1976, 2,166 (weighted); 1980, 1,325; 1984, 1,814; 1988, 1,909.

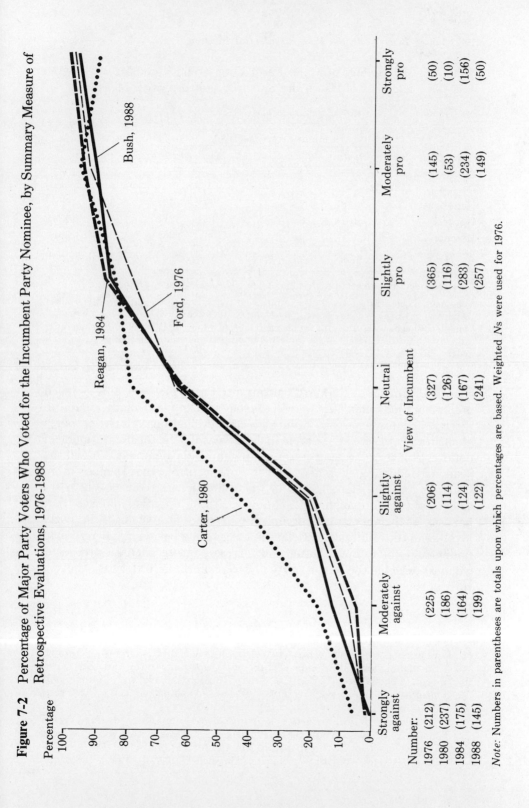

Figure 7-2 Percentage of Major Party Voters Who Voted for the Incumbent Party Nominee, by Summary Measure of Retrospective Evaluations, 1976-1988

Percentage

	Strongly against	Moderately against	Slightly against	Neutral	Slightly pro	Moderately pro	Strongly pro
Number:				View of Incumbent			
1976	(212)	(225)	(206)	(327)	(365)	(145)	(50)
1980	(237)	(186)	(114)	(126)	(116)	(53)	(10)
1984	(175)	(164)	(124)	(167)	(283)	(234)	(156)
1988	(145)	(199)	(122)	(241)	(257)	(149)	(50)

Note: Numbers in parentheses are totals upon which percentages are based. Weighted *N*s were used for 1976.

Table 7-7   Percentage of Major Party Voters Who Voted for Bush by Balance of Issues and Summary Retrospective Measures, 1988

Balance of issues[a]	Summary retrospective[b]							
	Republican		Neutral		Democratic		Total	
	%	(*N*)	%	(*N*)	%	(*N*)	%	(*N*)
Republican	98	(198)	78	(79)	29	(72)	79	(349)
Neutral	87	(181)	65	(111)	14	(161)	56	(453)
Democratic	78	(77)	41	(51)	4	(233)	25	(361)
Total	90	(456)	64	(241)	11	(466)	53	(1,163)

Note: Numbers in parentheses are totals upon which percentages are based.

[a]The neutral category is a score of −1, 0, or 1 on the full measure, while the Republican (Democratic) category is any score greater than 1 (less than −1) on the full measure.

[b]The neutral category is the same as on the full scale, while the Republican (Democratic) category is the combination of all three Republican (Democratic) categories on the full scale.

chapters, provides a powerful means for the typical citizen to reach preliminary judgments. As we will see, partisanship is strongly related to these judgments, especially to retrospective evaluations. Moreover, party identification plays a central role in debates about the future of American politics. Will there be a partisan realignment? a dealignment? Or will the years of federal government under split control, the Democrats in Congress and the Republicans in the White House, continue in a so-called split-level realignment? Many political scientists believe that partisan realignments can occur only if there are changes in party loyalties in the electorate as well as in their voting behavior. Therefore, to understand voter choice better and to assess future partisan prospects, we must examine the role of party loyalties, and it is to this task that we turn in the next chapter.

Notes

1. For our conclusions about these two elections, see Paul R. Abramson, John H. Aldrich, and David W. Rohde, *Change and Continuity in the 1980 Elections,* rev. ed. (Washington, D.C.: CQ Press, 1983), chap. 7; and *Change and Continuity in the 1984 Elections,* rev. ed. (Washington, D.C.: CQ Press, 1987), chap. 7.
2. V. O. Key; Jr., *Politics, Parties, and Pressure Groups,* 5th ed. (New York: Thomas Y. Crowell, 1964), 568. Key's theory of retrospective voting is most fully developed in *The Responsible Electorate: Rationality in Presidential Voting, 1936-1960* (Cambridge, Mass.: Harvard University Press, 1966).

3. Anthony Downs, *An Economic Theory of Democracy* (New York: Harper & Row, 1957).
4. Morris P. Fiorina, *Retrospective Voting in American National Elections* (New Haven, Conn.: Yale University Press, 1981), 83.
5. See Benjamin I. Page, *Choices and Echoes in Presidential Elections: Rational Man and Electoral Democracy* (Chicago: University of Chicago Press, 1978). He argues that "party cleavages" distinguish the party at the candidate and mass levels.
6. See Arthur H. Miller and Martin P. Wattenberg, "Throwing the Rascals Out: Policy and Performance Evaluations of Presidential Candidates, 1952-1980," *American Political Science Review* 79 (June 1985): 359-372.
7. Each respondent assesses governmental performance on the problem he or she considers the most important. In the four most recent surveys, respondents were asked, "How good a job is the government doing in dealing with this problem—a good job, only fair, or a poor job?" In 1988, respondents were specifically asked how good a job "the government in Washington" was doing.
8. Negative evaluations are not surprising. After all, if you thought the government had been doing a good job with the problem, then it probably would not be your major concern.
9. Since 1976, this question has been worded as follows: "Which political party do you think would be most likely to get the government to do a better job in dealing with this problem—the Republicans, the Democrats, or wouldn't there be much difference between them?"
10. See Gerald H. Kramer, "Short-Term Fluctuations in U.S. Voting Behavior, 1896-1964," *American Political Science Review* 65 (March 1971): 131-143; Fiorina, *Retrospective Voting;* M. Stephen Weatherford, "Economic Conditions and Electoral Outcomes: Class Differences in the Political Response to Recession," *American Journal of Political Science* 22 (November 1978): 917-938; D. Roderick Kiewiet and Douglas Rivers, "A Retrospective on Retrospective Voting," *Political Behavior* 6: 4 (1984): 369-393; Kiewiet, *Macroeconomics and Micropolitics: The Electoral Effects of Economic Issues* (Chicago: University of Chicago Press, 1983); and Michael S. Lewis-Beck, *Economics and Elections: The Major Western Democracies* (Ann Arbor: University of Michigan Press, 1988).
11. John E. Mueller, *War, Presidents and Public Opinion* (New York: John Wiley & Sons, 1973).
12. Edward R. Tufte, *Political Control of the Economy* (Princeton, N.J.: Princeton University Press, 1978). For a perceptive critique of the business cycle formulation, see James E. Alt and K. Alec Chrystal, *Political Economics* (Berkeley: University of California Press, 1983).
13. Fiorina, in *Retrospective Voting,* provides an analysis of these questions in earlier surveys. He also shows that these variables have an impact on the vote independent of the economic measures.
14. See Abramson, Aldrich, and Rohde, *Change and Continuity in the 1980 Elections,* rev. ed., 151 and Table 7-6, 152.
15. Fiorina, *Retrospective Voting.*
16. In the 1984 and 1988 surveys, this question was asked both in the preelection and in the postelection waves of the survey. Since attitudes held by the public before the election are what counts in influencing their choice, we use the first question. In both surveys, approval of Reagan's performance was more positive in the postelection interview: 66 percent approved of his performance in 1984, 68 percent approved in 1988.

17. To construct this measure, we awarded respondents two points if they approved of the president's performance (from the preelection wave of the survey), one if they had no opinion, and none if they disapproved. Second, respondents received two points if they thought the government was doing a good job in handling the most important problem facing the country, one if they thought the government was doing only a fair job, and none if they thought it was doing a poor job. Finally, respondents received two points if they thought the incumbent president's party would do a better job in handling the most important problem, one point if they thought there was no difference between the parties, and no points if they thought the challenger's party would do a better job. For all three questions, "don't know" and "not ascertained" responses were scored as 1, but respondents with more than one such response were excluded from the analysis. Scores on our measure were the sum of the individual values for the three questions, and thus ranged from a low of 0 (strongly against the incumbent's party) to a high of 6 (strongly for the incumbent's party). Thus, the measure has seven possible values, corresponding to the seven categories in Figures 7-1 and 7-2. Our summary measure of retrospective evaluations cannot be created with the 1972 NES survey. The presidential approval question was asked of a different half of the sample than was asked the most important problems question.

18. For data from the 1976 and 1980 elections, see Abramson, Aldrich, and Rohde, *Change and Continuity in the 1980 Elections,* rev. ed., Table 7-8, 156. For data from the 1984 elections, see Abramson, Aldrich, and Rohde, *Change and Continuity in the 1984 Elections,* rev. ed., Table 7-8, 204.

Chapter 8

Party Loyalties, Policy Preferences, Performance Evaluations, and the Vote

Political parties are central institutions in our political and electoral system. In most election years, all major presidential candidates are members of one of the two major parties, and all run for their party's nomination. Most citizens identify with a political party; this identification influences their political attitudes and, ultimately, their behavior. In the 1950s and 1960s the authors of *The American Voter*, along with other scholars, began to emphasize the importance of party loyalties.[1] Although today few would deny that partisanship is central to political attitudes and behavior, many scholars question the interpretation of the evidence gathered during that period. Indeed, what is party identification and how does it actually structure other attitudes and behavior? We will try to answer these questions before examining the role that party identification played in the 1988 presidential election.

Party Identification:
The Standard View

According to the authors of *The American Voter*, party identification is "the individual's affective orientation to an important group-object in his environment," in this case the political party.[2] In other words, Americans see that there are two major political parties that play significant roles in elections and develop an affinity for one of them. Most Americans develop a liking for either the Republican or the Democratic party. Most of the rest are independents, who are not only unattached to a party but also relatively unattached to politics in general.[3] They are less interested, informed, and active than their attached peers. Partisanship is, therefore, an evaluation of the two parties, but its implications extend to a wider variety of political phenomena. Angus Campbell and his colleagues measured partisanship simply by asking respondents which party they identified with and how strongly that identification was held.[4] If the individual does not identify with either party, he or she may lean toward a party or, if not, be "purely" independent. The small percentage who cannot relate to the party identification questions is "apolitical."[5]

Partisan identification in this view becomes an attachment or loyalty not unlike that observed between the individual and other groups or organizations in society, such as a religious body, social class, or even a favorite sports team. As with loyalties to many of these groups, partisan affiliation often begins early. One of the first political attitudes children develop is partisan identification, and it develops well before they acquire policy preferences and many other political orientations. Furthermore, as with other group loyalties, once an attachment to a party develops, it tends to endure. Some people do switch parties, of course, but they usually do so only if their social situation changes, if there is an issue of overriding concern that sways their loyalties, or if the political parties themselves change substantially.

Party identification, then, stands as a base or core orientation to electoral politics. It is formed at an early age and endures for most people throughout their lives.[6] Once formed, this core orientation, predicated on a general evaluation of the two parties, affects many other specific orientations. Democratic loyalists tend to evaluate Democratic candidates and officeholders more highly than Republican candidates and officeholders, and vice versa. In effect, one is predisposed to evaluate the promises and performance of one's party leaders relatively higher. It follows, therefore, that Democrats are more likely to vote for Democratic candidates than are Republicans, and vice versa.

Party Identification:
An Alternative View

In *The Responsible Electorate,* published in 1966, V. O. Key, Jr., argued that party loyalties contributed to electoral inertia, with many partisans voting as "standpatters" from election to election.[7] That is, in the absence of any information to the contrary, or if the attractions and disadvantages of the candidates are fairly evenly balanced, partisans are expected to vote for the candidate of their party. Voting for their party's candidates is their standing decision, until and unless they are given good reasons not to. In recent years, scholars have reexamined the reasons for such behavior. In this new view, citizens who consider themselves Democrats have a standing decision to vote for the Democratic nominee because of the past positions of Democrats compared with Republicans and because of their comparative past performances while in office. In short, this view of partisan identification presumes that it is a running tally of past experiences (mostly in terms of policy and performance), a sort of summary expression of political memory, according to Morris P. Fiorina.[8]

Furthermore, when in doubt about what, say, a Democratic candidate is likely to do on civil rights in comparison to the Republican opponent, it is reasonable to assume the Democrat will be more liberal than the Republican—at least until the candidates indicate otherwise. Because the political parties tend to be consistent on the basic historical policy cleavages for lengthy periods of time, summary judgments of parties and their typical candidates will not change radically or often.[9] As a result, one's running tally serves as a good first approximation, changes rarely, and can be an excellent device for saving time and effort that would be spent gathering information in the absence of this memory.

Many of the major findings used in support of the conventional interpretation of party identification are completely consistent with this more policy oriented view. We do not have the evidence to assert that one view is superior to the other. Indeed, the two interpretations are not mutually exclusive. Moreover, they share the important conclusion that party identification plays a central role in shaping voters' decisions.

Party Identification in the Electorate

If partisan identification is a fundamental orientation for most citizens, then the distribution of partisan loyalties is of crucial importance. The National Election Studies (NES) have monitored the party loyalties of the American electorate since 1952, and in Table 8-1 we show the basic distributions of partisan loyalties during the 1980s. Most Americans identify with a political party. In 1988 nearly two-thirds of the sample claimed to think of themselves as a Democrat or Republican, and another one-quarter, who initially said they were independent or had no partisan preference, nonetheless said they felt closer to one of the major parties than the other.[10] Only one in ten was purely independent of a party, and barely one in fifty was classified as apolitical. There was virtually no change in partisan loyalties between the 1984 (preelection) and 1988 surveys. Beginning in the mid-1960s, more people claimed to be independents.[11] This growth stopped, however, in the late 1970s and early 1980s. Similarly, as we saw in Chapter 4, the percentage of strong partisans declined in the same period. Again, this decline stopped and has been partially reversed.

Table 8-1 also shows that more people think of themselves as Democrats than as Republicans. Over the past thirty-six years, the balance between the two parties has favored the Democrats by a range of about 55 to 45 percent to about 60 to 40 percent. While the results from

Table 8-1 Party Identification in Pre- and Postelection Surveys, 1980-1988

Party identification	1980 pre-election	1980 post-election	1982 post-election	1984 pre-election	1984 post-election	1986 post-election	1988 pre-election
Strong Democrat	18%	17%	21%	17%	18%	18%	18%
Weak Democrat	24	24	25	20	22	23	18
Independent, leans Democratic	12	11	11	11	10	11	12
Independent, no partisan leanings	13	12	11	11	7	12	11
Independent, leans Republican	10	12	8	13	14	11	14
Weak Republican	14	14	15	15	15	15	14
Strong Republican	9	10	10	13	15	11	14
Total	100%	100%	101%	100%	101%	101%	101%
(N)	(1,577)	(1,376)	(1,383)	(2,198)	(1,941)	(2,120)	(1,999)
Apolitical	2%	2%	2%	2%	2%	2%	2%
(N)	(35)	(26)	(28)	(38)	(32)	(46)	(33)

Note: In the midterm years, 1982 and 1986, NES conducted only a postelection survey. The 1988 NES survey measured party identification only in the preelection interview.

the last two presidential election years still fall within that range, they show a clear shift toward the Republicans. In the 1980 (preelection) survey, 35 percent of the partisans were Republicans; in 1984, 42 percent were; and in 1988, 44 percent were. Moreover, if independents who lean to a party are counted as partisans, the percentage of Republicans rises from 38 percent (1980 preelection) to 45 percent (1984 preelection) to 47 percent (1984 postelection and 1988 preelection). Thus, the Democratic advantage in loyalties in the electorate has narrowed, an edge made even smaller in practice by the tendency of the Republicans to have a higher rate of turnout than Democrats (see Chapter 4).

The shift toward Republican party loyalties during the 1980s is also revealed in other surveys. The most useful data are provided by the General Social Surveys conducted by the National Opinion Research Center (NORC) of the University of Chicago, since NORC surveys are based upon in-person interviews employing multistage probability sampling, and since their measure of party identification is very similar to that employed by the NES.[12] The NORC surveys show that the percentage of party identifiers calling themselves Republicans rose from 37 percent in early 1980 to 40 percent in early 1984. By early 1985, the percentage rose to 43 percent. Since then, the percentage identifying as Republican has fluctuated slightly, falling to 40 percent in early 1986, but inching upward to 41 percent in early 1987, and returning to 43 percent in early 1988. In early 1989, 47 percent of all party identifiers were Republicans. Moreover, in most of these years, the percentage supporting the Republican party is slightly higher if independents who lean toward a party are included in the calculations. These surveys still show that more Americans identify as Democrats than Republicans, but the Democratic advantage was reduced substantially during Ronald Reagan's presidency.

Gallup surveys, which have been monitoring party loyalties since 1937, also found a sizable shift toward the GOP during the 1980s. The Gallup Organization also conducts representative surveys of the adult population that rely upon in-person interviews, and, although their measure of partisanship differs from that of the NES, Gallup surveys provide a useful data base for studying change.[13] In 1980, 46 percent of the Gallup respondents claimed to be Democrats, while only 24 percent said they were Republicans, giving the Democrats a nearly two-to-one lead among party identifiers. The Republicans made few gains through 1983, but in 1984 the Democrats fell to 40 percent support, while some 31 percent identified with the Republicans. By 1985, the Democrats' strength fell to 38 percent, with the Republicans' rising to 33 percent. Forty-six percent of the party identifiers supported the GOP. Although Republican strength in the Gallup polls has ebbed slightly since 1985, the Republicans are still substantially stronger than they were back in 1980. For example, surveys of 3,088 respondents conducted from July through

Table 8-2 Party Identification Among Whites, 1952-1988

Party identification[a]	1952	1954	1956	1958	1960	1962	1964	1966	1968
Strong Democrat	21%	22%	20%	26%	20%	22%	24%	17%	16%
Weak Democrat	25	25	23	22	25	23	25	27	25
Independent, leans Democratic	10	9	6	7	6	8	9	9	10
Independent, no partisan leanings	6	7	9	8	9	8	8	12	11
Independent, leans Republican	7	6	9	5	7	7	6	8	10
Weak Republican	14	15	14	17	14	17	14	16	16
Strong Republican	14	13	16	12	17	13	12	11	11
Apolitical	2	2	2	3	1	3	1	1	1
Total percent	99%	99%	99%	100%	100%	101%	99%	101%	100%
(N)	(1,615)	(1,015)	(1,610)	(1,638)[b]	(1,739)[b]	(1,168)	(1,394)	(1,131)	(1,387)

[a]The percentage supporting another party has not been presented; it usually totals less than 1 percent and never totals more than 1 percent.
[b]Weighted Ns.

September of 1988 found that 40 percent said they were Democrats while 31 percent said they were Republicans. Forty-four percent of the party identifiers were Republicans.

Not only have the Republicans made substantial gains in winning party loyalties in the electorate, during the 1980s they have had relatively high levels of support from young Americans. The 1988 NES survey, for example, reveals that among party identifiers born after 1963 ($N = 101$), 53 percent identified as Republicans. Among young white party identifiers ($N = 79$), 65 percent were Republicans. Among the approximately 650 eighteen- to twenty-nine-year-olds surveyed by Gallup from July through September of 1988, 34 percent were Democrats and 33 percent were Republicans. Studies based upon surveys conducted by a variety of polling organizations show that during the mid- to late 1980s, the Republicans have tended to fare better among young Americans than they have among the electorate as a whole.[14]

The shift toward the Republican party is a phenomenon concentrated among white Americans. As we saw in Chapter 5, the sharpest social division in U.S. electoral politics is race, and this division has been reflected in partisan affiliations for decades. Moreover, this division appears to be widening. While the distribution of partisanship in the electorate as a whole is virtually the same in 1988 as it was in 1984, this

1970	1972	1974	1976	1978	1980	1982	1984	1986	1988
17%	12%	15%	13%	12%	14%	16%	15%	14%	14%
22	25	20	23	24	23	24	18	21	16
11	12	13	11	14	12	11	11	10	10
13	13	15	15	14	14	11	11	12	12
9	11	9	11	11	11	9	13	13	15
16	14	15	16	14	16	16	17	17	15
10	11	9	10	9	9	11	14	12	16
1	1	3	1	3	2	2	2	2	1
99%	99%	99%	100%	101%	101%	100%	101%	101%	99%
(1,395)	(2,397)	(2,246)[b]	(2,490)[b]	(2,006)	(1,405)	(1,248)	(1,931)	(1,798)	(1,693)

stability masks a growth in Republican identification among whites, and, of course, a compensating growth of already strong Democratic affiliations among black Americans. In Table 8-2 we report the party identification of whites between 1952 and 1988, and in Table 8-3 we report the affiliation of blacks. As we can see, black and white patterns in partisan affiliation have been very different throughout this period. There was a sharp shift in black loyalties in the mid-1960s. Before then, about 50 percent of blacks were strong or weak Democrats, but from that time, 60 percent, 70 percent, and even greater percentages of blacks considered themselves Democrats.

The party affiliations of whites have changed more slowly. Still, the percentage of self-professed Democrats among whites has declined over the Reagan years, while the percentage of Republicans has increased. In the last two elections, then, affiliation by race has changed, this time due to shifts among whites. In 1984, there was about an even balance among whites between the two parties, if independent leaners are included. By 1988, Republican strength had increased. This time, the number of strong and weak Democrats and strong and weak Republicans was virtually the same. For the first time, there were more strong Republicans than strong Democrats among whites. And adding in the two independent leaning groups gives Republicans a clear advantage in identification among whites.

Table 8-3 Party Identification Among Blacks, 1952-1988

Party identification[a]	1952	1954	1956	1958	1960	1962	1964	1966	1968
Strong Democrat	30%	24%	27%	32%	25%	35%	52%	30%	56%
Weak Democrat	22	29	23	19	19	25	22	31	29
Independent, leans Democratic	10	6	5	7	7	4	8	11	7
Independent, no partisan leanings	4	5	7	4	16	6	6	14	3
Independent, leans Republican	4	6	1	4	4	2	1	2	1
Weak Republican	8	5	12	11	9	7	5	7	1
Strong Republican	5	11	7	7	7	6	2	2	1
Apolitical	17	15	18	16	14	15	4	3	3
Total percent	100%	101%	100%	100%	101%	100%	100%	100%	101%
(*N*)	(171)	(101)	(146)	(161)[b]	(171)[b]	(110)	(156)	(132)	(149)

[a]The percentage supporting another party has not been presented; it usually totals less than 1 percent and never totals more than 1 percent.
[b]Weighted *N*s.
* Less than 1 percent.

Including the independent leaners as partisans, 53 percent of white partisans are Republicans. Although the increased Republicanism of the white electorate is partly the result of long-term forces, such as generational replacement, the actual movement between 1964 and 1988 appears to result from two shorter-term increases in Republican identification. There is a 5-point movement toward the GOP between 1964 and 1968, and a 10-point movement toward the GOP between 1982 and 1988.

The Gallup polls also reveal a substantial movement toward the Republicans among the white electorate. In 1977, before vigorous Republican party efforts for the 1978 congressional elections, Gallup found that 46 percent of the whites surveyed said they were Democrats, and only 22 percent said they were Republicans. By the fall of 1984, this two-to-one edge disappeared entirely, and the Republicans held a 4-point advantage among whites.[15] Gallup surveys conducted from July through September of 1988 revealed that the Democrats once again had an advantage, but it was negligible. Thirty-six percent of whites interviewed said they were Democrats, while 34 percent said they were Republicans.[16] Forty-nine percent of white party identifiers were Republicans.

Party identification among blacks is very different. In 1988, there were very few black Republicans. To be sure, their numbers have

1970	1972	1974	1976	1978	1980	1982	1984	1986	1988
41%	36%	40%	34%	37%	45%	53%	32%	42%	39%
34	31	26	36	29	27	26	31	30	24
7	8	15	14	15	9	12	14	12	18
12	12	12	8	9	7	5	11	7	6
1	3	*	1	2	3	1	6	2	5
4	4	*	2	3	2	2	1	2	5
0	4	3	2	3	3	0	2	2	1
1	2	4	1	2	4	1	2	2	3
100%	100%	100%	99%	100%	100%	100%	99%	99%	101%
(157)	(267)	(224)[b]	(290)[b]	(230)	(187)	(148)	(247)	(322)	(267)

increased slightly since 1984, especially among weak Republicans. Still, 91 percent of strong and weak identifiers among blacks are Democrats (compared with 50 percent of whites), and, adding in leaners, 87 percent of blacks are Democrats (compared with 47 percent of whites).

These racial differences in partisanship are of long standing, and changes over time have deepened this division. Between 1952 and 1962, blacks were primarily Democratic, but about one in seven supported the Republicans. Black partisanship shifted massively and abruptly even further toward the Democratic party in 1964. In that year over half the black electorate considered themselves *strong* Democrats. Since then, well over half have identified with the Democratic party. Black Republican identification also fell to barely a trace in 1964 and has edged up only very slightly since then.

The reason for the changes in black loyalties in 1964 can be attributed to the two presidential nominees. President Lyndon B. Johnson's advocacy of civil rights legislation appealed directly to black voters, and his Great Society programs in general made an only slightly less direct appeal. Sen. Barry M. Goldwater, the Republican nominee, voted against the 1964 Civil Rights Act, a vote criticized even by his Republican peers. In 1968, Hubert H. Humphrey, the Democratic nominee, was a longtime champion of black causes. The proportion of blacks who were strong Democrats peaked in 1968 and declined some-what since then.

The proportion of blacks considered apolitical dropped from the teens to very small proportions, similar to those among whites, in 1964 as well. This shift can also be attributed to the civil rights movement, the contest between Johnson and Goldwater, and the passage of the Civil Rights Act. The civil rights movement stimulated many blacks, especially in the South, to become politically active. And the 1965 Voting Rights Act enabled many of them to vote for the first time.

There are some signs that the Democratic advantage among blacks may be weakening. The proportion of weak and independent leaning Republicans among blacks increased somewhat between 1984 and 1988. Also, while the proportion of strong Democrats increased, the propor-tion of weak Democrats decreased noticeably, some of them apparently moving to the independent leaning Democratic category. Gallup polls also show a slight movement of blacks away from the Democratic party between 1984 and 1988. Among the approximately 700 blacks inter-viewed by Gallup in the fall of 1984, 13 percent said they were independents; among the approximately 350 blacks interviewed in the polls conducted from July through September of 1988, 16 percent said they were independents. In these 1984 polls, only 7 percent of the blacks interviewed said they were Republicans; in the 1988 polls, 10 percent reported Republican identification. During these four years the percent-age of blacks identifying as Democrats fell from 80 percent to 74 percent. Only time (and party and candidate strategies) will tell whether these small signs of change portend genuine Republican gains among blacks.

Party Identification and the Vote

As we saw in Chapter 4, partisanship is related to turnout. Strong supporters of either party are more likely to vote than weak supporters, and independents who lean toward a party are more likely to vote than independents without partisan leanings. Republicans are somewhat more likely to vote than Democrats. While partisanship influences whether people go to the polls, it is more strongly related to *how* people vote.

Table 8-4 reports the percentage of white, major party voters who voted for the Democratic candidate across all categories of partisanship since 1952. Clearly, there is a strong relationship between partisan affiliation and candidate choice. With the single exception of the 1972 election, the Democratic nominee has received more than 80 percent of the vote of strong Democrats and majority support from both weak Democratic partisans and independent leaners. In 1988, these figures

Table 8-4 Percentage of White Major Party Voters Who Voted Democratic for President, by Party Identification, 1952-1988

Party identification	1952	1956	1960	1964	1968	1972	1976	1980	1984	1988
Strong Democrat	82	85	91	94	89	66	88	87	88	93
Weak Democrat	61	63	70	81	66	44	72	59	63	68
Independent, leans Democratic	60	65	89	89	62	58	73	57	77	86
Independent, no partisan leanings	18	15	50	75	28	26	41	23	21	35
Independent, leans Republican	7	6	13	25	5	11	15	13	5	13
Weak Republican	4	7	11	40	10	9	22	5	6	16
Strong Republican	2	*	2	9	3	2	3	4	2	2

Note: To approximate the numbers upon which these percentages are based, see Table 8-2. Actual *N*s will be smaller than those that can be derived from Table 8-2 because respondents who did not vote (or who voted for a minor party) have been excluded from these calculations. Numbers also will be lower since the voting report is provided in the postelection interviews that usually contain about 10 percent fewer respondents than the preelection interviews in which party identification is measured.

* Less than 1 percent.

were generally higher than at any time since the Democratic landslide of 1964, at least among strong Democrats and independents who leaned Democratic. The picture is even clearer among Republicans. Since 1952, strong Republicans have given the Democratic candidate less than one vote in ten. In 1988, weak Republicans and independents who leaned toward the Republican party voted for Michael S. Dukakis more than they had for Walter F. Mondale in 1984, but, even so, only about one in seven voted Democratic. The pure independent vote, which fluctuates substantially, tends to be Republican, with the exception of 50 percent for John F. Kennedy in 1960 and 75 percent for Johnson in 1964. In strong Republican years, their vote is clearly Republican, and barely more than one in three voted Democratic in 1988.

Among whites, then, partisanship leads to loyalty in voting. The 1988 election continues the resurgence in the importance of party identification at the polls that began in 1984. In 1984, the relationship between party identification and the presidential vote was higher than in any of the five elections between 1964 and 1980.[17] Nonetheless, while the partisan cast to the presidential vote in 1988 was about as strong as in 1984, the partisan basis of the vote in congressional elections remained low (see Chapter 10). Thus, the 1988 election data provide mixed signals about whether parties are continuing to decline in electoral significance or whether they are gathering new strength in the public.

As we saw in Chapter 5, blacks have voted overwhelmingly Democratic since 1964. Because the vast majority of blacks vote Democratic (90 percent in 1988), there is no meaningful relationship between partisanship and the vote among the black electorate.

Partisanship is related to the way people vote, but why do partisans support their party's candidates? As we will see, party identification affects behavior because it helps structure (or, according to Fiorina, is structured by) the way voters view both policies and performance.

Policy Preferences and Performance Evaluations

In their study of voting in the 1948 election, Bernard R. Berelson, Paul F. Lazarsfeld, and William N. McPhee discovered that Democratic voters attributed to their nominee, incumbent Harry S Truman, positions on key issues that were consistent with their own beliefs—whether those beliefs were liberal, moderate, or conservative.[18] Similarly, Republicans tended to see their nominee, Gov. Thomas E. Dewey (N.Y.), taking whatever positions they preferred. Since then, research has emphasized the roles of party identification in the "projection" on the preferred candidate of positions similar to the voter's own views and in influencing policy preferences in the public.[19] We will use four examples to illustrate the strong relationship between partisan affiliation and perceptions, prefer- ences, and evaluations of presidential candidates and other election- specific factors.

First, more partisans evaluate a president of their party as having done a good job than do independents and, especially, than do those who identify with the other party. This can be seen in Figure 8-1, which shows the percentage of each of the seven partisan groups that approves of the way the incumbent has handled his job as president (as a proportion of those approving or disapproving) in the last five presiden- tial elections. Strong Republicans have overwhelmingly approved of the last three Republican incumbents, and even three of four strong Demo- crats approved of the generally unpopular Carter presidency. In all cases, the differences between the Democrats and Republicans is very clear. The "pure" independents have favored the Republicans on this measure, but most disapproved of Jimmy Carter. Overall, partisanship is clearly not directly translated into approval or disapproval (for instance, weak Democrats consistently give higher marks to Republican incumbents than do independents who lean toward the Democratic party), but it is closely related to it.

Second, the relationship between partisanship and evaluation of presidential performance can be extended to show a strong relationship between party loyalties and approval of Ronald Reagan's handling of the economy in the last two election surveys. Table 8-5 shows this distribu- tion for all seven partisan categories.

In both election years, over three-quarters of each of the three Republican groups approved of Reagan's handling of the economy, while over half and often over two-thirds of all three Democratic groups disapproved. In 1984, the pure independents gave very strong approval to Reagan, but this declined in 1988. Nonetheless, a clear majority of independents approved of his handling of the economy that year. This provided Bush not only with a legacy of generalized approval of Reagan among Republicans, independents who leaned toward the Republicans, as well as independents with no partisan leanings, but also with one focused on one of the most important policy areas, economic policy. Of course, the high levels of disapproval of Reagan's economic performance among Democrats, as well as independents who leaned toward the Democrats, made it that much harder for Bush to make inroads among them.

NES surveys conducted before 1984 did not ask the same question about whether the respondent approved of the president's handling of the economy, but they did ask questions that clearly suggest that party identification was closely related to similar evaluations. In 1972, for example, respondents were asked which political party would better handle the problem of inflation and unemployment; in 1976 and 1980

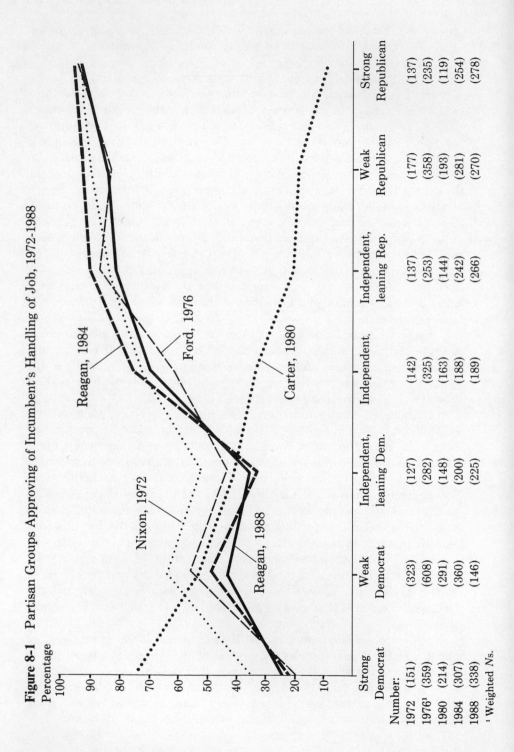

Figure 8-1 Partisan Groups Approving of Incumbent's Handling of Job, 1972-1988

Percentage

	Strong Democrat	Weak Democrat	Independent, leaning Dem.	Independent	Independent, leaning Rep.	Weak Republican	Strong Republican
Number:							
1972	(151)	(323)	(127)	(142)	(137)	(177)	(137)
1976[1]	(359)	(608)	(282)	(325)	(253)	(358)	(235)
1980	(214)	(291)	(148)	(163)	(144)	(193)	(119)
1984	(307)	(360)	(200)	(188)	(242)	(281)	(254)
1988	(338)	(146)	(225)	(189)	(266)	(270)	(278)

[1] Weighted *N*s.

Table 8-5 Approval of Incumbent's Handling of the Economy Among Partisan Groups, 1984 and 1988

	Party identification							
	Strong Democrat	*Weak Democrat*	*Independent, leans Democratic*	*Independent*	*Independent, leans Republican*	*Weak Republican*	*Strong Republican*	Total
1984								
Approve	17%	41%	32%	68%	84%	86%	95%	58%
Disapprove	83	59	68	32	16	14	5	42
Total percent (N)	100% (309)	100% (367)	100% (207)	100% (179)	100% (245)	100% (277)	100% (249)	100% (1,833)
1988								
Approve	19%	35%	32%	57%	76%	79%	92%	54%
Disapprove	81	65	68	43	24	21	8	46
Total percent (N)	100% (337)	100% (332)	100% (229)	100% (185)	100% (262)	100% (262)	100% (269)	100% (1,876)

they were asked separate questions about which party would better handle the problem of unemployment and which would better handle the problem of inflation. Although the relationships were not as strong as those presented in Table 8-5, there was a substantial relationship between party identification and assessments about which party would better handle these economic problems. The tendency of strong partisans to believe their party was better to solve economic problems was particularly noteworthy. In 1976, for example, only 16 percent of all respondents thought the Republican party would be better at solving both the problems of inflation and unemployment, but among strong Republicans 58 percent did and only 5 percent thought the Democrats would be better at solving both problems. In 1980, only 21 percent of all respondents thought the Democratic party would be better at solving both problems, but among strong Democrats 57 percent thought the Democratic party would be better and only 6 percent thought the Republican party would be.[20]

Third, partisans' policy preferences tend to put them closer to the policy positions of their party's nominee. In Table 8-6 we present the relationship between partisan affiliation and our balance of issues measure, which summarizes the overall Democratic or Republican leanings of each respondent on the issue scale questions analyzed in Chapter 6.[21] As we saw, these issues favored the Republicans in 1972, 1976, and 1980, but have worked slightly to the Democrats' favor in 1984 and 1988.

As the table shows, there is a clear, if moderately strong, relationship between partisanship and the balance of issues measure in the last three elections. The strength of the relationship for 1972 and 1976 was similar to that of the three most recent elections. However, there were some differences in the pattern of results during the last five elections. Until 1984 the relationship had been stronger among the Republicans than among the Democrats (the 1980 data in Table 8-6 are similar to those for the two preceding elections). But in 1984 the relationship was, if anything, stronger among the Democrats than among the Republicans, and in 1988 it was about the same for both Democrats and Republicans. The reason for this change is very likely the change in the political context. In 1980, for example, most people, Democrats as well as Republicans, were closer to the median position of Reagan than to that of Carter on such important issues as defense spending and cutting income taxes. Reagan, however, pushed both greatly increased defense spending and income tax cuts through Congress in his first term, as well as reducing the growth in spending for many domestic programs. By 1984, then, the public no longer favored as great an increase in defense spending and was more supportive of increased spending on domestic programs. These issues tended to divide the electorate along party lines, and in the last two elections Democrats became closer to their party's

Table 8-6 Balance of Issues Positions Among Partisan Groups, 1980-1988

Issue position closer to:[a]	Party identification							
	Strong Democrat	Weak Democrat	Independent, leans Democratic	Independent	Independent, leans Republican	Weak Republican	Strong Republican	Total
1980								
Democratic candidate	26%	23%	27%	20%	12%	10%	9%	19%
Neutral	34	37	33	43	40	43	31	37
Republican candidate	40	40	40	37	48	48	60	43
Total percent	100%	100%	100%	100%	100%	101%	100%	99%
(N)	(245)	(317)	(161)	(176)	(150)	(202)	(127)	(1,378)
1984								
Democratic candidate	57%	49%	59%	35%	23%	29%	14%	39%
Neutral	32	37	28	48	46	40	39	38
Republican candidate	11	14	13	17	32	32	47	23
Total percent	100%	100%	100%	100%	101%	101%	100%	100%
(N)	(331)	(390)	(215)	(213)	(248)	(295)	(256)	(1,948)
1988								
Democratic candidate	49%	36%	50%	33%	21%	21%	11%	32%
Neutral	34	40	38	48	46	43	35	40
Republican candidate	17	24	12	19	33	36	53	29
Total percent	100%	100%	100%	100%	100%	100%	99%	101%
(N)	(355)	(359)	(240)	(215)	(270)	(281)	(279)	(1,999)

[a]The neutral category consists of scores of −1, 0, or 1 on the full measure, while the Republican (Democratic) category is any score greater than 1 (less than −1) on the full measure.

Table 8-7 Retrospective Evaluations Among Partisan Groups, 1980-1988

Summary measure of retrospective evaluations[a]	Party identification							
	Strong Democrat	Weak Democrat	Independent, leans Democratic	Independent	Independent, leans Republican	Weak Republican	Strong Republican	Total
1980								
Democratic	45%	29%	18%	11%	8%	7%	4%	20%
Neutral	26	21	25	22	8	9	2	17
Republican	29	50	57	68	85	84	93	62
Total percent	100%	100%	100%	101%	101%	100%	99%	99%
(N)	(299)	(294)	(157)	(160)	(144)	(197)	(123)	(1,304)
1984								
Democratic	77%	54%	65%	27%	9%	9%	5%	37%
Neutral	12	17	13	22	15	18	5	14
Republican	12	29	21	52	76	73	90	49
Total percent	101%	100%	99%	101%	100%	100%	100%	100%
(N)	(303)	(356)	(197)	(181)	(241)	(270)	(239)	(1,787)
1988								
Democratic	79%	61%	64%	32%	20%	17%	6%	42%
Neutral	11	19	24	34	32	28	19	23
Republican	10	20	12	35	48	55	75	36
Total percent	100%	100%	100%	101%	100%	100%	100%	101%
(N)	(287)	(305)	(199)	(167)	(228)	(239)	(245)	(1,670)

[a]The neutral category is the same as that on the full scale, while the Democratic (Republican) category is the combination of all three Democratic (Republican) categories on the full scale.

candidate than to the Republican candidate. The result is a sharper and more balanced relationship between party identification and the balance of issues measures.

Finally, we find a strong relationship between party identification and our summary measure of retrospective evaluations in the last three elections.[22] Table 8-7 shows the basic relationships in 1980, 1984, and 1988, collapsing the summary retrospective measure into the three categories of pro-Democratic, neutral, and pro-Republican.[23] In all years, a majority of each Republican category tended to evaluate Republican performance favorably. Even in 1976, when only about one respondent in three was favorable to the Republicans, more than 60 percent of the Republicans were favorable. Among strong Republicans 71 percent were favorable to the GOP, and only 6 percent were favorable to the Democrats. And in 1976, 1984, and 1988, more than three of five Democratic identifiers assessed the Democratic party favorably. In 1980 only 20 percent of the electorate gave favorable assessments of Democratic performance, but among all Democratic identifiers, 36 percent did, and 45 percent of strong Democrats did so.

We have seen that both party identification and retrospective evaluations are related to the vote, but the two are also strongly related to each other. Do they still both contribute independently to the vote? The answer, as can be seen in Table 8-8, is yes. In this table, we have examined the combined impact of party identification and retrospective evaluations upon voting choices in the last four presidential elections. To simplify the presentation we have regrouped party identification into the three basic categories: strong and weak Republicans, all independents, and strong and weak Democrats. We also present the results for the three basic categories of our summary measure of retrospective evaluations.

Table 8-8 shows the percentage of major party voters who voted Republican for both party identification and retrospective evaluations in the last four elections. Reading across the rows reveals that in all elections, retrospective evaluations are strongly related to the vote, regardless of the respondent's partisanship. Reading down each column shows that in all elections, party identification is related to the vote, regardless of the respondent's retrospective evaluations. Moreover, party identification and retrospective evaluations have a combined impact upon how people voted. For example, in 1988 among Republican identifiers with pro-Republican evaluations, 97 percent voted for George Bush; among Democratic identifiers with pro-Democratic evaluations, only 5 percent did. Note as well the overall similarity of the 1984 and 1988 portions of the table. While there are some differences (for example, Bush did well, but not as well, among independent neutrals as Reagan did four years earlier), the most important reason that the 1988 election

Table 8-8   Percentage of Major Party Voters Who Voted for the Republican Candidate, by Party Identification and Summary Retrospective Measures, 1976-1988

Party identification[a]	Summary retrospective[b]						
	Republican		Neutral		Democratic		Total

A. Percentage Who Voted for Ford, 1976[c]

Republican	96	(269)	90	(98)	35	(54)	87	(421)
Independent	85	(183)	73	(133)	16	(187)	56	(503)
Democratic	53	(111)	30	(96)	5	(404)	18	(611)
Total	84	(563)	65	(327)	11	(645)	49	(1,535)

B. Percentage Who Voted for Reagan, 1980

Republican	100	(217)	75	(12)	33	(12)	95	(241)
Independent	82	(183)	36	(36)	24	(25)	69	(244)
Democratic	51	(135)	6	(78)	7	(140)	24	(353)
Total	81	(535)	21	(126)	11	(177)	58	(838)

C. Percentage Who Voted for Reagan, 1984

Republican	99	(344)	86	(42)	39	(18)	95	(404)
Independent	91	(230)	77	(62)	10	(110)	67	(402)
Democratic	72	(97)	32	(62)	5	(333)	22	(492)
Total	93	(671)	63	(166)	8	(461)	59	(1,298)

D. Percentage Who Voted for Bush, 1988

Republican	97	(277)	93	(84)	46	(37)	91	(398)
Independent	86	(124)	64	(94)	15	(131)	54	(349)
Democratic	67	(54)	27	(63)	5	(296)	16	(413)
Total	91	(455)	64	(241)	11	(464)	53	(1,160)

Note: Numbers in parentheses are totals upon which percentages are based.

[a] Democratic (Republican) identifiers were those classified as strong and weak Democrats (Republicans). Independents include those who lean toward either party and "pure" independents.

[b] The neutral category is the same as that on the full scale, while the Democratic (Republican) category is the combination of all three Democratic (Republican) categories on the full scale.

[c] Weighted *N*s.

was closer appears to be due to the less positive retrospective evaluations in the electorate.

In sum, partisanship appears to affect the way voters evaluate incumbents and their performance. Positions on issues are a bit different. Partisans are likely to be closer to their party's nominee and his policy platform, and in recent elections this linkage has grown among Democrats. But the connection between partisanship, issue preferences, and the perception of where candidates stand on the issues is not particularly strong. Policy-related evaluations in general are influenced partly by history and political memory and partly by the candidate's campaign strategies. Partisan attachments, then, limit the ability of candidates to control their fate in the electorate, but the limits are not entirely rigid. Candidates may be fairly tightly constrained by prior performance, especially that of the incumbent, as seen in partisan terms, but they are less limited by partisanship in their ability to receive support based on issues.

Conclusion

Party loyalties affect how people vote, how they evaluate issues, and how they judge the performance of the incumbent and his party. In recent years, research has suggested that the influence may work both ways: issue preferences, perceptions, and evaluations may also affect partisanship. The relationship between partisanship and issue preferences is more complex than any model assuming a one-way relationship would suggest. Doubtless, evaluations of incumbent performance may also affect party loyalties.[24]

As we saw in this chapter, there was a substantial shift toward Republican loyalties over the 1980s, and among whites, the advantage the Democrats enjoyed over the past four decades appears to be gone. To some extent, this shift in party loyalties must reflect Reagan's appeal, as well as his successful performance in office, as judged by the electorate. It also appears that he was able to shift some of that appeal on to Bush in 1988 directly, by the connection between performance judgments and the vote, but also indirectly, through shifts in party loyalties among white Americans.

To what extent did Bush benefit from the shift in party loyalties toward the Republicans? One way to answer this question is to ask what share of the vote Bush would have received if the party loyalties of the electorate had been as Democratic as they were eight years earlier, when Reagan first won the presidency. In making our estimates we will assume that each party identification category had the same turnout as that observed in the 1988 NES vote validation study (see Table 4-5), and that the percentage of each group voting for Bush was the same as we observed in the 1988 NES survey. The only change in these calculations for 1988 from that observed in the 1988 NES survey, then, is the proportions in the various categories of party identification. For example, in our hypothetical estimates, Bush would win the same support among strong Republicans as he actually did win, but there would be fewer strong Republicans, reflecting the smaller proportion of strong Republicans in 1980 compared with 1988. According to our estimates, Bush would have received only 47 percent of the vote if there had been no shift in the party loyalties of the electorate, whereas, according to the NES survey, he won 52 percent. Similar estimates were developed assuming that the distribution of party identification was the same in 1988 as it was in 1976, and they yield similar results. If the party loyalties of the electorate had been the same in 1988 as they were during the 1976 contest between Gerald R. Ford and Carter, Bush would have won 48 percent of the vote—the actual percentage Ford won.

Even with 48 percent of the vote to Carter's 50 percent, Ford came very close to winning an electoral vote majority, so we cannot say how the actual outcome of the 1988 contest would have been affected if party loyalties had not changed during the 1980s. However, viewed from this perspective, it appears that Bush's election resulted in large part from the shift in party identification toward the Republican party. Without that shift the contest would have been very close, with Dukakis holding a popular vote edge.[25]

Clearly, party loyalties are still an important force in the electoral process. If anything, they have been more strongly related to the vote in the last two elections than in any election from 1964 through 1980. As we saw, party loyalties are related to issue preferences and are strongly related to retrospective evaluations. Given these relationships, the shift toward Republican party identification in the electorate could have long-term consequences. One of the major advantages the Democrats enjoyed during the postwar years was a substantial lead in partisan loyalties. Because Republicans are somewhat more likely to vote than Democrats and because they are usually more loyal to their candidate than Democrats are to theirs, this shift in party loyalties toward the Republicans could become an additional burden for the Democrats, at least in their quest to regain the presidency. Obviously, the Republicans hope to continue their gains in party loyalties among whites and seek to create at least some inroads among blacks. But even if they merely keep the gains they made between 1980 and 1988 they will have substantially improved their competitive position.

If partisanship affects voting behavior generally, much of what we have written in this chapter should apply to congressional voting as well. Of course, partisan loyalties do affect the way people vote for Congress. And yet, despite the Republican gains in partisanship during the 1980s, in 1986 the Republicans lost control of the U.S. Senate, which they had won in 1980, and in 1988 they lost an additional Senate seat. Given the tendency for the party holding the White House to lose U.S. House seats in midterm elections, the loss of five seats by the GOP in the House in 1986 was a relatively modest setback. In 1988, however, the GOP lost three additional seats, the first time since 1960 that the party winning the presidency lost ground in the House. Why did the substantial shift in party loyalties, which clearly helped the Republicans hold the White House, have so little apparent effect in the congressional elections? Do the Democrats have advantages that help them retain congressional control? We will examine these questions in our next two chapters, when we turn to the other national elections.

Notes

1. Angus Campbell, Philip E. Converse, Warren E. Miller, and Donald E. Stokes, *The American Voter* (New York: John Wiley & Sons, 1960).
2. Ibid., 121. For a brief recent statement of this standard view, see Warren E. Miller and Santa A. Traugott, *American National Election Studies Data Sourcebook, 1952-1986* (Cambridge, Mass.: Harvard University Press, 1989), 79.
3. Only a very few identify with another party.
4. For the full wording of the party identification questions, see Chapter 4, note 46.
5. For the most detailed discussion of how the NES creates its summary measure of party identification, see Arthur H. Miller and Martin P. Wattenberg, "Measuring Party Identification: Independent or No Partisan Preference?" *American Journal of Political Science* 27 (February 1983): 106-121.
6. For evidence on the relatively high level of partisan stability among individuals over time, see M. Kent Jennings and Gregory B. Markus, "Partisan Orientations over the Long Haul: Results from the Three-Wave Political Socialization Panel Study," *American Political Science Review* 78 (December 1984): 1000-1018.
7. V. O. Key, Jr., *The Responsible Electorate: Rationality in Presidential Voting 1936-1960* (Cambridge, Mass.: Harvard University Press, 1966), 52.
8. Morris P. Fiorina, "An Outline for a Model of Party Choice," *American Journal of Political Science* 21 (August 1977): 601-625; Fiorina, *Retrospective Voting in American National Elections* (New Haven, Conn.: Yale University Press, 1981).
9. Benjamin I. Page provides evidence of this. See his *Choices and Echoes in Presidential Elections: Rational Man and Electoral Democracy* (Chicago: University of Chicago Press, 1978). Anthony Downs, in *An Economic Theory of Democracy* (New York: Harper & Row, 1957), develops a theoretical logic for such consistency in party stances on issues and ideology over time.
10. There is some controversy over how to classify these independent leaners. Some argue that they are mainly "hidden partisans" who should be considered identifiers. For the strongest statement of this position, see Bruce E. Keith et al., "The Partisan Affinities of Independent 'Leaners,'" *British*

Journal of Political Science 16 (April 1986): 155-185. In our view, however, the evidence on the proper classification of independent leaners is mixed. On balance, the evidence suggests that they are more partisan than independents with no partisan leanings, but less partisan than weak partisans. See Paul R. Abramson, *Political Attitudes in America: Formation and Change* (San Francisco: W. H. Freeman, 1983), 80-81, 95-96. For an excellent discussion of this question, see Herbert B. Asher, "Voting Behavior Research in the 1980s: An Examination of Some Old and New Problem Areas," in *Political Science: The State of the Discipline,* ed. Ada W. Finifter (Washington, D.C.: American Political Science Association, 1983), 357-360.

11. See, for example, Martin P. Wattenberg, *The Decline of American Political Parties, 1952-1988* (Cambridge, Mass.: Harvard University Press, 1990).

12. The results in this paragraph are based upon our calculations using codebooks for the General Social Surveys. These surveys of some 1,500 respondents have been conducted by NORC since 1972 and have been carried out in every subsequent year except 1979 and 1981. The basic party identification question in these surveys is, "Generally speaking, do you usually think of yourself as a Republican, Democrat, Independent, or what?" Follow-up questions are used to distinguish between strong and weak partisans and between independents who lean toward one of the two parties and those who do not.

13. Unless otherwise indicated, the Gallup results reported in this chapter are based upon George Gallup, Jr., and Alec Gallup, "Despite Presidential Win Streak, GOP Remains a Minority Party," *Gallup Poll,* December 22, 1988. The basic Gallup question is as follows: "In politics, as of today, do you consider yourself a Republican, a Democrat, or an Independent?" No follow-up questions are used to distinguish between strong and weak partisans or among various categories of independents.

14. For a study based upon the NES surveys, see Paul R. Abramson, "Generations and Political Change in the United States," *Research in Political Sociology* 4 (1989): 263-270; for an analysis of Gallup surveys, see Everett Carll Ladd, "The 1988 Elections: Continuation of the Post-New Deal System," *Political Science Quarterly* 104 (Spring 1989): 10-13; and for an analysis of CBS News/*New York Times* telephone surveys, see Helmut Norpoth, "Under Way and Here to Stay: Party Realignment in the 1980s?" *Public Opinion Quarterly* 51 (Fall 1987): 381-387.

15. See George Gallup, Jr., "GOP Affiliation Climbs to Highest Level in 30 Years," *Gallup Poll,* November 25, 1984, 3.

16. Gallup and Gallup, "Despite Presidential Win Streak," 3.

17. For details, see Paul R. Abramson, John H. Aldrich, and David W. Rohde, *Change and Continuity in the 1984 Elections,* rev. ed. (Washington, D.C.: CQ Press, 1987), 216. Note that there was a sizable third-party vote for president in the 1968 and 1980 elections. Since Table 8-4 excludes such voters, it tends to exaggerate the impact of party identification. For the distribution of votes among whites for the three major candidates in these two elections, see Abramson, Aldrich, and Rohde, *Change and Continuity in the 1980 Elections,* rev. ed. (Washington, D.C.: CQ Press, 1983), Table 8-8, 177.

18. Bernard R. Berelson, Paul F. Lazarsfeld, and William N. McPhee, *Voting: A Study of Opinion Formation in a Presidential Campaign* (Chicago: University of Chicago Press, 1954), 215-233.

19. See Richard A. Brody and Benjamin I. Page, "Comment: The Assessment of Policy Voting," *American Political Science Review* 66 (June 1972): 450-458;

Page and Brody, "Policy Voting and the Electoral Process: The Vietnam War Issue," *American Political Science Review* 66 (September 1972): 979-995; and Fiorina, "An Outline for a Model of Party Choice."

20. See Abramson, Aldrich, and Rohde, *Change and Continuity in the 1980 Elections,* rev. ed., Table 8-6, 173.
21. For a description of this measure, see Chapter 6. Since this measure uses the median placement of the candidates on the issue scales in the full sample, much of the "projection" effect is eliminated. To conserve space, we have not reported the relationship between party identification and the balance of issues measure in 1972 and 1976. For those relationships, see Abramson, Aldrich, and Rohde, *Change and Continuity in the 1980 Elections,* rev. ed., Table 8-5, 171.
22. For a description of this measure, see Chapter 7. As we note in Chapter 7 (note 17), this measure cannot be constructed with the 1972 NES survey.
23. To conserve space, we do not report the 1976 results in our table. For these results, see Abramson, Aldrich, and Rohde, *Change and Continuity in the 1984 Elections,* rev. ed., Table 8-7, 223.
24. For two important articles assessing some of these relationships, see Gregory B. Markus and Philip E. Converse, "A Dynamic Simultaneous Equation Model of Electoral Choice," *American Political Science Review* 73 (December 1979): 1055-1070; and Benjamin I. Page and Calvin C. Jones, "Reciprocal Effects of Policy Preferences, Party Loyalties and the Vote," *American Political Science Review* 73 (December 1979): 1071-1089. For a brief discussion of these articles, see Richard G. Niemi and Herbert F. Weisberg, "What Determines the Vote?" in *Controversies in Voting Behavior,* 2d ed., ed. Niemi and Weisberg (Washington, D.C.: CQ Press, 1984), 89-95. For an excellent discussion of complex models of voting behavior and the role of party identification in these models, see Asher, "Voting Behavior Research in the 1980s," 341-354.
25 Candidates' campaign strategies also affect election results, of course. We cannot conclude that Dukakis would have narrowly won the popular vote majority in 1988 if the electorate had party loyalties similar to those of 1976 or 1980, nor can we conclude that, say, Ford would have defeated Carter in 1976 had they faced an electorate with partisan loyalties similar to those of 1988. The candidates might have run different types of campaigns knowing they were facing electorates with different party loyalties than they actually faced. These estimates do indicate, however, how much more difficult it was for any Democratic presidential nominee to win in 1988 than it was for a Democratic candidate to win in 1976 or 1980.

The 1988
Congressional Election

So far we have focused on the presidential contest, the major event of the 1988 elections. The president, however, does not govern alone, but shares responsibility with Congress, which must approve major appointments and enact the legislative program. Having concluded our analysis of George Bush's election, we now turn to the selection of the Congress that serves with him. In Part 3 we will consider the selection of Congress and the policy implications of the electorate's choices.

There were many elections in 1988. In addition to twelve governors and thousands of state and local officials, the electorate chose thirty-three U.S. senators and 435 members of the House of Representatives. Unlike the 1980 elections, when the Republicans won control of the Senate, the 1988 elections held no major surprises. The Democrats had regained control of the Senate in the 1986 midterm elections and easily retained control in 1988. They gained one Senate seat, giving them a 55 to 45 seat margin over the Republicans. The Democrats have controlled the House since the 1954 midterm election, and in 1988 they actually gained three House seats—the first election since 1960 in which the party winning the presidency lost seats in the House of Representatives. The Democrats won 260 House seats, the Republicans only 175.

Although the Republicans could celebrate their continued domination in presidential elections, the 1988 congressional election was a major disappointment for them. By election day Republicans had little hope of regaining the Senate, and they had no hope of winning control of the House. But by actually losing House seats, they made future prospects of GOP congressional control dimmer. To control the House, the Republicans would need to win 43 seats. The Republicans could still hope to make major gains in 1992, for the reapportionment and redistricting that will occur after the 1990 census provides opportunities for change. But their poor results in congressional elections belied the claims of an imminent realignment that Republicans had made after their 1980 and 1984 presidential victories.

Why did the Republicans fare so poorly in 1988? Will the poor showing by his party make it difficult for Bush to govern? Why do the Democrats continue to dominate congressional elections, despite their failure to win presidential contests? And what prospects do the Republicans have in future Senate and House elections?

Chapter 9 examines candidates' resources and their effect on electoral outcomes. The crucial factor in determining congressional success—especially in House elections—is incumbency. We begin by looking at patterns of success for incumbents, studying changes over the past three decades. Although the Democrats have been the majority party in the House for more than three decades, and although they have held a majority in the Senate for all but six of these years, there have been dramatic shifts in regional patterns. We will examine these changes and see how the erosion of regional differences affected congressional as well as presidential voting. We will then study factors that affect the likelihood of success in congressional races—the background of the candidates, incumbency, and campaign spending. Next, we will study the likely impact of the 1988 election upon public policy. We will speculate on the outcome of the 1990 midterm election, showing how academic models of congressional voting behavior aid in predicting and understanding electoral outcomes.

As we saw in the introduction to Part 1, many political scientists argue that there will not be a pro-Republican realignment unless the Republicans gain a majority in the House. Some maintain that there has been a "split-level" realignment but doubt that there will ever be a full-fledged realignment in which the GOP gains control of both the presidency and Congress. Others say that the very term *realignment* no longer has much utility. But some Republicans believe that they still have realistic prospects of becoming the clear majority party. Their main hope of winning the House lies in the constitutional requirement that congressional seats be reallocated among the states after every decennial census. Moreover, as a result of Supreme Court decisions requiring House districts to have roughly equal populations, most House districts must be redrawn even if a state neither gains nor loses representatives. The Republicans hope to capitalize upon the changes that will occur after the 1990 census, and at the very least to minimize what they view as an unfair Democratic advantage in current congressional districting. We will examine Republican prospects for gains after 1990 and assess the GOP's long-term prospects of winning control of Congress.

Chapter 10 explores the way voters make congressional voting decisions—one of the most exciting and rapidly growing areas of research since the National Election Studies (NES) introduced new questions in 1978 to study congressional voting behavior. Because the composition of the Senate's electorate changes dramatically from election to election, our analysis will focus on voting for the House. Chapter 10 examines how social factors influence voters' choices and compares the relationship of these forces in congressional and presidential voting. The effects of issue preferences, partisan loyalties, and incumbency upon voters' decisions are also assessed. We will attempt to explain why the shift in party loyalties to the GOP, which played an important role in aiding Bush, does not lead to GOP victories in many House elections. We will then consider the thesis that a congressional voting decision is a referendum on the performance of the individual member of Congress as well as on the president. We will attempt to explain why Bush lacked coattails that might have aided Republican congressional candidates. Last, we will present additional evidence about the importance of campaign spending and further observations about the advantages of incumbency.

Chapter 9

Candidates and Outcomes

In the 1988 presidential election the voters, deliberately or not, endorsed the status quo by electing George Bush to succeed Ronald Reagan. In the congressional elections they also endorsed the status quo, but this collective choice returned Democratic majorities to both houses of Congress. Indeed, the 1988 congressional elections are most remarkable for how little change in Congress resulted from them. With Ronald Reagan's first election in 1980, the Republicans also took control of the Senate and gained 33 House seats; with Bush's victory, the Republicans lost seats in both Houses. In the Senate the Republicans lost 1 seat, giving the Democrats a 55 to 45 margin of control. In the House of Representatives, the Democrats gained 3 seats, making their margin 260 to 175 seats. This was 17 fewer seats than the Republicans held after Reagan's first victory in 1980, and 7 fewer than after his reelection in 1984. Indeed, the Republican share of House seats, 40.2 percent, was the lowest proportion won by the party of a victorious presidential candidate in the nation's history.

Thus, while the Republican party could draw encouragement from their continued domination at the presidential level, the 1988 results for Congress offered a less positive message. In this chapter we will look in some detail at the pattern of congressional outcomes for 1988 and how they compared with outcomes in previous years. We seek to explain why the 1988 results took the shape they did—what factors led to the overwhelming success of incumbent candidates, and what permitted some challengers to run better than others. We also try to anticipate the effect the election results are likely to have on the politics of the 101st Congress. Finally, we will discuss the implications of the 1988 results for the 1990 midterm elections and for subsequent elections through the rest of the century.

Election Outcomes in 1988

Patterns of Incumbency Success

Probably the most important generalization one can make regarding congressional elections is that most races involve incumbents and most incumbents are reelected. Although this generalization has been true for a long time, incumbents have been increasingly successful in recent years, particularly in House elections. Table 9-1 presents information on election outcomes for House and Senate races involving incumbents between 1954 and 1988.[1] During this period, an average of 93 percent of the House incumbents and 81 percent of the Senate incumbents who sought reelection were successful. The results also show that most defeats occur in general elections rather than in party primaries. While House incumbent defeats during these years have never been frequent—the success rate has never fallen below 86 percent—the last elections have yielded reelection percentages of 98 percent. In both 1986 and 1988, only six incumbents were beaten in the general election for the House.

During the period covered by Table 9-1, House and Senate outcomes have not always demonstrated the same pattern. Between 1968 and 1980, House incumbents were notably more successful than Senate incumbents, and the rates of success for the two groups were moving in opposite directions. In the three elections between 1976 and 1980, House incumbents' success averaged more than 90 percent, while for the Senate the rate was only about 60 percent. In the next two elections, however, the rates were very similar, and in the two most recent election years the House incumbents again exhibited more success than their Senate counterparts.

It appears that these results are the consequence of at least two factors, the first primarily statistical and the second substantive. The statistical factor simply involves the number of cases: House elections routinely involve about 400 incumbents, and Senate races usually involve fewer than 30. A comparatively small number of cases is more likely to produce volatile results over time. Thus, the proportion of successful incumbents in Senate races tends to jump around more than for the House. The substantive factor is that a Senate race is more likely to be vigorously contested than a House race. In 1988, for example, seventy-four House incumbents (or about 18 percent) had no opponent from the other major party, and a large share of the remainder had opponents who were inexperienced or underfunded or both. In Senate races, on the other hand, every incumbent faced a major party opponent. Most of these

Table 9-1 House and Senate Incumbents and Election Outcomes, 1954-1988

Year	Incumbents running (*N*)	Primary defeats (*N*)	(%)	General election defeats (*N*)	(%)	Reelected (*N*)	(%)
House							
1954	(407)	(6)	1.5	(22)	5.4	(379)	93.1
1956	(410)	(6)	1.5	(15)	3.7	(389)	94.9
1958	(394)	(3)	0.8	(37)	9.4	(354)	89.8
1960	(405)	(5)	1.2	(25)	6.2	(375)	92.6
1962	(402)	(12)	3.0	(22)	5.5	(368)	91.5
1964	(397)	(8)	2.0	(45)	11.3	(344)	86.6
1966	(411)	(8)	1.9	(41)	10.0	(362)	88.1
1968	(409)	(4)	1.0	(9)	2.2	(396)	96.8
1970	(401)	(10)	2.5	(12)	3.0	(379)	94.5
1972	(392)	(13)	3.3	(13)	3.3	(366)	93.4
1974	(391)	(8)	2.0	(40)	10.2	(343)	87.7
1976	(383)	(3)	0.8	(12)	3.1	(368)	96.1
1978	(382)	(5)	1.3	(19)	5.0	(358)	93.7
1980	(398)	(6)	1.5	(31)	7.8	(361)	90.7
1982	(393)	(10)	2.5	(29)	7.4	(354)	90.1
1984	(411)	(3)	0.7	(16)	3.9	(392)	95.4
1986	(393)	(2)	0.5	(6)	1.5	(385)	98.0
1988	(409)	(1)	0.2	(6)	1.5	(402)	98.3
Senate							
1954	(27)	(0)	—	(4)	15	(23)	85
1956	(30)	(0)	—	(4)	13	(26)	87
1958	(26)	(0)	—	(9)	35	(17)	65
1960	(28)	(0)	—	(1)	4	(27)	96
1962	(30)	(0)	—	(3)	10	(27)	90
1964	(30)	(0)	—	(2)	7	(28)	93
1966	(29)	(2)	7	(1)	3	(26)	90
1968	(28)	(4)	14	(4)	14	(20)	71
1970	(28)	(1)	4	(3)	11	(24)	86
1972	(26)	(1)	4	(5)	19	(20)	77
1974	(26)	(1)	4	(2)	8	(23)	88
1976	(25)	(0)	—	(9)	36	(16)	64
1978	(22)	(1)	5	(6)	27	(15)	68
1980	(29)	(4)	14	(9)	31	(16)	55
1982	(30)	(0)	—	(2)	7	(28)	93
1984	(29)	(0)	—	(3)	10	(26)	90
1986	(27)	(0)	—	(6)	22	(21)	78
1988	(26)	(0)	—	(3)	12	(23)	88

opponents had previously won elective office and were reasonably well funded. Thus, a large number of House races involve incumbents who are virtually guaranteed reelection. Had all House races been as heavily contested as Senate races in the late 1970s, the rate of defeat for House incumbents might have been substantially higher. We will consider the substantive point again later in this chapter.

We next turn from the consideration of incumbency to party. Figure 9-1 portrays the proportion of seats in the House and Senate won by Democrats in each election since 1952. In House elections, high rates of incumbent participation, coupled with the high rates of incumbent success, lead to fairly stable partisan control. Most important, the Democrats have won a majority in the House in every election since 1954, and have now won eighteen consecutive general elections. This is by far the longest period of dominance of the House by the same party in American history.[2] The Democrats' share of the House seats has been stable for the last four elections, varying only between 58 and 62 percent. In the more volatile Senate, however, the range of partisan change has been greater over the same period (46 to 55 percent). Moreover, there have been two shifts in Senate control during the past decade (with the Republicans gaining a majority in 1980 and the Democrats regaining power in 1986). These patterns suggest that while Democratic control of the Senate may be in some doubt in the near future, the same is not likely to be true with regard to the House. We will consider this matter in more detail below.

The combined effect of party and incumbency in 1988 is shown in Table 9-2. Overall the Democrats won 60 percent of the races for House seats and 58 percent for the Senate. Democratic incumbents in both bodies were overwhelmingly successful, as were House Republicans. While in percentage terms Republican Senate incumbents won a smaller share of their races, the small numbers involved meant that they lost only two incumbents to one for the Democrats.[3] In open House races, each party did very well, holding on to seats they had previously controlled (and much better than 1986, when each retained only about two-thirds of these seats).[4] Neither party was as successful in holding their open Senate seats, although only three of these seats changed hands. The important point is that in 1988, neither party in either chamber was able to make significant inroads into the seats held by the opposition. This seemingly neutral result represents a potentially important lost opportunity for the Republicans in their struggle to regain control of Congress, especially with regard to the Senate. In a year when their presidential candidate won by a comfortable margin, congressional Republicans failed to gain ground. In 1988, the Democrats were defending the majority of Senate seats up for contest (nineteen of thirty-three). In 1990, the Republicans will control eighteen of the thirty-four seats having elections. That, coupled with the traditional difficulties of the president's party in

Figure 9-1 Democratic Share of Seats in the House and Senate, 1953-1989

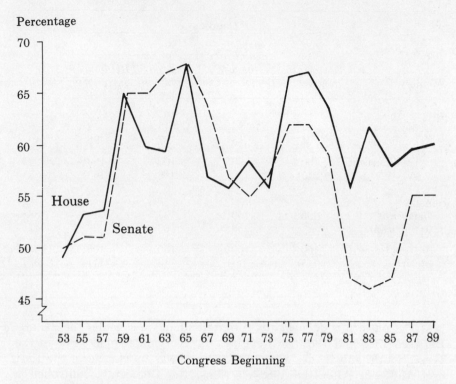

midterm elections, which we will consider shortly, will make the Republican quest for Senate control even more difficult.

Regional Bases of Power

The geographic pattern of 1988 election outcomes in the House and Senate can be seen in the partisan breakdowns by region presented in Table 9-3.[5] For comparison we also present breakdowns for 1979 (before the Republicans took control of the Senate in Reagan's first election) and for 1953 (the last Congress in which the Republicans controlled both chambers). In the House, the Reagan-Bush years have yielded the Republicans some gains in every region but the Midwest. Ironically, in that area—which was historically the Republican heartland and where the GOP held 76 percent of the seats in 1953—they lost some ground. These results also offer another perspective on the Republicans' inability to make congressional gains in 1988: despite Bush's solid electoral showing nationally, the Democrats won a majority of House seats in every one of the five regions.

Table 9-2   House and Senate General Election Outcomes, by Party and
Incumbency, 1988

| | Candidates | | | | |
Winners	Democratic incumbent	No incumbent (seat was Democratic)	No incumbent (seat was Republican)	Republican incumbent	Total
House					
Democrats	99%	92%	13%	2%	60%
Republicans	1	8	87	98	40
Total Percent	100%	100%	100%	100%	100%
(*N*)	(245)	(12)	(15)	(163)	(435)
Senate					
Democrats	93%	50%	33%	18%	58%
Republicans	7	50	67	82	42
Total Percent	100%	100%	100%	100%	100%
(*N*)	(15)	(4)	(3)	(11)	(33)

The pattern is only slightly different when we consider the Senate. Between 1979 and 1989 the Republicans have made small gains in the West, South, and border states, while there was no change in the East and Midwest. After the 1988 elections, the Democrats controlled a majority of the seats in all regions but the West, where Republican strength in the mountain states yields them numerical dominance.

The 1989 results are even more interesting when viewed from the longer historical perspective. In 1953 there were sharp regional differences in party representation in both houses. In the intervening years these differences have greatly diminished. The most obvious changes occurred in the South. The percentage of southern seats in the House held by Democrats declined from 94 percent in 1953 to 66 percent in 1989. In 1953 the Democrats held all twenty-two southern Senate seats, but in 1989 they controlled only fifteen of these twenty-two seats. While the regional shift is not as drastic as in presidential elections (see Chapter 3), the South is no longer a guaranteed Democratic stronghold for congressional candidates.

This change in the partisan share of the South's seats in Congress has had an important impact on that region's influence within the two parties. The South used to be the backbone of Democratic congressional representation. This, and the tendency of southern members of Congress to build seniority, gave southerners disproportionate power within the

Table 9-3 Party Shares of Regional Delegations in the House and
Senate, 1953, 1979, and 1989

| | 1953 | | | 1979 | | | 1989 | | |
| | Demo-crats (%) | Repub-licans (%) | (N) | Demo-crats (%) | Repub-licans (%) | (N) | Demo-crats (%) | Repub-licans (%) | (N) |
Region									
House									
East	35	65	(116)	66	34	(105)	58	42	(96)
Midwest	23	76	(118)[a]	51	49	(111)	57	43	(104)
West	33	67	(57)	62	38	(76)	53	47	(85)
South	94	6	(106)	71	29	(108)	66	34	(116)
Border	68	32	(38)	77	23	(35)	68	32	(34)
Total	49	51	(435)	64	36	(435)	60	40	(435)
Senate									
East	25	75	(20)	55	45	(20)	55	45	(20)
Midwest	14	86	(22)	59	41	(22)	59	41	(22)
West	45	55	(22)	46	54	(26)	38	62	(26)
South	100	0	(22)	73	27	(22)	68	32	(22)
Border	70	30	(10)	70	30	(10)	60	40	(10)
Total	49	51	(96)	59	41	(100)	55	45	(100)

Note: The figures are for the opening of the Congress each year. For our definition of each region, see note 5.

[a]Includes one independent.

Democratic party in Congress. Because of the decline in Democratic electoral success, the numerical strength of southern Democrats in Congress has waned. In 1947, with the Republicans in control of both houses of Congress, southerners accounted for about half of the Democratic seats in the House and Senate. During the late 1940s and the 1950s, southern strength was fairly stable at something over 40 percent. It then began to decline, and by the 1970s it stabilized again at about one-fourth of the Democratic seats in Congress.

A consideration of the South's share of Republican congressional representation presents the reverse picture. Minuscule or nonexistent at the end of World War II, it steadily began to grow, reaching about 20 percent in 1981 and later. As a consequence of these changes, southern influence has declined in the Democratic party and grown in the GOP. Because southerners of both parties tend to be on average somewhat more conservative than their colleagues from other regions, these shifts in strength have tended to make the Democratic party in Congress more liberal and the Republican party more conservative.[6]

Other regional changes since 1953, while not as striking as those in the South, are also significant. In the 1953 House, the Republicans controlled the East and West by two-to-one margins, and the Midwest by a margin of three to one; in 1989, they controlled none of these regions, and the party proportions were very similar among the three. In the 1953 Senate, the Republicans had a massive lead in the East and Midwest and a slight lead in the West; by 1989, party control was much more evenly split in both the East and Midwest, although Republican strength in the West had increased. On balance, what we have witnessed in the last three decades is the "de-regionalization" of congressional elections. Although some regional differences are still apparent, the similarities are much more striking than the differences. The Congress of 1989 is regionally homogeneous compared with that of 1953.

Candidates' Resources and Election Outcomes

Seats in the House and Senate are highly valued posts for which candidates vigorously compete. In contests for these offices candidates draw on whatever resources they have available. To understand the results of congressional elections we must consider the comparative advantages and disadvantages of the various candidates. In this section we will consider the most significant resources available to candidates, and their impact on the outcomes of congressional elections.

Candidate Quality

One major resource that candidates can draw on is the set of personal political abilities that foster electoral success.[7] There are few constituencies today that provide certain victories for one of the two major parties, so election outcomes usually depend heavily on candidate quality. A strong, capable candidate is a significant asset; a weak, inept one is a disability that is difficult to overcome. In his study of the activities of House members in their districts, Richard F. Fenno, Jr., describes how members try to build support within their constituencies, establishing bonds of trust between constituent and representative.[8] Members attempt to convey to their constituents a sense that they are qualified for their job, a sense that they identify with their constituents, and a sense of empathy with them. Challengers of incumbents and candidates for open seats engage in similar activities to win support. The winner of a contested congressional election will usually be the candidate who is better able to establish these bonds of support among constituents and convince them that he or she is the person for the job.

One indicator of candidate quality is previous success at winning elective office. The more important the office a candidate has held, the more likely it is that he or she had to overcome significant opposition to obtain that office. Moreover, the visibility and reputation for performance that usually accompany public office can also be a significant electoral asset. For example, a state legislator running for a House seat can appeal to the electorate on the basis that his or her prior experience was a good preparation for congressional service. A state legislator also would have previously constructed a successful electoral organization that could be useful in a congressional campaign. Finally, success in an electoral arena suggests that these candidates are more likely to be able to run strong campaigns. Less adept candidates have already been screened out at lower levels of competition. For these and other reasons, an experienced candidate would have an electoral advantage over a candidate who had held no previous elective office. Moreover, the higher the office previously held, the stronger the candidate will likely be in the congressional contest.

In Table 9-4, we present data on which candidates were successful in 1989 House and Senate elections, controlling for office background, party, and incumbency.[9] The vast majority of candidates who challenged incumbents lost regardless of their office background or party, although in previous election years the relationship between office background and success against incumbents was quite marked.[10] In races without incumbents, however, candidates with previous office experience were more successful than those without such experience. Given the importance of this factor, it is worth noting that the proportion of House races in which incumbents faced challengers with elective office backgrounds has been declining. In 1980, 17.6 percent of incumbents faced such challenges; in 1984, 14.7 percent did; and in 1988 only 10.5 percent did.[11]

Whether experienced politicians actually run for the House or Senate is, of course, not an accident. These are significant strategic decisions made by politicians with much to lose if they make the wrong choice. The choices will be governed by a host of factors that relate to the perceived chances of success, the potential value of the new office relative to what will be lost if the candidate fails, and the costs of running.[12] The chances of success of the two major parties vary from election to election both locally and nationally. Therefore, each election offers a different mix of experienced and inexperienced candidates from the two parties for the House and Senate.

Certainly the most influential factor governing the choice of a potential candidate is whether there is an incumbent in the race. High reelection rates tend to discourage potentially strong challengers from running, which in turn makes it more likely that incumbents will win. In addition to the general difficulty of challenging incumbents, factors related to specific years will affect decisions to run. For example, the Republican party had difficulty recruiting qualified candidates in 1986 because of fear of a potential backlash from the Iran-contra scandals. Moreover, actions of incumbents can influence the choices of potential challengers. Sen. James Exon (D-Neb.), facing reelection in 1990, was

Table 9-4   Success in House and Senate Elections, Controlling for Office
Background, Party, and Incumbency, 1988

Candidate's last office	Candidate is opponent of:				No incumbent in district			
	Democratic incumbent		*Republican incumbent*		*Democratic candidate*		*Republican candidate*	
	(%)	(N)	(%)	(N)	(%)	(N)	(%)	(N)
House								
State legislature or U.S. House	0	(8)	6	(17)	77	(13)	80	(5)
Other elective office	0	(10)	0	(8)	29	(7)	83	(6)
No elective office	1	(168)	2	(123)	17	(7)	33	(15)
Senate								
U.S. House	0	(2)	—	(0)	0	(3)	75	(4)
Statewide elective office	—	(0)	33	(6)	100	(2)	100	(1)
Other elective office	20	(5)	0	(3)	—	(0)	0	(1)
No elective office	0	(7)	0	(2)	50	(2)	0	(1)

Note: Percentages show that proportion of candidates in each category who won; numbers
in parentheses are the totals on which percentages are based.

thought to be potentially vulnerable. To counter this image, the Exon
camp began raising funds and conducted various other campaign activities early in 1989. As a consequence, two potentially strong Republican
challengers, Rep. Doug Bereuter and former representative Hal Daub,
announced in early June that they would not seek the seat.[13]

Ironically, there are times when parties do not try to recruit strong
challengers. If a party's chances are not good, a strong challenger, while
losing, may increase turnout for the opposition and thus affect other
races in the same election. For example, in Texas in 1988, the Republican
party fielded no candidates against eleven Democratic House incumbents
in order to hold down Democratic turnout. This strategy, however, is not
supported by the new leadership at the National Republican Congressional Committee.[14]

Of course, as we have seen, most congressional races don't involve
challengers with previous office experience. Given their small chances of
winning, why do challengers without experience run at all? As Jeffrey
Banks and D. Roderick Kiewiet point out,[15] although the chances of
success against incumbents may be small for such candidates, in the long
run it may be the best chance they have. If inexperienced challengers put
off their candidacy until a time when there is no incumbent, their

opposition is likely to include *multiple* experienced candidates in *both* parties. Moreover, as David Canon demonstrates,[16] some candidates without previous elective office experience can still have significant political assets and be formidable challengers.

Incumbency

One reason most incumbents win is that incumbency itself is a significant resource. Actually, incumbency is not a single resource, but rather a status that usually gives a candidate a variety of benefits. In some respects, incumbency works to a candidate's advantage automatically. For example, incumbents tend to be more visible to voters and to be viewed more favorably than their challengers.[17] Moreover, the plurality of the electorate in many districts will identify with the incumbent's political party. In other respects, incumbents can use their status to gain advantages. Incumbents usually raise and spend more campaign funds than challengers, and they usually have a better developed and more experienced campaign organization. They also have assets, provided at public expense, that assist in performing their jobs, but that also provide electoral advantages.

Since the mid-1960s the margins by which incumbents have been reelected have increased (although the pattern is less clear and more erratic in the case of Senate elections).[18] These changing patterns have interested analysts both for their own sake and because it was believed that the disappearance of marginal incumbents would mean less congressional turnover and a locking-in of current office occupants.

One explanation of the increased incumbent margins was offered by Edward R. Tufte, who argued that redistricting protected incumbents of both parties.[19] This argument seemed plausible because the increase in margins occurred around the same time as the massive redistricting required by Supreme Court decisions of the mid-1960s. But other analysts showed that incumbents had won by larger margins both in states that had redistricted and in those that had not, as well as in Senate races.[20] Thus, redistricting cannot be the dominant reason for the change.

Another explanation of the increased incumbency advantage was that it was a consequence of the growth in the perquisites of members— and of the greater complexity of government. Morris P. Fiorina has noted that in the post-New Deal period the level of federal services and the bureaucracy that administers them have grown tremendously.[21] More complex government means that many people will encounter problems in gaining services, and people who have problems frequently contact their representative to complain. Fiorina contends that in the mid-1960s new members of Congress placed greater emphasis on such constituency problem solving than did their predecessors. This expanded constituency service was translated into a reservoir of electoral support. Although analyses of the electoral impact of constituency services have produced mixed conclusions, it is likely that the growth of these services offers a partial explanation for changing incumbent vote margins and for the incumbency advantage generally.[22]

The declining impact of party loyalties offers a third explanation for the growth in incumbent vote margins. Until the mid-1960s there was a very strong linkage between party identification and congressional voting behavior: most people identified with a political party, many identified strongly, and most voters supported the candidate of their chosen party. Since then, however, the impact of party identification has decreased. John A. Ferejohn, drawing on data from the National Election Studies (NES), has shown that the strength of party ties has generally weakened and that within any given party identification category the propensity to support the candidate of one's party declined.[23] An analysis by Albert D. Cover shows that between 1958 and 1974 voters who did not identify with the party of a congressional incumbent were increasingly more likely to defect from their party and support the incumbent, while there had been no increase in defections from party identification by voters of the same party as incumbents.[24] Thus, in effect, weakened party ties produce a substantial net electoral benefit for incumbents.

Whatever the relative importance of these factors in explaining the increase in incumbents' victory margins, the increase has been continuing since the 1970s. In 1976, 72 percent of the incumbents seeking reelection received at least 60 percent of the vote, and 41 percent of them got 70 percent or more. In 1986, the proportions were 86 percent and 59 percent, respectively.

Campaign Spending

A third resource that has an important impact on congressional elections is campaign spending. The analysis of the effects of campaign spending has received a great deal of attention in the last decade as a consequence of the availability of more dependable data.[25] The data on spending have consistently shown that incumbents generally outspend their challengers, often by large margins. For example, 1982 data show that in House races Democratic incumbents outspent their challengers by an average of 91 percent, and Republican incumbents did so by 125 percent. Senate challengers tend to be better funded, so the incumbent spending advantage in 1982 Senate races was only 64 percent for Democrats and 40 percent for Republicans.[26] Patterns are similar for elections stretching back at least to 1972.

These disparities in campaign spending are linked to the increase in incumbent election margins. Beginning in the 1960s, congressional campaigns began to rely more heavily on campaign strategies that cost money—for example, media time, campaign consulting, and direct mailing—and over time these items have become more and more expensive. At the same time, candidates were progressively less likely to have available pools of campaign workers from established party organizations or from interest groups, making expensive media and direct mail strategies relatively more important. Many challengers, however, are unable to raise significant campaign funds. Neither the individuals nor groups who are interested in the outcomes of congressional elections like to throw money away; before making contributions they usually need to be convinced that the candidate has a chance. Yet we have seen that over time few incumbents are beaten. Thus potential contributors are difficult to convince, and contributions are often not forthcoming. This inclination by potential contributors is reinforced by incumbents who build up large war chests long before a potential challenge is launched, keeping the money on hand—just in case. Two of the leading House fund raisers for the 1988 election were incumbents who had no serious opposition: Robert K. Dornan (R-Calif.) and Joseph P. Kennedy II (D-Mass.), each of whom raised over $1.2 million.[27] Indeed, after the 1988 election twenty representatives already had over $515,000 on hand for 1990, and three had over $1 million.[28] Most challengers are unable to raise sufficient funds to wage a competitive campaign.

The ability to compete, rather than the simple question of relative amounts of spending, is the core of the issue. We have noted that incumbents have many inherent advantages that the challenger must overcome if he or she hopes to win. But often the money is not there to overcome them. In 1986, for example, more than 40 percent of challengers spent $25,000 or less.[29] Similarly, in 1976, a third of the challengers of House incumbents spent less than $10,000.[30] With so little money available, challengers are unable to make themselves visible to the electorate or to convey a convincing message. Under such circumstances, most voters—being unaware of the positions, or perhaps even the existence, of the challenger—vote for the incumbent.

Available data on campaign spending and election outcomes seem consistent with this argument. Table 9-5 shows the relationship between the incumbent's share of the two-party vote in the 1986 House elections and the amount of money spent by challengers. It is clear that there is a strong negative relationship between how much challengers spend and how well incumbents do. In races where challengers spent less than $26,000, every incumbent received at least 60 percent of the vote. At the other end of the spectrum, in races where challengers spent $200,000 or more, almost two-thirds of the incumbents received less than 60 percent of the vote, and more than one-third won under 55 percent. These results are consistent with those of earlier House races for which comparable data are available.[31]

These findings are reinforced by other research which shows that challenger spending has a much greater influence on election outcomes

Table 9-5   Incumbents' Share of the Vote in the 1986 House Elections, by Challenger Campaign Spending

Challenger spending[a]	Incumbents' share of the two-party vote					
	70 percent or more	60-69 percent	55-59 percent	Less than 55 percent	Total	(N)
0-25	80.0%	20.0	0.0	0.0	100.0%	(135)
26-75	53.6%	39.1	7.2	0.0	99.9%	(69)
76-125	28.0%	68.0	0.0	4.0	100.0%	(25)
126-199	5.3%	68.4	15.8	10.5	100.0%	(19)
200 or more	5.5%	30.1	30.1	34.2	99.9%	(73)
All	48.9%	33.0	9.3	8.7	99.9%	(321)

Note: Percentages read across.

[a]In thousands of dollars.

than does incumbent spending.[32] This generalization has been questioned recently on methodological grounds,[33] but further research by Gary C. Jacobson reinforces these findings. Using both aggregate and survey data, he finds that "the amount spent by the challenger is far more important in accounting for voters' decisions than is the amount of spending by the incumbent." [34] Parallel results have been found for Senate elections.[35]

It is, of course, true that challengers who appear to have good prospects will find it easier to raise money than those whose chances seem dim. Thus, one might wonder whether these data are simply a reflection of the fulfillment of expectations, in which money flows to challengers who would have done well regardless of spending. Other research, however, indicates that this is probably not the case. In an analysis of the 1972 and 1974 congressional elections, Jacobson concludes, "Our evidence is that campaign spending helps candidates, particularly non-incumbents, by bringing them to the attention of voters; it is not the case that well-known candidates simply attract more money; rather, money buys attention." [36]

From this perspective, adequate funding is a necessary but not a sufficient condition for a closely fought election contest. This does not mean that heavily outspending one's opponent guarantees victory; we do not believe elections can be bought. If an incumbent outspends the challenger, the incumbent can still lose if the challenger is adequately funded. The 1982 elections offer clear evidence of this. In twenty-one of the twenty-three House general election contests where incumbents lost (excluding six races where two incumbents faced each other due to redistricting), the loser outspent the winner. In these races, incumbents outspent challengers by an average of more than 50 percent. Nor is a spending advantage any kind of guarantee to a challenger. In an extreme example from 1986, in the eleventh district of Pennsylvania, Republican Marc Holtzman spent $1.35 million in his race against Democratic incumbent Paul E. Kanjorski, who spent about $714,000. Holtzman received only 29 percent of the vote. Instead, our view can be summarized as follows: if a challenger is to attain visibility and get his or her message across to the voters—overcoming the incumbent's advantages in name recognition and perquisites of office—the challenger needs to be adequately funded. If both sides in a race are adequately funded, the outcome of the race will tend to turn on factors other than money, and it will matter little whether one candidate heavily outspends another.

This argument carries us full circle back to our earlier discussion, and leads us to bring together the three elements that we have been considering—candidate experience, incumbency, and campaign spending. Table 9-6 presents data on the combination of the three elements in the 1986 House elections. We have categorized challenger experience as weak or strong depending on whether the challenger previously had held a significant elective office;[37] challenger spending was classed as low or high depending on whether it was less than or more than $125,000. The data show that each of the elements exerts its own independent effect. When challengers have weak experience and low spending, all incumbents win, and the vast majority win with more than 60 percent of the vote. In the opposite situation, where the challenger has both strong experience and substantial spending, a majority of the races are relatively close. The intermediate circumstances each yield similar results, with the incumbents being less likely either to win overwhelmingly or to be contested very closely.

This combination of factors also helps to explain the greater volatility of outcomes in Senate races. Previous analysis has shown that data on campaign spending in Senate races are consistent with what we have found true for House races: if challenger spending is above a certain threshold level, the race is likely to be quite close; if it is below that level, the incumbent is likely to win by a large margin.[38] In Senate races, however, the mix of well-funded and inadequately funded challengers is different. Senate challengers are more likely than House challengers to be able to raise significant amounts of money. Senate challengers, moreover, are also more likely to possess significant experience in office. Thus, in Senate races incumbents often will face well-funded and experienced challengers, and the stage is then set for their defeat if other circumstances work against them.

The 1986 Senate campaigns appear to provide additional evidence for the argument that if challengers have sufficient money to wage an

Table 9-6 Incumbents' Share of the Vote in the 1986 House Elections, by Challenger Campaign Spending and Office Background

Challenger experience	Challenger spending	70 percent or more	60-69 percent	55-59 percent	Less than 55 percent	Total	(N)	Percentage of incumbents defeated
Weak	Low	66.7%	31.0	1.9	0.5	100.1%	(216)	0
Strong	Low	61.5%	30.8	7.7	0.0	100.0%	(13)	0
Weak	High	6.2%	44.6	24.6	24.6	100.0%	(65)	3.1
Strong	High	3.7%	22.2	33.3	40.7	99.9%	(27)	14.8

Note: Percentages read across. Strong challengers have held a significant elective office (see note 37). High spending challengers spent more than $125,000.

adequate campaign, it does not matter if they are outspent by incumbents. In the sixteen most competitive Senate races, the Republicans outspent the Democrats by $1 million on average—$3.8 million to $2.8 million—yet they lost eleven of the races.[39] In some races the incumbent's advantage was even greater. Republican Mark Andrews spent $2.3 million defending his Senate seat in North Dakota, while his victorious Democratic challenger Kent Conrad spent $900,000. The lesson appears to be captured by the statement made by David Johnson, the director of the Democratic Senatorial Campaign Committee, to Rep. Richard C. Shelby of Alabama, who was challenging Republican senator Jeremiah Denton. Shelby, who won, was concerned that he did not have enough money, since Denton was outspending him two to one. Johnson responded: "You don't have as much money, but you're going to have enough—and enough is all it takes to win." [40]

The 1988 Election: The Impact on Congress

When Ronald Reagan was first elected president, the impact of the congressional elections on Congress was substantial. The Republican party had unexpectedly taken control of the Senate from the Democrats and had gained thirty-three seats in the House of Representatives. Most of the incoming Republican senators and representatives were extremely conservative, shifting the ideological balance of Congress noticeably to the right. The massive Reagan victory and Republican congressional gain also had an impact on the behavior of many southern Democrats. Reagan's popularity in the South and their own conservative inclinations led many to support Reagan's early policy initiatives on taxes and the budget. Southern Democratic support provided the margin of victory on those measures.

The results of the 1988 elections were very different. As a consequence of the great incumbency success we have discussed, membership turnover was the smallest in history. Only 8 percent of the membership of the 101st Congress consists of freshmen; the next lowest percentage was 8.8 percent four years earlier.[41] With so few new members, not only is the shift in party balance very small; so also is the ideological change. In contrast to 1980, when many of the new members were much more conservative than the members they replaced, in 1988 the new members and the departing members appear to be quite similar on average, with new conservative replacements of liberals balanced by shifts elsewhere in the opposite direction. Nor were the members who were returning from the previous Congress markedly different from those who departed. If one compares the support for Democratic versus Republican party positions[42] among departing and returning members in both parties and both houses, the average party support scores differ by more than 2 points only among Senate Republicans, and that is due largely to the departure of a single member, Lowell P. Weicker, Jr., of Connecticut. Weicker voted more often with the Democrats in 1988 than any other congressional Republican.

Because of the small change in membership, there is substantial potential to accentuate the political deadlock between Congress and the president that existed in Reagan's second term. Due to the frequent existence of sharp differences in preferences between the branches, many issues received only partial, negotiated solutions after long periods of conflict, and many other issues were not dealt with effectively at all.

Yet there are many reasons to expect that there will be no across-the-board deadlock on policy. First, this is a new administration that will need a record of achievement on which to seek a second term. President Reagan won a number of significant victories in his first term, and in his second term he was often content to hold the line against reversing what had been won. This negative orientation was often served well by deadlock. The Bush administration, on the other hand, has new initiatives it wants to see enacted into law. It, therefore, has a stronger incentive to reach accommodation with Congress and move toward Democratic positions, at least on issues on which it places a high priority.

Reinforcing this tendency is the fact that Bush simply has different preferences and priorities from Reagan's. Bush is not as "antigovernment" as his predecessor, and he is thus inclined to press for positive action in more areas. The new president is, moreover, less conservative than Reagan, and so there is frequently less of a gap to close between his positions and those of the Democrats in Congress. Finally, Bush is in a weaker political position than Reagan was at the outset of his presidency. Reagan carried with him a Republican Senate, and in the House there frequently were enough Republicans and conservative Democrats to carry the day. Bush faces a Democratic Senate, and there are fewer Republicans and fewer congenial Democrats to support his cause.

As a consequence of all these factors, the Bush administration has clearly been willing to seek accommodation with Congress on a wide range of issues right from the outset. For example, during his confirmation hearings as secretary of state in early January 1989 (even before Bush's inauguration), James Baker said that Congress and the executive needed to work together. "Simply put, we must have bipartisanship to succeed." [43] Demonstrating that this was not empty rhetoric, Baker and the administration reached a compromise with Congress on the thorny issue of contra aid in March of 1989. The Democrats agreed to provide humanitarian aid until 1990 (when elections were scheduled), in return for forgoing military aid and granting the Congress an informal veto over the humanitarian aid after November 30, 1989.[44]

Soon after this, the two sides also reached an agreement on the fiscal 1990 budget. The package involved both spending cuts and revenue increases. Many critics, particularly those outside of government, regarded the agreement as purely cosmetic and based on unrealistic economic assumptions. The important point here, however, is that it really was bipartisan. The agreement found critics both among conservative Republicans and liberal Democrats, and it was endorsed on the floor of both houses by remarkably similar proportions of both parties. In the House 63.5 percent of the Republicans and 62.1 percent of the Democrats supported the budget resolution, while in the Senate the respective percentages were 68.1 and 69.1.[45]

The ability to find common ground between the president and Congress will probably also be enhanced by changes in the personalities involved. It is likely that it will be easier for Bush to find acceptable compromises with Senate Majority Leader George J. Mitchell and Speaker Tom Foley than it was for Ronald Reagan to reach agreements with Sen. Robert C. Byrd and Speaker Jim Wright. Indeed, there are indications that President Bush may sometimes find more opposition among his own partisans than among Democrats. For example, some Republicans in both houses were bitter about the contra deal. Rep. Duncan Hunter (R-Calif.), said: "Nicaragua is lost. The hope of freedom is gone. The dark curtain of the Sandinista Gestapo has descended on Nicaragua." [46]

These anticipations of cooperation between Bush and Congress should not be carried too far. There is no reason to expect that the high levels of partisan disagreement exhibited within Congress in recent years[47] will markedly decline. Furthermore, there will continue to be issues on which the president and Congress will not be able to find any early compromise, such as Bush's veto of an appropriation bill that included funds for abortions. We believe, however, that the president and congressional Democrats will find deadlock easier to avoid during the 101st Congress than it was in Reagan's second term.

The 1990 Congressional Election and Beyond

The Election of 1990

As we noted earlier, the Republicans already control a majority of the Senate seats up for election in 1990 (eighteen of thirty-four), and they thus will have an uphill fight in seeking to regain control of that body. In assessing which seats will be most vulnerable in the next election, there are certain systematic forces and individual circumstances we can take into account.

Two important considerations in assessing vulnerability are the previous election margins and the length of service of incumbents. As of early 1990, thirty-one incumbents were seeking reelection, fifteen Republicans and sixteen Democrats. While large margins of victory do not guarantee the next win, narrow wins frequently mean future vulnerability because they tend to attract strong, well-funded challengers. First-term incumbents also tend to be more vulnerable than long-serving members who have had greater time to solidify their positions. Only three of the Democrats and one of the Republicans seeking reelection are freshmen elected with 55 percent of the vote or less. (Two Democrats and one Republican were first elected in 1984 by larger margins.) Among nonfreshmen, two Democrats and one Republican seeking reelection were last elected by 55 percent or less. Since open seats are more vulnerable to partisan change, it is important to note that all three of the seats that will have no incumbents are currently held by Republicans.

These data indicate that there are relatively few seats up in 1990 with characteristics that would lead us to consider them highly vulnerable to party switching, and that the Republicans have no particular advantage regarding those seats. This suggests that the GOP will find it difficult to regain Senate control this election cycle, although our earlier discussion shows that the actual outcomes will depend heavily on the quality of challengers and their level of campaign funding. (There were indications during the summer of 1989 that the Republicans are having better luck than the Democrats at recruiting Senate challengers.)[48] It is likely that 1990 will merely set the stage for the Senate elections of 1992, when the group of seats that produced the switches in party control of 1980 and 1986 will again be contested.

The Republicans have virtually no chance to win control of the House in 1990. There is a strong historical tendency for the president's party to lose House seats in midterm elections, although the losses tend to be greater after the president's second election than after the first. In the last decade or so, a number of scholars have constructed and tested models of congressional election outcomes, focusing especially on midterms, seeking to isolate the factors that most heavily influence the fluctuating results.

The first models, constructed by Tufte[49] and by Jacobson and Samuel Kernell,[50] focused on two variables: presidential approval (often termed popularity) and a measure of the state of the economy. Tufte hypothesized a direct influence on voter choice and outcomes. The theory was that an unpopular president or a poor economic situation would cause the president's party to lose popular votes and, therefore, seats in the House. In essence, the midterm election was viewed as a referendum on the performance of the president and his party. Jacobson and Kernell, on the other hand, saw more indirect impact for presidential approval and the economy. They argued that these forces affected election results by influencing the decisions of potential congressional candidates. If the president is unpopular and the economy is in bad shape, potential candidates will expect the president's party to perform poorly. As a consequence, strong potential candidates of the president's party will be inclined to forgo running until a better year, and strong candidates from the opposition party will be more inclined to run because they foresee good prospects for success. According to Jacobson and Kernell, this mix of weak candidates from the president's party and strong opposition candidates will lead to a poor election performance by the party occupying the White House. To measure this predicted relationship, their model relates the division of the vote to presidential approval and the economic situation early in the election year, when, they argue, decisions to run for office are being made, rather than at the time of the election. This has come to be called the "strategic politicians" thesis.[51]

More recent research has built from this base. One model, developed by Alan I. Abramowitz, Albert D. Cover, and Helmut Norpoth, brings a new variable under consideration: short-term party evaluations.[52] They argue that voter attitudes about the economic competence of the political parties affect the impact of presidential approval and economic performance on voting decisions. If the electorate judges that the party holding the presidency is better able to deal with the problems voters regard as most serious, the negative impact in midterm elections of an unpopular president or a weak economy will be reduced. The authors conclude from analysis of both aggregate votes and responses to surveys in midterm elections that there is evidence for their "party competence" hypothesis.

All of the models we have discussed used the division of the popular vote as the variable to be predicted, and focused only on midterm elections. Some recent work has merged midterm results with those of presidential years, contending that there should be no conceptual distinction between them, and has sought to predict changes in seats directly without reference to the division of the vote. For example, a study by Bruce I. Oppenheimer, James A. Stimson, and Richard W. Waterman argues that the missing piece in the congressional election puzzle is the degree of "exposure," or "the excess or deficit number of seats a party holds measured against its long-term norm."[53] If a party wins more House seats than normal, those extra seats will be vulnerable in the next election, and the party is likely to suffer losses. Thus, the party that wins a presidential election does not automatically benefit in House elections. But if the president's party does well in the House elections, it will be more vulnerable in the subsequent midterm election. Indeed, the May 1986 article by Oppenheimer and his colleagues predicted only small Republican losses for 1986 because Reagan's large 1984 victory did not bring substantial congressional gains to his party. The actual result was consistent with this prediction, for the Republicans lost only five seats.

Another model of House elections we consider is that constructed by Robin F. Marra and Charles W. Ostrom, Jr.[54] They develop a "comprehensive referendum voting model" of both presidential year and midterm elections, and include factors such as foreign policy crises, scandals, unresolved policy disputes, party identification, and the change in the level of presidential approval. The model also incorporates measures reflecting hypotheses in the models we discussed earlier: the level of presidential approval, the state of the economy, the strategic politicians hypothesis, exposure, and party competence. The model was tested on data from all congressional elections from 1950 through 1986.

The Marra-Ostrom analysis shows significant support for most of the hypothesized relationships. The results indicate that the most powerful influences affecting congressional seat changes are presidential approval (directly and through various events) and exposure. The model is striking in its statistical accuracy; the average error in the predicted change is only four seats. The average error varies little whether presidential or midterm years are predicted, and the analysis demonstrates that the usually greater losses for the president's party in second midterm years result from negative shifts in presidential approval, exposure, and scandals.

Drawing on the insights of these various models, we can see how many of the factors may influence outcomes in the 1990 House elections. How well the economy is doing and how much the voters approve of Bush's performance early in the year may encourage or discourage high quality potential challengers. The same variables close to election time may lead voters to support or oppose Republican candidates because of voter reaction to the performance of the Bush administration. It is important to note that because the Republicans did so poorly in the 1988 House elections, their exposure is low. Therefore we would expect Republican success in 1990 to be greater than would be anticipated based on other influences. Finally, the impact of events like crises and scandals in the Marra-Ostrom model reminds us that there are many unforeseeable events that may influence the 1990 congressional election results.

There is a final factor, one we noted in discussing the Senate elections, that we should consider in closing: the number of open seats and their partisan distribution. If incumbents are insulated from challenges, then partisan gains are more likely to come from open seats, and the party that has more open seats will be at a disadvantage. As of this writing relatively few decisions to vacate House seats have been firmly announced, and comparatively few members seem ready to retire from politics. (A larger number of retirements seems likely in 1992, when reapportionment will disrupt most district lines.) On the other hand, a number of representatives are considering running for senator or governor, and they appear to be disproportionately Republicans. If most of the open House seats in 1990 are previously Republican, that party's chances of making a good showing will be reduced considerably.

Republican Prospects in Congressional Elections

Although Republicans have little chance to regain control of the Senate in 1990, and virtually no chance to win the House, they may be more hopeful about their longer term prospects. Assessing these prospects sheds light on the possibility of a full-fledged partisan realignment, in which the Republicans can control both the presidency and Congress. To close this chapter, we will briefly consider Republican prospects in future Senate elections, and then offer a more detailed analysis of the outlook for Republicans in the House. As we have said, the connection between partisan identification and congressional voting is weaker today than it used to be. Thus, even if the shift toward the Republicans in party identification we discussed in Chapter 8 proves to be long lasting, it is unlikely to produce a stable voting bloc that will guarantee continuing Republican majorities in Congress. For Senate elections, we argue that this means that outcomes will continue to be volatile and erratic, influenced to some degree by national trends, but even more so by the one-on-one competition of strong, well-funded Republican candidates facing strong, well-funded Democratic candidates in most elections. For the House, there are a number of other factors, including party organizations, gerrymandering, and presidential coattails, that we must consider before rendering a judgment on future prospects.

The Republican party's supposed comparative advantage in terms of national organization in House elections has received a good deal of attention.[55] In the 1982 House races, for example, the Republican party outspent the Democratic party almost six to one in direct contributions and coordinated spending.[56] More recently, in 1989 the National Republican Congressional Committee hired Ed Rollins (who managed Ronald Reagan's reelection campaign in 1984) as co-chairman, at a salary of $250,000 a year, to develop a strategy to win control of the House.

Yet things are not so one-sided or simple as this summary might suggest. Even though the Republicans were first to organize and develop their national congressional campaign organization, the Democrats are catching up. The party improved its fund raising and organization over the last few elections. In 1988 the ratio of Republican to Democratic campaign committee spending in House races was less than two to one.[57] Moreover, the Democrats have followed other strategies that do not show up in the kind of spending figures we have cited. For example, the Democratic Congressional Campaign Committee has concentrated on helping candidates get money from political action committees (PACs), rather than simply raising it themselves and donating it to candidates.

Democrats argue that their party controls the House and will continue to do so for the rest of the century, so the PACs would be well advised to support their candidates. The strategy has worked well. In the 1988 election cycle, Democratic candidates received $69.4 million in PAC contributions, while Republicans raised only $30.3 million. Of course, much of this advantage is due to the fact that there are more Democratic than Republican incumbents, but Democrats also received more PAC money in open seats ($5.8 million to $3.6 million), and Democratic challengers got $8.1 million to Republican challengers' $2.4 million.[58]

Another factor that many think is related to the potential for future Republican success is the pattern of House districting in the United States. Republicans believe that Democrats have drawn district lines to their advantage and against the Republicans, depriving the GOP of its rightful share of House seats according to the national vote. Citing 1984 as an example, Republicans point out that they got 47 percent of the national House vote but only 42 percent of the House seats. Republicans have, therefore, made it a high priority to win state legislative seats and governorships so they can increase their control of House redistricting after the 1990 census.

To be sure, some states—California for example[59]—are gerrymandered against Republican candidates. However, other states, such as Indiana, are gerrymandered in the opposite direction, and in still other states, mostly where political control of the state government was divided between the parties, districts were drawn to the advantage of incumbents of both parties.[60] The net effect of redrawn congressional districts would seem to be less one-sided than Republicans suggest.

Even if current districting were one-sided, moreover, Republican chances of significantly altering the situation in their favor seem limited.[61] The chances of partisan benefit from reapportionment and redistricting[62] are usually best for a party if it controls the governorship and both houses of the state legislature.[63] After the November 1989 elections in New Jersey and Virginia, the Republicans held this kind of control in only four states with a total of 11 House seats, while the Democrats controlled fifteen states with a total of 117 representatives. The remaining states had split party control. Of course, the important question is the balance of partisan control after the 1990 election, for that is when the next reapportionment will take place. But the Republicans have a long way to go before they will be well positioned to take advantage of the reapportionment and redistricting that will result from the 1990 census.

Finally, even if the Republicans were in full control of the redistricting process in a large number of states, there is no guarantee that their districting plans would have the intended effect. Indiana offers an excellent example. In 1981 the Republicans controlled the governorship and both houses of the state legislature, and they were determined to draw the House district lines in a way that would erase the six to five Democratic advantage in House seats. Analyses of the plan they imposed anticipated a six to four, or even seven to three, outcome in favor of the Republicans.[64] (The state lost one House seat in the reapportionment.) Instead the outcome in 1982 was an even five-five split, and in 1986 the Democrats gained another seat to make it six to four. The Democrats also came within forty-seven votes in 1986 of winning the seat held by Republican John Hiler. Finally, to add insult to injury, in 1989 the Republicans lost a special election called to fill the vacancy caused by the appointment of Republican representative Dan Coats to fill Vice President Dan Quayle's former Senate seat. This gave the Democrats control of the delegation, seven to three.

Nor is it even clear that the basic Republican claim of bias is well-supported. Norman J. Ornstein has pointed out that the gap between the share of seats and share of the vote for the Republicans seems to be more a consequence of the single-member district system employed in this country and the higher turnout among Republicans.[65] The single-member district system means that a party can win a seat with 51 percent of the vote as well as with 80 percent. If one party wins districts across the country by larger margins than the other party, the former party will "waste" a lot of votes even if there is no bias in districting. Districts are, moreover, apportioned on the basis of population, not voter turnout. As Table 9-7 shows, Democrats tend to do very well in districts in which relatively few people vote, and Republicans win a lot of districts with higher turnout. When these votes are added up for the nation as a whole, the total vote of the two parties is closer than it would be if turnout were equal in all districts. Thus the Republican "disadvantage" appears to be more a consequence of our electoral system than of deliberate Democratic design, and Republican hopes for substantial gains when districts are redrawn after 1990 may turn out to be little more than wishful thinking.

A third consideration relevant to the Republican party's future in House elections is the link between House outcomes and presidential voting, or rather the lack of such a link. Despite an enormous presidential landslide in 1984 and a solid win in 1988, Republican presidential candidates were unable to induce voters also to elect substantial numbers of House Republicans. In 1984, Reagan ran ahead of Mondale in 372 congressional districts, but Democratic House candidates carried a majority (191) of them. Walter Dean Burnham, writing about 1984, asked: "If Ronald Reagan could not provide the incentive for straight party voting, who will be able to do so in the future?"[66] Well, it wasn't George Bush in 1988,[67] and there is no reason to expect that any other presidential candidate will do so either.

Perhaps nothing better illustrates the difficulty Republicans have had in moving toward control of the House than their performance over

Table 9-7　Election Outcomes by Party in 1984 House Races, by Total Votes Cast in District

Winner	Less than 125,000	125,000-150,000	150,000-175,000	175,000-200,000	200,000-225,000	More than 225,000
Democrat	93%	93%	73%	57%	42%	50%
Republican	7	7	27	43	58	50
Total	100%	100%	100%	100%	100%	100%
(*N*)	(27)	(30)	(51)	(91)	(121)	(98)

Source: Adapted from Norman J. Ornstein, "Genesis of a Gerrymander," *Wall Street Journal,* May 7, 1985, 34.

Note: Because there is relatively little difference in the size of the voting-age population among congressional districts, the total number of votes cast provides a rough measure of the relative turnout among the districts. Uncontested seats have been excluded from these calculations.

the last decade in open-seat elections. In these instances all their disadvantages in challenging Democratic incumbents were stripped away. These races offered their best chance for gaining ground. Yet in the five general elections between 1980 and 1988, the Republicans gained only 10 seats net in 177 open-seat races. Moreover, most of those minimal gains were concentrated in 1980, when Reagan was first elected. If we consider only the last four elections, the Republicans gained the munificent total of *1 seat* in 134 open races.[68] At that rate, a majority will be a long time coming.

After consideration of all these factors, one must conclude that the likelihood of the Republicans' winning control of the House of Representatives in the near future, say through the mid-1990s, is relatively small. The Republicans would have to make a net gain of forty-three House seats over the number they held at the beginning of the 101st Congress to take control. But after the 1990 midterm contest, the Republicans might need fifty or more seats for control. It is not easy to see where such substantial Republican gains are likely to come from. We must therefore conclude that, barring any strong pro-Republican national tide, which seems most unlikely, the Democratic hold on the House is likely to be secure. Thus, even if the Republicans continue to dominate presidential election contests, they may still have achieved only a split-level realignment.

Notes

1. The definition of incumbent here is limited to elected incumbents. This includes all members of the House because the only way to become a representative is by election. In the case of the Senate, however, vacancies

Candidates and Outcomes 257

may be filled by appointment. Appointed senators are not counted as incumbents.

2. The Republicans won control of the House in eight consecutive elections between 1894 and 1908, far short of the current Democratic series of successes.

3. The Republicans also lost the Nebraska seat, which was held by an appointed Republican incumbent.

4. Paul R. Abramson, John H. Aldrich, and David W. Rohde, *Change and Continuity in the 1984 Elections,* rev. ed. (Washington, D.C.: CQ Press, 1987), 312-313.

5. The regional breakdowns used in this chapter are as follows: East: Connecticut, Delaware, Maine, Massachusetts, New Hampshire, New Jersey, New York, Pennsylvania, Rhode Island, and Vermont; Midwest: Illinois, Indiana, Iowa, Kansas, Michigan, Minnesota, Nebraska, North Dakota, Ohio, South Dakota, and Wisconsin; West: Alaska, Arizona, California, Colorado, Hawaii, Idaho, Montana, Nevada, New Mexico, Oregon, Utah, Washington, and Wyoming; South: Alabama, Arkansas, Florida, Georgia, Louisiana, Mississippi, North Carolina, South Carolina, Tennessee, Texas, and Virginia; border: Kentucky, Maryland, Missouri, Oklahoma, and West Virginia. This classification differs somewhat from the one we used in other chapters, but it is commonly used for congressional analysis.

6. Over the years changes in the southern electorate have also made southern Democratic constituencies more like northern Democratic constituencies and less like Republican constituencies, North and South. These changes have also enhanced the homogeneity of preferences within partisan delegations in Congress. See David W. Rohde, " 'Something's Happening Here; What It Is Ain't Exactly Clear': Southern Democrats in the House of Representatives," in *Home Style and Washington Work: Studies of Congressional Politics,* ed. Morris P. Fiorina and David W. Rohde (Ann Arbor: University of Michigan Press, 1989), 137-163; and Rohde, " 'The Reports of My Death Are Greatly Exaggerated': Parties and Party Voting in the House of Representatives," in *Changing Perspectives on Congress,* ed. Glenn R. Parker (Knoxville: University of Tennessee Press, 1990).

7. See Gary C. Jacobson and Samuel Kernell, *Strategy and Choice in Congressional Elections,* 2d ed. (New Haven, Conn.: Yale University Press, 1983), esp. Chaps. 2-4, for a corroborating analysis.

8. Richard F. Fenno, Jr., *Home Style: House Members in Their Districts* (Boston: Little, Brown, 1978).

9. The data on office backgrounds were taken from "1988 Candidates for Senate and House," *Congressional Quarterly Weekly Report,* October 15, 1988, 2955-2966.

10. See, for example, Abramson, Aldrich, and Rohde, *Change and Continuity in the 1984 Elections,* rev. ed., 240-242.

11. The data for earlier years are taken from ibid., and from Paul R. Abramson, John H. Aldrich, and David W. Rohde, *Change and Continuity in the 1980 Elections,* rev. ed. (Washington, D.C.: CQ Press, 1983), 198.

12. See Jacobson and Kernell, *Strategy and Choice;* Gary C. Jacobson, "Strategic Politicians and Congressional Elections, 1946-1980" (Paper delivered at the Annual Meeting of the American Political Science Association, New York, September 3-6, 1981); Jon R. Bond, Gary Covington, and Richard Fleisher, "Explaining Challenger Quality in Congressional Elections," *Journal of Politics* 47 (May 1985): 510-529; and David W. Rohde, "Risk-Bearing and

Progressive Ambition: The Case of Members of the United States House of Representatives," *American Journal of Political Science* 23 (February 1979): 1-26.

13. Charles E. Cook, "Odd-Numbered Years Determine Hill Winners," *Roll Call,* June 12-18, 1989, 6. See also Jonathan S. Krasno and Donald Philip Green, "Preempting Quality Challengers in House Elections," *Journal of Politics* 50 (November 1988): 920-936.

14. Rhodes Cook, "Is Competition in Elections Becoming Obsolete?" *Congressional Quarterly Weekly Report,* May 6, 1989, 1062-1063.

15. Jeffrey S. Banks and D. Roderick Kiewiet, "Explaining Patterns of Candidate Competition in Congressional Elections," *American Journal of Political Science* 33 (November 1989): 997-1015.

16. David Canon, *Actors, Athletes and Astronauts: Political Amateurism in the United States Congress* (Chicago: University of Chicago Press, forthcoming).

17. See Thomas E. Mann and Raymond E. Wolfinger, "Candidates and Parties in Congressional Elections," *American Political Science Review* 74 (September 1980): 617-632.

18. See David R. Mayhew, "Congressional Elections: The Case of the Vanishing Marginals," *Polity* 6 (Spring 1974): 295-317; Robert S. Erikson, "The Advantage of Incumbency in Congressional Elections," *Polity* 3 (Spring 1971): 395-405; Erikson, "Malapportionment, Gerrymandering, and Party Fortunes in Congressional Elections," *American Political Science Review* 66 (December 1972): 1234-1245; Warren Lee Kostroski, "Party and Incumbency in Postwar Senate Elections: Trends, Patterns, and Models," *American Political Science Review* 67 (December 1973): 1213-1234; and Donald Gross and David Breaux, "Historical Trends in U.S. Senate Elections" (Paper delivered at the Annual Meeting of the Midwest Political Science Association, Chicago, April 13-15, 1989).

19. Edward R. Tufte, "Communication," *American Political Science Review* 68 (March 1974): 211-213. The communication involved a discussion of Tufte's earlier article, "The Relationship Between Seats and Votes in Two-Party Systems," *American Political Science Review* 67 (June 1973): 540-554.

20. See John A. Ferejohn, "On the Decline of Competition in Congressional Elections," *American Political Science Review* 71 (March 1977): 166-176; Albert D. Cover, "One Good Term Deserves Another: The Advantage of Incumbency in Congressional Elections," *American Journal of Political Science* 21 (August 1977): 523-541; and Albert D. Cover and David R. Mayhew, "Congressional Dynamics and the Decline of Competitive Congressional Elections," in *Congress Reconsidered,* 2d ed., ed. Lawrence C. Dodd and Bruce I. Oppenheimer (Washington, D.C.: CQ Press, 1981), 62-82.

21. Morris P. Fiorina, *Congress: Keystone of the Washington Establishment,* 2d ed. (New Haven, Conn.: Yale University Press, 1989), esp. Chaps. 4-6.

22. See several conflicting arguments and conclusions in the *American Journal of Political Science* 25 (August 1981): John R. Johannes and John C. McAdams, "The Congressional Incumbency Effect: Is It Casework, Policy Compatibility, or Something Else? An Examination of the 1978 Election," 512-542; Morris P. Fiorina, "Some Problems in Studying the Effects of Resource Allocation in Congressional Elections," 543-567; Diana Evans Yiannakis, "The Grateful Electorate: Casework and Congressional Elections," 568-580; and John C. McAdams and John R. Johannes, "Does Casework Matter? A Reply to Professor Fiorina," 581-604. See also John R. Johannes, *To Serve the People: Congress and Constituency Service* (Lincoln: University of Nebraska Press,

1984), esp. Chap. 8; and Albert D. Cover and Bruce S. Brumberg, "Baby Books and Ballots: The Impact of Congressional Mail on Constituent Opinion," *American Political Science Review* 76 (June 1982): 347-359. The evidence in Cover and Brumberg for a positive electoral effect is quite strong, although the result may be applicable only to limited circumstances.

23. Ferejohn, "On the Decline of Competition," 174.
24. Cover, "One Good Term," 535.
25. The body of literature has now grown to be quite large. Some salient examples are: Gary C. Jacobson, "The Effects of Campaign Spending in Congressional Elections," *American Political Science Review* 72 (June 1978): 469-491; Jacobson, *Money in Congressional Elections* (New Haven, Conn.: Yale University Press, 1980); Jacobson, "Parties and PACs in Congressional Elections," in *Congress Reconsidered,* 4th ed., ed. Lawrence C. Dodd and Bruce I. Oppenheimer (Washington, D.C.: CQ Press, 1989), 117-152; Jacobson, "Money in the 1980 and 1982 Congressional Elections," in *Money and Politics in the United States: Financing Elections in the 1980s,* ed. Michael J. Malbin (Chatham, N.J.: Chatham House, 1984), 38-69; Jacobson and Kernell, *Strategy and Choice;* John A. Ferejohn and Morris P. Fiorina, "Incumbency and Realignment in Congressional Elections," in *The New Direction in American Politics,* ed. John E. Chubb and Paul E. Peterson (Washington, D.C.: Brookings Institution, 1985), 91-115.
26. Jacobson, "Money in the 1980 and 1982 Congressional Elections," 56-57. The analysis includes only incumbents with major party opposition.
27. *Roll Call,* November 13, 1988, 5. The figures are through September 20, 1988.
28. "Congressional War Chests," *Washington Post,* February 13, 1989, A21.
29. The 1986 election was the last for which complete spending data were available at the time this analysis was conducted. Data were taken from *Politics in America: The 100th Congress,* ed. Alan Ehrenhalt (Washington, D.C.: CQ Press, 1987). Our analysis excludes races with no major party opposition.
30. Abramson, Aldrich, and Rohde, *Change and Continuity in the 1980 Elections,* rev. ed., 201.
31. Ibid., 200-203; Abramson, Aldrich, and Rohde, *Change and Continuity in the 1984 Elections,* rev. ed., 246.
32. See, for example, Gary C. Jacobson, "Money and Votes Reconsidered: Congressional Elections, 1972-1982," *Public Choice* 47 (No. 1, 1985): 7-62; and the works cited above in note 25.
33. Donald Philip Green and Jonathan S. Krasno, "Salvation for the Spendthrift Incumbent: Reestimating the Effects of Campaign Spending in House Elections," *American Journal of Political Science* 32 (November 1988): 884-907.
34. Gary C. Jacobson, "The Effects of Campaign Spending in House Elections: New Evidence for Old Arguments," *American Journal of Political Science* 34 (May 1990): 334-362.
35. Alan I. Abramowitz, "Explaining Senate Election Outcomes," *American Political Science Review* 82 (June 1988): 385-403.
36. Gary C. Jacobson, "Campaign Spending and Voter Awareness of Congressional Candidates" (Paper presented at the Annual Meeting of the Public Choice Society, New Orleans, May 11-13, 1977), 16.
37. Significant elective offices included U.S. representative, statewide office, state legislature, countywide (supervisor or prosecutor), or citywide (mayor or prosecutor) offices.

38. Abramson, Aldrich, and Rohde, *Change and Continuity in the 1980 Elections,* rev. ed., 202-203.

39. Thomas B. Edsall, "GOP's Cash Advantage Failed to Assure Victory in Close Senate Contests," *Washington Post,* November 6, 1986, A46.

40. Quoted in Angelia Herrin, "Big Outside Money Backfired in GOP Loss of Senate to Dems," *Detroit Free Press,* November 17, 1986, 12A.

41. Julie Rovner, "Turnover in Congress Hits an All-Time Low," *Congressional Quarterly Weekly Report,* November 19, 1988, 3362-3365.

42. This discussion is based on a comparison of the average party support scores for members of both houses for 1988, which measures the proportion of votes on which a member supports his or her party when party majorities oppose one another. The data are taken from *Congressional Quarterly Weekly Report.*

43. Quoted in John Felton, "Baker Woos Hill With Call for Bipartisanship," *Congressional Quarterly Weekly Report,* January 21, 1989, 125.

44. See John Felton, "Bush, Hill Agree to Provide Contras With New Aid," *Congressional Quarterly Weekly Report,* March 25, 1989, 655-657.

45. "Senate Votes; House Votes," *Congressional Quarterly Weekly Report,* May 6, 1989, 1083-1084.

46. Quoted in John Felton, "Hill Gives Contra Package Bipartisan Support," *Congressional Quarterly Weekly Report,* April 15, 1989, 833.

47. See Rohde, "The Reports of My Death."

48. Helen Dewar, "GOP Looking to Move Up in Senate While Democrats Hope to Stay Even," *Washington Post,* July 2, 1989, A4.

49. Edward R. Tufte, "Determinants of the Outcomes of Midterm Congressional Elections," *American Political Science Review* 69 (September 1975): 812-826; and Tufte, *Political Control of the Economy* (Princeton, N.J.: Princeton University Press, 1978).

50. Jacobson and Kernell, *Strategy and Choice in Congressional Elections,* esp. chap. 3.

51. The Jacobson-Kernell hypothesis was challenged by Richard Born in "Strategic Politicians and Unresponsive Voters," *American Political Science Review* 80 (June 1986): 599-612. Born argued that economic and approval data at the time of the election were more closely related to outcomes than were data earlier in the year. Jacobson, however, offers renewed support for the hypothesis in an analysis of both district-level and aggregate data. See Gary C. Jacobson, "Strategic Politicians and the Dynamics of House Elections, 1946-1986," *American Political Science Review* 83 (September 1989): 773-793.

52. Alan I. Abramowitz, Albert D. Cover, and Helmut Norpoth, "The President's Party in Midterm Elections: Going from Bad to Worse," *American Journal of Political Science* 30 (August 1986): 562-576.

53. Bruce I. Oppenheimer, James A. Stimson, and Richard W. Waterman, "Interpreting U.S. Congressional Elections: The Exposure Thesis," *Legislative Studies Quarterly* 11 (May 1986): 228.

54. Robin F. Marra and Charles W. Ostrom, Jr., "Explaining Seat Change in the U.S. House of Representatives 1950-86," *American Journal of Political Science* 33 (August 1989): 541-569.

55. See, for example, Gary C. Jacobson and Samuel Kernell, "Party Organization and the Efficient Distribution of Campaign Resources: Republicans and Democrats in 1982" (Paper presented at the Weingart-Caltech Conference on the Institutional Context of Elections, California Institute of Technology,

Pasadena, February 16-18, 1984); and Jacobson, "The Republican Advantage in Campaign Finance," in *The New Direction in American Politics,* 143-173.

56. Jacobson, "The Republican Advantage," 156.
57. "Political Party Committee Activity, 1987-88," *Congressional Quarterly Weekly Report,* April 1, 1989, 718. The figures were $5.69 million for the Republicans and $3.10 million for the Democrats.
58. The data are reported in "PACs: The Givers and the Takers," *Washington Post,* April 10, 1989, A7.
59. See Bruce E. Cain, "Assessing the Partisan Effects of Redistricting," *American Political Science Review* 79 (June 1985): 320-333; and Cain, *The Reapportionment Puzzle* (Berkeley: University of California Press, 1984).
60. See Abramson, Aldrich, and Rohde, *Change and Continuity in the 1980 Elections,* rev. ed., 256-263.
61. Richard Born concludes that between 1952 and 1982, the partisan effects of redistricting have been modest and have weakened over time. See "Partisan Intentions and Election Day Realities in the Congressional Redistricting Process," *American Political Science Review* 79 (June 1985): 305-319.
62. Reapportionment is the process through which the 435 seats in the U.S. House of Representatives are redistributed among the states to reflect changes in population. Redistricting is the process through which congressional district lines within each state are redrawn.
63. Abramson, Aldrich, and Rohde, *Change and Continuity in the 1980 Elections,* rev. ed., 261-263. See also Alan I. Abramowitz, "Partisan Redistricting and the 1982 Congressional Elections," *Journal of Politics* 45 (August 1983): 767-770.
64. Christopher Buchanan, "Classic Gerrymander by Indiana Republicans," *Congressional Quarterly Weekly Report,* October 17, 1981, 2017-2022.
65. Norman J. Ornstein, "Genesis of a Gerrymander," *Wall Street Journal,* June 24, 1985, 14.
66. Walter Dean Burnahm, "A Continuing Political Gridlock," *Wall Street Journal,* June 24, 1985, 14.
67. Bush carried 299 congressional districts, of which 136 were won by Democratic House candidates. Richard E. Cohen, "Lonely Runner," *National Journal,* April 29, 1989, 1048.
68. In 1980 through 1988, the Democrats held ninety-five of the seats before the elections and eighty-five after. For 1982 through 1988, it was sixty-eight before and sixty-seven after. These open races exclude new seats created as a result of the redistricting before the 1982 election.

Chapter 10

The Congressional Electorate

In the preceding chapter we viewed congressional elections at the district and state level and saw how those outcomes come together to form a national result. In this chapter we consider congressional elections from the point of view of the individual voter, using the same National Election Studies (NES) surveys we employed to study presidential voting. We discuss how social forces, issues, partisan loyalties, incumbency, and evaluations of congressional and presidential performance influence the decisions of voters in congressional elections. We also try to determine the existence and extent of presidential coattails and to shed additional light on the effects of adequate or inadequate campaign resources on the part of challengers.

Social Forces and the Congressional Vote

In general, social forces relate to the congressional vote much as they do to the presidential vote.[1] But in 1988 Democratic congressional candidates did better than their presidential candidate, Michael S. Dukakis, in every single category used in the presidential vote analysis (Table 5-1.)[2] Consider the relationship between voting and race, for example. Democratic candidates for the House ran 14 points better than Dukakis among white voters and 2 points better even among black voters, from whom Dukakis received 90 percent of the vote. While Dukakis received only a little over two-fifths of the white vote, the NES survey shows that 55 percent of white voters supported Democratic House candidates.[3]

Keeping in mind the gap in relative support that we have discussed, we find that presidential and congressional voting patterns are similar not only with respect to race, but also for other social categories, including union membership, occupation, religion, and family income. (Except for voting by race, the discussion here, as in Chapter 5, is limited to white voters.) Members of union families were 11 points more likely to vote Democratic than voters from nonunion families; working-class voters were 9 points more Democratic than middle-class voters. Catholics were 16 points more likely to vote Democratic than Protestants. The gap between voters with annual family incomes of less than $10,000 and families that earned $50,000 or more is very large: 22 points. Like presidential voting, however, most of the difference in voting on this variable is captured by these extreme categories. If we exclude them, there is comparatively little variation in congressional vote by party along the income spectrum. For these and the other social forces, the comparison with the Democratic presidential vote is similar: in virtually every instance the direction of the relationship is the same.

Of particular interest is the relationship between House voting and gender. In Chapter 5, we saw that there was a small gender gap in the presidential vote, with women somewhat more likely to vote Democratic than men. With regard to the congressional vote, however, there is no gender gap at all. The proportion of men and women voting Democratic was identical. This is a change from 1984, when there was a small gender gap in voting for both president and Congress.

One clear exception to the similar patterns in presidential and congressional voting relates to comparisons of voting across regions. Here the presidential pattern is reversed. The election results demonstrate that the South was Bush's best region, and the NES survey shows he did especially well among southern whites. In House voting, the highest rate of support for Democrats was in the border states (where the number of respondents is relatively small),[4] and in the South. Sixty-four percent of southern whites voted Democratic for Congress, whereas only 37 percent voted for Dukakis. Despite the shattering of Democratic party ties at the presidential level in the South, white southerners still tend disproportionately to support Democratic congressional candidates.

Issues and the Congressional Vote

In Chapter 6 we analyzed the impact of issues on the presidential vote in 1988. Any attempt to conduct a parallel analysis for congressional elections is hampered by limited data. Because we do have data on voters' positions on many issues, however, one approach we can take is to see whether those positions are systematically related to the portion of the congressional vote going to one party or another. Table 10-1 shows the relationship between issue positions and voting for the House on the same seven issues analyzed in Chapter 6.[5] Because we would expect a

Table 10-1 Percentage Voting Democratic for the House, 1988, Controlling for Party Identification and Positions on Seven Issues

Party identification[a]	Issue position					
	Liberal		Middle		Conservative	
	(%)	(N)	(%)	(N)	(%)	(N)
Government Spending/Services						
Democrat	93	(59)	82	(166)	78	(23)
Independent	84	(31)	56	(140)	40	(35)
Republican	54	(13)	24	(164)	18	(68)
Defense Spending						
Democrat	95	(77)	82	(169)	85	(20)
Independent	73	(51)	58	(153)	38	(26)
Republican	43	(21)	23	(201)	21	(43)
Government Health Insurance						
Democrat	87	(91)	85	(131)	76	(33)
Independent	73	(48)	57	(113)	47	(49)
Republican	30	(37)	25	(114)	21	(101)
Jobs and Standard of Living						
Democrat	94	(52)	84	(154)	80	(49)
Independent	71	(21)	62	(113)	46	(80)
Republican	30	(10)	28	(116)	20	(132)
Aid to Minorities						
Democrat	87	(55)	88	(145)	78	(60)
Independent	81	(26)	62	(130)	47	(68)
Republican	30	(10)	23	(149)	26	(98)
Relations with Russia						
Democrat	86	(78)	86	(134)	83	(46)
Independent	62	(69)	61	(122)	44	(34)
Republican	30	(61)	22	(162)	22	(36)
Role of Women						
Democrat	87	(180)	79	(82)	88	(26)
Independent	64	(146)	51	(69)	62	(21)
Republican	26	(144)	23	(99)	21	(28)

Note: Numbers in parentheses are totals on which percentages are based. For each of the scales we group positions 1 and 2, positions 3 through 5, and positions 6 and 7. The "liberal" positions on these issues are: favor government spending and services; for reducing defense spending; favor government health insurance; government action on jobs and standard of living; favor aid for blacks/minorities; for cooperation with Russia; and for women having an equal role. See Figures 6-1 and 6-2, and Chapter 6, note 6, for more information about these scales.

[a] In this table and in Tables 10-3 through 10-8, independents who lean to one of the parties are classified as independents, strong and weak Democrats as Democrats, and strong and weak Republicans as Republicans.

relationship between issue positions and party identification and between party identification and the congressional vote, we control for party identification in the table. Reading across each row, we see that in most instances the more liberal the position of the voter, the more likely the voter is to vote Democratic. It is clear, however, that this relationship is not completely consistent, and there is considerable variation in its strength. Indeed, there is a much weaker relationship between issue positions and congressional voting in 1988 than our analysis showed for 1984.[6] Reading down each column, on the other hand, shows that party identification is consistently and strongly related to the way people vote, regardless of the respondents' position on these issues. Party identification categories consistently produce greater voting differences than do varying issue positions.

A more interesting perspective on issues in the congressional vote is to ask whether voters are affected by their perceptions of where candidates stand on the issues. Previous analysis has shown that there was a relationship between voter perception of House candidates' position on a liberal-conservative issue scale and the voter's choice.[7] Unfortunately, the 1988 NES survey does not contain similar questions on the perceived position of House candidates on issues. We can, however, draw on other research to shed further light on this question. In two articles Alan I. Abramowitz used NES surveys to demonstrate a relationship between candidate ideology and voter choice in both House and Senate elections.[8] For the 1978 Senate election, Abramowitz classified the contests according to the clarity of the ideological choice the two major party candidates offered to voters. He found that the higher the ideological clarity of the race, the more likely voters were to perceive some difference between the candidates on a liberalism-conservatism scale, and the stronger the relationship was between voters' positions on that scale and the vote. Indeed, in races with a very clear choice, ideology had approximately the same impact on the vote as party identification. In an analysis of House races in 1980 and 1982, Abramowitz found that ideology had a positive impact on voting in both cases (in other words, the more liberal the voter the more likely the voter was to vote Democratic), but that the relationship was statistically significant only in 1982.

Another point of view is offered in an analysis by Robert S. Erikson and Gerald C. Wright.[9] They examined the positions of 1982 House candidates on a variety of issues (expressed in response to a CBS News/*New York Times* poll) and found that, on most issues, most of the districts were presented with a liberal Democrat and a conservative Republican. They also found that moderate candidates did better in attracting votes than more extreme candidates.

So far, we have seen that both issue positions and party identification appear to have an independent impact on voter choice in congressional elections, with the impact of partisanship consistently being stronger. It is also clear, however, that neither of these factors, nor both together, accounts for all the variation in voting, so we must also consider other influences on the vote. Before moving on, we will provide more information on the effect of party identification on House voting.

Party Identification and the Congressional Vote

As our discussion in the preceding chapters demonstrates and data presented here indicate, party identification has a significant effect on voters' decisions. Table 10-2, which corresponds to Table 8-4 on the presidential vote, reports the percentage of whites voting Democratic for the House across all categories of partisanship from 1952 through 1988. Even a casual inspection of the data reveals that the proportion of voters who cast ballots in accordance with their party identification has declined substantially over time.

Consider first the strong identifier categories. In every election between 1952 and 1964, at least nine strong party identifiers out of ten supported the candidate of their party. After that, the percentage dropped, falling to four out of five in 1980, then fluctuating somewhat through 1988. The relationship between party and voting among weak party identifiers shows a similar decline over time, and the rates of defection are higher. By 1984 fully a third of the weak identifiers in both parties were voting for House candidates of the opposition, although there was some resurgence of partisanship within this group in 1988. Independents who lean to one party or the other show a more erratic pattern, although in most years defection rates tend to be higher since the 1970s than earlier.

Despite this increase in defections from party identification since the mid-1960s, strong party identifiers continue to be more likely to vote in accord with their party than weak identifiers. Weak Republicans are more likely to vote Republican than independents who lean toward the Republicans. Weak Democrats were more likely to vote Democratic than independents who leaned Democratic in most of the elections between 1952 and 1978, although in four of the last five elections this pattern was reversed.

As we saw in Chapter 8, however, the proportion of the electorate that strongly identifies with a political party has declined. Thus strong Democrats, for example, not only are less likely to vote Democratic than before, but also fewer voters identify themselves as strong Democrats. The impact of party on voting, therefore, has suffered a double weakening.

If party identifiers have been defecting more frequently in House elections, to whom have they been defecting? As one might expect from the preceding chapter, the answer is: to incumbents.

Table 10-2   Percentage of White Major Party Voters Who Voted
Democratic for the House, by Party Identification,
1952-1988

Party identification	1952	1954	1956	1958	1960	1962	1964	1966	1968
Strong Democrat	90	97	94	96	92	96	92	92	88
Weak Democrat	76	77	86	88	85	83	84	81	72
Independent, leans Democratic	63	70	82	75	86	74	78	54	60
Independent, no partisan leanings	25	41	35	46	52	61	70	49	48
Independent, leans Republican	18	6	17	26	26	28	28	31	18
Weak Republican	10	6	11	22	14	14	34	22	21
Strong Republican	5	5	5	6	8	6	8	12	8

Notes: To approximate the numbers upon which these percentages are based, see Table
8-2. Actual *N*s will be smaller than those that can be derived from Table 8-2 because
respondents who did not vote (or who voted for a minor party) have been excluded from
these calculations. Numbers also will be lower for the presidential election years because

Incumbency and the Congressional Vote

In Chapter 9 we mentioned Albert D. Cover's analysis of congressional
voting behavior between 1958 and 1974.[10] Cover compared the rates of
defection from party identification between voters who were of the same
party as the incumbent and those who were of the same party as the
challenger. The analysis showed no systematic increase over time in
defection among voters who shared identification with incumbents, and
the proportions defecting varied between 5 percent and 14 percent.
Among voters who identified with the same party as challengers, however, the rate of defection—that is, the proportion voting for the
incumbent instead of the candidate of their own party—increased
steadily from 16 percent in 1958 to 56 percent in 1972, then dropped to 49
percent in 1974. Thus the decline in the strength of the relationship
between party identification and House voting appears to be due in large
measure to increased support for incumbents.

Data on the percentage of respondents who voted Democratic for
the House and Senate in 1988, controlling for party identification
and incumbency, are presented in Table 10-3. In House voting we find
the same relationship as Cover did. As we present the percentage

1970	1972	1974	1976	1978	1980	1982	1984	1986	1988
91	91	89	86	83	82	90	87	91	86
76	79	81	76	79	66	73	66	71	80
74	78	87	76	60	69	84	76	71	86
48	54	54	55	56	57	31	59	59	66
35	27	38	32	36	32	36	39	37	37
17	24	31	28	34	26	20	33	34	29
4	15	14	15	19	22	12	15	20	23

the voting report is provided in the postelection interviews that usually contain about 10 percent fewer respondents than the preelection interviews in which party identification was measured. The 1954 survey measured voting intention shortly before the election. Except for 1954, the off-year election surveys are based upon a postelection interview.

of major party voters who voted Democratic, the defection rate for Democrats is the reported percentage subtracted from 100 percent. Among Republicans, the reported percentage is the defection rate. (By definition, independents cannot defect.) The proportion of voters defecting from their party identification is very low when that identification is shared by the incumbent: 4 percent among Democrats and 3 percent among Republicans.[11] When, however, the incumbent belongs to the other party, the rates are much higher: 47 percent among Democrats and 52 percent among Republicans. Note also that the support of the independents is skewed sharply in favor of the incumbent. When there was an incumbent Democrat running, three-fourths of the independents voted Democratic; when there was an incumbent Republican, three-fourths of the independents voted Republican.

A similar pattern is apparent from the data on Senate voting, although the pull of incumbency appears to be somewhat weaker. When given the opportunity to support a Republican House incumbent, 47 percent of the Democratic identifiers defected. Faced with the opportunity to support an incumbent Republican senator, only 31 percent defected. Because the proportion of the electorate that has the chance to

Table 10-3   Percentage Voting Democratic for the House and Senate, 1988, by Party Identification and Incumbency

| Incumbency | Party identification | | | | | |
| | Democrat | | Independent | | Republican | |
	(%)	(N)	(%)	(N)	(%)	(N)
House						
Democrat	96	(214)	75	(152)	52	(121)
None	80	(20)	70	(20)	4	(28)
Republican	53	(68)	24	(70)	3	(130)
Senate						
Democrat	94	(156)	73	(130)	41	(133)
None	91	(34)	59	(46)	17	(41)
Republican	69	(108)	39	(82)	8	(107)

Note: Numbers in parentheses are totals upon which percentages are based.

vote for Democratic and Republican senatorial candidates will vary greatly from election to election, it is difficult to make generalizations about the overall effects of incumbency in Senate contests. But the results in Table 10-3 show that in the House elections the Democrats are the clear beneficiaries of the tendency to support incumbents. Over two-fifths of all Republican identifiers lived in a district in which a Democratic incumbent was seeking reelection. On the other hand, just over a fifth of the Democratic identifiers lived in a district with a Republican incumbent running. Among independents, 63 percent lived in a district with a Democratic incumbent seeking reelection and 29 percent in a district with a Republican incumbent. In the remainder of this chapter we will further explore this relationship among party identification, incumbency, and congressional voting.

The Congressional Vote as a Referendum

In Chapter 7 we analyzed the effect of perceptions of presidential performance on the vote for president in 1988, more or less viewing that election as a referendum on Reagan's job performance. A similar conception can be applied here, employing different perspectives. On the one hand, a congressional election can be considered a referendum on the performance of a particular member of Congress in office; on the other, it can be viewed as a referendum on the performance of the president. We will consider both possibilities here.

For some time, public opinion surveys have shown that the approval ratings of the performance of congressional incumbents are very high, even when judgments on the performance of Congress as an institution are not. While traveling with House incumbents in their districts, Richard F. Fenno, Jr., noted that the people he met overwhelmingly approved of the performance of their own representative, although at the time the public generally disapproved of the job the institution was doing.[12] Data in the 1988 survey again indicate widespread approval of House incumbents: among respondents who had an opinion, an average of 91 percent endorsed their members' job performance. Approval was widespread, regardless of the party identification of the voter or the party of the incumbent. Indeed, an examination of all combinations of these two variables shows that the *lowest* approval rate for incumbents is the 75 percent level achieved by Republican members among Democratic party identifiers.[13]

Further evidence indicates, moreover, that the level of approval is electorally consequential. Table 10-4 shows the level of proincumbent voting among voters who share the incumbent's party and among those who are of the opposite party, controlling for whether they approve or disapprove of the incumbent's job performance. If voters approve of the member's performance and share his or her party identification, support is almost complete. At the opposite pole, among voters from the opposite party who disapprove, support is virtually nil. In the mixed categories, more than two-thirds of the voters support the incumbent. Because approval rates are very high even among members of the opposite party, most incumbents are reelected by large margins.

In Chapter 9 we pointed out that midterm congressional elections were influenced by public evaluations of the president's job performance. Voters who think the president is doing a good job are more likely to support the congressional candidate of the president's party. Less scholarly attention has been given to this phenomenon in presidential election years, but the 1988 NES survey provides us with the data needed to explore the question.

On the surface at least, there would appear to be a strong relationship. Among voters who approved of Reagan's job performance, only 40 percent voted Democratic for the House; among those who disapproved of the president's performance, 83 percent supported Democrats. In 1980 there was a similar relationship between the two variables, but when controls were introduced for party identification and incumbency, the relationship all but disappeared.[14] Approval of Carter increased the Democratic House vote by a small amount among Democrats, but had virtually no effect among independents and Republicans. In 1988, however, the results are very different. Table 10-5 presents the relevant data on House voting, controlling for party identification, incumbency,

Table 10-4　Percentage of Voters Supporting Incumbents in House Voting, 1988, by Party and Evaluations of Incumbent's Performance

	Voter's evaluation of incumbent's job performance			
	Approve		*Disapprove*	
Incumbent is of:	(%)	(N)	(%)	(N)
Same party as voter	98	(290)	[6]	(7)
Opposite party from voter	67	(134)	3	(29)

Notes: Numbers in parentheses are totals upon which percentages are based. The total number of cases is markedly lower than for previous tables because we have excluded respondents who did not evaluate the performance of the incumbent and those who live in a district with no incumbent running. The number in brackets is the number supporting the incumbent when the total *N* is less than 10.

and evaluation of Reagan's job performance. We find that even with these controls, there is still a noticeable impact on House voting from evaluations of the president's job. To be sure, Democrats are still more likely both to disapprove of Reagan and to vote Democratic than are Republicans. Yet even after controlling for the pull of incumbency, within each party identification category, those who disapprove of Reagan's job performance are noticeably more likely to vote Democratic for the House than are those who approve, and the difference in every category is larger than the corresponding difference in 1980. The results for 1984 are similar to those for the 1988 election. Further research is necessary to reconcile these conflicting findings. At this point, all we know is that in the three elections a popular incumbent appeared to be of some substantial benefit to House candidates of his party, while an unpopular incumbent seemed to have little negative effect on his party's candidates.

Presidential Coattails and the Congressional Vote

Another perspective on the congressional vote, somewhat related to the presidential referendum concept we have just considered, is the impact of the voter's presidential vote decision, or the "length" of a presidential candidate's coattails. That is, does a voter's decision to support a presidential candidate make him or her more likely to support a congressional candidate of the same party, permitting the congressional candidate, as the saying goes, to ride into office on the president's coattails?

Table 10-5 Percentage Voting Democratic for the House, 1988, Controlling for Evaluation of Reagan's Performance, Party Identification, and Incumbency

Party identification	Evaluation of Reagan's job							
	Incumbent is Republican				*Incumbent is Democrat*			
	Approve		Disapprove		Approve		Disapprove	
	(%)	(N)	(%)	(N)	(%)	(N)	(%)	(N)
Democrat	32	(22)	64	(45)	90	(59)	98	(150)
Independent	12	(43)	46	(26)	66	(101)	91	(45)
Republican	3	(116)	8	(12)	49	(110)	82	(11)

Note: Numbers in parentheses are totals upon which percentages are based.

Expectations regarding presidential coattails have been shaped in substantial measure by the period of the New Deal realignment. Franklin D. Roosevelt won by landslide margins in 1932 and 1936 and swept enormous congressional majorities into office with him. Research has indicated, however, that such strong pulling power by presidential candidates may have been a historical aberration, and in any event, that candidates' pulling power has declined in recent years.[15] In an analysis of the coattail effect since 1868, John A. Ferejohn and Randall L. Calvert point out that the effect is a combination of two factors: how many voters a presidential candidate can pull to congressional candidates of his party and how many congressional seats can be shifted between the parties by the addition of those voters.[16] (The second aspect is called the seats-votes relationship, or the swing ratio.)

Ferejohn and Calvert discovered that the relationship between presidential voting and congressional voting between 1932 and 1948 was virtually the same as it was between 1896 and 1928 and that the impact of coattails was strengthened by an increase in the swing ratio. In other words, the same proportion of votes pulled in by a presidential candidate produced more congressional seats than in the past. After 1948, they argue, the coattail effect declined because the relationship between presidential and congressional voting decreased. Analyzing data from presidential elections from 1956 through 1980, Ferejohn and Calvert reached similar conclusions about the length of presidential coattails.[17] They found that although every election during the period exhibited significant coattail voting, over time the extent of such voting probably declined.

Table 10-6 Percentage of Respondents Voting Democratic for House and Senate, 1988, Controlling for Party Identification and Presidential Vote

Presidential vote	Party identification					
	Democrat		*Independent*		*Republican*	
	(%)	*(N)*	*(%)*	*(N)*	*(%)*	*(N)*
House						
Bush	58	(40)	40	(132)	21	(257)
Dukakis	89	(254)	85	(102)	65	(20)
Senate						
Bush	64	(42)	40	(135)	21	(259)
Dukakis	88	(246)	83	(115)	74	(19)

Note: Numbers in parentheses are totals upon which percentages are based.

Data on the percentage of respondents who voted Democratic for the House and Senate in 1988, controlling for their presidential vote and their party identification, are presented in Table 10-6. For both congressional offices, a strong relationship is apparent. Within each party identification category, the proportion of Bush voters who supported Democratic congressional candidates is substantially lower than the proportion of Dukakis voters who cast their congressional ballots that way.

Because we know that this apparent relationship could be just an accidental consequence of the distribution of different types of voters among Democratic and Republican districts, in Table 10-7 we present the same data on House voting in 1988, but this time controlling for the party of the House incumbent. Despite this additional control, the relationship holds up very well. Within every category, Bush voters support Democratic candidates at substantially lower rates than do Dukakis voters. These data are consistent with the interpretation that Bush was an electoral asset to Republican congressional candidates in 1988. However, this asset did not provide a net benefit for the Republicans, since, as we saw in Chapter 9, they lost three House seats. It is also important to note that the results in both Table 10-6 and 10-7 are very similar to the corresponding data from 1980 and 1984. Within the various categories of party identification and congressional incumbency, the relationship between presidential voting and congressional voting seems to be substantially the same in these three elections.[18]

Table 10-7 Percentage of Respondents Voting Democratic for the
House, 1988, Controlling for Presidential Vote, Party
Identification, and Incumbency

	Presidential vote							
	Incumbent is Democrat				*Incumbent is Republican*			
	Dukakis		Bush		Dukakis		Bush	
Party identification	(%)	(N)	(%)	(N)	(%)	(N)	(%)	(N)
Democrat	98	(182)	78	(27)	61	(54)	17	(12)
Independent	99	(66)	57	(83)	50	(28)	3	(38)
Republican	100	(12)	46	(108)	[1]	(5)	2	(124)

Note: Numbers in parentheses are totals upon which percentages are based. Numbers in brackets are the number voting Democratic for the House where the total *N* is less than 10.

Incumbency and Candidate Resources Revisited

In Chapter 9 and this one, we have consistently seen the impact of incumbency both on congressional election outcomes and on the decisions of individual voters. In Chapter 9 we discussed the relationship between incumbency and candidate resources and argued that the larger victory margins of House incumbents, observed since the mid-1960s, may be primarily the consequence of the challengers' inability to raise enough money to compete effectively. The 1988 election study contains a number of questions that provide, we believe, further support for this position.

In addition to the various questions about attitudes and voting behavior we have employed so far, respondents in the 1988 survey were asked a number of questions about contacts they had with incumbents and challengers in House races.[19] Recalling our earlier discussion of incumbency and resources, we would expect that most voters were contacted in some way by their House incumbent, but that a large share of the electorate was not contacted by challengers, because many of the challengers lacked the resources to do so. There are as many as 400,000 persons of voting age in each district, and contacting them is an expensive task. The survey data bear out this expectation. Among congressional voters who live in contested districts with incumbents running, 41 percent report some contact with both candidates, but an additional 50 percent remember only contact with the incumbent. Nine

Table 10-8   Percentage Supporting House Incumbents, 1988, Controlling for Party of Voter and Incumbent and for Contact by Incumbent and Challenger

| | Voter is contacted by: | | | | | |
| | Only the incumbent | | Both candidates | | Neither candidate | |
Voter is:	(%)	(N)	(%)	(N)	(%)	(N)
Same party as incumbent	98	(192)	95	(113)	89	(35)
Independent	89	(102)	61	(100)	74	(19)
Opposite party from incumbent	60	(81)	45	(92)	69	(13)

Note: Numbers in parentheses are totals upon which percentages are based.

percent of the voters report no contact with either candidate, and less than 1 percent report being contacted only by the challenger. These results are also consistent with the earlier survey research studies on name recognition advantages of incumbents that we discussed in Chapter 9.

The next step is to assess whether these patterns of contact have electoral consequences. Table 10-8 presents data on voter support for incumbents controlling for party identification and contacts between voters and congressional candidates. (Because there were so few cases where voters were contacted only by the challenger, this category is excluded.) The results appear to be fairly strong and consistent with our expectations. When voters share partisanship with the incumbent, support rates tend to be very high across all categories, although there is some slippage when the incumbent and the challenger both fail to contact the voter. Among independents and voters who identify with the same party as the challenger, however, the variations across categories are substantial. When only the incumbent contacts independent voters, the incumbent wins nearly nine out of ten votes. But incumbents win only three out of five votes when both candidates contact the voters, although they win three out of four votes among the few respondents contacted by neither candidate. Similarly, among voters of the challenger's party, the defection rate is 60 percent when only the incumbent has contacted the voter, but it is lower when both candidates have contacted the voter. These results seem to support our hypothesis that a significant part of the electoral advantage of House incumbents is due to the inability of challengers to get their message across to voters.

Conclusion

In this chapter we have considered a variety of possible influences on voters' decisions in congressional elections. We found that social forces, with the exception of race, have a modest impact on that choice. Party identification and issues both apparently have an effect, with the former generally stronger than the latter.

Consistent with our discussion in the preceding chapter, we find here that incumbency has a major and consistent impact on voters' choices. It solidifies the support of the incumbent's partisans, attracts independents, and leads to defections by voters who identify with the challenger's party. Incumbent support is linked to positive evaluation of the representative's job by the voters and apparently also to greater contact with voters. The tendency to favor incumbents appears to be of particular benefit to the Democratic party in House races. Within the context of this incumbency effect, voters' choices also seem to be affected by their evaluations of the job the president is doing and by their vote choice for president.

Notes

1. As we saw in Chapter 5, the 1988 NES survey results for the presidential vote were very close to the actual election results revealed by the official election statistics. However, the 1988 NES survey somewhat overestimated the Democratic congressional vote. According to the survey, the Democrats received 58.9 percent of the major party vote; official election results show they actually received only 53.9 percent. See "Counting the Vote: Nationwide Totals for 1988 Elections," *Congressional Quarterly Weekly Report*, May 6, 1989, 1063.
2. We will confine our attention in this section to voting for the House because this group of voters is more directly comparable to the presidential electorate. Except for our comparison of whites and blacks, our social comparisons refer to white voters only. We here employ the same definitions for social and demographic categories used in Chapters 4 and 5.
3. In this instance, the overrepresentation of the Democratic vote in the 1988 NES survey might affect our conclusions. As the Democrats received only 53.9 percent of the major party vote, they could not have received 55 percent of the white vote. A figure of 50 percent seems more likely. However, there is no doubt that a substantially larger proportion of whites voted for Democratic House candidates than voted for Dukakis.
4. The reported Democratic vote in the border states is 83 percent, but this result is based upon only sixty-five voters. We are using the standard definition of regions employed in the NES studies, and thus the border states include Kentucky, Maryland, Oklahoma, Tennessee, West Virginia, and the District of Columbia. The South includes Alabama, Arkansas, Florida, Georgia, Louisiana, Mississippi, North Carolina, South Carolina, Texas, and Virginia.
5. To simplify the presentation, we have eliminated from consideration votes for minor party candidates in all the tables in this chapter. Furthermore, to

ensure that our study of choice is meaningful, in all tables except Table 10-2 we include only voters who lived in congressional districts in which both major parties ran candidates.

6. For our analysis of the 1984 results, see Paul R. Abramson, John H. Aldrich, and David W. Rohde, *Change and Continuity in the 1984 Elections,* rev. ed. (Washington, D.C.: CQ Press, 1987), 265-266.

7. Paul R. Abramson, John H. Aldrich, and David W. Rohde, *Change and Continuity in the 1980 Elections,* rev. ed. (Washington, D.C.: CQ Press, 1983), 215-216.

8. Alan I. Abramowitz, "Choices and Echoes in the 1978 U.S. Senate Elections: A Research Note," *American Journal of Political Science* 25 (February 1981): 112-118; and Abramowitz, "National Issues, Strategic Politicians, and Voting Behavior in the 1980 and 1982 Congressional Elections," *American Journal of Political Science* 28 (November 1984): 710-721.

9. Robert S. Erikson and Gerald C. Wright, "Voters, Candidates, and Issues in Congressional Elections," in *Congress Reconsidered,* 3d ed., ed. Lawrence C. Dodd and Bruce I. Oppenheimer (Washington, D.C.: CQ Press, 1985), 91-116.

10. Albert D. Cover, "One Good Term Deserves Another: The Advantage of Incumbency in Congressional Elections," *American Journal of Political Science* 21 (August 1977): 523-541. Cover includes in his analysis not only strong and weak partisans, but also independents with partisan leanings.

11. It should be noted that the 1988 NES survey may contain biases that inflate the percentage who report voting for House incumbents (see note 19 below).

12. Richard F. Fenno, Jr., "If, as Ralph Nader Says, Congress Is 'the Broken Branch,' How Come We Love Our Congressmen So Much?" in *Congress in Change: Evolution and Reform,* ed. Norman J. Ornstein (New York: Praeger, 1975), 277-287. This theme is expanded and analyzed in Richard F. Fenno, Jr., *Home Style: House Members in Their Districts* (Boston: Little, Brown, 1978).

13. The 1984 and 1988 surveys show that there has been a shift in the approval level of the job Congress has been doing. In the 1980 NES survey there was only a 41 percent approval level, while in 1984 and 1988, 60 percent of the respondents approved.

14. Abramson, Aldrich, and Rohde, *Change and Continuity in the 1980 Elections*, rev. ed., 220-221. For the 1984 results, see Abramson, Aldrich, and Rohde, *Change and Continuity in the 1984 Elections,* rev. ed., 272.

15. Opinion on this last point is not unanimous, however. See Richard Born, "Reassessing the Decline of Presidential Coattails: U.S. House Elections from 1952-80," *Journal of Politics* 46 (February 1984): 60-79.

16. John A. Ferejohn and Randall L. Calvert, "Presidential Coattails in Historical Perspective," *American Journal of Political Science* 28 (February 1984): 127-146.

17. Randall L. Calvert and John A. Ferejohn, "Coattail Voting in Recent Presidential Elections," *American Political Science Review* 77 (June 1983): 407-419.

18. See Abramson, Aldrich, and Rohde, *Change and Continuity in the 1980 Elections,* rev. ed., 222-223, for the corresponding data on 1980; and Abramson, Aldrich, and Rohde, *Change and Continuity in the 1984 Elections,* rev. ed., 273-275, for the data on 1984.

19. Researchers have argued that the NES surveys from 1978 through 1982 have a built-in bias among the respondents in favor of incumbents because the question on congressional voting is preceded by a set of questions about the respondent's perceptions of and contacts with the incumbent, and in many of

these questions the incumbent is mentioned by name. See Robert B. Eubank and David John Gow, "The Pro-Incumbent Bias in the 1978 and 1980 National Election Studies," *American Journal of Political Science* 27 (February 1983): 122-139; and David John Gow and Robert B. Eubank, "The Pro-Incumbent Bias in the 1982 National Election Study," *American Journal of Political Science* 28 (February 1984): 224-230. This problem was alleviated in the 1984 survey because the incumbent-perception and contact questions were asked after the voting behavior questions. In the 1986 and 1988 surveys, however, questions about contacts by the incumbent preceded the questions about congressional voting behavior. Further research is necessary to determine the impact of this change upon responses to questions about voting behavior.

PART 4

The 1988 Elections in Perspective

A careful analysis of past voting patterns can provide some evidence for speculating about future elections. Admittedly, unexpected developments may dramatically change political life. The breakdown of Communist rule in Eastern Europe during the last two months of 1989, as well as reforms in the Soviet Union, provide startling reminders that unexpected developments can occur. Indeed, these changes, if they persist, may alter American politics by reducing Cold War tensions, thus diminishing the importance of foreign policy concerns in future elections. The way George Bush responds to these developments will not only affect prospects for world peace, but will also affect his relationships with conservative members of his own party.

Other international developments may also affect American domestic politics. As the economies of advanced industrial societies become more interdependent, the ability of domestic political leaders to affect their own economies may be reduced. Thus, the movement of the European Economic Community toward greater economic integration in 1992 may affect the American economy in ways that political leaders cannot control. At least in the short run, economic changes may substantially affect both congressional and presidential elections. Both long-term forces and short-term changes affect election outcomes. In our analysis, we have carefully documented several long-term patterns, but we cannot predict the short-term changes that can affect specific elections.

Despite the unpredictability of all politics, the American political system has constitutional features that make it somewhat more predictable than the political systems of most other democracies, and far more predictable than the political systems of dictatorships. Most important, both congressional and presidential elections take place according to a constitutionally fixed schedule. Thus, we know that all 435 seats in the House of Representatives will be filled in 1990 and again in 1992. We know that a census will be held in 1990, that some states will gain representation, and that others will lose. We know that most congressional districts will be redrawn, creating more opportunities for change in 1992 than in 1990. Moreover, we know that Bush's first term is scheduled to end on January 20, 1993. Although the actual election date is not constitutionally fixed, we can be confident that the next general election for president will take place on November 3, 1992.

The pattern of past midterm election results suggests that the Republicans have virtually no chance to win control of the House in 1990, and thus the 1992 elections provide the first opportunity to end the divided partisan control of the Congress and the White House that has characterized postwar American politics. In analyzing the insights that the 1988 election provides about the future, we first turn to divided partisan rule. We show that divided rule is not unprecedented, but earlier periods of divided rule were substantially different from the present period. Moreover, we examine the factors that have contributed to eighteen consecutive Democratic victories in the House. We believe that there are powerful systemic forces that contribute to this Democratic advantage. Although divided partisan control of the government will eventually end, it seems more likely that it will end by the Democrats regaining the White House than by the Republicans gaining a majority in the House of Representatives.

We therefore turn to the prospects for continued Republican dominance in presidential elections, considering four possibilities. First, the Republicans may extend their winning streak and become increasingly dominant in winning the White House. Second, the Democrats could return to dominance. Although a single presidential win would not make the Democrats the majority party, it would provide them an opportunity to reshape the political agenda and thereby return to dominance. Third, a new political party could emerge and win the presidency, although we believe there are powerful systemic factors that make such a development unlikely. Last, a Democratic presidential victory might reestablish the pattern of electoral volatility that ended, at least temporarily, with the Republican presidential victory of 1988. Evaluating these alternative possibilities allows us to return to a basic question we raised at the outset of this book. Has there been, or will there soon be, a partisan realignment?

Chapter 11

The 1988 Elections and the Future of American Politics

The 1988 election brought a new president to power, but George Bush represented continuity as well as change. As Ronald Reagan's loyal vice president, he pledged to maintain many of Reagan's policies, and he was especially committed to resist new taxes. Bush offered new policy proposals, but he faced a House and Senate solidly controlled by the Democrats.

Expectations for change were low. Unlike Reagan in 1981, who had a Republican Senate and a House in which Republicans and conservative Democrats often formed a working majority, Bush realized that he would be heavily dependent upon the cooperation of the congressional Democratic leadership. In his first four months in office, he compromised with the Democratic Congress by reaching an agreement on the fiscal 1990 budget that cut spending and increased revenues. He also reached an agreement on aiding the contras in Nicaragua, defusing a potentially divisive foreign policy issue.

But the prospects for new programs were limited. As Bush began his presidency the national debt reached $2.8 trillion. The estimated deficit for fiscal 1989 was $164 billion, and the total national debt was projected to reach $3 trillion. The national debt and the budget deficits that created them limited new expenditures and would doubtless have imposed severe limits even if Michael S. Dukakis had been elected. Moreover, new problems had emerged. Massive federal expenditures were needed to rescue many of the nation's savings and loan institutions, and the compromise solution reached by Bush and Congress may ultimately cost taxpayers some $162 billion. By the end of 1989, it appeared that improved relations with the Soviet Union might enable the government to reduce defense spending, but Bush argued that there would be no "peace dividend" that could finance new domestic programs.[1]

The choice of Bush over Dukakis will probably have important policy consequences because the Supreme Court is closely divided on many issues and because Bush is likely to make one or more appointments. The Supreme Court term that ended in July 1989 clearly demonstrated that Reagan's three appointments—Sandra Day O'Connor, Antonin Scalia, and Anthony M. Kennedy—had turned the Court in a conservative direction.[2] Several important cases were decided by a five to four majority.[3] In future antidiscrimination actions, employees would have to prove that job requirements screening out women or minority group members were not based upon business necessities. The Court ruled that white workers could challenge affirmative action agreements in subsequent legal actions, and the Court narrowed the scope of an 1866 civil rights law that banned discrimination in private employment. By similar five to four votes the Court ruled that states could execute murderers who are mentally retarded as well as those who were sixteen when they committed murder. The Court also ruled that inmates on death row did not have the constitutional right to a lawyer in making a second round of appeals to state courts.

Not all the five to four decisions resulted in conservative victories. The Court ruled that burning the American flag as a political protest is constitutionally protected by the First Amendment. But in *Webster v. Reproductive Health Services,* a major decision on a Missouri abortion law, the Court upheld the right of the state to place sharp restrictions on abortions. Although the Supreme Court did not overturn the 1973 *Roe v. Wade* decision, which prohibited states from outlawing abortion, by the end of its term this decision seemed in jeopardy.

Of course, the president does not have a free hand in making Court appointments, since they must be approved by a majority of the Senate. The Senate rejected Reagan's appointment of Robert H. Bork to the Supreme Court in 1987, because Bork's outspoken conservative policies were too controversial. But it could not ultimately block Reagan's appointment of a conservative, and, by appointing Kennedy, he created a conservative Court majority on many issues. If Bush gains the opportunity to make even one new appointment to the Supreme Court, he may push the balance even more clearly in a conservative direction.

While the division of partisan control between the Senate and the president may have little effect on Bush's ability to appoint conservative justices, divided control between Congress and the president may make it difficult to initiate new domestic policies. Although the president has considerable autonomy in making foreign policy decisions, he needs congressional cooperation in making economic policies and in raising revenues for new programs. The nation still has massive budget deficits, a negative trade balance, and a decaying infrastructure of roads, bridges, and railways. Dramatic solutions to these problems seem unlikely. As Gerald M. Pomper writes, "A divided government is unlikely to be an active government, for the Congress provides no substitute for the Presidency as a continuing source of energy and policy direction." [4] Apart from the policy consequences of divided government, we may ask why divided government has become the prevailing pattern in postwar American politics, and whether divided partisan control of the presidency and Congress is likely to end.

Divided Government

Many scholars argue that no realignment has occurred because the Republicans have failed to take control of Congress. Some argue that, at most, there has been a split-level realignment, and others maintain that contemporary American politics render the very concept of realignment useless. Clearly, the postwar years have been characterized by divided partisan control of the presidency and Congress. Partisan division briefly occurred in the 80th Congress, elected in 1946, when the Democrats under Harry S Truman lost control of the House and Senate. But Truman held the presidency in 1948, and the Democrats regained control of Congress. In his landslide victory of 1952, Dwight D. Eisenhower brought with him Republican majorities in the House and Senate, but the Republicans lost control of both houses in the 1954 midterm elections. They never regained control of the House, and the Democrats have now won control of the House in eighteen consecutive general elections, by far the longest period of continuous partisan control in the nation's history. The Democrats retained majorities in the Senate through 1980, but the Republicans captured the Senate in Reagan's 1980 triumph, losing it six years later in the 1986 midterm election.

Regardless of what happens in the 1990 midterm election, the thirty-six years between 1955 and 1991 (the 84th through the 101st Congresses) will have witnessed twenty-four years of divided partisan control. And the twenty-two years between 1969 and 1991 (the 91st through the 101st Congresses) will have witnessed eighteen years of divided control.

Divided partisan control is not unprecedented, but for most of American history the same party has controlled both the presidency and Congress. And parties that have captured the presidency in previous realignments have also managed to win both houses of Congress. [5] When Abraham Lincoln won the presidency for the Republicans, the party won both houses of Congress and held both branches until the 1874 midterm election. The Republicans had already captured both houses of

Congress two years before William McKinley's 1896 victory over William Jennings Bryan. Although the GOP lost House seats in 1896, they easily held control, and they maintained control of both chambers until the 1910 midterm election. And when Franklin D. Roosevelt won the presidency in 1932, the Democrats also won control of both houses of Congress, then held control of both chambers until the 1946 midterm election.

The only lengthy periods of divided partisan control, apart from the present, were from 1843 to 1861 (the 28th through the 36th Congresses) and from 1875 to 1897 (the 44th through the 54th Congresses). During six of the eighteen years between 1843 and 1861 Whig presidents faced a Democratic House (and for four of these years a Democratic Senate), for two years a Democratic president faced a Whig House, and for four years Democratic presidents shared power with a Republican House. During ten of the twenty-two years between 1875 and 1897 Republican presidents faced a Democratic House of Representatives (and for two of these years a Democratic Senate). For four years Democrat Grover Cleveland faced a Republican Senate, and for another two years the Republicans controlled both chambers. During these periods there was considerable electoral volatility in presidential elections, for, as we saw in Chapter 3, the party controlling the presidency lost four consecutive elections between 1840 and 1852 and again between 1884 and 1896. There was also great volatility in congressional elections. Partisan control of the House changed six times during the nine elections from 1842 through 1858, and it changed six times during the eleven elections from 1874 through 1894. These periods of volatility and divided partisan control both ended with "critical" elections, the 1860 election, which brought the Republicans to power, and the 1896 election, which solidified Republican rule.

These earlier periods of divided partisan control provide few clues about the present, however. The dynamics of House elections were vastly different, with incumbents much more vulnerable to defeat. Moreover, with the exception of the 80th Congress, after World War II divided government has always resulted from the Republican party controlling the presidency with the Democrats controlling Congress. And, unlike the earlier period, in which there were numerous changes of partisan control in the House, the Democrats will have held the House for thirty-six consecutive years when the 101st Congress ends.

Divided control in these earlier periods eventually ended when polarizing elections raised new issues and created a new partisan balance. In 1860 divided control ended with a new party winning the presidency. But in 1896 it ended because the party that won most of the presidential elections during the late nineteenth century gained firm control over Congress as well. But there is no reason to believe that the present period of divided control will end soon, and even less reason to believe it will end by the Republicans gaining control of the House of Representatives. Let us briefly review the evidence.

In the first place, Democratic dominance of the House is unprecedented. No previous period of American history has seen such lengthy dominance by a single party. Moreover, as Figure 9-1 showed, the Democrats have never come close to losing control, for after 1956 they held 56 percent of the House seats even in their three worst showings (1968, 1972, and 1980). This dominance alone strongly suggests that there are powerful forces favoring the Democrats in House elections.

One Democratic advantage has clearly been reduced, however. During the entire postwar era, and back into the 1930s, the Democrats held a lead in party loyalty among the electorate. This advantage has eroded. Unfortunately for the Republicans, the relationship of party identification to congressional voting preferences has declined, mainly, as we saw in Chapter 10, because many partisans desert their party to support incumbents. As there are more Democratic incumbents, these defections tend to benefit the Democrats.

Because they have more incumbents, the Democrats enjoy some advantages in fund raising, especially from political action committees (PACs), and the Democratic National Committee has developed strategies for helping candidates raise PAC funds. In 1988, even Democrats running for open seats raised more PAC money than Republicans seeking such seats, and Democratic challengers raised more PAC funds than Republican challengers. Given these disparities, it is easy to see why the Democrats viewed Bush's proposal to outlaw PAC contributions as an attempt to gain partisan advantage. Bush argued that his reform would reduce the ironclad grip incumbents have on their seats, but Ronald H. Brown, the newly elected Democratic National Committee chairman, was quick to condemn the proposal as a "fat cat protection scheme." While some campaign reforms may be enacted by Congress, it seems highly unlikely that Bush's proposal will be taken seriously.

Some argue that the Democrats gain from partisan efforts in drawing congressional districts. This advantage, the Republicans hope, could prove temporary. After every census, many states gain congressional seats while many others lose seats, and, as a result, existing district boundaries must be redrawn. Even if a state retains its present number of House seats, districts usually need to be redrawn to assure that all districts within the state have roughly equal population. Some claim that the Democrats have redrawn district boundaries to their advantage, noting that the Democratic share of seats in the House is larger than their total share of the popular vote. But this bias, as we saw, results mainly from the tendency of Democratic candidates to win in districts where turnout is low. Moreover, even though parties can sometimes reap substantial benefits by redrawing district boundaries, they are well positioned to make favorable changes only if they control both the governorship and both houses of the state legislature. As of early 1990, the Republicans held full partisan control in only four states with a total of 11 House seats, while the Democrats held full control in fifteen states with a total of 117 seats. The key question is who will have partisan control after the 1990 elections, for that is when new district boundaries will be drawn. But the Republicans currently have a long way to go before they can take advantage of the reapportionment and redistricting that will result from the 1990 census.

The Republicans can hope to score a presidential landslide in 1992, and with it bring many Republicans to Congress. But, as we have seen, in the last two presidential elections Republican candidates have had virtually no coattails. One might expect coattails to be longer in an election that occurs after redistricting, for redistricting often reduces the advantages of incumbency. Many representatives who seek reelection are forced to run in districts in which there are many voters who are new constituents. Even so, the last presidential election to be held after reapportionment and redistricting brought the Republicans few gains. Nixon won 61 percent of the popular vote in 1972 and carried forty-nine states, but the GOP gained only twelve House seats.

Some contend that the Democrats are advantaged because voters prefer divided government. We doubt that many voters consciously vote for divided government. As Gary C. Jacobson reasons, if this were the case, voters who switched from Reagan in 1984 to Dukakis in 1988 would have also switched from a Democratic vote for Congress to a Republican vote.[6] We doubt that many voters made such a switch.[7]

A more reasonable argument is that voters believe that the president and Congress perform different jobs and represent different interests. According to Byron E. Shafer, for example, split partisan control is based upon a new structuring of political issues. After the 1968 election, he writes, "The presidency was to be pre-eminently about foreign policy and cultural values; the Republican party was to gain the majority position on these issues. . . . The House was to remain centered on social welfare and service provision," and the Democrats held the majority position on these issues. And, according to Shafer, the Senate became competitive because it "was to be *centered* on social welfare and economics, but to be amenable to foreign policy and cultural values as well, so that it would lean Democratic but be available to the Republicans." [8]

Jacobson makes a similar argument, maintaining that "divided control of the presidency and Congress is more a byproduct of the electorate's self-contradictory preferences than the fulfillment of sophisticated ideological balancing." For example, voters favor a balanced budget and lower taxes, but they also favor a strong national defense; government aid to the poor and elderly; and government spending to protect the environment, to support education, and to provide medical services. "During the 1980s," Jacobson writes, "partisan (Republican, Democratic) and institutional (president, Congress) differences combined to give voters the chance to express their contradictory preferences at the polls." [9]

The arguments by Shafer and Jacobson seem plausible, but they need to be tested. In some cases, the data do not appear to support their claims. For example, both maintain that the Republicans clearly benefit from foreign policy issues. Yet the data on issue preferences presented in Chapter 6 reveal that the average voter was somewhat closer to the public's perception of where Dukakis stood on defense spending than to where Bush stood. The data also show that the public saw little difference between Bush's and Dukakis's views on cooperation with Russia (see Figure 6-2). Clearly, further research is needed to determine the extent to which contradictory issue preferences help the Democrats maintain congressional control.

Last, the Democrats may benefit because voters see Congress as the institution designed to protect special interests. The Republicans win the presidency, Pomper argues, because they seem to defend basic American values. The job of Congress, he writes, is "to deal with the particularistic needs of constituents and the distinctive demands of interest groups. . . . Because Democrats are more trusted to 'care about people like me,' or to be 'on your side,' Democrats continue to control the House and Senate. Divided government is the result of a divided American political mind." [10] In a similar argument, Jacobson maintains that a split vote "is consistent with differences in the duties that voters assign to presidents and members of Congress." Presidents are expected to safeguard the broad national interest. "Members of Congress," Jacobson writes, "are expected to protect constituents from damaging government policies regardless of the broader benefits to the nation as a whole. . . . On election day it is not so much that voters balance Democrats in one branch against Republicans in the other to get a government that is closer to their centrist views but that majorities prefer a president committed to a set of diffuse collective goods and congressional representatives who promise to minimize what voters have to give up to achieve them." [11]

If these arguments are correct, it is hard to see how the Republicans can gain control of the House of Representatives. Eventually, divided control may end. But despite the dismal record of Democratic candidates in the last three presidential elections, it seems more likely that divided government will end by the Democrats regaining the presidency than by the Republicans winning the House. Therefore, we must ask to what extent future Republican control of the White House is assured.

Continued Republican Dominance

The Republicans have now won five of the last six presidential elections. But what of the future? Can they continue their dominance of the White House through the end of the century and into the next?

Winning three presidential elections in a row is a clear sign of party dominance, and the Republicans exhibited such dominance in the 1980s. They came close to winning six straight elections, because even after the Watergate scandal, Gerald R. Ford, the unelected Republican incumbent who had pardoned Nixon, came close to winning the White House.[12] As we saw in Chapter 3, there are many states, especially in the West, that the Republicans consistently win, giving them a substantial electoral vote base. The 1980, 1984, and 1988 elections suggest that the GOP has an equally strong—perhaps even stronger—base of electoral votes in the South.

Many political scientists think that the most positive development for future Republican prospects is the shift in party identification toward the Republicans. The results in Chapter 8 suggest that the substantial shift in party loyalties between 1980 and 1988 was a major factor contributing to Bush's victory. To date, this shift in party loyalties has not aided the Republicans much beyond the White House. But Republicans can hope that the shift in party loyalties will eventually allow them to win more lower offices as well. The shift has been most dramatic in the South, where, according to some surveys, more whites now identify with the Republicans than with the Democrats.[13]

As we saw in Chapter 8, in the nation as a whole the Republicans have pulled nearly even with the Democrats in party identification. The major shift toward the GOP occurred shortly before the 1984 presidential election, and this shift was registered in the National Election Studies (NES) surveys.[14] The Michigan party identification measure is highly regarded because it is specifically designed to measure long-term commitment to a political party.[15] In 1980, the NES surveys found no evidence of a shift in party loyalties to the GOP, even in the survey conducted shortly after the election, and the 1982 NES survey also revealed no shift toward the GOP. In 1984, these surveys registered a sizable pro-Republican shift. Although the GOP has not made further gains in subsequent NES surveys, the gains registered in the fall of 1984 persisted in the 1986 and 1988 surveys (see Table 8-1). Moreover, as we saw, both the National Opinion Research Center (NORC) General Social Surveys and the Gallup polls show similar shifts in party loyalties toward the Republicans. Admittedly, the Democrats still hold a slight edge in party identification. But because Republicans are consistently more likely to vote than Democrats, Republican parity in party loyalties might be enough to make the GOP the majority party.

Moreover, as we noted in Chapter 8, Republican loyalties are strongest among the young, a finding documented by the NES surveys, as well as analyses of Gallup surveys, and surveys conducted by CBS News and the *New York Times*. More recent CBS News/*New York Times* surveys provide further evidence.[16] The surveys used to monitor party loyalties across time are telephone surveys, and the questions used are similar to those employed by the NES.[17] According to these surveys, in 1981, 49 percent of the respondents identified with or leaned toward the Democratic party, while only 39 percent were Republicans. The Democratic advantage narrowed markedly in 1984, and in 1985 the Democrats held only a 47 percent to 43 percent lead. In surveys based upon 4,178 respondents conducted in early 1989, the Democratic lead had shrunk even further. Forty-six percent of the respondents identified with or leaned toward the Democratic party, while 44 percent identified with or leaned toward the Republicans. Moreover, the shift among young voters has been dramatic. Among eighteen- to twenty-nine-year-olds interviewed in 1981, the Democrats held a 47 percent to 42 percent lead. But in 1985, the Republicans held a 48 percent to 42 percent lead over the Democrats. In the surveys conducted in early 1989, the Republican lead among the young had widened. Among respondents below the age of 30, 52 percent identified with or leaned toward the Republicans, while only 38 percent identified with or leaned toward the Democrats.

It should be emphasized, however, that GOP gains in party identification have not led to Republican dominance beyond the presidency. Despite GOP gains in party identification in the South, for example, the Democrats won 77 of the 116 southern House seats in 1988. And, although the Republicans held the governorship in five of the eleven southern states, the Democrats held majority control of both houses of the state legislature in all eleven states, and held a two to one margin in both houses in six of the eleven states. Of course, if Republican gains in party loyalties increase they may lead to Republican victories beyond the presidency. The decline in Democratic loyalties among the electorate deprives the Democrats of a valuable asset, and concerted Republican efforts to convert both party activists and voters are underway in many states, especially in the South.

Despite their strengths the Republicans have liabilities as well, and these liabilities may ultimately cost them the presidency. First, the Republicans are far to the right politically, and are far more conservative than the electorate. As we saw in Chapter 6, the electorate was on average less conservative than it viewed Bush as being on all seven issues for which appropriate measures were available. But many Republicans view Bush as too moderate. Bush was able to capture the Republican nomination because of his close ties to Reagan, and because he was the only candidate with the money and organization to compete in a heavily frontloaded nomination campaign. But Bush may still have felt the need to placate the far right of his party by choosing Dan Quayle as his running mate. As we saw, the average citizen was on balance somewhat closer to where Dukakis was viewed on the issues than to where Bush was viewed. If the Republicans nominated a candidate who was clearly on the right of their party, and if he lacked Reagan's political skills, they would jeopardize their control of the presidency. They would be especially at risk if the Democrats moved to the political center, for the Democrats could easily field a candidate who would be substantially closer to the policy preferences of the electorate.

Second, the Republicans may be at risk if social issues dominate the political agenda. In response to the Supreme Court decision in June 1989 that burning the U.S. flag was constitutionally protected as an expression of free speech, Bush was quick to grasp the popular side of an emotional issue. He proposed a constitutional amendment to allow Congress and the states to outlaw the "physical desecration" of the flag. But the Supreme Court decision in July 1989 upholding a Missouri law placing restrictions on abortion raises far more difficult political questions. Although the Court did not overturn the 1973 *Roe v. Wade* decision, it signaled that it was willing to grant states more authority to restrict, although not outlaw, abortions. Thus, even if the Supreme Court does not overturn *Roe v. Wade,* abortion may become an overriding issue in state politics during the next several years. At the national level, the Democrats have endorsed a "pro-choice" position, whereas the Republicans have endorsed "pro-life" policies. The actual struggle over restrictions on abortions will be fought mainly at the state level, however, and the contest may or may not divide legislators along partisan lines. But if the Republicans are too closely identified with anti-abortion policies, it may weaken their support among young voters. Many young Americans may support the Republicans as the party most likely to provide conditions for economic opportunity, but young Americans often oppose restrictive abortion legislation.

Some Republican leaders have expressed concern about the abortion controversy. "An emerging group for us, baby boomer women, is really concerned with this issue," according to Mary Matalin, chief of staff at the Republican National Committee. "We have to be very careful on how we allow this debate to be framed." [18] On the other hand, some Democrats were hopeful that the abortion controversy would help their party. For example, Colorado representative Patricia Schroeder maintained that anti-abortion voters had helped the Republicans in the past, but she argued that voters who support abortion rights might help the Democrats in future contests. "I think you're going to see a total flip," she said shortly after the Supreme Court decision upholding the Missouri law restricting abortions.[19] William Schneider argues that "the abortion issue could drive a stake through the heart of the Reagan coalition." He maintains that the New Deal coalition held together until the Supreme Court forced civil rights onto the political agenda. "By overturning *Roe v. Wade*," Schneider argues, "the Court would force the Republican party to deliver on its commitments to the religious right—and face the consequences." [20]

Last, we find it difficult to view any party as a majority party when only 53 percent of the potential electorate votes. For the Republicans the large body of nonvoters poses a potential danger because nonvoters are found disproportionately among those social groups that might be expected to vote Democratic. But recent presidential elections demonstrate that these nonvoters may be very difficult to mobilize. In our view, there is no reasonable scenario in which increased turnout by the disadvantaged would have altered the presidential election result. But in a closer contest the Democrats might benefit from increased turnout by blacks, Hispanics, and poor whites. The Democrats, however, might face a problem getting these groups to the polls without losing support among working-class and middle-class whites. Although it is unrealistic for the Democrats to pin their hopes on higher turnout, the potential for increased participation by disadvantaged Americans still poses a danger for the Republicans.

A Resurgent Democratic Party

The Democratic party has survived since 1828 when Andrew Jackson defeated the incumbent president, National Republican John Quincy Adams, and it would be foolish to ignore its chances to return to power. Admittedly, those chances currently look poor. The Democrats lack a regional base, and would need to rely upon an across-the-board win that would somehow earn them 270 electoral votes. The New Deal coalition that provided their electoral dominance from the 1930s through 1964 seems defunct, with one of its major components, southern whites, voting heavily Republican for president. One of the major Democratic advantages, a solid lead in party identification, has been substantially narrowed. Moreover, the party is currently leaderless. Competing leaders recognize the need to change the Democratic party's appeals but cannot agree on the appropriate strategy.

The basic debate among Democrats is whether to attempt to mobilize nonparticipants or whether to attempt to attract Republican voters. These are not mutually exclusive strategies, of course, but they call for different emphases. In 1988, Jesse Jackson emerged as the leader of the left of the Democratic party, because, except for Sen. Paul Simon of Illinois, he was the only candidate to espouse traditional New Deal values. Jackson stressed the need to mobilize new voters and played down the need to win back Democratic defectors. Shortly after the November 1988 election, Jackson argued that "we can't become preoccupied with retrieving those who choose to leave." Jackson said that it was necessary to "inspire massive turnout among traditional Democrats," as well as to mobilize the young, the poor, and blue-collar workers.[21]

As nearly half the eligible electorate does not vote, there is obviously some logic to a strategy based upon bringing new voters to the polls. But many Democratic leaders argue that the party needs to appeal to middle-class whites and to win back Democratic defectors. At the annual conference of the Democratic Leadership Council in March 1989, Sen. Sam Nunn of Georgia argued that "we are losing the working and middle-class Americans who used to be the mainstay of our party's governing coalition." Sen. Charles S. Robb of Virginia argued that Jesse Jackson's class-based appeals were counterproductive. "The public's perception that we're dividing the country, I believe, is not conducive to the electoral success we're looking for." Jackson directly challenged Nunn and Robb, arguing that the Democrats need to focus on mobilizing the poor, blacks, and Hispanics to vote. His position was based not just upon strategic considerations, but also on moral concerns. "The issue, finally, is not who leads us but who needs us," Jackson asserted.[22]

Sen. Lloyd Bentsen of Texas, whose vice-presidential campaign had increased his stature as a party leader, argued that the Democrats needed both to increase turnout among the disadvantaged and to regain support from the middle class. But, he concluded, "when the two come into conflict, I come down on the side of reaching out.... When you've decided your house is too small it's all very well to do some shoring up and strengthening of the foundation. But at some point, you've got to build where nothing existed before." [23]

Conflicts over the future of the party have been inconclusive. The election of Ronald Brown as the national party chairman suggested that the Democrats had not moved toward the political center, for Brown is a black politician who worked in presidential campaigns for Edward M. Kennedy and Jesse Jackson. Future conflicts may provide further clues to the direction of the national party. At the Democratic convention in Atlanta, Dukakis refused to concede ground on the party platform, but he allowed changes in party rules that might facilitate a future Jackson candidacy. With the newly adopted rules the allocation of delegates will more closely reflect the division of the popular vote in the primaries and caucuses by allowing fewer deviations from proportional representation. Such rules, in both 1984 and 1988, would have increased Jackson's share of the delegates. Some Democrats want to challenge these rules well before the 1992 primary and caucus season, but others argue that continued conflict over the party's rules would be counterproductive. As

Brown warned, if a battle over party rules became a fight over Jackson, the results could be "bloody." [24]

The ultimate test for the Democrats is not their choice of party chairperson, or what rules they adopt, but rather the kind of candidate they nominate in 1992. Dukakis was a technocrat, not an ideologue, as he reminded the voters in his acceptance speech at the Democratic National Convention. All the same, he was successfully branded as a liberal by Bush's negative campaigning. Dukakis appealed to the electorate neither as a populist who could mobilize the disaffected nor as a moderate technocrat who could offer acceptable alternatives to a relatively attractive status quo. It might be difficult to find a candidate who can simultaneously appeal to traditional Democrats and who can stir up enough enthusiasm to boost Democratic voting among the relatively disadvantaged. But this task might still be possible. And, of course, the Democrats might be lucky. Many economists expect a recession but disagree about its timing. If it occurs early in Bush's presidency, the political costs may be minimal, just as the 1982 recession left no lasting damage to Reagan's chances for reelection. But if a recession is delayed until 1991 or 1992, the Republicans may be vulnerable.

Simply winning one election would not restore the Democrats to dominance. But once a party controls the White House, it has the opportunity to reshape the political agenda. A Democratic win would at least create the opportunity for the Democrats to once again emerge as the majority party.

A New Political Party

The political struggle need not be confined to the Republican and Democratic parties. Admittedly, no new political party has emerged to capture the presidency since the Republicans replaced the Whigs in the 1850s. But third parties have three sources of hope. First, approximately one-third of all Americans of voting age claim to have no party ties. Second, and perhaps more important, only three adults in ten claim to be strongly committed to either of the two major parties. Third, there are more than 80 million nonvoters, who, if brought to the polls, could transform any political movement into a majority party. Even though all minor party candidates together won only 900,000 votes in 1988 (just under 1 percent of the votes cast), eight years earlier John B. Anderson, an independent candidate, won 5,700,000 votes or 6.6 percent of the total. Clearly, a new political party could emerge, but how likely is such a development, and what would such a party's ideological stripe be?

The only third parties since World War II that have gained a single electoral vote have been parties of the political right—the States' Rights Democrats in 1948 and the American Independent Party in 1968—with all these votes coming from states of the old Confederacy. But it is hard to see how a conservative political party can compete with the Republicans. Admittedly, some Americans believe that even the Republicans favor too much governmental involvement. The Libertarian party represents such a position and favors very little government interference either in the economy or in the lives of individuals. In 1980, Ed Clark, the Libertarian presidential candidate, was on the ballot in all fifty states and gained 920,000 votes—only 1 percent of the votes cast. He finished behind Reagan, Jimmy Carter, and Anderson in every state but Alaska, where he finished third behind Reagan and Carter. But the Libertarians won only 230,000 votes nationwide, and in 1988 they won 430,000. As we saw in Chapter 6, Bush is viewed as more conservative than the average voter views himself or herself. A party that favors even less governmental involvement in the economy and even less support for social programs is unlikely to have a large pool of potential supporters.

A far greater number of social conservatives may be dissatisfied with Reagan and with Bush for failing to push for constitutional amendments banning abortion and legalizing school prayer. In principle, a third party could emphasize these social issues. But because most voters in national elections are concerned with economic issues, parties that push for social and moral issues are probably doomed to failure.[25] Most social conservatives are likely to continue supporting the Republicans, although they might become disaffected in the unlikely event that the Republicans chose a presidential candidate who did not at least espouse their goals. There seems to be little basis for a successful political party based on social issues.

Anderson's candidacy of 1980 illustrates the problems facing a third party of the center. According to Anthony Downs, the center is the logical place for each party to strive toward, but one of the two major parties is likely to hold that space already.[26] A third party of the center finds it difficult to present a distinctive policy agenda. On most issues, a majority of the electorate did not know where Anderson stood, despite his attempts to articulate clear policy positions.[27] A centrist party has a chance only if the two major parties veer too far to the right and left simultaneously, or if both major parties nominate unpopular candidates. Moreover, even when the major parties have moved to the right or left, it is usually easy for at least one of them to recapture some of the center ground.

A left-wing party has plenty of room on the American political landscape and would find even more space if the Democratic party clearly moved to the political center. A leftist party could draw support from disadvantaged social groups that have had very low turnout in recent elections. However, a party of the left faces severe organizational difficulties. To be successful it must extend its reach beyond the upper-middle-class liberals who may have supported a candidate like Eugene McCarthy (independent) in 1976 or Barry Commoner (Citizens party) in 1980. Thus, we would agree with critics who argue that the decision in July 1989 by the National Organization for Women to explore founding a new political party is unrealistic, for a party aiming at feminist goals would have little mass appeal.[28] To be successful, a party of the left must win support from blacks, the poor, and from working-class whites.

Where would the impetus for such a party come from? In his bids for the Democratic presidential nomination, Jackson relied heavily upon black churches. But even though about one-fifth of all Democratic party identifiers are black, Jackson had very little chance of winning the Democratic presidential nomination. Although some commentators discussed Jackson's prospects for actually winning the Democratic nomination after his victory in the Michigan caucuses, his most realistic hope was to hold the balance of delegate votes between two white candidates. Those chances ended after Albert Gore, Jr., withdrew from the race following the New York primary. Although Jackson was given a place of honor at the Democratic National Convention in Atlanta, as at the party convention in San Francisco four years earlier, he had little input on the platform or on Walter F. Mondale's or Dukakis's vice-presidential selections.

Despite Jackson's dissatisfaction, and despite the disappointment of his supporters, there is no logical basis for a black third-party candidacy. Blacks make up only 11 percent of the electorate, and, even in the most heavily black state, Mississippi, they make up only 31 percent. A black political party running a national campaign would probably win only the three electoral votes of the District of Columbia. Even if the Democrats stop supporting policies favored by blacks, this segment of the electorate may have no attractive alternative. Of course, blacks could vote Republican. Blacks could also support a black third-party candidate, but except for the message this might convey, such a vote would have the same effect as abstaining.

For a party of the left to succeed it would have to be a multiracial coalition. To some extent Jackson developed a multiracial coalition in his bid to win the 1988 Democratic presidential nomination. But that coalition failed even within a constituency of Democratic party supporters who have more liberal views than the electorate as a whole. It seems extremely unlikely that such a coalition could actually win a general election for the presidency.

Labor unions could in principle provide the organizational basis for a party of the left. As Ira Katznelson reminded us in an essay written shortly after the 1980 presidential election, "Over three decades ago C. Wright Mills observed that the only mass, multiracial, progressive organizations in the United States were trade unions; and the future of social policy depended heavily on the zeal of their members and the choices of their leaders." Mills was pessimistic about the prospects for unions taking a lead in social reforms, and, according to Katznelson, there was less reason for optimism in the early 1980s than in the 1950s. As Katznelson concludes, "Organized labor has become increasingly disinclined to engage in larger political battles." [29]

Organized labor did become more politically involved after 1980, but only as a traditional force within the Democratic party. In October 1983 the AFL-CIO formally endorsed Mondale, and labor unions provided major organizational and financial support that helped him win the nomination. In 1988, the AFL-CIO declined to endorse any of the Democratic candidates before the convention, although it formally endorsed Dukakis after he won the nomination. Dukakis was clearly acceptable to organized labor, even though he was probably not the first choice of most labor leaders. But even if labor leaders are disappointed with the 1992 Democratic nominee, it seems unlikely that they would support a left-of-center movement. In many respects unions and blacks have differing interests. Union leaders are often interested in protecting the privileges of their members, and black leaders are more likely to make broader claims for the redistribution of resources. This is seen most concretely in the insistence of union leaders that seniority be the major criterion for job security, while black leaders often demand preferential treatment for minority group members to compensate for past injustices.

The absence of any social structure that could provide the organizational basis for a third party of the left greatly reduces the chances that there will be a successful third-party movement—even if the Democrats clearly move to the political center in 1992. But there are also structural features to the American electoral system that tend to protect the Republican and Democratic parties from the challenge of new political parties.

Most obviously, there is the electoral college system, which requires a party to receive a plurality of the vote within a state or D.C. to obtain any electoral votes. This places any new party at a disadvantage unless it has a regional base. But there are other features as well. Third parties have a difficult time getting on the ballot, despite court decisions that have made it somewhat easier.[30] Even more difficult is raising money, and here the federal election laws place an additional burden on third-party candidates. Democratic and Republican nominees are guaranteed full federal funding merely by gaining their party's nomination, but third-party candidates receive funding only if they attain 5 percent of the vote in the November election. Thus, in 1980 Anderson was forced to ask supporters to lend him money, on the promise that it would be repaid if he met conditions for federal support. Given the importance of money for polling, travel, media, and organizational expenses, the built-in federal funding for major party nominees provides a tremendous advantage.

Even more important, nomination by a major political party provides a huge bonus of votes because, at the very least, a major party nominee can count on the support of strong party identifiers. This bonus, already large in 1980, grew substantially for the Republicans because of the increasing percentage of strong Republican identifiers. How many votes can a major party nominee count on? Assuming there are 173 million Americans of voting age, there are about 30 million strong Democrats. If we assume that three-fifths of these Democrats actually vote, and that seven out of ten vote Democratic (a smaller number than has ever supported the Democratic candidate in an NES survey), these voters would provide the Democratic candidate with 13 million votes. There are fewer strong Republicans, but they are more likely to vote, and are more consistently loyal to their party. Assuming that two-thirds of these Republicans vote, and that nine out of ten vote Republican (the NES surveys have always registered at least 90 percent support), these Republicans would provide their nominee with more than 14 million votes. Of course, neither the Democratic nor Republican candidate can win with only 13 or 14 million votes, but this is a substantial base with which to start.

A third-party candidate has no such base of support. Even Americans who call themselves independents have felt no loyalty to third-party candidates, such as George C. Wallace in 1968 or Anderson in 1980, who label themselves independent. Although such candidates do fare better among independents than among party identifiers, Wallace received only a fifth of the vote among independents with no partisan leaning (his best group), and Anderson received just over a fifth of the vote among independents who leaned Democratic (the category in which he fared best.)[31]

Last, the openness of the current nomination process encourages most candidates who wish to become president to seek their goal by attempting to win the Democratic or Republican party nomination. The party reforms introduced by the Democrats between 1968 and 1972 made it far more difficult for party leaders to influence the choice of the nominee. Perhaps this is why Wallace, who earned nearly 10 million votes as the American Independent party candidate in 1968, decided four years later to seek the Democratic party nomination. The nomination of George S. McGovern in 1972 and of Carter in 1976 attest to the openness of the system. The creation of superdelegates in 1984 slightly increased the influence of elected officials, and, even though this reform was relatively minor, it helped Mondale lock up his nomination victory. But Gary Hart's strong challenge in 1984 demonstrates that the system is still relatively open. Although the Republican party did not engage in a similar series of reforms, it was affected by many of the changes wrought by the Democrats, and in 1988 three-fourths of the Republican delegates were chosen by primaries.

Wresting a party's nomination away from an incumbent president is still a formidable task. Even an unelected president, Ford, was able to hold off Reagan in 1976, and four years later Carter was able to outrun Kennedy. But at least one party's nomination is always open, and sometimes, as in 1988, both are. The relatively open structure of the nominating process makes aiming at a major party nomination the most reasonable strategy for most potential presidential candidates, and contributes to the absence of attractive candidates to lead third party movements.[32]

A Return to Electoral Volatility

As we have seen, Bush's election may solidify continued Republican dominance of the presidency, although we see few prospects for a realignment in which the Republicans dominate both elected branches of government. The Democrats, however, could regain the White House, and with skill and luck again become the dominant party. The least likely alternative is the emergence of a new political party as a major political force. But even if the Democrats do not regain their majority party status, they can win the presidency under circumstances that favor their cause. If the Democrats win in 1992, a period of volatility will return.

During most of the postwar era there has been a great deal of electoral volatility. From 1952 through 1984, neither party was able to win more than two presidential elections in a row. The greatest volatility occurred in 1976 and 1980 when the party controlling the White House lost two elections in a row—the only two successive losses for the incumbent president in this century (Table 3-2). Moreover, there have been wide swings in the presidential vote from election to election, the most dramatic being the 24-point drop in the Democratic vote between 1964 and 1972.

Volatility may return if economic conditions deteriorate shortly before a presidential election. Several scholars have argued that elections reflect a response to short-term economic conditions. Although economic models have been applied mainly to the study of Congress, they can also be applied to the study of the presidency.[33] Unlike leaders in parliamentary systems, who have at least some control over the scheduling of elections, the party holding the White House must face elections at constitutionally fixed intervals. In recent years, the Republicans have had the good fortune to run during periods of economic expansion. Given the limited ability of the president to control the economy, the Republicans will ultimately be forced to face the electorate in periods of rising unemployment, inflation, or both. We do not think continued Republican success is merely a matter of timing or luck. There have been major shifts in voting patterns, as well as a sizable shift in the partisan loyalties of the electorate. But even apart from the possibility that economic misfortunes could end Republican rule, there are factors that suggest that volatility could return in presidential elections.

First, the party loyalties of the electorate are relatively weak. Even though party loyalties became stronger between 1980 and 1988, they are considerably weaker than they were between 1952 and 1964—the years Philip E. Converse labels the steady-state period in American party loyalties.[34] During that period, 22 percent of the electorate was classified as independents; in the 1988 NES survey, 36 percent was. While being an independent does not necessarily signify commitment to "independence" as a principle, it does reveal a lack of strong commitment to a party.[35] Moreover, even though the percentage of strong partisans rose between 1980 and 1988 (due to an increase in strong Republicans), the percentage of strong partisans was clearly lower than during the steady-state period. In the period between 1952 and 1984, 36 percent of the electorate claimed to have strong partisan ties; in 1988 only 31 percent did. Weak partisans and self-classified independents are much more volatile in their voting choices than individuals who claim strong party ties.

Second, the evidence suggests that most of the gains in Republican partisanship occurred very suddenly in the fall of 1984. Although these gains have persisted through early 1989, there must be a large number of Republican identifiers who have voted Republican for only a few elections. These new Republicans cannot yet have developed a strong pattern of habitual partisan voting that, according to the *American Voter* thesis, would contribute to strong party ties.[36] Of course, the shift toward the Republicans may turn out to be durable. But during the 1980s there have been short-term shifts in partisan support that lasted for relatively short periods. For example, there were substantial gains in Republican party loyalties in early 1981, but they vanished by the end of 1982.[37] These fluctuations suggest that the electorate has relatively volatile partisan loyalties.

Last, social forces (other than race) have less and less influence on voting behavior—a trend that is likely to contribute to electoral volatility. Today, few voters are bound to a party by social class, ethnic, or religious ties. This increases the proportion of the electorate that is likely to switch from election to election.

Ultimately, at least short-term electoral volatility in presidential elections will return. Despite their problems, the Democrats will eventually enter an election with the economy weak, with the Republican candidate unpopular, and with the Democratic party relatively united. But an occasional Democratic victory will not necessarily end overall Republican dominance in presidential elections. A Republican majority in the House, on the other hand, would be a transformation of major proportions, especially if, unlike 1952, Republican control could be sustained for more than one election. The Republicans would, at long last, become the majority party.

Notes

1. James McCartney, "Bush: Peace Won't Buy New Programs at Home," *Detroit Free Press,* December 5, 1989, 10A.
2. In addition, Reagan had appointed William H. Rehnquist, an associate justice of the Supreme Court, to chief justice.
3. Linda Greenhouse, "The Year the Court Turned to the Right," *New York Times,* July 7, 1989, A1, A10.
4. Gerald M. Pomper, "The Presidential Election," in *The Election of 1988: Reports and Interpretations,* Gerald M. Pomper et al. (Chatham, N.J.: Chatham House, 1989), 149.
5. It should be borne in mind that U.S. senators were chosen by state legislatures until the Seventeenth Amendment was ratified in 1913.
6. Gary C. Jacobson, "Congress: A Singular Continuity," in *The Elections of 1988,* ed. Michael Nelson (Washington, D.C.: CQ Press, 1989), 127-152.
7. Although respondents in the 1988 NES survey were asked about their 1984 presidential vote, they were not asked how they voted for Congress in 1984. Therefore, we cannot test this possibility empirically.
8. Byron E. Shafer, "The Election of 1988 and the Structure of American Politics: Thoughts on Interpreting an Electoral Order," *Electoral Studies* 8 (April 1989): 11.
9. Jacobson, "Congress: A Singular Continuity," 144, 145.
10. Pomper, "The Presidential Election," 149.
11. Jacobson, "Congress: A Singular Continuity," 145.
12. Our analysis of the 1976 NES survey strongly suggests that Ford's pardon of Richard Nixon lost him votes. See Paul R. Abramson, John H. Aldrich, and David W. Rohde, *Change and Continuity in the 1980 Elections,* rev. ed. (Washington, D.C.: CQ Press, 1983), 151-152. Of course, if Ford had won in 1976, the high levels of inflation that damaged Carter might have been blamed on the GOP, so the Republicans might not have won the 1980 election.
13. See the poll evidence reported in Paul R. Abramson, John H. Aldrich, and David W. Rohde, *Change and Continuity in the 1984 Elections,* rev. ed. (Washington, D.C.: CQ Press, 1987), 350. The 1988 NES surveys clearly show that white southerners have become more Republican, but the Democrats still hold an edge among white party identifiers. Among southern white party identifiers ($N = 220$) only 44 percent are Republicans. If independents who lean toward a party are included (increasing the N to 311), 47 percent are Republicans.
14. For evidence on the timing of this shift, see Abramson, Aldrich, and Rohde, *Change and Continuity in the 1984 Elections,* rev. ed., 210-212.
15. Philip E. Converse and Roy Pierce, "Measuring Partisanship" (Paper delivered at the World Congress of the International Political Science Association, Paris, July 15-20, 1985). For the exact wording of the questions the Michigan Survey Research Center uses to measure party identification, see chapter 4, note 46.
16. R. W. Apple, Jr., "Public Rates Bush Highly but Sees Mostly Style," *New York Times,* April 20, 1989, B12. For a more systematic analysis of the CBS News/*New York Times* polls, see Helmut Norpoth, "Under Way and Here to

Stay: Party Realignment in the 1980s?" *Public Opinion Quarterly* 51 (Fall 1987): 376-391.

17. Telephone surveys are often not as representative of the population as surveys based upon in-person interviews because telephone surveys tend to overrepresent better-educated Americans and those with higher income and occupational levels. Therefore, there is the possibility that these surveys may tend to overestimate Republican strength. Even if there are such biases with the CBS News/*New York Times* surveys, however, they clearly show a strong trend toward the Republican party.

18. E. J. Dionne, Jr., "Abortion Ruling Shakes Up Races for Legislatures," *New York Times,* July 10, 1989, B8.

19. Ibid.

20. William Schneider, "Trouble for the GOP," *Public Opinion* 12 (May/June 1989): 2, 60. For an alternative view, see Everett Carll Ladd, "Trouble for Both Parties," *Public Opinion* 12 (May/June 1989): 3-8.

21. Joe Atkins, "Democrats' Post-mortem Likely to be Painful," *Lansing* [Michigan] *State Journal,* November 10, 1988, 13A.

22. E. J. Dionne, Jr., "Party Told to Win Middle-Class Vote," *New York Times,* March 12, 1989, L32.

23. Ibid.

24. E. J. Dionne, Jr., "Again, Democrats Agonize over the Rules," *New York Times,* May 21, 1989, E5.

25. The Republicans emerged as a major party in the 1850s by opposing the extension of slavery into the territories, but for both northern farmers and southern slave owners this was largely an economic issue that would determine the availability of western land.

26. Anthony Downs, *An Economic Theory of Democracy* (New York: Harper & Row, 1957). As Steven J. Brams points out, there are disadvantages to the middle position in multicandidate races. See *The Presidential Election Game* (New Haven, Conn.: Yale University Press, 1978), 13-18.

27. Abramson, Aldrich, and Rohde, *Change and Continuity in the 1980 Elections,* rev. ed., 178-180.

28. See Dan Balz, "NOW's Talk of a New Party Attacked as Self-Defeating," *Washington Post,* July 28, 1989, A5.

29. Ira Katznelson, "A Radical Departure: Social Welfare and the Election," in *The Hidden Election: Politics and Economics in the 1980 Presidential Campaign,* ed. Thomas Ferguson and Joel Rogers (New York: Pantheon), 1982, 331, 332.

30. For a discussion of restrictions to ballot access, see Steven J. Rosenstone, Roy L. Behr, and Edward H. Lazarus, *Third Parties in America: Citizen Response to Major Party Failure* (Princeton, N.J.: Princeton University Press, 1984), 19-25.

31. See Abramson, Aldrich, and Rohde, *Change and Continuity in the 1980 Elections,* rev. ed., Table 8-8, 177. Our table presents the results for whites, but including blacks would have little effect on the overall percentage of Wallace or Anderson voters among these partisan categories.

32. We are grateful to Joseph A. Schlesinger for this insight.

33. See Robert S. Erikson, "Economic Conditions and the Presidential Vote," *American Political Science Review* 83 (June 1989): 567-573; and Douglas A. Hibbs, Jr., *The American Political Economy: Macroeconomics and Electoral Politics* (Cambridge, Mass.: Harvard University Press), 195-200.

34. Philip E. Converse, *The Dynamics of Party Support: Cohort-Analyzing Party Identification* (Beverly Hills, Calif.: Sage, 1976).
35. For the strongest evidence supporting this conclusion, see Martin P. Wattenberg, *The Decline of American Political Parties, 1952-1988* (Cambridge, Mass.: Harvard University Press, 1990), 36-49.
36. See Angus Campbell, Philip E. Converse, Warren E. Miller, and Donald E. Stokes, *The American Voter* (New York: John Wiley & Sons, 1960), 161-165. Morris P. Fiorina, on the other hand, views the relationship between length of attachment to a party and strength of partisan identification as more problematic. See *Retrospective Voting in American National Elections* (New Haven, Conn.: Yale University Press, 1981), 91.
37. For a review of this evidence, see Abramson, Aldrich, and Rohde, *Change and Continuity in the 1980 Elections*, rev. ed., 286-287.

PART 5

1990 Election Update

The American midterm election is a unique political institution. Unlike legislative elections in parliamentary democracies, it does not affect the term of service of the executive, or, as in France, threaten to weaken the president's basic political powers. The U.S. president, elected for a four-year term, serves regardless of his legislative support. Yet the very system of biennial elections for all members of the House of Representatives and for one-third of the Senate often reduces the capacity of the president to govern effectively.

More than a quarter of a century ago, V. O. Key, Jr., noted that the electorate's behavior in midterm elections followed a highly predictable pattern:

> Since the electorate cannot change administrations at midterm elections, it can only express its approval or disapproval by returning or withdrawing legislative majorities. . . . The President's party, whether it basks in public favor or is declining in public esteem, ordinarily loses House strength at midterm—a pattern that, save for one exception, has prevailed since the Civil War.[1]

Seven midterm elections have been held since Key wrote these words, and the president's party has lost seats in all of them. The 1934 midterm election, conducted during Franklin D. Roosevelt's first term, was the only contest since the Civil War in which the president's party gained strength in the House, and that election occurred during a major realigning period in which the Democrats were emerging as the majority party.[2]

In the 1990 midterm election the Republicans suffered moderate losses: nine House seats, one Senate seat, and one or two governorships. A year before the midterm, Republican leaders actually hoped to gain seats in the House thereby breaking the historical pattern of midterm losses. Such gains, if they had occurred, might well have been seen as a clear signal of a pro-Republican realignment. Instead, the 1990 midterm election provided little hope for future Republican control of the House and for becoming a true majority party. But the 1990 midterm did little to diminish Republican prospects for holding the presidency.

Part 5 analyzes American politics in light of the 1990 election. Chapter 12 looks directly at the election and its impact on Congress. We begin by examining the success of incumbents seeking reelection. In 1990 many critics expected a tidal wave of resentment against incumbents. As we shall see, House incumbents were somewhat less successful in 1990 than in 1986 and 1988, but only one incumbent senator failed to win reelection. We ask: Which party "won" the election? This question must be answered in terms of historical patterns, the expectations experts held shortly before the election, and the academic models of congressional elections. We then examine the impact of national level trends and local factors on the congressional election and return to the question of incumbency. We will find that although the vast majority of incumbents won reelection to the House, the margin by which incumbents won declined.

In Chapter 12 we also will examine George Bush's success in campaigning, the impact of national party organizations in providing funding and recruiting candidates, and local factors that affect the chances of defeating incumbents. Elections are mechanisms for choices about public policy, and we will assess the impact of the 1990 election on the policies the 102d Congress will attempt to implement.

We conclude Chapter 12 with a look toward the 1992 congressional election. That election provides greater prospects for change—as a result of reapportionment, eight states will gain one or more House members and thirteen states will lose one or more seats. Even in states which neither gain nor lose seats, districts will still need to be redrawn. We will examine Republican prospects for gaining seats as a result of reapportionment and redistricting, and conclude that although the Republicans are likely to gain House seats in 1992, their prospects for winning control of the House are very low. Beginning with the 1954 midterm, the Democrats have won control of the U.S. House of Representatives in nineteen consecutive general elections, and they are likely to extend that winning streak. An analysis of open seat races from 1983 through 1990 suggests that Democratic dominance of the House does not result from advantages of incumbency or from their ability to draw congressional districts to their advantage.

Chapter 13 explores what may happen in future elections in light of the events of 1990 and early 1991. Here we deal with great uncertainty. Although the Iraqi invasion of Kuwait had relatively little impact on the 1990 midterm election, the war in the Persian Gulf could dramatically alter Republican prospects for retaining the presidency. In the short term, the crisis in the Persian Gulf may have led many Democrats to postpone their decision about whether or not to run for president, making a discussion of the 1992 presidential nomination highly problematic. Even so, we know that in early 1992 the parties will begin choosing delegates to their respective nominating conventions.

We begin Chapter 13 by discussing the delegate selection process and how party rules may affect the nominations. In fact, we expect relatively modest changes in Democratic party rules, although there may be changes in the scheduling of the primaries and caucuses.

As of February 1991, there are no clear Democratic presidential contenders, but many possible candidates have been mentioned. We discuss twelve of these Democrats and evaluate their strengths and weaknesses. Although we cannot predict specific candidates, we believe that the overall pattern of the Democratic nomination process will be similar to other open contests in the post-1968 era, that is, contests in which an incumbent president does not seek his party's renomination. We expect many Democrats eventually to run, and expect that through a winnowing process the winner will emerge as a result of the primary and caucus season—well before the Democratic party national nominating convention.

The shape of the general election contest also is uncertain, but we believe that the Republicans have several advantages that may help them retain the presidency. We discuss Republican assets, which include the ability to field an incumbent president, a slight advantage from the effects of congressional reapportionment on the electoral college, Republican gains in partisan loyalties among the American electorate, Democratic losses among blacks, and the possible emergence of affirmative action as a political issue.

But the Republicans have some liabilities as well. These include divisions that have emerged within the Republican party, the likelihood that Bush will retain Dan Quayle as his running mate, and the possible emergence of abortion as an issue if *Roe v. Wade* is overturned. In addition, some suggest that the Democrats could make inroads if they successfully capitalize on the theme that the Republican policies have benefited wealthy Americans, a theme that Dukakis largely avoided in 1988. On balance, we think Republican assets outweigh their liabilities, and that Bush, if he seeks reelection, has a good chance of winning. Divided government seems likely to continue.

Notes

1. V. O. Key, Jr., *Parties, Politics, and Pressure Groups,* 5th ed. (New York: Crowell, 1964), 567, 568.

2. In the 1902 election, held during Republican Theodore Roosevelt's first term, both the Republican and the Democratic parties gained seats. This was possible because the overall size of the House of Representatives increased after the 1900 census. The Republicans gained nine seats, but the Democrats gained twenty-five. This midterm result is consistent with Key's generalization because the party holding the White House lost strength relative to the opposition party.

Chapter 12

The 1990 Congressional Election

In the 1990 midterm election, voters cast their ballots in a variety of races across the country. In this chapter we will discuss the pattern of outcomes in these races to determine whether there is any collective message in the individual results and to assess whether these outcomes have any implications for future elections. On the surface this may appear to be an easy task because the postelection results were quite similar to what existed prior to election day. The Democrats won eighteen of the thirty-five Senate contests, for a total of fifty-six seats in the 102d Congress—a one-seat gain. In the House, the Democrats won 267 seats to the Republicans' 167, with one seat won by an independent.[1] The GOP suffered a loss of nine seats in the House. Meanwhile, in thirty-six gubernatorial contests, the Republicans won fourteen seats and the Democrats took nineteen. In addition, two governorships were won by independent candidates, and one race was undecided[2] resulting in a loss of one (or two) governorships for the Republicans. Our attempt to discover whether a more complex pattern is hidden beneath these results begins with a closer examination of the congressional outcomes.

The Pattern of Outcomes

The data on incumbency and electoral success in Table 12-1 update the information found in Table 9-1. In the House races, the reelection rate was slightly below the historic high of the two previous elections—but only slightly. Of the 407 representatives seeking another term, 96.1 percent were successful. That is only two percentage points below 1986 and 1988 and is higher than all but two of the other years displayed in

Table 12-1   House and Senate Incumbents and Election Outcomes, 1990

Year	Incumbents running (N)	Primary defeats (%)	Primary defeats (N)	General election defeats (%)	General election defeats (N)	Reelected (%)	Reelected (N)
House	(407)	0.2	(1)	3.7	(15)	96.1	(391)
Senate	(30)	—	(0)	3.3	(1)	96.7	(29)

Note: For the results between 1954 and 1988, see Table 9-1 on page 233.

Table 9-1. Only sixteen representatives lost their reelection bids, one in a primary election and the others in the general election. In the Senate contests, incumbents' success was even greater: the 96.7 percent rate was the highest during the entire period we have considered. Only one incumbent senator—Rudy Boschwitz (R-Minn.)—was defeated.

Table 12-2 shows the combined effects of party and incumbency in the 1990 general election. In the House contests, the Republican incumbents fared somewhat worse than the Democrats, but again by only a little; nine Republican incumbents and six Democratic incumbents

Table 12-2   House and Senate General Election Outcomes, by Party and Incumbency, 1990

Winners	Candidates Democratic incumbent	No incumbent (seat was Democratic)	No incumbent (seat was Republican)	Republican incumbent	Total
House					
Democrats	98%	100%	33%	6%	62%
Republicans	2	0	67	94	38
Total Percent	100%	100%	100%	100%	100%
(N)	(248)	(11)	(18)	(158)	(435)
Senate					
Democrats	100%	100%	0	7%	49%
Republicans	0	0	100%	93	51
Total Percent	100%	100%	100%	100%	100%
(N)	(16)	(1)	(4)	(14)	(35)

Note: For the 1988 results, see Table 9-2 on page 236.

were defeated. The overwhelming success of representatives who wanted to remain in office continued for both parties, although as we will see below, the electorate was not quite so placid or as evenhanded between the parties in these races as the results suggest. In the relatively small number of contests for open House seats, the partisan results were much more one sided. The Democrats held onto all of their former districts, plus they took one-third of those belonging to the Republicans, for a gain of six seats. Indeed, two-thirds of the Republicans' nine-seat loss in the House was a result of races in open districts.

The Senate elections display even less change or partisan advantage. Only the Republicans' loss of the Minnesota seat prevented a perfect pattern of defense of what each party held before the election. None of the five seats without incumbents switched partisan control.[3]

In the wake of these small changes in membership, the shifts in the party shares of regional delegations displayed in Table 9-3 (see page 237) also are small. The proportion of seats held by Democrats in the East, Midwest, and West grew between two and four points: to 60 percent in the East and Midwest and to 57 percent in the West. Thus, after the 1990 elections, there was even less variation across the regions than there had been in the past. Across the regions the highest Democratic share of the seats was 68 percent in the South, while the lowest was 57 percent in the West—a range of only eleven points. Of course there was even less change in the Senate. The shift in control of the Minnesota seat increased the Democratic share of senators from the Midwest from 59 percent to 64 percent. The balance in all of the other regions was the same as after the 1988 elections.

Assessing Victory and Explaining the Results

One question that obviously comes to mind regarding these results is: Which party won and which party lost? This question is of real consequence to political actors because politicians use their interpretation of election results to infer the political desires of voters. Ronald Reagan's convincing electoral vote victory over Jimmy Carter in 1980 and substantial gains made by the Republicans in the House and Senate (taking control of the latter for the first time since 1955) was interpreted as an endorsement of the Republican agenda of tax cuts, reductions in social spending, and increases in defense expenditures. As a consequence, all of these measures were enacted into law in the next Congress.

For us to determine which party was victorious, we must apply some standard—a "yardstick"—to measure victory. The yardstick provides us with a set of expectations against which the actual results can be compared. In addition, as we saw in Chapter 9, expectations or hypotheses about election outcomes can be combined in models of the electoral

Table 12-3   House Seat Losses by the President's Party in Midterm Elections, 1946-1986

All elections	By term of administration	
	First term	*Later term*
1946: 55 Democrats	1954: 18 Republicans	1946: 55 Democrats
1950: 29 Democrats	1962: 4 Democrats	1950: 29 Democrats
1954: 18 Republicans	1970: 12 Republicans	1958: 47 Republicans
1958: 47 Republicans	1978: 11 Democrats	1966: 47 Democrats
1962: 4 Democrats	1982: 26 Republicans	1974: 43 Republicans
1966: 47 Democrats		1986: 5 Republicans
1970: 12 Republicans	Average: 14.2	
1974: 43 Republicans		Average: 37.7
1978: 11 Democrats		
1982: 26 Republicans		
1986: 5 Republicans		
Average: 27.0		

process that can provide explanations as well as predictions. We will, in turn, consider the historical pattern, the expectations of participants, and the insights from academic models.

Historical Trends

The first column in Table 12-3 presents data on losses in the House by the party that controlled the White House for every midterm election since World War II. In these eleven elections, the average loss was twenty-seven seats. There was, however, a range of outcomes, from the fifty-five-seat loss by Democrats in 1946 to the four-seat Democratic loss in 1962. So while the president's party has invariably lost seats, as occurred in 1990, we have no obvious ground to judge the magnitude of that loss from the outcomes of postwar midterms.

Another consideration related to the president, however, sharpens the context for judgment somewhat. If a president is facing his first midterm election, he can make a plausible appeal that he has had little time to bring about substantial change or to secure many achievements. Moreover, even if things are not going very well, voters may not be inclined to place the blame on a president who has served for such a short time. But four years later (if the president is fortunate enough to face a second midterm election), appeals of too little time in office are likely to be unpersuasive. After six years, if the economy or foreign policy is not going well, voters may seek a policy change by reducing the president's partisans in Congress.

The second and third columns in Table 12-3 indicate that this is what has happened in the past. Losses by the president's party in the first midterm election of a presidency tend to be much less than the losses in future midterms.[4] Indeed, with the exception of the result in 1986, the two categories yield two fairly homogeneous sets of outcomes that are sharply different from one another. In the five midterm elections that took place during a first term, the president's party lost between four and twenty-six seats, with an average loss of fourteen seats. In the five elections after the first term (excluding 1986), the range of losses was between twenty-nine and fifty-five seats, with an average loss of forty-four seats. (We will discuss the atypical 1986 result below.)

Within this historical context, one would have expected the Republican losses in 1990 to be fairly small, and they were. The nine-seat decline for the GOP was similar to, but somewhat smaller than, the fourteen-seat average for first midterm elections.[5] Thus, by a purely historical yardstick, the Republicans did reasonably well.

Observers' Expectations

The preelection expectations of politicians and media analysts provide another standard for judging election outcomes. Even if a party loses ground, it may try to claim victory (at least a "moral victory") if it performs noticeably better than was expected. These public expectations are shaped in part by the historical standards we have discussed, but they also are influenced by polls and by recent political events.

The publicly voiced anticipations of politicians during elections are a mixture of predictions, hopes, and public relations statements; thus, they cannot be taken entirely at face value. Despite this caveat, it is interesting to note that Republican expectations for 1990 changed markedly over the course of the two years after George Bush's victory in 1988, declining as events turned against them. With a popular president and a newly revitalized Republican congressional campaign committee, GOP leaders were talking confidently of breaking the historical pattern of losses for the president's party and gaining as many as ten seats in the House.[6] They also anticipated at least modest gains in the Senate, setting the stage for a determined battle for control in 1992. As Bush's approval ratings waned during early 1990, as the economy stagnated, and as difficulties mounted recruiting candidates, Republican officials began to scale back their predictions, especially for the House.

This trend against GOP prospects was not as strongly reflected in the predictions of more objective observers, because the early anticipation of House gains was never shared. In a February 1990 analysis, *Roll Call* (an independent congressional newspaper) indicated that a Democratic gain of three to five seats in the House was most likely, and that it was possible that the two parties could break even. In the Senate races, the expectation was that the Republicans were likely to gain two seats.

The six Senate seats judged to be the "top contests" were all held by Democrats.[7] Similarly, the *Cook Political Report* stated in March that "The worst case scenario for Democrats this election cycle is to lose three or four [Senate] seats." At that time, all of the Republican seats were rated as at least leaning toward the GOP, while three Democratic seats were listed as "toss ups." [8]

By September the estimates of GOP chances had slipped only slightly from these levels. The *Cook Political Report* was predicting a Republican gain of one or two seats in the Senate and a Democratic increase of one to seven seats in the House. Then, as election day approached, the *Cook Political Report* saw the tide turning against the GOP. The prediction on October 30, 1990, was for the Senate to break even and for Democratic gains in the House to number ten to fifteen seats. We now know that the Republican party did not fare as well in 1990 as it had originally anticipated, and worse than independent observers had predicted earlier in the season. By either of those standards, the actual results were a modest victory for the Democrats.

Academic Insights

We can now draw on the academic models discussed in Chapter 9 for additional insights to assist us in evaluating the 1990 results. The analyses of Gary C. Jacobson and Samuel Kernell indicated that the proportion of challengers to incumbents who have political experience has an important effect on the number of incumbents who are defeated in a given election. We will consider this factor in evaluating the 1990 midterm election later in this chapter. Here we will discuss two other variables that the models showed had an influence on election outcomes: presidential approval and "exposure."

Much of the research discussed in Chapter 9 demonstrated that the level of presidential approval by the public had a potent impact on congressional elections, especially in midterm years. The data indicated that midterm elections are, to a degree at least, referenda on the performance of the president. If the president is doing well in the eyes of the voters, his party can be expected to do relatively well at the ballot box. If, however, the president's approval level is low, his party can be expected to suffer significant losses. In light of this relationship, it is no wonder that Republicans were sanguine about their prospects for 1990. Bush's approval level had peaked at 80 percent in late 1989 and early 1990. Bush's approval ratings fell somewhat through July 1990, but public approval rose after Iraq invaded Kuwait, and a CBS News/*New York Times* poll conducted in August 1990 showed that 76 percent of those polled approved of Bush's performance as president.

During the election campaign, however, a number of developments combined to undermine Bush's standing with the voters, including the prospects of war in the Persian Gulf, the growing belief that the economy was moving toward a recession, and the difficulties that the president had in securing congressional agreement on a deficit-reduction package. Particularly damaging during the budget debate was his reversal of his "read-my-lips" promise of 1988 not to raise taxes. In the two months from August to October, the CBS News/*New York Times* poll showed that Bush's approval level had dropped twenty-four points to 52 percent (with 37 percent of the people polled disapproving).[9]

Of course, these shifts in public opinion shaped the predictions of the observers we discussed above, and the evidence from the academic models indicates that both the earlier and later anticipations were justified. If Bush's popularity had remained above 70 percent, the Republicans might well have been insulated from congressional losses and might have even gained some ground. The sharp drop in public approval dashed those prospects, however, and set the stage for significant potential Republican losses. But Bush's approval level stabilized in the week or two before the election—and remained above 50 percent—probably limiting the damage to the GOP. (As we will see later, many Republican incumbents survived by narrow margins.)

The level of "exposure" for congressional Republicans offers a final measure for evaluating the 1990 results. Recall that the degree of exposure is the number of seats held by a party relative to its long-term norm. One major reason that the president's party has historically suffered significant losses in midterm House elections is that presidents have often carried with them a substantial number of new House members in the preceding presidential election. Thus, in these instances, the level of exposure would have been high. For example, in Lyndon B. Johnson's landslide election in 1964, the Democrats won 295 House seats compared to the 259 seats they had won two years earlier. Then, in the midterm election of 1966, the high level of Democratic exposure, coupled with Johnson's low approval level and a bad economy, dropped the Democrats to 248 seats.

As we know, however, Bush did not stimulate significant Republican gains in the House when he was elected in 1988. In fact, the Republicans actually lost seats. Consequently their level of exposure was low in 1990. Indeed, the GOP was defending the fewest House seats possessed by a president's party in his first midterm election in the history of American congressional races. As a consequence, one should not have expected substantial Democratic gains in 1990, and it is not surprising that they did not reach the average gain for the "out" party in first midterms. These factors also help to explain the small Republican losses in 1986 that we noted earlier. In 1986 Republican exposure also was low (the GOP had gained relatively few seats in Reagan's 1984 landslide), and the president's approval rating was comparatively high for the sixth year of a presidency.

To summarize, historical patterns, public expectations, and academic analyses provide a context within which we can evaluate the relative success of the two parties in 1990. In light of these combined standards, the most accurate characterization of the results is between a draw and a marginal Democratic victory. The House and Senate losses for the president's party were, respectively, slightly below and slightly above their historical levels, but GOP exposure for the House was so low that a nine-seat decline cannot be seen as a positive result. It had been reasonable for the Republicans to anticipate doing better than they did, but as the elections approached, political conditions turned against them, and their chances of reversing historical patterns for midterm elections slipped away.

National and Local Influences in Congressional Elections

Thomas P. "Tip" O'Neill, Jr., the former Democratic Speaker of the House, was well known for asserting that "all politics is local." Yet as our evaluation of the 1990 results indicates, this characterization is not entirely correct. National-level factors, like approval of the president's job performance or the state of the economy, also can influence congressional election outcomes. Thus, each election is affected both by local and national forces, although the impact of each varies from year to year. In this section we will examine some factors that were relevant to the 1990 congressional elections.

Incumbency: Pro or Con?

In earlier chapters we analyzed the advantages of incumbency. Incumbents have rarely been defeated in recent years. They tend to be better known than their challengers, they have a number of advantageous perquisites by virtue of holding office, and they usually find it easier to raise campaign funds. One would assume that, short of being personally involved in a scandal, incumbency is an unquestionable asset. In 1990, however, it appeared that this might not be the case, for this was the year of the "anti-incumbent mood."

Early in 1990 pollsters and commentators began to perceive stronger anti-Congress sentiments among the electorate.[10] Of course there was nothing new about Congress being unpopular; it has long suffered ups and downs in approval just like the president. What was different in 1990 was that Congress's unpopularity appeared to be undermining the approval of members by their own constituents. In July 1990, Geoff Garin, a pollster for Democratic candidates, said, "The conventional wisdom, which held that voters could hate Congress while liking their own Congressman, is rapidly becoming outdated." "The feeling," Garin claimed, "is starting to seep from one over to the other."[11] A number of campaign consultants indicated that many of their incumbents were running well behind the levels of their previous elections. Among the issues leading to these negative attitudes were the savings-and-loan crisis and the cost of the bailout, the congressional pay raise, the possibility of higher taxes, and a number of ethics scandals.

These perceptions were reinforced by particular events as the midterm campaign wore on. In Michael S. Dukakis's home state, the "Massachusetts miracle" had unraveled, and the state's budget was in a shambles. In the face of precipitous declines in his standing with voters, Dukakis declined to run again. The voters blamed not just the departing governor, but the entire Democratic establishment. In the September primary, a record voter turnout rejected all but one statewide candidate who had the official party endorsement.[12] For governor, the Democratic nomination went to John Silber, a controversial anti-establishment newcomer (he was president of Boston University). The same month in Oklahoma the voters adopted, by a two-to-one margin, a constitutional amendment that limited state lawmakers to twelve years in office.[13] In addition, many former members of Congress were having difficulty in seeking a return to political office. To some observers, this was due to the anti-incumbent climate.[14] Then in late September and early October, Congress and President Bush deadlocked in an attempt to reach a budget agreement, and analysts detected another drop in incumbents' standing with the voters.[15]

Despite these indicators, however, the existence of an anti-incumbent mood remained questionable. Of the 407 representatives seeking reelection, 307 had no primary opposition, and among the remainder 67 received more than 75 percent of the primary vote.[16] No senator and only one congressman—Donald E. Lukens of Ohio who had been convicted of having sex with a minor—was defeated in a primary. And in the general election few incumbents were defeated. Even in Massachusetts, the supposed hotbed of anti-incumbent feelings, every incumbent representative (ten Democrats and one Republican) was reelected, and Democratic senator John Kerry coasted to a comfortable 57 percent to 43 percent reelection victory.

The Return of the Marginals?

Does this ultimate success by incumbents conclusively refute the idea of an anti-incumbent mood? Not necessarily. We must again look below the surface for a more complete picture. While not many incumbents actually lost, a large number came close to losing. In addition to the nine Republican and six Democratic representatives who were defeated, ten Republicans and seven Democrats won with 52 percent or less of the vote. Similarly, in the Senate races, in addition to the defeat of Boschwitz, four other senators (three Republicans and one Democrat)

Table 12-4   Average Vote Percentages of House Incumbents, Selected
Years, 1974-1990

Election year	Democrats	Republicans	All incumbents
1974	68.5	55.2	61.7
1980	64.0	67.9	65.5
1982	67.9	59.9	64.1
1984	64.2	68.2	65.9
1986	70.2	65.6	68.2
1988	68.8	67.5	68.2
1990	65.8	59.8	63.5

Note: Based on incumbents with major party opposition (Democrats with Republican
opponents and Republicans with Democratic opponents).

also survived with 52 percent or less of the vote.

These percentages are particular manifestations of a more general
trend in 1990: a decline in the average vote percentage received by House
incumbents. It was the first such decline since 1982, as the data in Table
12-4 show.[17] Also, for the first time since 1982, the proportion of
incumbents receiving 60 percent or more of the vote (the benchmark
percentage often used to categorize members as marginal) declined as
well, from 86 percent in 1988 to 75 percent in 1990.[18] In some cases the
drop in vote margins was expected, such as where members were saddled
with the taint of the savings-and-loan scandal. In other instances,
however, members who were being vigorously challenged did a good deal
worse than had been anticipated. For example, Newt Gingrich (R-Ga.),
the outspoken conservative Minority Whip of the House, won by less
than 1,000 votes in a race that he was expected to win by a comfortable
margin.

Finally in some contests, defeat or narrow survival was completely
unexpected. For example, Herbert H. Bateman's (R-Va.) victory margin
fell from 73 percent of the vote in 1988 to 51 percent in 1990, while Doug
Walgren (D-Pa.) dropped from 63 percent to a losing share of 49 percent.
Both of these representatives had been classified as "safe" in *Congressional Quarterly Weekly Report*'s preelection analysis in October 1990.
While there are always some surprises in an election, the number of
unexpected results this time was much higher than usual. Indeed, of the
thirty-two incumbents who lost or won by narrow margins (52 percent of
the vote or less), twelve (38 percent) had been categorized as safe by
Congressional Quarterly.

The data in Table 12-4 also show that the reduction in vote margins
in the House was not equally distributed between the parties. The
average vote received by Republican incumbents in 1990 declined by

almost 8 percentage points from 1988, while it dropped only 3 percentage points for the Democrats. The average vote share for Republican incumbents was as low as in 1982 when twenty-eight GOP incumbents lost. (It is interesting to note that the 167 seats won by the Republicans in 1990 was only one more than the number they won in 1982.) Among Democratic incumbents who faced Republican opposition, only 6 percent lost or survived by narrow margins, while this was true of 15 percent of GOP incumbents opposed by Democrats. Had conditions been worse for Republicans, their losses in the House could have been much greater. In particular, if the Democratic challengers had been stronger, their success rate would likely have been higher. (We will return to this issue below.) This increase in close margins may stimulate more competitive contests in 1992. In any event, the results discussed here indicate that there were some national forces at work in the 1990 congressional elections, and that they affected one party's candidates more than the other's. The results also suggest that there is nothing immutable about the high reelection rates of incumbents; they can still lose if conditions are right.

The Role of President Bush

Another potential national influence on congressional elections is the president. During presidential elections, the winning presidential candidate can potentially have a direct influence on congressional outcomes by pulling in House and Senate candidates of his party on his coattails, as we discussed in Chapter 10. In midterm elections, presidents can affect outcomes because of voters' reactions to their job performance. Presidents also can try to influence voters more directly by campaigning for candidates of their party.

As we argued above, Bush's declining popularity may have taken a toll on Republican congressional chances. As the president's approval ratings declined, expectations about GOP chances also declined, and the party ended up not doing as well as observers had anticipated earlier in the year. There is also more direct evidence on this point: In an exit poll, voters who approved of the job Bush was doing reported voting Republican 60 percent to 40 percent, while those who disapproved voted Democratic 73 percent to 27 percent.[19]

President Bush was a fairly active campaigner during the election, but his strategy shifted as time passed. In September, when his popularity was still quite high, Bush's rhetoric on the stump was not very partisan. This was a deliberate decision because of his efforts to govern by consensus rather than by confrontation as Reagan had.[20] That decision was reinforced by his desire for bipartisan support in the Persian Gulf crisis, and by the need to come to an agreement with congressional Democrats on the budget. In October, after negotiations on the budget had deadlocked, the president attacked the opposition more frequently.

Then in the last week of the campaign, he again softened his rhetoric, in part because his political advisers didn't believe that he could get away with strong attacks on the Democrats over matters like high taxes so soon after working with them on a compromise budget package.[21]

In the end the results were disappointing both generally and in the particular races where Bush campaigned. The three big states with Republican governors where the president campaigned most intensively were the greatest cause for regret. While the GOP retained the California governor's chair, they lost the election in Florida (where Bush visited three times) and in Texas (where he spent the last three days of the campaign).[22] Thus, it appears that the president's declining popularity undermined Republican chances, and that his personal intervention in individual contests did little to produce positive Republican results.[23]

National Parties: Candidate Recruitment and Campaign Dollars

The analysis presented in Chapter 9 indicated that there were three factors that were extremely important in determining how competitive a congressional race would be: whether an incumbent was involved, how well-funded a challenger or open seat candidate was, and whether the candidates had experience in elective office. While these may properly be considered local influences, national forces have an impact on them. First of all, as Jacobson and Kernell argued in connection with their strategic politicians hypothesis, a party's national prospects influence the decisions of potential candidates of that party whether or not to seek office that particular year. Beyond that, however, national party organizations have a more direct impact by recruiting candidates and contributing money to them.

In 1990 both parties were active in recruiting candidates with mixed results—especially for Senate seats. Democratic party officials tried to persuade former vice president (and senator) Walter F. Mondale of Minnesota, former governor Jim Hunt of North Carolina, former governor Gerald L. Baliles of Virginia, and popular representative Ron Wyden of Oregon to take on Republican incumbents in their states. All decided not to run. Indeed, as we will see below, no Democratic statewide office holders or incumbent congressmen ran against Republican senators, and there were relatively few experienced Democratic candidates running against Republican representatives.

The Republicans were more successful at candidate recruitment, partly because they had the persuasive powers of an incumbent president and other executive branch officials on their side. Eight incumbent representatives and a lieutenant governor were persuaded to run against vulnerable Democratic senators or for open seats.[24] Because of the upcoming reapportionment and redistricting after the census, Republican party officials also were active in recruiting candidates for state legislative seats.[25] But despite strong efforts, the party frequently failed in efforts to find House candidates, or had candidates drop out after deciding to run. In a number of instances, the prospective candidates attacked the National Republican Congressional Committee (NRCC) for inadequately supporting their candidacies.[26]

The Republicans maintained their advantage in fundraising, although it became less pronounced between both parties' Senate campaign committees. The Democratic Senatorial Campaign Committee's contributions increased, while those of its Republican counterpart declined. For the House committees, both parties' receipts declined, with the Republicans falling to $28.5 million and the Democrats to $8.2 million.[27]

With its larger base of funding and its new leadership (under co-chairman Ed Rollins),[28] the NRCC continued to be more active and aggressive than its Democratic counterpart and the Senate campaign committees. This was, of course, a reflection of the greater effort needed in the continuing unsuccessful attempt to achieve majority status in the House. It is much easier for the Democrats to defend their dominance than it is for the Republicans to achieve it. For example, after the September 1989 House vote on the capital-gains tax rate (on which a majority of representatives supported the Bush position to cut the rate), the NRCC targeted about eighty of the districts of Democrats who voted with their party leadership against the cut. It sent press releases and radio announcements to media in those districts charging the Democrats with supporting high taxes.[29] The committee also had tried similar tactics with votes on federal subsidies for allegedly obscene art and random drug testing for State Department staff.[30]

Certainly the most controversial action by Rollins and the NRCC in their pursuit of electoral success for GOP House candidates was a memorandum Rollins wrote to them in October 1990. In it he noted that the committee's poll analysis indicated that the mood of voters had turned pessimistic about the direction of the country, that Bush's approval ratings had slipped "precipitously" because of the lack of a clear Republican position on taxes and spending, and that voters believed that Republicans were more interested in protecting tax breaks for the rich than in cutting taxes for average citizens. He then said: "My best advice today is to urge you to oppose taxes, specifically gas and income taxes. Do not hesitate to oppose either the President or proposals being advanced in Congress." [31] Such advice undermined the administration's efforts to secure a budget agreement, and the president and his staff were furious. There were even reports that Bush wanted Rollins fired from his position; Rollins announced his resignation in January 1991.

Thus, party committees are another national level influence on congressional elections, one that affects the local forces that are most

Table 12-5   Success in House and Senate General Elections, Controlling
for Office Background, Party, and Incumbency, 1990

Candidate's last office	Candidate is opponent of:				No incumbent in district			
	Democratic incumbent		Republican incumbent		Democratic candidate		Republican candidate	
	(%)	(N)	(%)	(N)	(%)	(N)	(%)	(N)
House								
State legislature or U.S. House	8	(13)	22	(9)	67	(12)	50	(16)
Other elective office	0	(10)	29	(7)	83	(6)	33	(6)
No elective office	3	(179)	5	(108)	36	(11)	33	(6)
Senate								
U.S. House or statewide elective office	0	(6)	—	(0)	50	(2)	80	(5)
Other elective office	0	(2)	0	(5)	0	(3)	—	(0)
No elective office	0	(6)	14	(7)	—	(0)	—	(0)

Note: Percentages show the proportion of candidates in each category who won; numbers in parentheses are the totals on which percentages are based. For the 1988 results, see Table 9-4 on page 240.

important in determining outcomes. The committees seek to recruit strong candidates,[32] and they then provide those candidates with money and strategic advice as their campaigns progress. As our discussion shows, their impact in 1990 was decidedly mixed.

Local Forces: Candidate Quality and Incumbents' Problems

As our earlier analysis showed, one of the most important influences on outcomes in individual races is the quality of candidates seeking office. Table 12-5 shows the results in House and Senate races in 1990, controlling for the previous experience of challengers to incumbents and of candidates in open seat races. (This corresponds to the 1988 data in Table 9-4.) Only one Senate incumbent lost, so no relationship is visible regarding those races, but in House contests candidates with elective experience were more successful than those without. In open House races, the data show again that experienced candidates were more likely to win, and in Senate races no inexperienced candidates even won nomination.

In addition to affecting victory or defeat, the data in Table 12-6 show that challenger experience also was related to the incidence of close contests for victorious House incumbents. In both parties, experienced challengers were more likely to win and were more likely to run close

Table 12-6 Election Margins for House Incumbents in the 1990
Elections, Controlling for Party and Elective Office
Experience of Challengers

Party of challenger	Challenger experienced?	Incumbent won with more than 55%	Incumbent won with less than 55%	Incumbent lost	Total	(N)
Democrat	No	87.0%	8.3	4.6	99.9%	(108)
Democrat	Yes	50.0%	25.0	25.0	100.0%	(16)
Republican	Yes	65.2%	30.4	4.3	99.9%	(23)
Republican	No	93.3%	3.9	2.8	100.0%	(179)
All		87.1%	8.3	4.6	100.0%	(326)

unsuccessful races than were challengers without such backgrounds. The
data also show, however, that experienced challengers were again rare in
1990 as they had been in 1988. Slightly less than 10 percent of all
incumbents (and only 12 percent of those with major party opponents)
had experienced challengers, continuing the decline from previous years.
Democrats were slightly less likely (9 percent versus 10 percent) than
Republicans to field strong challengers—the first time that has been true
since we began our analyses of national elections in 1980. Indeed,
Jacobson has said that the proportion of experienced Democratic challengers in 1990 was the lowest since the end of World War II and down
precipitously from 1982 when about 40 percent of the challengers had
held elective office.[33]

Beyond the incidence of weak challengers, it is important to note
that eighty House incumbents (20 percent) had no major party opponent
at all, which is also a slight increase over previous elections. (In 1986 and
1988 the proportion was about 18 percent.) As with experienced challengers, the Republicans had a marginal advantage by having more unop-
posed incumbents running than did the Democrats (21 percent versus 19
percent). This, however, was a major change from earlier years. In 1988,
for example, 24 percent of Democratic incumbents had no major party
opposition, while this was true of only 9 percent of Republicans. Thus in
1990, Democrats fielded a collectively weak challenge to Republicans in
House elections. As a result they probably harvested fewer gains from
what turned out to be advantageous political conditions than would have
been the case with a stronger corps of candidates.[34]

There also were many idiosyncratic elements that influenced the
outcomes in some races. As in 1988, a number of defeated incumbents
were touched by scandal. In 1990 this was true for about half of the

sixteen losers, including five who were linked to the savings-and-loan crisis (although some of these incumbents were not charged with personal wrongdoing, but with failing in their institutional responsibilities to oversee the issue).[35] In at least three districts, challengers supporting abortion rights succeeded in ousting antiabortion incumbents, but in other cases opponents of abortion survived comfortably.

In other races losses by incumbents seemed to spring from their complacency about their reelection chances. The most salient example of this was Robert W. Kastenmeier (D-Wis.), who was beaten after thirty-two years in office.[36] He had won a solid 59 percent victory in 1988 against a strong, well-funded, two-time challenger; as a result the NRCC had removed him from their target list. A month before the 1990 election, Kastenmeier's campaign polls showed him with 62 percent support, so his campaign organization stopped polling. In addition, the campaign also closed down its get-out-the-vote phone banks. Kastenmeier's challenger pressed a platform of anti-incumbent themes (including term limits and opposition to the congressional pay raise) during the last month, and he won 53 percent to 47 percent.[37]

Thus, the evidence linking local influences to outcomes provides a picture that meshes well with the national patterns we have seen. If a clever challenger faces an unprepared or uninvolved incumbent, the latter can be easy pickings. If an experienced challenger runs, he or she can give even an effective incumbent a tough race. And if an incumbent faces a weak challenger (or none at all), he or she will be virtually invincible.

The 1990 Election: The Impact on Congress

The change in membership for the 102d Congress is only slightly greater than the change resulting from the 1988 elections that we discussed in Chapter 9. Although the partisan and ideological changes that the elections produced in Congress will be minimal, the policy implications may turn out to be more substantial.

There are forty-four freshmen representatives in the 102d Congress—10 percent of the total membership. The House roster includes record numbers of women (twenty-eight) and blacks (twenty-five), although these groups remain underrepresented relative to their share of the population. Of the female members, nineteen are Democrats and nine are Republicans. Among the black members, freshman Gary Franks of Connecticut is the only Republican, and he is the first black Republican to serve in the House since the Great Depression.

The membership change in the House yields a modest, but noticeable shift to the left in political ideology. In addition to the simple effect of the nine-seat shift to the Democrats, the new Democrats include some very liberal members, while some of the departing Republicans were outspoken conservatives. The former group spans the country, from socialist Bernard Sanders of Vermont and Thomas H. Andrews of Maine, a community organizer and former head of his state's association of handicapped persons, to Neil Abercrombie of Hawaii, whose beard and shoulder-length hair remain from his days as an antiwar activist. The Republican departures included Chuck Douglas of New Hampshire, the newly elected chairman of the Conservative Opportunity Society (COS), an organization of conservative activists in the House, and Jack Buechner of Missouri, another COS member. In the Senate there are only four new members (three Republicans and one Democrat),[38] and little change in the character of the membership is visible.

As the members of both parties in the House came together for the new Congress, leadership contests gave some indication of the policy debates that were to come. Among the Democrats, the top party leaders were reelected without incident, but when the Democratic Caucus voted on committee chairmen, there were some significant surprises.[39] With almost no warning, the chairmen of both the Public Works and the House Administration committees were voted down and replaced. Additionally, eighty-nine votes were cast against the chairman of the Banking Committee, although he survived the challenge. "The agitation reflects a desire by many Democrats to make their caucus more assertive legislatively and politically in the run-up to the 1992 elections. Both [chairmen] were regarded as weak, ineffective leaders and were replaced by younger, more aggressive Democrats. ..."[40]

The changes in committee leadership were due in part to party members' concern about upcoming policy conflicts, and they wanted to make sure that adequate leadership would be available on those issues. For example, the Public Works Committee faced the prospect of securing passage for a major new highway bill that would likely require funding of $20 billion for four years. House Democrats "wanted an effective, aggressive chairman who would 'go to the mat' with the Appropriations Committee and the White House to obtain the funding that is necessary for the bill." [41] It is interesting to note that, unlike previous challenges to committee chairs, the top party leaders did not intervene strongly to try to save the committee leaders.

Among House Republicans, it was second-rank party leaders that came under challenge. While Minority Leader Robert H. Michel of Illinois and Minority Whip Newt Gingrich of Georgia were reelected without opposition, Jerry Lewis of California, chairman of the House Republican Conference, and NRCC chairman Guy Vander Jagt of Michigan were challenged. These contests reflected the continuing division in the House GOP between activist conservatives led by Gingrich, who favored confrontation with House Democrats on policy matters to secure electoral gains, and more moderate Republicans who sought compromises with the majority to influence policy.[42] Both of the challenges failed, but it was clear that the basic conflict would persist. For example, when Bush's budget director, Richard Darman, was critical of some of the ideas of the activist conservatives, Gingrich called for his resignation, describing him as a "technocrat" in the "Dukakis/ McNamara" mold. Gingrich went on to say that "Ideological battles matter.... If they didn't matter, we would be talking about President Dukakis...." [43]

Republicans in the Senate had their own ideological struggle over leadership positions. Here, too, the top leaders were routinely endorsed, but in contested elections for four second-rank positions, conservative senators·defeated more moderate ones. This included the ouster of John H. Chafee of Rhode Island as chairman of the Republican Conference by Thad Cochran of Mississippi. Conservatives resented Chafee because he had not only voted for cloture (to cut off debate) and to override Bush's veto of a hotly contested civil rights bill, but he was one of only three GOP senators to support cloture on a campaign finance bill. One of the conservatives, Dan Coats of Indiana, said that the leadership elections "May reflect the fact that there is a sense that business as usual is not going to serve us in 1992. We need an aggressiveness in defining differences between the two parties." [44]

Senator Coats's statement and the leadership contests described above reflect the increase in partisanship in Congress that has occurred since the 1970s. During those years the parties, and especially the Democrats, were beset by many policy divisions that usually occurred along regional lines. Subsequently, because of electoral changes,[45] the political preferences of the constituencies of northern and southern Democrats became more like one another and less like those of Republicans. As a consequence, Democrats found greater common ground on previously divisive issues, but this also led to greater conflict with the GOP.

This partisan context and the persistence of divided government will yield a continuation of the policy conflicts between the Democratic congressional majority and the White House that we saw throughout the 1980s. Presidential-congressional disagreement was frequent in Bush's first two years, with Bush coming out the loser in many confrontations. Despite his high approval scores among the public, the president won only 46.8 percent of the roll call votes in 1990 on which he took a position. This was the second lowest success rate in any year since 1953 when Congressional Quarterly began keeping track of these votes.[46] The president's lack of success is, of course, a reflection of the small number of Republicans in both chambers, particularly in the House where Bush lost 68 percent of these votes in 1990.

Many of the most divisive issues from the 101st Congress will carry over to the 102d Congress. For example, the Democrats will again press for passage of a civil rights bill, despite Bush's successful 1990 veto on the grounds that such a law would lead businesses to adopt racial quotas in hiring. GOP opposition to that bill, plus frequent attacks by Republicans against affirmative action programs, led House Majority Leader Richard A. Gephardt (D-Mo.) to charge that Republican strategists were trying "to divide white working people from black working people, and thereby distract them from their common interests." [47]

Continuing problems with the budget deficit are likely to provoke partisan disagreements. Despite the five-year deficit-reduction agreement between Bush and Congress, it is clear that the recession may require them to return to the budget debate much sooner. Even without the additional economic pressure, some elements of the earlier deal are not as settled as they are supposed to be. For example, one of the key parts of the agreement involved who would judge the cost of tax cuts and new spending programs. The negotiators had given that task to the Office of Management and Budget, a significant concession to the president. However, House Democrats—believing that those estimates would be politically motivated—endorsed a new House rule that would require such estimates to be made by the Congressional Budget Office. In a letter to Speaker Tom Foley, Bush said that such a rule would undercut "the credibility of the entire budget agreement. I will veto any bill that contains language such as that specified in the rule." [48] The House adopted the new rule early in 1991 anyway.

As Bush's letter suggests, much of the conflict between him and the 102d Congress revolves around the politics of vetoes. The president vetoed sixteen bills during the 1989-1990 congressional session, and none was overridden. Some of the vetoes, however, were sustained by narrow margins. For example the override vote on the civil rights bill in the Senate was 66-34 (failing by one vote), and a House override attempt on a textile bill lost 275-152 (failing by ten votes). With fewer Republicans, Bush may find success with this strategy more difficult. In addition, presidential electoral politics will more and more color the legislative process as the 1992 elections draw nearer. As Senate Majority Leader George J. Mitchell (D-Maine) has said, "There will be a political context as well as a legislative context." [49]

The 1992 Election and Beyond

In addition to the presidential election, which we will discuss in Chapter 13, 1992 will feature another round of congressional elections. In the Senate races, we will see a vigorous battle for party control of that body. The central feature of the House contests will be the impact of reappor-

Table 12-7   Vulnerability of Senate Seats to Be Contested in 1992

Very vulnerable (4D, 6R)	Potentially vulnerable (6D, 4R)	Safe (10D, 5R)
Adams (D, Wash.)[a]	Daschle (D, S.D.)[a]	Bond (R, Mo.)
Coats (R, Ind.)[a]	Garn (R, Utah)	Breaux (D, La.)[a]
Cranston's seat (D, Calif.)	Glenn (D, Ohio)	Bumpers (D, Ark.)
D'Amato (R, N.Y.)	Graham (D, Fla.)[a]	Conrad (D, N.D.)[a]
Fowler (D, Ga.)[a]	Murkowski (R, Alaska)	Dixon (D, Ill.)
Kasten (R, Wis.)	Packwood (R, Ore.)	Dodd (D, Conn.)
McCain (R, Ariz.)[a]	Sanford (D, N.C.)[a]	Dole (R, Kan.)
Reid (D, Nev.)[a]	Shelby (D, Ala.)[a]	Ford (D, Ky.)
Seymour (R, Calif.)[b]	Specter (R, Pa.)	Grassley (R, Iowa)
Symms (R, Idaho)	Wirth (D, Colo.)[a]	Hollings (D, S.C.)
		Inouye (D, Hawaii)
		Leahy (D, Vt.)
		Mikulski (D, Md.)[a]
		Nickles (R, Okla.)
		Rudman (R, N.H.)

Note: Except for the two California seats, the classifications are taken from *Roll Call,* November 19, 1990, 8.

[a] First-term members.   [b] Appointed to office.

tionment and redistricting that will take place in the wake of the 1990 census. In this section, we will focus on each of these subjects, and conclude by speculating about congressional elections for the rest of the decade.

1992: The Battle for Senate Control

While every election year involves an effort by both parties to achieve majority status in the Senate, 1992 is of particular importance because the group of Senate seats that is up for reelection is the same group that brought Republicans in 1980 their first Senate control since 1955, and the same one that lost them control in 1986. Since the 1986 election, the GOP has been looking forward to 1992 as its golden opportunity to regain the majority, because the Democrats will be defending twenty seats and the Republicans only fifteen seats. Moreover, eleven of the Democratic seats are held by freshmen, many of whom won by narrow margins, while only three Republicans are in their first term.[50]

Republican prospects, however, do not appear to be as bright as these numbers suggest. Some early state-by-state analyses indicate that the GOP may have more seats that it will have trouble holding onto than the Democrats. For example, in an overview published by *Roll Call* just after the 1990 elections,[51] the senators whose seats are to be contested were classified as "very vulnerable," "potentially vulnerable," and "safe" (see Table 12-7). Five Republicans and only three Democrats were listed as "very vulnerable," to which we have added the two California seats (one for each party). Six Democratic and four GOP seats were termed "potentially vulnerable," while ten Democrats and five Republicans were thought to be "safe."

Some of the "very vulnerable" senators have been placed in that category partly because they have potential high quality opponents who are actively campaigning or considering a race. For example, Sen. Bob Kasten (R-Wis.) won his first term in 1980 with 50.9 percent of the vote and was reelected in 1986 with only 50.8 percent of the vote. Among Kasten's potential challengers is Democratic representative Jim Moody of Milwaukee, who won 71 percent of the vote during his House campaign in 1990. To many observers the campaign had already begun in 1990 when Moody attacked Kasten for continuing to support a no-new-taxes position and a cut in the capital gains rate in the midst of the budget crisis. Kasten, in turn, criticized Moody's support for the congressional pay raise. Among the "potentially vulnerable" Democrats is Sen. Terry Sanford of North Carolina—all three Republican House members have expressed an interest in opposing him.

While conditions may change a great deal from these preliminary estimates, they do suggest that the Republican party will find it difficult to retake control of the Senate in 1992. Indeed, they may have trouble gaining any seats at all, and a loss of seats is even possible.

1992: Redistricting, Retirements, and the House Contests

The Republican party once hoped that 1992 might give it control of the House. They knew that the reapportionment after the 1990 census would redistribute House seats among the states, taking some seats from states with slow growing populations and transferring them to states with large increases in population. States would be required to redistrict, making all of the districts within each state as equal as possible in population. As we discussed in Chapter 9, Republicans have long argued that they have been denied majority status in the House because district lines were unfairly gerrymandered against them and the Democratic majority benefited from the advantage of incumbency. (We will reassess the accuracy of that claim below.) Therefore, one of their principal goals in 1990 was to increase their control of governorships and state legislatures in order to strengthen their hand in the redistricting process.

Like many other aspects of the 1990 elections, the GOP's hopes were frustrated in this instance as well. In addition to the loss of one or two governorships, they lost some ground in state legislatures. In the three states where they held the governorships before the election, and which would gain the greatest number of seats, the Republicans managed to retain control in California, but they lost both Texas and Florida. This was very damaging because Democrats control both houses of the legislature in all three states.

In late December 1990 the census figures were announced along with the redistribution of House seats. A total of nineteen seats will be shifted among the states, with thirteen states losing seats and eight states gaining seats. The big winners were as expected: California ($+7$), Florida ($+4$), and Texas ($+3$). The big losers were Illinois, Michigan, Ohio, and Pennsylvania (-2 each), and New York (-3).[52] Actually, the finality of these figures may only be theoretical because officials in many states that lost seats contend that the census figures are inaccurate, and they are seeking an adjustment of the figures. The Secretary of Commerce is under a court imposed deadline of July 15, 1991, to decide whether the census numbers should be statistically adjusted. Before or after that date, the courts or Congress may step in to impose a decision.

Seven states will have only one representative,[53] and Nebraska (with three seats) has a nonpartisan unicameral legislature. In the remaining states a political party may control the redistricting process if it controls the governorship and both houses of the state legislature. The Democrats hold the governorship and both houses of the state legislature in 18 states slated to have 154 House seats.[54] The Republicans control only two states (New Hampshire and Utah) with five seats. The remaining twenty-two states (with 266 seats) have divided partisan control. This situation is far from what the GOP was aiming for and is marginally worse than after the 1980 census, when Republicans completely controlled four states (forty-seven seats) to the Democrats' seventeen states (164 seats). It is clear that these figures do not guarantee that the Republicans will end up worse off at the end of the redistricting process than they are now. In states with split partisan control, the GOP can block any plan that damages its interests thereby forcing the Democrats to compromise or letting the courts handle the issues.

To bolster its efforts, the GOP also is supporting the efforts of black and Hispanic political groups to create more districts containing a majority of minority residents. They are aided in this effort by the Voting Rights Act, which protects the political rights of minorities and may require the creation of districts in which minority members make up a majority of the population, although that question has not been conclusively settled.[55] The minority groups are obviously interested in increasing the number of minority representatives in Congress. The Republicans are seeking to concentrate voters who tend to vote Democratic in a small number of districts, thereby undermining the safety of Democratic incumbents who formerly represented those voters.

Finally, many Republicans believe that because the population growth in those states that are gaining seats has occurred primarily in areas where their party is strong, the lion's share of the new seats will come to them automatically. Thus the gubernatorial and state legislative outcomes do not guarantee that the GOP will suffer as a result of the redistricting process. They do, however, mean that the party won't have as much influence over that process as it hoped to have.

Another cause for hope among Republicans comes from the prospect of an unusually large number of open seats in 1992. While the prospect that some have talked about—100 races without incumbents—is probably greater than what will actually take place, there surely will be more of these races than in recent years, and it is not unlikely that the number will be larger than after the last census. (There were fifty-six open seats in 1982.)

As a result of reapportionment, nineteen seats automatically will be vacant. A few other seats will likely open up due to deaths or resignations and an uncertain but probably significant number of members will leave to seek other offices. Some of these have already been announced; in California three Democrats have indicated they will seek a Senate seat. Other contests are probable, but not yet certain, such as the cases of Rep. Moody of Wisconsin and the three North Carolina Republicans mentioned earlier in the chapter. The twenty Democratic Senate seats are particularly likely to stimulate House Republicans to run. The combination of the greater influence of minority members in the Senate, the possibility of GOP Senate control, and the likely continuation of Republican minority status in the House make the prospect of a run for higher office quite attractive.

Finally, the number of retirements should be greater than usual. Some senior members have had the opportunity to convert excess campaign contributions to their personal use upon retirement. Under a new law, 1992 will be their last year to do so. Others have delayed retiring until the new pay raise goes into effect, so that their pensions will be greater. Still others will likely quit because of close electoral calls in 1990, or because their constituencies are significantly disrupted by redistricting. Thus, the number of open seats should be large, and Republicans hope that without the roadblock of Democratic incumbents in those districts, they will be able to make significant gains.

1992 and Beyond: Continued Democratic Dominance of the House?

Senate races are so independent of one other, and the party balance so close, that it is difficult to anticipate what will occur beyond 1992 until we know the results of those elections. Therefore, we will confine our attention to the House in this concluding section. As we have noted, Republicans have been looking forward to the 1992 elections because of their hope that the two alleged Democratic advantages—gerrymandering and incumbency—would be undermined. In Chapter 9 we questioned the validity of Republican claims of disadvantage based on those factors. Two years later, is there any reason to put more credence in GOP claims? We think not. Rather, additional evidence and analysis suggest that the causes of GOP failures in House elections lie elsewhere.

Our discussion of the prospects for redistricting indicates that the political balance is such that the Republicans will be unable to control the process in enough states to bias the results in their favor. However, in our previous discussion we questioned the ability to gerrymander itself. Gerrymandering depends on the existence of dependable, predictably partisan voting blocs that can be defined geographically and then allocated to particular districts to produce a desired result. But we continue to observe evidence, such as the high rate of ticket splitting, that such partisan blocs no longer exist in most places. If the preconditions for gerrymandering do not exist, gerrymandering may have little effectiveness.

This helps to explain why the intended Republican gerrymander in Indiana (see pages 254-255) was unsuccessful. Indeed, in 1990 the results were even worse, as Republican incumbent John Hiler fell to a Democratic challenger, and as Democrat Jill Long (who had won Dan Quayle's old seat in a 1989 special election) was reelected with 61 percent of the vote. Thus the redistricting plan that was supposed to produce a six to four or seven to three GOP advantage has yielded an eight to two Democratic delegation. Even in California, supposedly the most successful pro-Democratic gerrymander, two Democratic incumbents lost in 1990, as did one Republican incumbent. This suggests that the plan may have been successful more because each party *believed* in its supposed effects and refrained from challenging the other side's incumbents rather than because the district lines guaranteed a particular partisan result. Indeed, new analyses continue to undermine the claim that gerrymandering has had a significant role in continuing Democratic majority control.[56]

The incumbency advantage in maintaining the Democrats' majority that we discussed earlier (see pages 255-256) pointed out the lack of Republican success in winning open seats between 1980 and 1988 where this advantage was absent. In his more extensive analysis, Jacobson shows that between 1968 and 1988 the Democrats "have taken 27.6 percent of Republican open seats while losing 19.9 percent of their own." [57] In Table 12-8 we have updated our earlier analysis by showing the results for open seat races for the period after the 1982 elections through 1990. The advantage of this time period is that all of the preelection-postelection comparisons of outcomes take place within a common set of district lines.[58] Furthermore, this set of data, unlike the others we have discussed, includes open seat races that took place in special elections. A significant number of representatives were initially selected this way, so the inclusion of these races substantially improves

Table 12-8 Partisan Outcomes in Open Seat House Races, 1983-1990

Seats	Division before elections (D-R)	Division after elections (D-R)	Net seat change
All	71-73	75-69	+ 4D
Democratic seats	71-0	56-15	+ 15R
Republican seats	0-73	19-54	+ 19D
Republican districts won by Bush in 1988	0-68	16-52	+ 16D
Republican districts won by Bush with 60% or more of total vote	0-41	8-33	+ 8D

the completeness of the data.[59]

The data generally conform to those cited earlier. In 144 races, the partisan division was 71 Democrats and 73 Republicans before the elections, and 75 to 69 respectively after. The results yielded a net gain of four seats by the Democrats. Of course Republican partisans would likely argue that the open seat results show nothing. They would claim that many of these seats were gerrymandered against the GOP, so it is the interaction of districting and incumbency that matters. Since these races all take place within one set of district lines, we can test this claim.

Table 12-8 first breaks down the districts according to which party held each one before the open seat race, paralleling Jacobson's results cited earlier. The pattern is very similar. The Republicans won 21.1 percent of the Democratic seats, while 26.0 percent of the GOP seats went the other way. This substantially undermines Republican claims. If the majority of districts were gerrymandered against them, the Republican districts would have to be significantly *safer* for them than Democratic districts for the Democrats. This is the only way a bias (that is, more districts for the Democrats than they would be entitled to by their share of the vote) can be created. Without such a bias, there is no gerrymander. Since the GOP had already won the Republican seats in one or more races preceding the open seat election, it is logically impossible for them to claim that the seats were drawn in such a way that they could not win.

We can create additional subsets of the open seat data to shed even more light on Republican performance and the question of alleged bias. First we consider only the sixty-eight seats that were held by Republicans before the open seat election and were carried by Bush in 1988. Thus these districts have a double indication of Republican ability to achieve success within their boundaries. However, they lost 23.5 percent of these, a sixteen-seat loss. Finally, we show the results for the forty-one GOP seats Bush carried with 60 percent or more of the vote. It is exceedingly difficult to claim that these seats are biased against the Republican party; they lost 19.5 percent of those seats (-8).[60]

The analyses presented here indicate strongly that neither incumbency nor gerrymandering, separately or in combination, explains the Republicans' failures to win majority control of the House. Instead one must look to political problems rather than these structural ones to account for their continued minority status. As Jacobson states, "Republicans have failed to advance in the House because they have fielded inferior candidates on the wrong side of issues that are important to voters in House elections, and because voters find it difficult to assign blame or credit when control of the government is divided between the parties." [61] Because there is no reason to believe that these political conditions will change soon, there is no reason to expect the result to change. Republican gains in 1992 would not be surprising; indeed, because of their low level of exposure, their failure to gain seats would be a surprise. However, a Republican majority is unlikely in 1992 (and probably for at least the rest of the millennium), and neither the redrawing of district lines before the election nor the number of open seats will matter very much.

Notes

1. The independent candidate was Bernard Sanders of Vermont, formerly elected mayor of Burlington running as a socialist. He defeated incumbent Republican Peter Smith and Democratic candidate Dolores Sandoval. For convenience in presenting results, we will count Sanders as a Democrat in the rest of this chapter. This seems reasonable because Sanders stated that he would seek to join the House Democratic Caucus if he won (although he was eventually refused admission because he would not adopt the party label), because he voted with the Democrats to organize the House, and because Sandoval received only 3 percent of the vote while Sanders won 56 percent of the vote. This suggests that the voters were treating him as if he were the de facto Democratic candidate. (Unless otherwise indicated, all vote results used in this chapter are taken from *Congressional Quarterly Weekly Report*'s postelection issue, November 10, 1990.)
2. The Arizona race was undetermined because no candidate received a majority of the total vote cast as required by the Arizona constitution. The Republican candidate received 49.7 percent of the vote, a write-in candidate received slightly less than one percent, and the balance went to the Democrat. The runoff between the Democrat and the Republican was scheduled for February 26, 1991.
3. Recall that as we noted in Chapter 9, only *elected* members are counted as incumbents. Thus two seats that were occupied by appointed senators are counted here as seats without incumbents. In both cases Dan Coats (R-Ind.) and Daniel K. Akaka (D-Hawaii) won election.
4. Earlier research indicates that for these purposes voters may tend to regard a president whose predecessor either died or resigned from office as a continuation of the first president's administration. Therefore, these data are organized by term of administration, rather than term of president. See Paul R.

Abramson, John H. Aldrich, and David W. Rohde, *Change and Continuity in the 1980 Elections,* rev. ed. (Washington, D.C.: CQ Press, 1983), 252-253.

5. Senate elections, with their small number of races, fluctuate more than House outcomes, but still yield predictable patterns. In the five first-midterm elections, the president's party broke even, averaging 0 seats lost, while in the six later midterms the average loss was eight seats. That was exactly the result for 1986, so that year is not atypical for Senate elections. Thus for 1990, the outcome for the Senate was very close to the historical average.

6. *Cook Political Report,* September 21, 1990, 9-10.

7. *Roll Call,* February 19, 1990, 11-30.

8. *Cook Political Report,* March 20, 1990, 1.

9. "Opinion Outlook: Views on Presidential Performance," *National Journal,* December 15, 1990, 3053.

10. For example, a late-1989 poll for the American Medical Association PAC showed that the approval rating for Congress had dropped nine points over the previous year, from 62 percent to 53 percent. *Cook Political Report,* March 20, 1990, 3.

11. Quoted in Susan B. Glasser, "Anti-Incumbent Sentiment Runs Strong," *Roll Call,* July 16, 1990, 21.

12. William Schneider, "GOP Hoping for Anti-Incumbent Tide," *National Journal,* September 29, 1990, 2370.

13. Similar amendments were adopted in California and Colorado in the November general election.

14. See *Roll Call,* September 27, 1990, 12.

15. Charles E. Cook, "The Anti-Incumbent Mood Is on Again, This Time for Good," *Roll Call,* October 11, 1990, 6.

16. "1990 Candidates for Senate and House," *Congressional Quarterly Weekly Report,* October 13, 1990, 3359-3371.

17. These data are taken from "House Incumbents' Average Vote Percentage," *Congressional Quarterly Weekly Report,* November 10, 1990, 3800.

18. *Roll Call,* November 12, 1990, 10.

19. "Portrait of the Electorate: U.S. House Vote," *New York Times,* November 8, 1990, B7.

20. Ann Devroy, "Different Tack in Midterm Races: Campaigning Locally, Bush Rarely Strikes Partisan Stance," *Washington Post,* September 20, 1990, A10.

21. Maureen Dowd, "In Switch of Campaign Tactics, the Kinder, Gentler Bush Emerges," *New York Times,* November 3, 1990, 8.

22. Jack W. Germond and Jules Witcover, "Bush Takes a Hit," *National Journal,* November 10, 1990, 2732, 2734.

23. This lack of personal influence on outcomes is consistent with the historical pattern. Other popular presidents, including Franklin D. Roosevelt and Ronald Reagan, were unable to persuade voters to back their choices in midterm elections. It must be noted that presidential campaign visits are consistently productive for one purpose: fundraising.

24. GOP officials also were active in persuading potential candidates *not* to run. For example, President Bush met with conservative Chicago businessman Gary MacDougal and encouraged him to drop out of the Senate race in Illinois and instead endorse Republican representative Lynn Martin, the more moderate candidate. See *Roll Call,* July 13, 1989, 3.

25. David S. Broder, "For GOP's Statehouse Recruiters, 'Bait-and-Switch' Takes on New Meaning," *Washington Post,* October 8, 1989, A10.

26. Richard E. Cohen, "GOP Dropouts Hurting House Prospects," *National*

Journal, June 30, 1990, 1613-1614.

27. The figures used here are from the *Washington Post,* November 3, 1990, A8. Money raised does not necessarily correspond to money distributed to candidates. The House Republican committee had more than a three to one advantage in receipts in 1988, but (as the data in Chapter 9, note 57 show) its advantage in money distributed was less than two to one. Indeed, in a contest for chairmanship of the NRCC, the challenger, Rep. Don Sundquist (R-Tenn.), claimed that only 7 percent of the money raised went to candidates. See *Congressional Quarterly Weekly Report,* November 24, 1990, 3929.

28. See Chapter 9, page 253.

29. *Roll Call,* October 2-8, 1989, 5.

30. Tom Kenworthy, "GOP Tries to Turn Two Votes Against Democrats: Controversial Art Exhibit, Drug Tests Cited in Press Releases," *Washington Post,* July 19, 1989, A6.

31. The full text of the memo can be found in "The Rollins Remedy," *Washington Post,* October 25, 1990, A21.

32. One committee's activities can undermine the success of another committee of the same party. For example, of the eight GOP House seats left open because members were seeking a Senate seat, the Democrats took four seats, accounting for almost half of their 1990 gains.

33. *Roll Call,* November 12, 1990, 10.

34. Of course it may turn out that the Democrats had a large number of well-funded amateurs, but we will not know this until campaign spending data become available later in 1991. However, this seems unlikely because a preelection study by Common Cause showed that only twenty-three incumbents were involved in races in which opponents had raised even half as much money as they had. See *Roll Call,* October 8, 1990, 23.

35. Dave Kaplan, "The Tally: Democrats, Up Nine; Republicans, Down Eight," *Congressional Quarterly Weekly Report,* November 10, 1990, 3802.

36. This account is drawn from *Roll Call,* November 15, 1990, 6.

37. Another political disadvantage for House incumbents was to be Republican and named Smith. Of the five GOP Smiths who sought reelection, two lost—a 40 percent defeat rate.

38. There are also two senators, one from each party, who were serving by appointment.

39. As a result of reform rules adopted in the 1970s, the Democratic Caucus conducts an automatic secret ballot vote on each committee chairman at the beginning of every Congress. If a majority of the members vote against a chairman, there is a subsequent vote in the Caucus to fill the position. For a discussion of the adoption and use of these rules, see David W. Rohde, *Parties and Leaders in the Postreform House* (Chicago: University of Chicago Press, 1991), chapters 2-4.

40. Janet Hook, "Younger Members Flex Muscle in Revolt Against Chairmen," *Congressional Quarterly Weekly Report,* December 8, 1990, 4059.

41. Thomas J. Burger, "Wed. Night Massacre: How It All Happened," *Roll Call,* December 10, 1990, 22.

42. Gingrich supported the challenge to Lewis, but backed Vander Jagt's reelection.

43. Quoted in Gwen Hill, "Gingrich Escalates Criticism of Bush's Domestic Policy," *Washington Post,* December 1, 1990, A3.

44. Quoted in Janet Hook, "Senate Republican Conference Takes a Step to the

Right," *Congressional Quarterly Weekly Report,* November 17, 1990, 3871.

45. For a brief account of these changes and their consequences in both the House and Senate, see David W. Rohde, "Electoral Forces, Political Agendas, and Partisanship in the House and Senate," in *The Postreform Congress,* ed. Roger Davidson (New York: St. Martin's, forthcoming).

46. The lowest success rate was 43.5 percent in 1987, the next to last year of the Reagan administration. Bush's first-year success rate was the worst first year for any elected president. See George Hager, "Bush's Success Rate Sinks to Near-Record Low," *Congressional Quarterly Weekly Report,* December 22, 1990, 4183-4187.

47. Quoted in Thomas B. Edsall, "Gephardt Says GOP Playing Racial Politics: Stage Set for Renewal of Rights Bill Battle," *Washington Post,* December 7, 1990, A14.

48. Quoted in Ann Devroy, "Bush Counters House Democrats' Budget Tack with Veto Threat," *Washington Post,* December 22, 1990, A4.

49. Quoted in Richard E. Cohen, "Small Gains, Big Impact," *National Journal,* November 10, 1990, 2715.

50. This includes the California seat occupied by former Republican state senator John Seymour, the appointed replacement of former senator Pete Wilson who resigned after winning the governorship. Thus both California seats will be contested; the other is being vacated by Alan Cranston who is retiring.

51. *Roll Call,* November 19, 1990, 8.

52. The one-seat winners were Arizona, Georgia, North Carolina, Virginia, and Washington. The single-seat losers were Iowa, Kansas, Kentucky, Louisiana, Massachusetts, Montana, New Jersey, and West Virginia.

53. Alaska, Delaware, Montana, North Dakota, South Dakota, Vermont, and Wyoming.

54. Arkansas, Florida, Georgia, Hawaii, Kentucky, Louisiana, Maryland, Mississippi, Nevada, New Jersey, New Mexico, Oklahoma, Rhode Island, Tennessee, Texas, Virginia, Washington, and West Virginia.

55. See Peter Bragdon, "Democrats' Ties to Minorities May Be Tested by New Lines," *Congressional Quarterly Weekly Report,* June 2, 1990, 1739-1742.

56. As Jacobson states, Republican governor George Deukmejian, running for reelection in 1986, carried twenty of the twenty-seven Democratic House districts. He analyzed district outcomes since World War II and found no evidence of a pro-Democratic bias from redistricting. See Gary Jacobson, *The Electoral Origins of Divided Government: Competition in U.S. House Elections, 1946-1988* (Boulder: Westview, 1990), 93-96. Gary King and Andrew Gelman conclude, in a more complex analysis, that the electoral system has been biased in favor of the Republicans when the incumbency advantage has been controlled for. See King and Gelman, "Systemic Consequences of Incumbency Advantage in U.S. House Elections," *American Journal of Political Science* 35 (February 1991): 110-138.

57. Jacobson, *Electoral Origins,* 33.

58. Actually, eleven states redrew their district lines after 1982, but most of the changes were minimal, and none substantially affected the districts in the open seat set.

59. Only special elections that were held independently of the regular November general elections are included; there were twenty-eight. Two of these elections involved the wives of deceased representatives and were excluded, as was the 1983 race in Texas when Phil Gramm, who had been elected as a Democrat, resigned, and successfully won election as a Republican. For regular elections,

seats in which the incumbent was defeated in a primary are not counted as open, since the opposing party could not anticipate the vacancy, thus affecting the selection of its candidate.

60. By comparison, the Republicans did not win one of the fourteen open seat Democratic districts that Bush lost with less than 40 percent of the vote.
61. Jacobson, *Electoral Origins,* 105; also see Chapter 6 of *Electoral Origins* for evidence in support of this position.

Chapter 13

1992 and Beyond

On August 2, 1990, Iraq invaded Kuwait, precipitating a major crisis in the Persian Gulf. By the 1990 midterm election George Bush had sent 250,000 American troops to the Middle East to defend Saudi Arabia in Operation Desert Shield, and by the beginning of 1991 the United States had deployed more than 400,000 troops in the Gulf. Bush led a cooperative effort to gain worldwide support, including securing combat troops and diplomatic and financial aid from a wide range of countries. And Bush, who had once served as the U.S. ambassador to the United Nations, worked through the U.N. Security Council to get the council to pass a series of resolutions condemning Iraqi aggression, including a resolution authorizing the use of force if Iraq did not leave Kuwait by January 15, 1991. On January 16 Allied forces launched aerial attacks against Iraq, and Operation Desert Storm began.

The Gulf crisis had economic repercussions. Oil prices increased rapidly, leading to higher costs for gasoline, heating oil, and other petroleum-based products. There were already signs of a weak economy before the Gulf crisis, and by election day many economists believed that the United States was already in a recession. Most believed that the recession would be relatively mild. But as Alan Greenspan, chairman of the Federal Reserve Board, warned, a relatively long war could erode consumer confidence, contributing to a deep recession.[1]

Ending the Cold War made international cooperation against Iraq possible, but it brought unforeseen difficulties. Internal difficulties within the Soviet Union posed serious problems. Continued economic difficulties led to serious food shortages, and ethnic and regional strife threatened the stability of the Soviet Union and even raised the prospects of civil war.

These events remind us that politics is highly uncertain. Yet, as we explained earlier, the American political system has constitutionally mandated regularities. The United States held a presidential election during the American Civil War and during World War II, and will hold an election in 1992. We know that Bush's presidential term ends on January 20, 1993. Congressional legislation dictates other regularities as well. The popular vote to choose presidential electors will be held on the first Tuesday following the first Monday in November; in 1992 that is November 3. And in addition to the Constitution and legislation, political parties have created other procedures including the way presidential contenders are nominated. Therefore, despite great uncertainty about specific events, we can still speculate in general terms about the 1992 presidential election.

Delegate Selection

Presidential nomination campaigns effectively begin when the preceding midterm election is held. On the night of the midterm election, media commentators invariably speculate about the consequences of the midterm election for likely presidential candidates. Many candidates begin to think seriously about the upcoming presidential race. In early 1987, for example, we were able to compile a list of potential presidential candidates for the 1988 campaign.[2] We named five Republicans and five Democrats as likely contenders, and all ten actually ran. We chose another three Republicans and four Democrats as potential candidates, and two (including Michael S. Dukakis) actually ran. Moreover, those whom we labeled as likely candidates included Republicans Bush and Pierre "Pete" duPont and Democrats Bruce Babbitt and Richard A. Gephardt who had either formally declared their intention to run or filed a statement of candidacy with the Federal Election Commission.

In early 1991 the situation is quite different. No candidate has made a formal declaration for the 1992 presidential election and, except for George Bush, no candidacy can be considered likely. The absence of active Republican candidates is not surprising, but most commentators are surprised by the absence of visible planning among the Democrats. Ever since the post-1968 nomination reforms, party nominations have been won by campaigning among the electorate to win delegates to the party nominating conventions. This process places great demands on prospective candidates to create an organized national network of support, to raise funds needed to compete seriously, and to comply with the complex federal regulations necessary to earn federal campaign funds. Beginning early seems essential.

The 1992 contest also appears to differ from the five previous contests by the absence of significant changes in the nomination process. The Democratic National Committee changed its rules in ways that significantly affected campaigning in each contest from 1972 through 1984. Although the national party did not make substantial rules changes for the 1988 campaign, Democratic leaders in the South were instrumental in coordinating the actions of various state legislatures. Ten of the eleven states of the old Confederacy held their presidential primaries on March 8, 1988, as did six states outside the South, making that day a truly Super Tuesday (see Chapter 1).[3] Major changes, either as a result of changed party rules or state legislative action, seem unlikely for either of the parties in 1992.

The Democrats, however, did introduce some minor changes for 1992. The number of superdelegates will be reduced, and Democratic rules will reduce the extent to which states can deviate from proportional representation in the allocation of delegates. Individual states may decide to use primaries rather than caucuses to choose presidential delegates, and some may abandon primaries in favor of caucuses. And the specific dates that primaries and caucuses will be held will be altered.

California Considers Change

During 1990 the California state legislature considered moving its primary date from early June—at the end of the primary season—to a date soon after the New Hampshire primary, the first primary allowed by Democratic party rules.[4] While this would have been a case of only one state changing its procedures, California offers so many delegates to both the Republican and Democratic conventions that this single change could have had considerable consequences.

In 1988, for example, 363 of the 4,162 Democratic delegates were from California as were 175 of the 2,277 Republican delegates. An early California primary would have become the third major event of 1992 after the Iowa caucuses and the New Hampshire primary. In effect, an early California primary could have created a Super Tuesday and might have affected who decided to run. For example, prospective presidential candidates from California, or those who would appeal to Californians, would have an advantage. Some argue that the presence of an early regional southern primary helped persuade Sen. Albert Gore, Jr., of Tennessee to run for the presidency in 1988, and perhaps a candidate who expected to do well in an early California contest would be tempted to enter the race. Moreover, California is so large that candidates must rely on the media to get their message across. "Wholesale" campaigns that rely on the media rather than "retail" campaigns that rely on canvasing and small meetings are necessary. Candidates who were unlikely to raise substantial campaign funds might decide not to seek the nomination at all.

The California legislature decided not to move the California primary to an early date, although there is a small but unlikely chance that the primary will be rescheduled.[5] The decision not to move the primary to an early date was based largely on local considerations. The California presidential primary is used not only to select presidential delegates but to nominate candidates for other offices. Legislative leaders were reluctant to hold other nomination contests early in the election year, and they also were reluctant to pay for two separate primaries. In addition, statewide California elections are important for passing constitutional amendments and legislation through referendums. If Bush is uncontested, or if he has no significant competition for the Republican nomination, a primary for the presidency alone might attract many more Democratic than Republican voters, raising the chances for passing amendments or legislation that conservatives oppose.

The Future of Super Tuesday

As we discussed in Chapter 1, Super Tuesday was very important in both the Republican and Democratic nomination campaigns. Bush effectively won the GOP nomination with his overwhelming victory on Super Tuesday, and we believe that Dukakis's more limited success that day was a crucial part of his slower march to the Democratic nomination. The southern primary, however, did not fulfill the basic objective of southern Democratic leaders by selecting a nominee who could do well in the South. In addition, while Super Tuesday brought a great deal of attention to the South, most southern states received less media attention in 1988 than they had in 1984.[6]

Given the failure of Super Tuesday to meet its basic objective, enthusiasm for a regional primary has waned. Although many southern states may continue to hold their presidential primary on the same date, in early 1991 it is not clear whether there will be a single day with a very large number of primaries, and, if such a day occurs, the extent to which the contest will have a regional flavor. Several of the states that participated in Super Tuesday 1988 are considering moving their primary to a different date in order to play a more important role and to receive more attention for their individual state.

Still, in early 1991, the 1992 presidential nomination process appears to be similar to that of the 1988 process. The result is that the patterns in the 1992 nomination contest are likely to be similar to those patterns found in nomination contests under the post-1968 nomination system. The nomination also is likely to be won by the candidates who can succeed in mounting an effective nomination campaign among the electorate. But who are those contenders likely to be?

1992 Presidential Candidates

Barring some extraordinary or tragic event, Bush will seek renomination, as did incumbents Richard Nixon in 1972, Jimmy Carter in 1980, and Ronald Reagan in 1984. In addition, Gerald R. Ford, who became president in 1974 when Nixon resigned, sought his party's nomination in 1976. During the post-1968 period, the 1988 election has been the only contest in which the incumbent president did not seek his party's nomination.[7] In the four other contests the incumbent president was nominated. Ford faced strong competition from Reagan in 1976, but narrowly won the GOP nomination. In 1980 Carter faced a strong challenge from Sen. Edward M. Kennedy, but held off the challenge by a relatively comfortable margin.[8] Nixon faced two opponents in 1972: Rep. Paul N. McCloskey, Jr., of California ran as an opponent of Nixon's Vietnam policies, while Rep. John M. Ashbrook of Ohio presented himself as an ideologically conservative alternative. Nixon was able to defeat these opponents easily. In 1984 Reagan was unchallenged in his bid to win his party's renomination.

Potential Republican Candidates

Ronald Reagan in 1976 and Edward Kennedy in 1980 both were strong challengers who would have had an excellent chance of winning their party's nomination if they had not faced an incumbent president. Reagan, after all, won his party's nomination four years later. There are no Republican candidates with the strength of a Reagan or a Kennedy to challenge Bush; however, one or more conservative Republicans may run against him in 1992. Most likely, such an opponent, or opponents, would provide trivial opposition, such as Nixon faced in 1972.

If conservative candidates do challenge Bush, they will do so because he reneged on his promise not to raise taxes—his strongest campaign promise. As he said in his acceptance speech at the Republican nomination convention in New Orleans, and as he repeated throughout his campaign, "Read my lips. No new taxes." In the summer of 1990, however, Bush agreed that new revenues were needed, and he eventually signed a compromise budget package that included significant tax increases. Moreover, Bush had strongly argued that a cut in the capital gains tax should be part of any tax compromise, but the final budget package included no such cut. Conservatives were outraged.

Some speculate that former Delaware governor duPont, who ran an unsuccessful Republican presidential campaign in 1988, might challenge Bush for the nomination. In December 1990, duPont announced the formation of the Committee for Republican Leadership, which some observers believe may be a smokescreen to challenge Bush.[9] Other possible challengers include conservative columnist Pat Buchanan, former senator William L. Armstrong of Colorado, former U.N. ambassador Jeane Kirkpatrick, and the Rev. Pat Robertson, who also ran an unsuccessful campaign in 1988.[10] It is possible that conservative Republicans are talking about potential contenders merely as a threat to ensure that Bush pays renewed attention to the right wing of the party. But, as the 1976 and 1980 contests demonstrated, even a strong candidate is unlikely to deny an incumbent president his party's nomination.

Potential Democratic Candidates

The open contest for the Democratic nomination is harder to foresee. As we stated above, there is usually a great deal of maneuvering among potential candidates a year before delegates are actually chosen in the Iowa caucuses and the New Hampshire primary. But in early 1991, there has been little activity. All the same, there is considerable speculation about possible candidates.

Many believed that Sen. Bill Bradley of New Jersey and Gov. Mario Cuomo of New York would be the two strongest contenders for the 1992 Democratic nomination. Both suffered recent political setbacks, however. Bradley narrowly won reelection in the 1990 midterm over Republican Christine Todd Whitman, even though he outspent her by a ten-to-one margin. Although Bradley's poor showing was largely due to opposition to the policies of Democratic governor James Florio, the election diminished his presidential prospects. Cuomo is the most frequently mentioned liberal. Cuomo, like Bradley, won by a narrower margin than expected, although he still gained a majority of the votes in a three-candidate contest. But Cuomo faces problems as governor that may delay or derail a presidential bid; in early 1991 New York faced a $4 billion revenue shortfall. If he can solve these budgetary problems, Cuomo might be a formidable candidate for the Democratic nomination.[11] Still, some critics believe that a northeastern liberal might be a weak candidate in the general election.

Meanwhile, the Rev. Jesse Jackson, recently elected as a nonvoting "shadow senator" from the District of Columbia, continues to be a potential candidate for the 1992 Democratic nomination. If he decides to run, it will be his third attempt. As in 1984 and 1988, he would be a representative for causes important to blacks and other minorities. But in 1992, there might be another black candidate: Douglas Wilder. Wilder was elected governor of Virginia in 1989 and is considered a possible candidate if for no other reason than his ability to win the highest office in a former Confederate state. Unlike Jackson, Wilder is a moderate Democrat who says his message is "the new mainstream." In late 1990, Wilder was the most active of the various Democratic "noncandidates" and had given speeches in Iowa and New Hampshire.[12] Some speculate that a reasonable showing by Wilder in the presidential nomination contest might also position him to win the Democratic vice-presidential nomination.

Three white southerners also are frequently mentioned: Sen. Lloyd Bentsen of Texas, Sen. Albert Gore, Jr., of Tennessee, and Sen. Sam Nunn of Georgia. Nunn has gained prominence as chairman of the Senate Armed Services Committee, where he strongly opposed offensive military action in the Persian Gulf. Some think that Nunn's shift from a pro-life to a pro-choice position on abortion may signal that he is considering a presidential bid, while others point to his decision to cancel his membership in an all-white country club as another indication. Gore, as we saw in Chapter 1, was an unsuccessful presidential candidate in 1988, which we clearly view as a political liability. Candidates with liabilities usually do not seek the presidency, but there are exceptions to this generalization.[13] Bentsen also made an unsuccessful try for the Democratic presidential nomination, but his bid was in 1976. He is better remembered for his strong campaign for the vice presidency in 1988. Rep. Richard Gephardt of Missouri, another presidential candidate in 1988, is also sometimes mentioned as a potential candidate.

Two long-shot candidates also have been discussed: Gov. Bill Clinton of Arkansas and Sen. Bob Kerrey of Nebraska. Although Kerrey is a first-term senator, two first-term senators sought the Democratic nomination in 1988. And Kerrey, a Vietnam veteran, served one term as governor. Another first-term senator, Charles S. Robb of Virginia, also is mentioned as a potential contender. He, too, served one term as governor, but many believe Robb is more likely to run in 1996 rather than in 1992.

Lastly, in January 1991, George S. McGovern of South Dakota, the 1972 Democratic nominee, announced that he was considering another presidential bid. McGovern, who lost his Senate seat in 1980, ran unsuccessfully for the Democratic presidential nomination in 1984. A leading spokesman against the Vietnam War, McGovern said that if he ran in 1992 his campaign would focus on domestic economic and political issues.

Despite this long list, as of early 1991 no one can be called a likely contender. The remarkable thing is that so few have signaled any real signs of seriously contemplating a candidacy. This is true even though, as we shall see, Bush may be vulnerable.

Patterns in the Nomination Process

As uncertain as the 1992 nomination campaign appears, there are patterns in the nomination process that seem likely to be repeated in 1992. First, although we do not know who will run, we can predict what kinds of candidates will eventually choose to compete. Most notably, with the exceptions of Jackson and McGovern, all of the Democrats we mentioned hold high public office, and McGovern served as a U.S. senator for eighteen years.[14]

Among the five potential Republican challengers to Bush, none holds public office, and only duPont and Armstrong have ever held elective office. Kirkpatrick has held a Cabinet-level post, and Buchanan was a special assistant to Nixon, but Robertson has never held a government position. Few candidates without elective office experience are likely to run a strong presidential race. Strong candidates are likely to emerge only from the top of the "opportunity structure," and they are likely to risk a presidential candidacy only when a race for the presidency is unlikely to damage their future political careers if they fail.[15] Although ten of the twelve potential Democratic contenders we named hold elective office, only Gephardt, as a member of the U.S. House of Representatives, is up for reelection in 1992. Thus, if the others run they will not have to face a choice of running for reelection or for the presidency.

A second set of patterns concerns the Republican contest. Incumbent presidents are very difficult to defeat for nomination, and a serious attempt to challenge an incumbent president may divide the party. Strong challengers emerge only when incumbent presidents appear highly vulnerable, as Ford was in 1976 and as Carter was in 1980. Few candidates choose to challenge an incumbent president of their party, and few will challenge Bush in 1992.

On the Democratic side, we must examine patterns of competition in contests in which there was no incumbent seeking his party's nomination. Thus, precedents are provided by the 1972, 1976, 1984, and 1988 Democratic contests and by the 1980 and 1988 Republican contests. These races attracted a minimum of six contenders. Perhaps fewer than six Democrats will run in 1992, but the list of possible contenders is long.

Once the campaign formally begins, we should expect that the earliest events, notably the Iowa caucuses, New Hampshire primary, and (if it remains) Super Tuesday, will be the most important events of the contest. As a result, Democratic candidates will "frontload" their campaigns, spending disproportionate money and time in these early contests. Half the candidates will be winnowed out by these early events. Indeed, it is this winnowing process that underlines the importance for candidates to frontload their efforts in these states. Put differently, after the first major events of 1992, there may be no more than two or three candidates with any opportunity to raise the resources needed to continue effective campaigns. It is possible that a clear front-runner will emerge fairly early. Typically, after the early primaries, front-runners have been able to capitalize on their front-runner status to win the nomination, as Bush and Dukakis did in 1988. Thus, it seems highly likely that, as in past nomination contests in the post-1968 era, the nomination will be won before the party nomination convention actually convenes. That victory will be achieved by amassing the support of a majority of the delegates to the Democratic nominating convention by virtue of victory in the Democratic primaries and caucuses.

Uncertain Republican Prospects

As we have seen, the 1992 nomination contest has more than its share of uncertainty; and uncertainty appears even greater for the 1992 general election. At the beginning of 1991, the Republicans appear to be strongly positioned to continue to hold onto the presidency. But it is also easy to see how the Democrats could win the 1992 presidential election thereby ending a pattern of Republican presidential dominance. In early 1991, the chances of a Republican victory appear to depend largely on events over which Bush has limited control.

The crisis created by Iraq's invasion of Kuwait was not an issue in the 1990 midterm election. Bush's policies of preventing an invasion of Saudi Arabia and of imposing economic sanctions against Iraq had widespread public and congressional support. But two days after the midterm election, Bush shifted American policy by announcing the need to develop greater offensive capability against Iraq.

Many prominent Democrats urged Bush to refrain from military action, and to give economic sanctions more time to work. Bush claimed he had the authority to commit U.S. troops to combat without congressional approval, and congressional leaders seemed reluctant to call for a vote on Bush's Gulf policies. But as the U.N. deadline for Iraq to withdraw from Kuwait neared, Congress voted on competing resolutions—to continue to rely on economic sanctions and to authorize Bush to use military force.

The final votes on January 12, 1991, closely followed party lines. In the House, 164 Republicans voted to authorize Bush to use military force, while only three voted against the authorization; among Democrats, eighty-six voted to authorize force, and 179 voted against the measure. In the Senate, forty-two Republicans voted to support Bush, while only two voted "no"; among Democrats, ten voted to authorize force, while forty-five voted "no." [16] Among the congressional Democrats we named as possible presidential contenders, Gephardt and Nunn not only voted against authorizing the use of force, but led the fight for the competing resolution to continue economic sanctions. In addition, Bentsen, Bradley, and Kerrey voted against Bush; Gore and Robb voted to support the use of force.

The effect of these partisan divisions on the 1992 general election is difficult to predict, because it depends on the outcome of a war that, as of this writing, is only four weeks old. All the same, commentators were quick to suggest that the way Democrats voted had potential implications for their presidential ambitions: Nunn needed to demonstrate his liberal credentials, and Gore needed to show that he was a moderate. Clayton K. Yeutter, the newly named chairman of the Republican National Committee, argued that Democrats who voted against authorizing the use of force should be held politically accountable. "I would guess 90 percent of them wish they had cast their votes the other way," Yeutter said. "They picked the wrong side. If the conflict goes well, that will work against them." [17]

In the short term, the war boosted Bush's presidential approval to more than 80 percent. This was predictable. Analysts of presidential approval have demonstrated that there is often a "rally-'round-the-flag" phenomenon in times of international crisis.[18] But it also is predictable that this support eventually will fall. Even so, Bush's strong public support in early 1991 may further delay the decision of Democrats to run for president. If the war is over quickly, and if casualties are low, some Democrats may decide that 1996 is a better year to run for president than 1992. But if the war ultimately goes badly, Bush's prospects for reelection could be severely damaged. Even if the war goes well, Bush's prospects may be damaged if the conflict destabilizes the traditional Gulf states that are part of the coalition effort against Iraq, and especially if it destabilizes Saudi Arabia.

Just as events in the Gulf are partly beyond Bush's control, Bush has limited control over economic developments as well. In November 1990 unemployment reached 5.9 percent, a three-year high, removing any doubt that the United States had entered a recession. If the recession is not severe, and if it ends fairly early, it may have little impact on the November 1992 contest. During 1982 Ronald Reagan presided over the nation's worst postwar recession, but he won a landslide reelection in 1984. Of course, Bush will attempt to ensure that economic recovery comes well before the 1992 campaign, but presidents have limited influence over economic developments.

Lastly, Bush cannot control the Democratic strategies for 1992, and more importantly, he cannot choose his opponent. In 1984 Reagan was probably unbeatable, but he was aided by Walter F. Mondale's ineffective general election campaign. Even in 1988 when the Republicans were vulnerable, the Democrats chose a candidate who ran an ineffective campaign. As we have seen, the 1992 Democratic contest appears wide open, with no clear candidates, but many prospective nominees. Ever since the post-1968 reforms, the Democrats have chosen candidates who have run poor campaigns. Even Carter, the only Democrat after 1968 to win the presidency, began his campaign with a 20 percentage point lead in the polls, but wound up defeating Ford by only 2 percentage points. Nevertheless, several of the potential Democratic prospects we have discussed could run strong general election campaigns, but it remains to be seen who will choose to run.

Republican Assets

Although there are many uncertainties, there are some patterns that indicate a Republican advantage in the 1992 presidential contest. First, the Republicans can nominate the incumbent president as their standard bearer, and most incumbent presidents who seek to retain the presidency are successful. Between 1832 (when Andrew Jackson ran for reelection) and 1988, there have been twenty-two elections in which the party controlling the White House has nominated the incumbent president. The incumbent party won fifteen of those contests. There have been eighteen contests in which the incumbent party did not nominate its president.[19] The party controlling the White House won only eight of those elections. Of course, being able to run an incumbent does not provide an insurmountable advantage. As recently as 1976 and 1980, incumbent presidents were defeated in two consecutive elections.

Secondly, the Republicans may gain a marginal advantage as a result of the reapportionment that will occur after the 1990 census. In Chapter 2, Figure 2-1 shows the states that the Republicans won in at least four of the five elections between 1968 and 1984—elections that set the stage for the 1988 contest—and the number of electoral votes that each state had in 1988. In Figure 13-1, we show the states that the Republicans won in at least four of the five contests between 1972 and 1988 and the number of electoral votes these states are projected to have in 1992.[20] Figure 13-1 also illustrates that the Republicans won twenty-four states in all five of the last elections. These states are slated to have 221 electoral votes in 1992, whereas in 1988 they had 219 electoral votes. There are seventeen states that the Republicans have won in four of the last five elections. These states will probably have 212 electoral votes in 1992, whereas in 1988 they had 210 electoral votes. If we look only at the 1988 contest (see Map 3-1C), we find that four of the ten states Dukakis carried are slated to lose electoral votes in 1992, while one is to gain an electoral vote. These ten states (plus the District of Columbia) earned the Democrats 112 electoral votes in 1988, but would earn them only 107 in 1992. On balance, these shifts are small, but they could give the Republicans a slight advantage if the 1992 presidential race is close.

Thirdly, Republican gains in party identification have persisted, and appear to have grown slightly, at least through early 1990. The best available data to update the National Election Studies (NES) are provided by the General Social Surveys conducted by the National Opinion Research Center (NORC) of the University of Chicago.[21] As we saw in Chapter 8, by early 1989, 47 percent of Americans who identified with a political party were Republicans. The General Social Survey conducted in February, March, and April of 1990 revealed slight Republican gains: 48 percent of all party identifiers were Republicans. If

Figure 13-1   States That Voted Republican at Least Four Out of Five
Times, 1972-1988

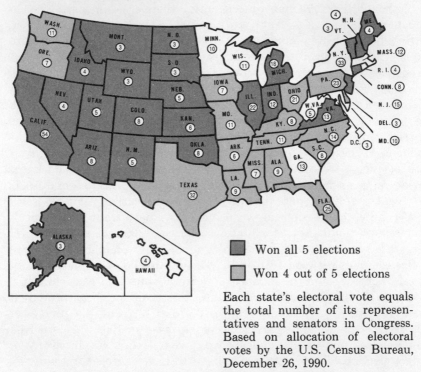

Won all 5 elections

Won 4 out of 5 elections

Each state's electoral vote equals
the total number of its representatives and senators in Congress.
Based on allocation of electoral
votes by the U.S. Census Bureau,
December 26, 1990.

Source: Election results based on *America Votes 18: A Handbook of Contemporary
American Election Statistics,* compiled and edited by Richard M. Scammon and Alice V.
McGillivray (Washington, D.C.: Congressional Quarterly Inc., 1989), 7-15. The number of
electoral votes for 1992 is based on information provided in Holly Idelson, "Census Adds
Seats in Eight States," *Congressional Quarterly Weekly Report,* December 29, 1990, 4240.

independents who lean toward a party are included in the calculations, 49
percent were Republicans. The 1990 NORC results show the highest level
of Republican support since the General Social Surveys began in 1972.
The shift toward the Republican party was a major asset in electing
George Bush president. Even if the Republicans merely manage to hold
their parity with the Democrats in partisan loyalties, the Republicans
may gain from this shift in partisan loyalties in the 1992 presidential
contest.

Gallup surveys also show marked Republican gains. As Michael B.
MacKuen, Robert S. Erikson, and James A. Stimson have shown, changes
in partisanship (as measured by Gallup) contribute to Democratic gains
or losses in both the congressional and presidential vote.[22] However, the
Gallup measure of party affiliation appears to vary much more than the
Michigan Survey Research Center measure partly because Gallup asks

respondents which party they support "as of today." [23] Even so, the Gallup measure provides valuable information about the short term strength of the Republican and Democratic parties. As we saw in Chapter 8, Gallup surveys also reveal substantial Republican gains, and these gains continued through the first quarter of 1990. During the first quarter of 1990 (the same time that the General Social Survey was conducted), 35 percent of the people surveyed were Republicans, 39 percent were Democrats, and 28 percent were independents. In other words, 47 percent of those who chose a political party were Republicans. In the most recent available quarterly results, based on surveys conducted during July, August, and September of 1990, the Democrats rebounded somewhat.[24] Thirty percent of the respondents said they were Republicans, 41 percent said they were Democrats, and 29 percent said they were independents. With these gains, 42 percent of those choosing a party were Republicans, still well above levels of Republican strength during most of the postwar years.

A fourth Republican advantage may emerge from GOP gains among black voters. Since 1964 the Democrats have gained an overwhelming portion of the black vote; this heavy black support was a major factor in many Democratic victories. As we saw in Chapter 5, Carter won the presidency in 1976 even though he carried less than half of the white votes cast. But in the 1990 midterm, exit polls based on 17,770 voters suggest that 22 percent of the blacks who voted supported Republican congressional candidates.[25] Black votes for Republican candidates grew despite Bush's veto of the 1990 Civil Rights bill, and despite several campaigns in which race-related issues emerged. Blacks, however, played a major role in some Democratic victories, most notably Ann Richards's win over Clayton Williams in the Texas gubernatorial race. But, according to Peter Applebome, "A number of experts said the [Democratic] party's move toward the political center and away from some of its more outspoken liberal positions could be hampering its ability to turn out black voters." [26] In many states, black turnout dropped markedly, and the gap between national white and black turnout increased. Even with their gains among black voters, the Republicans still stand to benefit from low black turnout, since more than three out of four black voters supported Democratic congressional candidates in the midterm election.

The Republicans may have gained another advantage in 1990, one that may cost them their inroads among blacks and may also stimulate black turnout. Some critics believe that the Republicans were successful in exploiting their opposition to racial quotas, and that affirmative action will emerge as an important issue in 1992. Bush's veto of the 1990 Civil Rights bill was based on his claim that the bill would force employers to establish percentage quotas for hiring women and minorities in an attempt to avoid lawsuits. Although the legislation specifically rejected quotas, Bush argued that it would lead to quotas in practice. Sen. Jesse Helms of North Carolina specifically used his opposition to quotas in his bid to fend off a challenge from his black Democratic opponent, Harvey Gantt. One of Helms's television ads showed white hands crumpling a job rejection letter. The narrator comments, "You needed that job, and you were the best qualified. But it had to go to a minority because of a racial quota."

Although many viewed Helms's appeal as racist, the ad may have been effective. Public opinion polls showed Gantt leading shortly before the election (although many questioned the reliability of these polls). In fact, Helms won by four percentage points. Moreover, some Republican leaders argue that quotas are a legitimate issue. William Bennett, who had been named by Bush to be the Republican National chairman, but who withdrew from consideration, seemed particularly eager to use quotas as an issue. The Democrats plan to reintroduce a civil rights bill in the 102d Congress, and argue that there is broad bipartisan support for the measure. But some Democrats believe they may be vulnerable on the issue of quotas. According to Mandy Grunwald, the media consultant for Gantt, the Democrats may be hurt by the quota issue when the economy is bad. "What you're talking about basically is the politics of resentment," Grunwald says.[27] Frederick Yang, a Democratic political consultant, argues, "A fundamental reason why the Democrats are vulnerable to attacks on issues such as affirmative action and race quotas is the perception that the Democratic Party has overlooked the needs and values of the average American." [28]

Republican Liabilities

Although we have focused on some Republican advantages, the Republicans face liabilities as well. Most importantly, Bush's willingness to support higher taxes led to open divisions between the administration and conservatives within the Republican party.

Bush's promise not to raise taxes was his strongest policy statement of the 1988 campaign. As we saw above, in the summer of 1990, in an effort to reduce the federal budget deficit, Bush acknowledged that increased revenues were necessary. Some Republican leaders, most notably Rep. Newt Gingrich of Georgia, the Republican House whip, were highly critical of Bush's decision to approve a tax increase. In both the House and Senate, a majority of Republicans voted against the final budget resolution. Bush signed the bill the day before the midterm election, but he had suffered political damage.

One Republican critic, Howard Phillips, chairman of the Conservative Caucus, argues that "Bush has participated in a historic act of deception of the American people. Nothing he does between now and the [1992] election can restore his credibility." [29] Only two days after the midterm election, Bush renewed his pledge not to raise taxes. Bush said he needed to do "remedial work" to heal divisions in a divided Republican party, and said he had "serious regrets" that he had been forced to abandon his campaign pledge not to raise taxes. Moreover, Bush vowed that he would "absolutely" refuse to accept any tax increases other than those he supported during the budget compromise.[30] Bush also pledged to renew his attempt to win a capital gains tax cut, but by late December he acknowledged that this goal could not be accomplished in 1991. Although Bush's renewed pledge to resist tax increases heartened Republicans, Bush has to deal with a House and Senate in which the Democrats have gained strength. As we saw in Chapter 12, it seems likely that partisan controversies over the budget will continue.

Despite Bush's renewed pledge not to raise taxes, the Republican party remains divided. As we discussed earlier, several conservative Republicans may challenge Bush for his party's nomination. Admittedly, these challengers seem unlikely to deny Bush the nomination, but a divided Republican party might be less likely to defeat a strong Democratic challenger in the 1992 presidential election.

Bush's problems with the conservative wing of his party make it more likely that he will face a second liability in 1992: Dan Quayle. Quayle was chosen by Bush in 1988 largely to satisfy the right wing of his party, and it might be politically costly among conservatives to remove him from the ticket. Indeed, Bush had announced that he was pleased with Quayle's performance as vice president and that if he sought reelection, he would want Quayle as his running mate.

According to estimates by Martin P. Wattenberg, which we discussed in Chapter 2, Quayle's presence on the ticket may have cost Bush about 2 percentage points in the popular vote. Moreover, positive assessments of Quayle appear to have declined during the Bush presidency. In a Gallup telephone poll of 1,000 registered voters conducted in October 1988, 46 percent said that Quayle was "qualified to serve as President if it becomes necessary." [31] But in a Gallup telephone survey of 1,200 respondents in March 1990, only 31 percent thought Quayle was qualified to be president. When asked whether Bush should keep Quayle on the ticket if Bush runs for reelection in 1992, only 35 percent agreed, while 49 percent thought he should "choose someone new." [32] And although the war in the Persian Gulf boosted Bush's approval ratings, it may have raised further doubts about Quayle. In a Cable News Network/*Time* poll conducted eight days after the war began, 1,000 American adults were asked, "If something happened to President Bush, are you confident that Vice President Quayle could lead the nation in war with Iraq?" Only 28 percent answered, "yes"; 55 percent said, "no." [33]

According to George Gallup, Jr., and Frank Newport: "The 'Dan Quayle factor' could shape up to be one of the most significant issues of the 1992 presidential election campaign." [34] Bush will be sixty-eight years old in 1992, and concerns about Quayle's competence could be important. In a close election having Quayle on the ticket could cost Bush his reelection. Of course, Bush could drop Quayle from the ticket, and the Republican nominating convention would accede to Bush's request. Ford dropped his appointed vice president, Nelson A. Rockefeller, in 1976, although an elected vice president has not been dropped from the ticket since 1944 when Franklin D. Roosevelt allowed the Democratic nominating convention to replace vice president Henry A. Wallace with Harry S Truman.

Thirdly, the Republican position against abortion could prove costly. With Republican gubernatorial defeats in 1989 in New Jersey and Virginia, the Republicans moved away from their strong antiabortion position. Lee Atwater, then the Republican National Committee chairman, declared that individual Republicans could choose their own position on the abortion controversy, and many Republicans were pro-choice in the 1990 contest. In the biggest contest of all—the California governorship—both Sen. Pete Wilson, the Republican winner, and ex-San Francisco mayor Dianne Feinstein supported abortion rights. On balance, abortion played a relatively small role in the 1990 midterm contest.

By virtue of making Supreme Court appointments, the president exercises greater influence on abortion rights than any other single American. Bush's appointment of David H. Souter to the Supreme Court in 1990 may have provided the vote that could overturn *Roe v. Wade*. As long as *Roe v. Wade* stands, middle-class women will be relatively free to obtain abortions. But if the Court does overturn *Roe v. Wade,* abortion rights could become a costly issue for the Republicans in the 1992 presidential election.

Lastly, the Democrats may be able to make inroads if they can successfully capitalize on the theme that Republican policies have benefited the wealthy. The Democratic failure to capitalize on this issue was highlighted in a recent book, *The Politics of Rich and Poor,* by Kevin Phillips.[35] Phillips documents the extent to which income redistribution during Ronald Reagan's presidency tended to favor the wealthy, and marvels at the failure of the Democrats to raise this issue. As he notes, Dukakis did raise some class-based themes around Labor Day, and came back to these themes late in the 1988 campaign. But for the most part, Dukakis was uncomfortable with populist issues. According to Phillips, Lee Atwater, Bush's campaign manager, worried about these issues, especially given Bush's upper class background. After the election, Atwater commented, "The way to win a presidential race against the Republicans is to develop the class warfare issue, as Dukakis did at the end. To divide up the haves and have nots and try to reinvigorate the

New Deal coalition and to attack." [36] According to Phillips, the only Democrat who emphasized these populist appeals in 1988 was Jesse Jackson, but Jackson lacked the ability "to crystallize these issues." "His race," Phillips writes, "limited his influence among white workers, and so did rhetoric that seemed to put Bolivian or West African interests on a par with jobs or prosperity in Steubenville, Ohio." [37]

Of course, this does not mean that the Democrats will choose to emphasize class-based appeals in 1992, or that they will succeed if they do. Still, Republican vulnerabilities did emerge during the budget negotiation debates in which Bush was forced to emphasize his objections against a surtax on persons earning more than $1 million a year. Class-based appeals are more likely to work in a period of high unemployment, and if prosperity returns by 1992 they may have limited impact.

Conclusion

The 1988 election clearly established the Republicans as the dominant party in American presidential elections, having won three elections in a row. The 1992 contest provides the Republicans with an opportunity to extend that dominance. But prospects for 1992 seem highly uncertain, and, as a result, by February 1991 no Democrat had publicly announced a decision to challenge Bush for the presidency. Depending on events that take place at home and in the Persian Gulf, Bush might be highly vulnerable, or he might prove difficult to defeat.

We have tried to outline potential Republican assets as well as liabilities. On balance, the assets seem greater than the liabilities. As we have seen, however, in the last four presidential elections voting choices have been largely shaped by evaluations of past performance. These evaluations, in turn, are affected by economic and political conditions. In 1992, as in four of the last five presidential contests, we expect to find an incumbent president seeking reelection. In such contests, retrospective evaluations may be especially important. If Bush runs for reelection in 1992, he will be judged largely by the outcome of the Persian Gulf War and by the state of the economy.

Whatever the outcome of the presidential contest, however, the Democrats are likely to retain control of the U.S. House of Representatives. And with the odds favoring a Republican presidential win, continued divided government seems likely. Political scientists can speculate about whether there has been a partisan realignment, dealignment, or a split-level realignment, or about whether we have entered a political era that renders these concepts irrelevant. But if divided government continues, party leaders must rethink the long term problems that continue to deny the Republicans legislative power and that continue to deny the Democrats the White House.

Notes

1. David Rosenbaum, "Greenspan Warns of a Deep Recession if War Lasts," *New York Times,* January 31, 1991, Y1, C5. (All citations in this chapter to the *New York Times* are to the National Edition.)
2. See Paul R. Abramson, John H. Aldrich, and David W. Rohde, *Change and Continuity in the 1984 Elections,* rev. ed. (Washington, D.C.: CQ Press, 1987), 340-344.
3. Five states also held Democratic caucuses on March 8, including Texas which held a primary and caucuses. One state held Republican caucuses.
4. California has held a presidential primary in each election cycle since 1912. From 1912 through 1944 the California primary was held in May. From 1948 through 1988 the California primary has been held in early June.
5. Lou Cannon, "Speaker Brown Girds to Have Final Say," *Washington Post,* December 21, 1990, A8.
6. See Paul-Henri Gurian, "Less Than Expected: Media Coverage of Super Tuesday, 1988," paper delivered at the Annual Meeting of the American Political Science Association, San Francisco, August 30-September 2, 1990.
7. Reagan was ineligible to be reelected in 1988 because of the Twenty-second Amendment.
8. In 1980, Gov. Jerry Brown of California also sought the Democratic nomination, but he had much less of an impact on the campaign than Kennedy had.
9. "Challengers on Ice," *Newsweek,* January 7, 1991, 30.
10. Jack Germond and Jules Witcover, "GOP right casting for candidates," *Lansing* [Michigan] *State Journal,* November 28, 1990, 6A.
11. Elizabeth Kolbert, "For Cuomo, Hard Times and Choices," *New York Times,* December 30, 1990, 1, 13.
12. William Schneider, "Is This the Era of the Noncandidate?" *National Journal,* December 22, 1990, 3118.
13. See Paul R. Abramson, John H. Aldrich, and David W. Rohde, "Progressive Ambition among United States Senators: 1972-1988," *Journal of Politics* 48 (February 1987): 3-35.
14. In recent contests, many candidates have been former holders of high elective office. A candidate who has left office under favorable circumstances may be in a better position to run for office than a politician who currently holds office.
15. The term *opportunity structure* refers to the loose hierarchy of offices that define the path of political careers within a political system. For a discussion of this concept, see Joseph A. Schlesinger, *Ambition and Politics: Political Careers in the United States* (Chicago: Rand McNally, 1966).
16. For an analysis of the vote on the authorization to use force, see Rhodes Cook and Ronald D. Elving, "Even Votes of Conscience Follow Party Lines," *Congressional Quarterly Weekly Report,* January 19, 1991, 190-195.
17. Quoted in Robin Toner, "War, Politics and Flux Embroil G.O.P. Parley," *New York Times,* January 25, 1991.
18. For the classic study of this effect, see John E. Mueller, *War, Presidents and Public Opinion* (New York: John Wiley & Sons, 1973). For a comprehensive summary of Gallup presidential approval from 1953 through 1988, see George C. Edwards III with Alec M. Gallup, *Presidential Approval: A Sourcebook* (Baltimore: Johns Hopkins University Press, 1990). See pages 143-152 for a discussion of the impact of "rally events" on presidential approval.
19. In two of the contests, 1960 and 1988, the incumbent president was ineligible

to run due to the Twenty-second Amendment.

20. These electoral vote projections are based on the census figures released by the U.S. Census Bureau on December 26, 1990. As we point out in Chapter 12, the allocation of House seats can be changed until July 15, 1991.
21. NORC employs the same questions to measure party identification as those used by NES. See Chapter 4, note 46 for the full wording of the party identification questions. For information about the NORC General Social Surveys, see Chapter 8, note 12.
22. See Michael B. MacKuen, Robert S. Erikson, and James A. Stimson, "Macropartisanship," *American Political Science Review* 83 (December 1989): 1125-1142.
23. For the full wording of the Gallup question, see Chapter 8, note 13. For evidence that the Gallup measure is more likely to respond to short term economic and political conditions than the Michigan measure, see Paul R. Abramson and Charles W. Ostrom, Jr., "Macropartisanship: An Empirical Reassessment," *American Political Science Review* 85 (March 1991): 181-192.
24. All the Gallup party affiliation results we report in this book are based on in-person interviews. The standard size for a Gallup survey is now about 1,000 respondents, and quarterly party affiliation results are usually based on several surveys. The results for the third quarter of 1990 were provided directly by the Gallup Poll.
25. "Portrait of the Electorate: U.S. House Vote," *New York Times,* November 8, 1990, A19. These results are based on questionnaires distributed by Voter Research and Surveys to voters after they left polling places, a combined venture by all the television networks.
26. Peter Applebome, "Blacks and the 1990 Elections: Was There a Signal? If So, What?" *New York Times,* November 18, 1990, Y1.
27. Robin Toner, "Issue of Job Quotas Sure to Affect Debate on Civil Rights in the '90's," *New York Times,* December 10, 1990, A13.
28. Quoted in ibid.
29. Quoted in David Shirbman and Michel McQueen, "President Now Faces More Hostile Congress, Pressure in Own Party," *Wall Street Journal,* November 8, 1990, A12.
30. Andrew Rosenthal, "Reacting to Vote, President Renews Anti-Tax Pledge," *New York Times,* November 9, 1990, A1.
31. The poll was conducted a few days after Quayle's vice-presidential debate with Bentsen. See George Gallup, Jr., and Alec Gallup, "Dukakis Fails to Exploit Quayle Factor; Bush Maintains Campaign Lead," *The Gallup Poll,* October 12, 1988.
32. George Gallup, Jr., and Frank Newport, "Almost One-Half Say Bush Should Replace Quayle with Someone New in 1992," *Gallup Poll Monthly,* March 1990, 17-23.
33. "The Quayle Question," *Time,* February 4, 1991, 15.
34. George Gallup, Jr., and Frank Newport, "Almost One-Half Say Bush Should Replace Quayle," 17.
35. Kevin Phillips, *The Politics of Rich and Poor: Wealth and the American Electorate in the Reagan Aftermath* (New York: Random House, 1990).
36. Quoted in ibid., 30.
37. Ibid., 49.

Suggested Readings

* Readings preceded by an asterisk include discussion of the 1988 elections.

Chapter 1: The Nomination Struggle

* Abramowitz, Alan I. "Viability, Electability, and Candidate Choice in a Presidential Primary Election: A Test of Competing Models." *Journal of Politics* 51 (November 1989): 977-992.

* Abramson, Paul R., John H. Aldrich, and David W. Rohde. "Progressive Ambition among United States Senators: 1972-1988." *Journal of Politics* 49 (February 1987): 3-35.

Aldrich, John H. *Before the Convention: Strategies and Choices in Presidential Nomination Campaigns.* Chicago: University of Chicago Press, 1980.

Bartels, Larry M. *Presidential Primaries and the Dynamics of Public Choice.* Princeton, N.J.: Princeton University Press, 1988.

Brams, Steven J. *The Presidential Election Game.* New Haven, Conn.: Yale University Press, 1978, 1-79.

* Cain, Bruce E., I. A. Lewis, and Douglas Rivers. "Strategy and Choice in the 1988 Presidential Primaries." *Electoral Studies* 8 (April 1989): 23-48.

* Germond, Jack W., and Jules Witcover. *Whose Broad Stripes and Bright Stars? The Trivial Pursuit of the Presidency, 1988.* New York: Warner, 1989, 65-395.

* Goldman, Peter, and Tom Mathews, with others. *The Quest for the Presidency 1988.* New York: Simon & Schuster, 1989, 42-330.

Hess, Stephen. " 'Why Great Men Are Not Chosen Presidents': Lord Bryce Reconsidered." In *Elections American Style,* edited by A. James Reichley. Washington, D.C.: Brookings, 1987, 75-94.

* Morrison, Donald, ed. *The Winning of the White House 1988.* New York: Time, 1988, 1-212.

Polsby, Nelson W., and Aaron Wildavsky. *Presidential Elections: Contemporary Strategies of American Electoral Politics,* 7th ed. New York: Free Press, 1988, 88-161.

* Pomper, Gerald M. "The Presidential Nominations." In *The Election of 1988: Reports and Interpretations,* by Gerald M. Pomper, with colleagues. Chatham, N.J.: Chatham House, 1989, 33-71.

Shafer, Byron E. *Bifurcated Politics: Evolution and Reform in the National Party Convention.* Cambridge, Mass.: Harvard University Press, 1988.

Wayne, Stephen J. *The Road to the White House: The Politics of Presidential Elections,* 3d ed. New York: St. Martin's Press, 1988, 87-167.

Chapter 2: The General Election Campaign

Aldrich, John H., and Thomas Weko. "The Presidency and the Election Process: Campaign Strategy, Voting, and Governance." In *The Presidency and the Political System,* 2d ed., edited by Michael Nelson. Washington, D.C.: CQ Press, 1988, 251-267.

Asher, Herbert B. *Presidential Elections and American Politics: Voters, Candidates, and Campaigns since 1952,* 4th ed. Chicago: Dorsey Press, 1988, 248-327.

Brams, Steven J. *The Presidential Election Game.* New Haven, Conn.: Yale University Press, 1978, 80-133.

* Germond, Jack W., and Jules Witcover. *Whose Broad Stripes and Bright Stars? The Trivial Pursuit of the Presidency, 1988.* New York: Warner, 1989, 399-467.

* Goldman, Peter, and Tom Mathews, with others. *The Quest for the Presidency 1988.* New York: Simon & Schuster, 1989, 333-411.

* Hershey, Marjorie Randon. "The Campaign and the Media." In *The Election of 1988: Reports and Interpretations,* by Gerald M. Pomper, with colleagues. Chatham, N.J.: Chatham House, 1989, 73-102.

Kessel, John H. *Presidential Campaign Politics: Coalition Strategies and Citizen Response,* 3d ed. Chicago: Dorsey Press, 1988, 79-235.

* Morrison, Donald, editor. *The Winning of the White House 1988.* New York: Time, 1988, 213-243.

Polsby, Nelson W., and Aaron Wildavsky. *Presidential Elections: Contemporary Strategies of American Electoral Politics,* 7th ed. New York: Free Press, 1988, 162-237.

Wayne, Stephen J. *The Road to the White House: The Politics of Presidential Elections,* 3d ed. New York: St. Martin's Press, 1988, 171-274.

West, Darrell M. *Making Campaigns Count: Leadership and Coalition Building in 1980.* Westport, Conn.: Greenwood, 1984.

Chapter 3: The Election Results

* *America Votes 18: A Handbook of Contemporary American Election Statistics,* compiled and edited by Richard M. Scammon and Alice V. McGillivray. Washington, D.C.: Congressional Quarterly, 1989.

Black, Earl, and Merle Black. *Politics and Society in the South.* Cambridge, Mass.: Harvard University Press, 1987.

Burnham, Walter Dean. *Critical Elections and the Mainsprings of American Politics.* New York: W. W. Norton, 1970.

Clubb, Jerome M., William H. Flanigan, and Nancy H. Zingale. *Partisan Realignment: Voters, Parties, and Government in American History.* Beverly Hills, Calif.: Sage, 1980.

Galderisi, Peter F., Michael S. Lyons, Randy T. Simmons, and John G. Francis, eds. *The Politics of Realignment: Party Change in the Mountain West.* Boulder, Colo.: Westview Press, 1987.

Kelley, Stanley, Jr. *Interpreting Elections.* Princeton, N.J.: Princeton University Press, 1983.

Lamis, Alexander P. *The Two-Party South,* expanded ed. New York: Oxford University Press, 1988.

* Pomper, Gerald M. "The Presidential Election." In *The Election of 1988: Reports and Interpretations,* by Gerald M. Pomper, with colleagues. Chatham, N.J.: Chatham House, 1989, 129-152.

Presidential Elections since 1789, 4th ed. Washington, D.C.: Congressional Quarterly, 1987.

Sundquist, James L. *Dynamics of the Party System: Alignment and Realignment of Political Parties in the United States*, rev. ed. Washington, D.C.: Brookings, 1983.

Chapter 4: Who Voted

Burnham, Walter Dean. "The Turnout Problem." In *Elections American Style*, edited by A. James Reichley. Washington, D.C.: Brookings, 1987, 97-133.

Conway, M. Margaret. *Political Participation in the United States*. Washington, D.C.: CQ Press, 1985.

Kleppner, Paul. *Who Voted? The Dynamics of Electoral Turnout, 1870-1980*. New York: Praeger, 1982.

Piven, Frances Fox, and Richard A. Cloward. *Why Americans Don't Vote*. New York: Pantheon, 1988.

Powell, G. Bingham, Jr. "American Voter Turnout in Comparative Perspective." *American Political Science Review* 80 (March 1986): 17-43.

* Teixeira, Ruy A. "Registration and Turnout." *Public Opinion* 11 (January/February 1989): 12-13, 56-58.

_____. *Why Americans Don't Vote: Turnout Decline in the United States, 1960-1984*. New York: Greenwood Press, 1987.

Uhlaner, Carole J. "Rational Turnout: The Neglected Role of Groups." *American Journal of Political Science* 33 (May 1989): 390-422.

* U.S. Department of Commerce, Bureau of the Census. *Voting and Registration in the Election of November 1988*. Washington, D.C.: U.S. Government Printing Office, Series P-20, No. 440, October 1989.

Wolfinger, Raymond E., and Steven J. Rosenstone. *Who Votes?* New Haven, Conn.: Yale University Press, 1980.

Chapter 5: Social Forces and the Vote

Alford, Robert R. *Party and Society: The Anglo-American Democracies*. Chicago: Rand McNally, 1963.

Axelrod, Robert. "Where the Votes Come From: An Analysis of Electoral Coalitions, 1952-1968." *American Political Science Review* 66 (March 1972): 11-20.

Huckfeldt, Robert, and Carol Weitzel Kohfeld. *Race and the Decline of Class in American Politics*. Urbana: University of Illinois Press, 1989.

* Ladd, Everett Carll. "The National Election." *Public Opinion* 11 (January/February 1989): 2-3, 60.

Lipset, Seymour Martin. *Political Man: The Social Bases of Politics*. Baltimore: Johns Hopkins University Press, 1981.

* "Opinion Roundup: The Exit Poll Results." *Public Opinion* 11 (January/February 1989): 24-26.

Petrocik, John R. "Realignment: New Party Coalitions and the Nationalization of the South." *Journal of Politics* 49 (May 1987): 347-375.

* Schneider, William. "Solidarity's Not Enough." *National Journal*, November 12, 1988, 2853-2855.

Stanley, Harold W., William T. Bianco, and Richard G. Niemi. "Partisanship and Group Support Over Time: A Multivariate Analysis." *American Political Science Review* 80 (September 1986): 969-976.

* "Vote by Groups in Presidential Elections Since 1952." *Gallup Report*, Report No. 278, November 1988, 6-7.

Chapter 6: Issues, Candidates, and Voter Choice

Asher, Herbert B. *Presidential Elections and American Politics: Voters, Candidates, and Campaigns since 1952,* 4th ed. Chicago: Dorsey Press, 1988, 124-210.

Brody, Richard A., and Benjamin I. Page. "Comment: The Assessment of Policy Voting." *American Political Science Review* 66 (June 1972): 450-458.

Campbell, Angus, Philip E. Converse, Warren E. Miller, and Donald E. Stokes. *The American Voter.* New York: John Wiley & Sons, 1960, 168-265.

Carmines, Edward G., and James A. Stimson. *Issue Evolution: Race and the Transformation of American Politics.* Princeton, N.J.: Princeton University Press, 1989.

Enelow, James M., and Melvin J. Hinich. *The Spatial Theory of Voting: An Introduction.* New York: Cambridge University Press, 1984.

* Farah, Barbara G., and Ethel Klein. "Public Opinion Trends." In *The Election of 1988: Reports and Interpretations,* by Gerald M. Pomper, with colleagues. Chatham, N.J.: Chatham House, 1989, 103-128.

Kessel, John H. *Presidential Campaign Politics: Coalition Strategies and Citizen Response,* 3d ed. Chicago: Dorsey Press, 1988, 239-338.

Page, Benjamin I. *Choices and Echoes in Presidential Elections: Rational Man and Electoral Democracy.* Chicago: University of Chicago Press, 1978.

Pomper, Gerald M. *Voters' Choice: Varieties of American Electoral Behavior.* New York: Dodd, Mead, 1975.

Rabinowitz, George, and Stuart Elaine Macdonald. "A Directional Theory of Issue Voting." *American Political Science Review* 83 (March 1989): 93-121.

Chapter 7: Presidential Performance and Candidate Choice

Abramowitz, Alan I., David J. Lanoue, and Subha Ramesh. "Economic Conditions, Causal Attributions, and Political Evaluations in the 1984 Presidential Election." *Journal of Politics* 50 (November 1988): 848-863.

Downs, Anthony. *An Economic Theory of Democracy.* New York: Harper & Row, 1957.

Fiorina, Morris P. *Retrospective Voting in American National Elections.* New Haven, Conn.: Yale University Press, 1981.

Key, V. O., Jr. *The Responsible Electorate: Rationality in Presidential Voting, 1936-1960.* Cambridge, Mass.: Harvard University Press, 1966.

Kiewiet, D. Roderick. *Macroeconomics and Micropolitics: The Electoral Effects of Economic Issues.* Chicago: University of Chicago Press, 1983.

Lewis-Beck, Michael S. *Economics and Elections: The Major Western Democracies.* Ann Arbor, Mich.: University of Michigan Press, 1988.

Marcus, George E. "The Structure of Emotional Response." *American Political Science Review* 82 (September 1988): 737-761.

Miller, Arthur H., Martin P. Wattenberg, and Oksana Malanchuk. "Schematic Assessments of Presidential Candidates." *American Political Science Review* 80 (June 1986): 521-540.

Riker, William H. *Liberalism Against Populism: A Confrontation Between the Theory of Democracy and the Theory of Social Choice.* San Francisco: W. H. Freeman, 1982.

Tufte, Edward R. *Political Control of the Economy.* Princeton, N.J.: Princeton University Press, 1978.

Chapter 8: Party Loyalties, Policy Preferences, Performance Evaluations, and the Vote

Abramson, Paul R. *Political Attitudes in America: Formation and Change.* San Francisco: W. H. Freeman, 1983.

Asher, Herbert B. "Voting Behavior Research in the 1980s: An Examination of Some Old and New Problem Areas." In *Political Science: The State of the Discipline,* edited by Ada W. Finifter. Washington, D.C.: American Political Science Association, 1983, 339-388.

Beck, Paul Allen. "The Dealignment Era in America." In *Electoral Change in Advanced Industrial Democracies: Realignment or Dealignment?* edited by Russell J. Dalton, Scott C. Flanagan, and Paul Allen Beck. Princeton, N.J.: Princeton University Press, 1984, 240-266.

Campbell, Angus, Philip E. Converse, Warren E. Miller, and Donald E. Stokes. *The American Voter.* New York: John Wiley & Sons, 1960, 120-167.

Carmines, Edward G., John P. McIver, and James A. Stimson. "Unrealized Partisanship: A Theory of Dealignment." *Journal of Politics* 49 (May 1987): 376-400.

Jennings, M. Kent, and Gregory B. Markus. "Partisan Orientations over the Long Haul: Results from the Three-Wave Political Socialization Panel Study." *American Political Science Review* 78 (December 1984): 1000-1018.

Kinder, Donald R., and David O. Sears. "Public Opinion and Political Action." In *Special Fields and Applications,* vol. 2 of *Handbook of Social Psychology,* 3d ed., edited by Gardner Lindzey and Elliot Aronson. New York: Random House, 1985, 659-741.

Miller, Warren E., and Santa A. Traugott. *American National Election Studies Data Sourcebook, 1952-1986.* Cambridge, Mass.: Harvard University Press, 1989.

Norpoth, Helmut. "Under Way and Here to Stay: Party Realignment in the 1980s?" *Public Opinion Quarterly* 51 (Fall 1987): 376-391.

* Wattenberg, Martin P. *The Decline of American Political Parties: 1952-1988.* Cambridge, Mass.: Harvard University Press, 1990.

Chapter 9: Candidates and Outcomes

Abramowitz, Alan I. "Explaining Senate Election Outcomes." *American Political Science Review* 82 (June 1988): 385-403.

* Baker, Ross K. "The Congressional Elections." In *The Election of 1988: Reports and Interpretations,* by Gerald M. Pomper, with colleagues. Chatham, N.J.: Chatham House, 1989, 153-176.

Campbell, James E. "Predicting Seat Gains from Presidential Coattails." *American Journal of Political Science* 30 (February 1986): 165-183.

Fenno, Richard F., Jr. *Home Style: House Members in Their Districts.* Boston: Little, Brown, 1978.

Fiorina, Morris P. *Congress: Keystone of the Washington Establishment,* 2d ed. New Haven, Conn.: Yale University Press, 1989.

* Jacobson, Gary C. "Congress: A Singular Continuity." In *The Elections of 1988,* edited by Michael Nelson. Washington, D.C.: CQ Press, 1989, 127-152.

Rohde, David W. " 'Something's Happening Here; What It Is Ain't Exactly Clear': Southern Democrats in the House of Representatives." In *Home Style and Washington Work: Studies in Congressional Politics,* edited by Morris P. Fiorina and David W. Rohde. Ann Arbor: University of Michigan Press, 1989, 137-163.

* Rothenberg, Stuart. "The House and the Senate." *Public Opinion* 11 (January/February 1989): 8-11, 59.

Schlesinger, Joseph A. *Ambition and Politics: Political Careers in the United States.* Chicago: Rand McNally, 1966.

——. "The New American Political Party." *American Political Science Review* 79 (December 1985): 1152-1169.

Chapter 10: The Congressional Electorate

Born, Richard. "Reassessing the Decline of Presidential Coattails: U.S. House Elections from 1952-80." *Journal of Politics* 46 (February 1984): 60-79.

Calvert, Randall L., and John A. Ferejohn. "Coattail Voting in Recent Presidential Elections." *American Political Science Review* 77 (June 1983): 407-419.

Erikson, Robert S., and Gerald C. Wright, Jr. "Voters, Candidates, and Issues in Congressional Elections." In *Congress Reconsidered,* 3d ed., edited by Lawrence C. Dodd and Bruce I. Oppenheimer. Washington, D.C.: CQ Press, 1985, 87-108.

Fenno, Richard F., Jr. "If, as Ralph Nader Says, Congress Is 'the Broken Branch,' How Come We Love Our Congressmen So Much?" In *Congress in Change: Elections and Reform,* edited by Norman J. Ornstein. New York: Praeger, 1975, 277-287.

Ferejohn, John A., and Randall L. Calvert. "Presidential Coattails in Historical Perspective." *American Journal of Political Science* 28 (February 1984): 127-146.

Herrnson, Paul. "Do Parties Make a Difference? The Role of Party Organizations in Congressional Elections." *Journal of Politics* 48 (August 1986): 589-615.

Hurley, Patricia A. "Partisan Representation and the Failure of Realignment in the 1980s." *American Journal of Political Science* 33 (February 1989): 240-261.

Jacobson, Gary C. *The Politics of Congressional Elections,* 2d ed. Boston: Little, Brown, 1987.

McAdams, John C., and John R. Johannes. "Congressmen, Perquisites, and Elections." *Journal of Politics* 50 (May 1988): 412-439.

Wright, Gerald C., Jr., and Michael B. Berkman. "Candidates and Policy in United States Senate Elections." *American Political Science Review* 80 (June 1986): 567-588.

Chapter 11: The 1988 Elections and the Future of American Politics

* Burnham, Walter Dean. "The Reagan Heritage." In *The Election of 1988: Reports and Interpretations,* by Gerald M. Pomper, with colleagues. Chatham, N.J.: Chatham House, 1989, 1-32.

* Goldman, Peter, and Tom Mathews, with others. *The Quest for the Presidency 1988.* New York: Simon & Schuster, 1989, 412-418.

* Ladd, Everett Carll. "The 1988 Elections: Continuation of the Post-New Deal System." *Political Science Quarterly* 104 (Spring 1989): 1-18.

* McWilliams, Wilson Carey. "The Meaning of the Election." In *The Election of 1988: Reports and Interpretations,* by Gerald M. Pomper, with colleagues. Chatham, N.J.: Chatham House, 1989, 177-206.

* Nelson, Michael. "Constitutional Aspects of the Elections." In *The Elections of 1988,* edited by Michael Nelson. Washington, D.C.: CQ Press, 1989, 181-209.

* Shafer, Byron E. "The Election of 1988 and the Structure of American Politics: Thoughts on Interpreting an Electoral Order." *Electoral Studies* 8 (April 1989): 5-21.

Additional Readings

The following readings on the 1988 and 1990 elections have appeared since the first edition of our book was published.

Abramson, Paul R., and William Claggett. "Racial Differences in Self-Reported and Validated Turnout in the 1988 Presidential Election." *Journal of Politics* 53 (February 1991): 186-197.

Ansolabehere, Stephen, and Gary King. "Measuring the Consequences of Delegate Selection Rules in Presidential Nominations." *Journal of Politics* 52 (May 1990): 609-621.

Bartels, Larry M., and C. Anthony Broh. "The Polls—A Review: The 1988 Presidential Primaries." *Public Opinion Quarterly* 53 (Winter 1989): 563-589.

Bennett, Stephen Earl, and David Resnick. "The Implications of Nonvoting for Democracy in the United States." *American Journal of Political Science* 34 (August 1990): 771-802.

Blumenthal, Sidney. *Pledging Allegiance: The Last Campaign of the Cold War.* New York: Harper Collins, 1990.

Campbell, James E., and Joe A. Sumners. "Presidential Coattails in Senate Elections." *American Political Science Review* 84 (June 1990): 513-524.

Fiorina, Morris P. "The Electorate in the Voting Booth." In *The Parties Respond: Changes in the American Party System,* edited by L. Sandy Maisel. Boulder: Westview, 1990, 116-133.

Ginsberg, Benjamin, and Martin Shefter. *Politics by Other Means: The Declining Importance of Elections in America.* New York: Basic Books, 1990.

Herrnson, Paul S. "Reemergent National Party Organizations." In *The Parties Respond: Changes in the American Party System,* edited by L. Sandy Maisel. Boulder: Westview, 1990, 41-66.

Jacobson, Gary C. *The Electoral Origins of Divided Government: Competition in U.S. House Elections, 1946-1988.* Boulder: Westview, 1990.

John, Kenneth E. "The Polls—A Report: 1980-1988 New Hampshire Presidential Primary Polls." *Public Opinion Quarterly* 53 (Winter 1989): 590-605.

Kamarck, Elaine Ciulla. "Structure as Strategy: Presidential Nominating Politics in the Post-Reform Era." In *The Parties Respond: Changes in the American Party System,* edited by L. Sandy Maisel. Boulder: Westview, 1990, 160-186.

Ladd, Everett C. "Like Waiting for Godot: The Uselessness of Realignment for Understanding Change in Contemporary American Politics." *Polity* 22 (Spring 1990): 511-525.

Miller, Warren E. "The Electorate's View of the Parties." In *The Parties Respond: Changes in the American Party System,* edited by L. Sandy Maisel. Boulder: Westview, 1990, 97-115.

Phillips, Kevin. *The Politics of Rich and Poor: Wealth and the American Electorate in the Reagan Aftermath.* New York: Random House, 1990.

Rapoport, Ronald B., Walter J. Stone, and Alan I. Abramowitz. "Sex and the Caucus Participant: The Gender Gap and Presidential Nominations." *American Journal of Political Science* 34 (August 1990): 725-740.

Rothenberg, Stuart. "The 1992 Shakeup in Congress." *The American Enterprise* 1 (May/June 1990): 92-93.

Schneider, William, and Patrick Reddy. "Altered States: The Demographic Changes and Partisan Shifts of Four Decades." *The American Enterprise* 1

(July/August 1990): 45-55.

Stone, Walter J., Ronald B. Rapoport, and Alan I. Abramowitz. "The Reagan Revolution and Party Polarization in the 1980s." In *The Parties Respond: Changes in the American Party System,* edited by L. Sandy Maisel. Boulder: Westview, 1990, 67-93.

Taylor, Paul. *See How They Run: Electing the President in an Age of Mediaocracy.* New York: Knopf, 1990.

U.S. Department of Commerce, Bureau of the Census. *Projections of the Voting-Age Population for States: November 1990.* Washington, D.C.: U.S. Government Printing Office, Series P-25, No. 1059, April 1990.

Valelly, Richard. "Vanishing Voters." *The American Prospect* 1 (Spring 1990): 140-150.

Index